BEST ROAD TRIPS CANADA

ESCAPES ON THE OPEN ROAD

Regis St Louis
Ray Bartlett, Oliver Berry, Gregor Clark, Shawn Duthie, Steve Fallon, Carolyn Heller, Anna Kaminski, Adam Karlin, John Lee, Craig McLachlan, Liza Prado, Brendan Sainsbury, Phillip Tang

SYMBOLS IN THIS BOOK

Top Tips

History & Culture

Essential Photo

Link Your Trips

Family

Walking Tour

Tips from Locals

Food & Drink

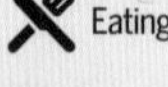
Eating

Trip Detour

Outdoors

Sleeping

Telephone Number
Opening Hours
Parking
Nonsmoking
Air-Conditioning
Internet Access
Wi-Fi Access
Vegetarian Selection
Swimming Pool
English-Language Menu
Family-Friendly
Pet-Friendly

MAP LEGEND

Routes
Trip Route
Trip Detour
Linked Trip
Walk Route
Tollway
Freeway
Primary
Secondary
Tertiary
Lane
Unsealed Road
Plaza/Mall
Steps
Tunnel
Pedestrian Overpass
Walk Track/Path

Boundaries
International
State/Province
Cliff

Hydrography
River/Creek
Swamp/Mangrove
Canal
Water
Dry/Salt/ Intermittent Lake
Glacier

Route Markers
Trans-Canada Hwy
Provincial/ Territorial Hwy
US National Hwy
US Interstate Hwy
US State Hwy

Trips
Trip Numbers
Trip Stop
Walking tour
Trip Detour

Population
Capital (National)
Capital (State/Province)
City/Large Town
Town/Village

Areas
Beach
Cemetery (Christian)
Cemetery (Other)
Park
Forest
Reservation
Urban Area
Sportsground

Transport
Airport
Cable Car/ Funicular
Metro/Muni station
Parking
Subway station
Train/Railway
Tram

Note: Not all symbols displayed above appear on the maps in this book

PLAN YOUR TRIP

ON THE ROAD

CONTENTS

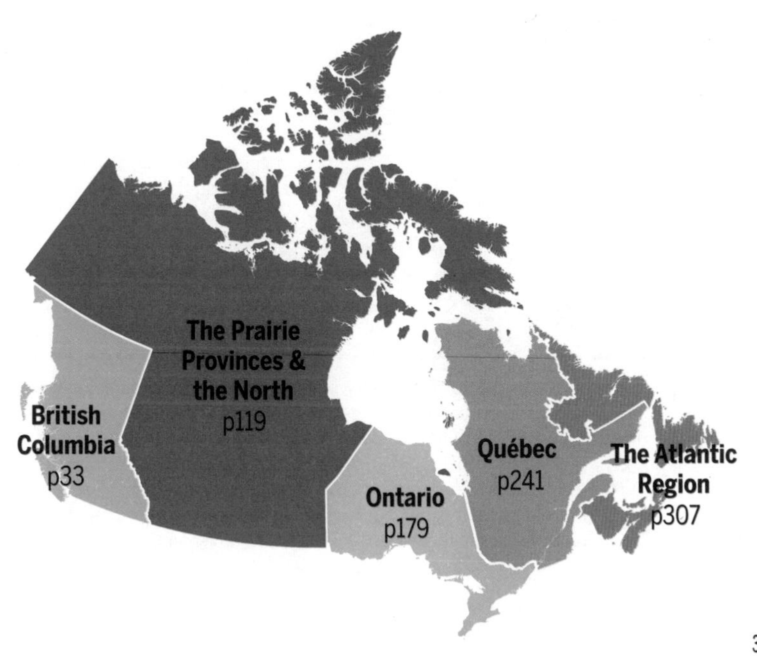

The Prairie Provinces & the North
p119
British Columbia
p33
Ontario
p179
Québec
p241
The Atlantic Region
p307

Contents cont.

TERRITORY ACKNOWLEDGEMENT

Lonely Planet would like to acknowledge and pay respect to the Indigenous people throughout this country. This guide was written on and is written about land which includes their traditional lands, unceded territories and Treaty territories. We also recognise the ongoing efforts of Indigenous peoples for reconciliation, justice, and social, cultural, and economic self-determination. We hope you can use the opportunity of your travels to connect with the people and learn about Indigenous culture and society.

COVID-19

We have re-checked every business in this book before publication to ensure that it is still open after the COVID-19 outbreak. However, the economic and social impacts will continue to be felt long after the outbreak has been contained, and many businesses, services and events referenced in this guide may experience ongoing restrictions. Some businesses may be temporarily closed, have changed their opening hours and services, or require bookings; some unfortunately could have closed permanently. We suggest you check with venues before visiting for the latest information.

Nova Scotia Fishing boats in Peggy's Cove (p321)

Miss Peggy's Cove

WELCOME TO CANADA

The awe-inspiring power of nature is on full display in the second-biggest country on earth. Sky-high mountains, glinting glaciers, spectral rainforests and remote beaches are all here, spread across six time zones. They're the backdrop for plenty of 'ah'-inspiring moments – and for a big cast of local characters. That's big as in polar bears, grizzly bears, whales and everyone's favorite, moose.

Whether you want to drive into the remote, tundra-filled northern wilderness or follow the sinewy roads past rugged, lighthouse-dotted shores, the 32 road trips in this book will take you there.

If you're game for burgeoning food markets in the Québécois countryside, wild-fiddling Celtic parties in Cape Breton or mist-cloaked indigenous villages on Haida Gwaii, we've got you covered. And if you've only got time for one journey, pick from our 9 Classic Trips, which take you on a tour of the very best of Canada. Turn the page for more.

Grizzly bear, Grouse Mountain (p40), British Columbia
DAVID J. MITCHELL/SHUTTERSTOCK ©

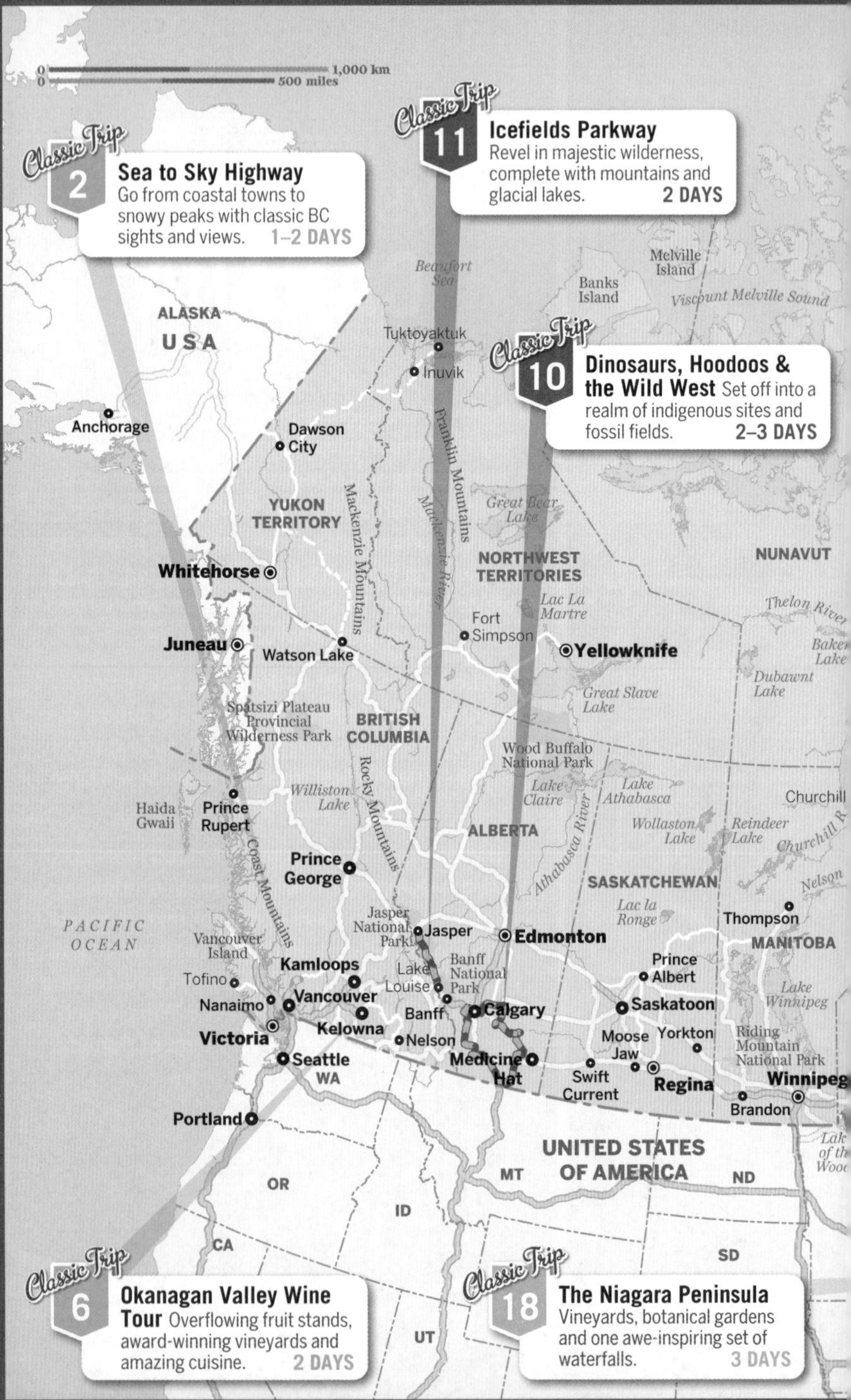

Classic Trip

2 Sea to Sky Highway

Go from coastal towns to snowy peaks with classic BC sights and views. **1–2 DAYS**

Classic Trip

11 Icefields Parkway

Revel in majestic wilderness, complete with mountains and glacial lakes. **2 DAYS**

Classic Trip

10 Dinosaurs, Hoodoos & the Wild West

Set off into a realm of indigenous sites and fossil fields. **2–3 DAYS**

Classic Trip

6 Okanagan Valley Wine Tour

Overflowing fruit stands, award-winning vineyards and amazing cuisine. **2 DAYS**

Classic Trip

18 The Niagara Peninsula

Vineyards, botanical gardens and one awe-inspiring set of waterfalls. **3 DAYS**

0 — 1,000 km
0 — 500 miles

ALASKA
USA
Anchorage
Beaufort Sea
Banks Island
Melville Island
Viscount Melville Sound
Tuktoyaktuk
Inuvik
Dawson City
YUKON TERRITORY
Mackenzie Mountains
Franklin Mountains
Mackenzie River
Great Bear Lake
NORTHWEST TERRITORIES
NUNAVUT
Whitehorse
Lac La Martre
Fort Simpson
Thelon River
Juneau
Watson Lake
Yellowknife
Baker Lake
Dubawnt Lake
Great Slave Lake
Spatsizi Plateau Provincial Wilderness Park
BRITISH COLUMBIA
Wood Buffalo National Park
Haida Gwaii
Prince Rupert
Williston Lake
Rocky Mountains
Lake Claire
Lake Athabasca
Churchill
Athabasca River
Wollaston Lake
Reindeer Lake
Churchill R
ALBERTA
Coast Mountains
Prince George
SASKATCHEWAN
Nelson
Lac la Ronge
Thompson
PACIFIC OCEAN
Jasper National Park
Jasper
Edmonton
MANITOBA
Vancouver Island
Kamloops
Lake Louise
Banff National Park
Prince Albert
Tofino
Nanaimo
Vancouver
Banff
Calgary
Saskatoon
Lake Winnipeg
Victoria
Kelowna
Nelson
Moose Jaw
Yorkton
Riding Mountain National Park
Seattle
Medicine Hat
Swift Current
Regina
Winnipeg
WA
Brandon
Portland
UNITED STATES OF AMERICA
MT
ND
OR
ID
CA
SD
UT
Lake of the Woods

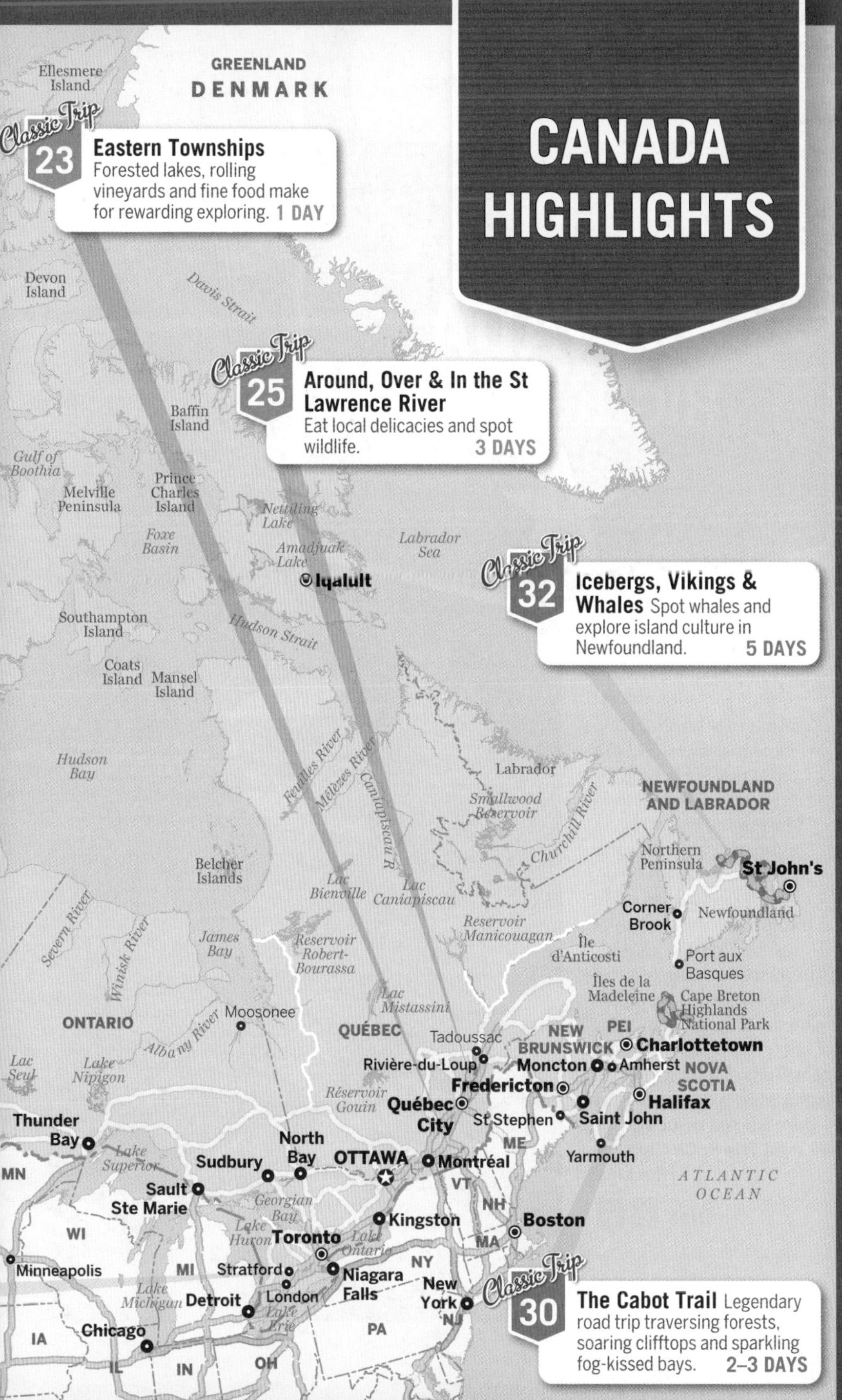
CANADA
HIGHLIGHTS
Classic Trip
23
Eastern Townships
Forested lakes, rolling vineyards and fine food make for rewarding exploring. 1 DAY
Classic Trip
25
Around, Over & In the St Lawrence River
Eat local delicacies and spot wildlife. 3 DAYS
Classic Trip
32
Icebergs, Vikings & Whales Spot whales and explore island culture in Newfoundland. 5 DAYS
Classic Trip
30
The Cabot Trail Legendary road trip traversing forests, soaring clifftops and sparkling fog-kissed bays. 2–3 DAYS
GREENLAND
DENMARK
Ellesmere Island
Devon Island
Davis Strait
Baffin Island
Gulf of Boothia
Melville Peninsula
Prince Charles Island
Foxe Basin
Nettiling Lake
Amadjuak Lake
Iqaluit
Labrador Sea
Southampton Island
Hudson Strait
Coats Island
Mansel Island
Hudson Bay
Feuilles River
Mélèzes River
Caniapiscau R
Labrador
Smallwood Reservoir
Churchill River
NEWFOUNDLAND AND LABRADOR
Northern Peninsula
St John's
Belcher Islands
Lac Bienville
Lac Caniapiscau
Corner Brook
Newfoundland
Severn River
Winisk River
James Bay
Reservoir Robert-Bourassa
Reservoir Manicouagan
Île d'Anticosti
Port aux Basques
Îles de la Madeleine
Cape Breton Highlands National Park
Lac Mistassini
ONTARIO
Moosonee
Albany River
QUÉBEC
Tadoussac
NEW BRUNSWICK
PEI
Charlottetown
Lac Seul
Lake Nipigon
Rivière-du-Loup
Moncton
Amherst
NOVA SCOTIA
Fredericton
Réservoir Gouin
Québec City
Halifax
Thunder Bay
St Stephen
Saint John
North Bay
ME
Yarmouth
MN
Lake Superior
Sudbury
OTTAWA
Montréal
ATLANTIC OCEAN
Sault Ste Marie
VT
Georgian Bay
NH
Kingston
Boston
WI
Lake Huron
Toronto
Lake Ontario
MA
NY
Minneapolis
MI
Stratford
Niagara Falls
Lake Michigan
Detroit
London
New York
Lake Erie
NJ
IA
Chicago
PA
IL
IN
OH

Canada's best sights and experiences, and the road trips that will take you there.

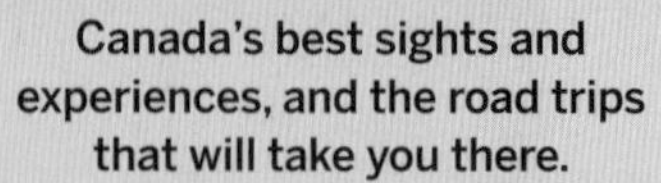

CANADA HIGHLIGHTS

★

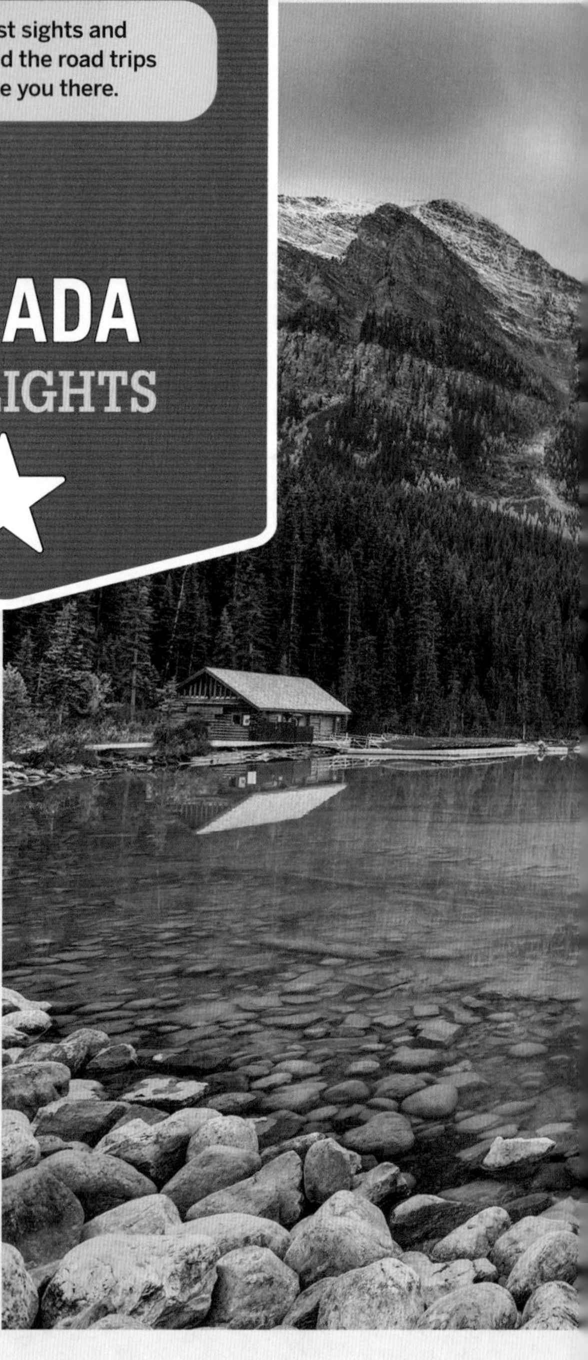

Lake Louise

No one should leave this mortal coil without first setting eyes on the robin-egg-blue waters of Lake Louise nestled bellow the icy hue of the Victoria Glacier and ringed by an impressive amphitheater of mountains. True, selfie sticks can often outnumber walking poles on the crowded lakeside promenade, but take a less obvious path to an alpine teahouse or through a valley of larch trees and you'll find that Homo sapiens soon get replaced by wilder company (bears if you're lucky). See it on **Trip 8: Circling the Rockies**.

Trips 8 11

BGSMITH/SHUTTERSTOCK ©

Lake Louise (p102) Stunning emerald-green water and tall, snowy peaks

Dawson City (p164) One of the most historic and evocative towns in Canada

Dawson City

Dawson, with its brightly painted Klondike-era buildings, once drew thousands in the search for gold. Today, instead of miners, the city attracts artists and rugged individualists, with a doors-always-open atmosphere. On **Trip 14: Klondike Highway**, you can give gold panning a go in the icy rivers or try your hand at poker in the historic saloon. Then soak up some of the spectacular sub-Arctic scenery.

Trip 14

Wine Tasting in the Okanagan

Enjoying a trip around the bucolic, vine-striped hills of the Okanagan Valley region is the best way for any tipple-loving visitor to spend their time in Western Canada. On **Trip 6: Okanagan Valley Wine Tour**, you'll pass numerous wineries. One thing is certain: you won't go thirsty. Nominate a designated driver, and don't forget to dine: many winery tasting rooms are adjoined by excellent restaurants.

Trip 

Haida Gwaii

Once known as the Queen Charlotte Islands, this dagger-shaped archipelago 80km off BC's coast is a magical trip. Colossal spruce and cedars cloak the wild landscape. Bald eagles and bears roam the ancient forest, while sea lions and orcas cruise the waters. But the islands' real soul is the resurgent Haida people, best known for their war-canoe and totem-pole carvings. See the lot on **Trip 7: Haida Gwaii Adventure**.

Trip 7

JUSTIN FOULKES/LONELY PLANET © MARKUS THOMPSON/500PX ©

Haida Gwaii An eagle perches on a totem pole in Old Masset (p95)

BEST ROADS FOR DRIVING

Highway 1 Dazzling views near Lake Louise. **Trips** 8 11

Sea to Sky Highway Waterfalls, misty shorelines and jaw-dropping panoramas. **Trip** 2

Cabot Trail Clifftop vistas over valleys, fishing villages and rugged shores. **Trip** 30

Icefields Parkway Wilderness of glacial lakes, waterfalls and soaring peaks. **Trip** 11

Highway 60 Look for moose, otters and bald eagles along forested Algonquin Provincial Park. **Trip** 19

Peggy's Cove

Despite being clogged with tour buses all summer long, Peggy's Cove enchants all who visit. The lighthouse, the blue-grey sea and the tiny sheltered bay scattered with crab traps and Popeye-esque boat docks are all straight out of a sailor's yarn. On **Trip 29: South Shore Circular**, take time to meander and experience a glimpse of life in a very, very small Maritime village.

Trip 

Icefields Parkway (p133) This road leads you through Canada's magnificent Rocky Mountain wilderness

Icefields Parkway

There are amazing road trips, then there's **Trip 11: Icefields Parkway**, a 230km-long ribbon of asphalt that parallels the Continental Divide between Lake Louise and Jasper, passing through some of Canada's most elemental landscapes en route. Giant mountains, mammoth moose, craning trees and gargantuan glaciers brood moodily from the sidelines. Most drive it, but it also makes for a challenging multiday bike ride giving you more time to contemplate stops at Peyto Lake, powerful Athabasca Falls and the hikeable Athabasca Glacier.

Trip 11

BEST SMALL TOWNS

Tobermory A charming village on Bruce Peninsula surrounded by crystal-clear waters. **Trip** 20

Brigus Picture-perfect coastal Newfoundland town with 17th-century roots. **Trip** 32

Nelson Lakeside village with an arts-loving vibe. **Trip** 9

Baie St Paul Québécois gem on the St Lawrence and birthplace of Cirque de Soleil. **Trip** 25

Niagara-on-the-Lake Historic town packed with architectural treasures. **Trip** 18

VINCENT MCNULTY/EYEEM/GETTY IMAGES ©

Niagara Falls This cacophonous cascade straddles the border between Canada and the US

N1924/SHUTTERSTOCK ©

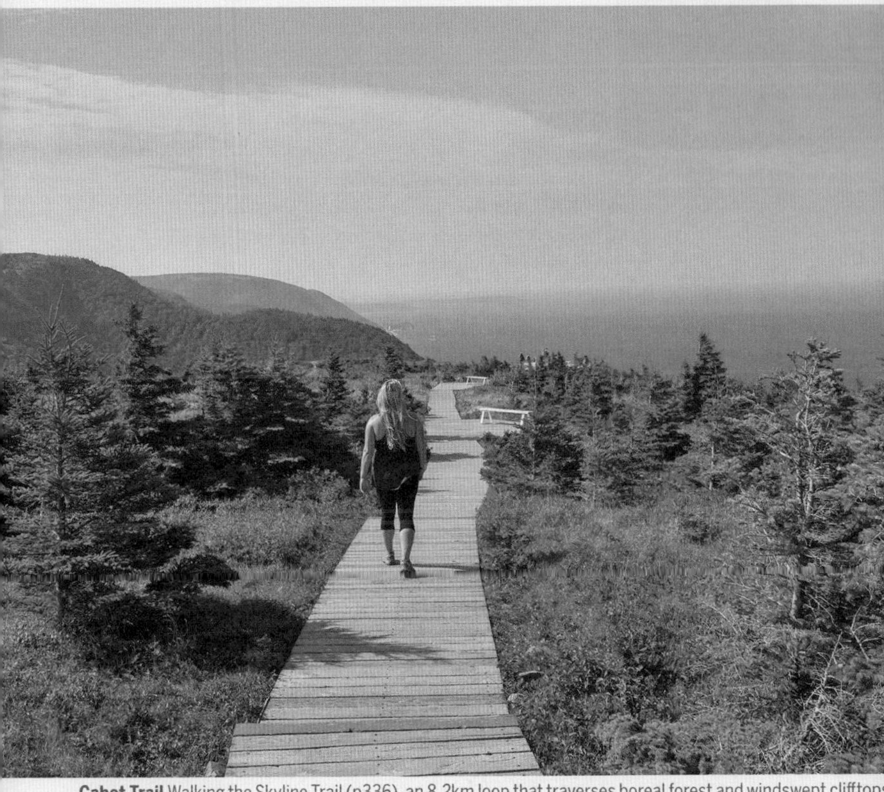

Cabot Trail Walking the Skyline Trail (p336), an 8.2km loop that traverses boreal forest and windswept clifftops

Prince Edward Island National Park

Dune-backed beaches and grassy bluffs that stretch for miles and miles – that's what you'll find in this hugely popular national park on **Trip 31: Two Islands, Three Provinces**. Stretching from the Greenwich Dunes all the way east to Cavendish, a total distance of 42km, it's sunbathing central in summer – but it's worth seeing at any time of year.

Trip 31

Niagara Falls

Crowded? Cheesy? Well, yes. Niagara is short, too – it doesn't even crack the top 500 worldwide for height. But c'mon, when those great muscular bands of water arc over the precipice like liquid glass, roaring into the void below, and when you sail toward it in a mist-shrouded little boat, Niagara Falls impresses big time. You won't regret stopping by on **Trip 18: Niagara Peninsula**. Nowhere in North Amcrica beats its thundering cascade.

Trip 18

Cabot Trail

The 300km Cabot Trail, named for explorer John Cabot, is a highway that winds and climbs over stunning coastal mountains, with heart-stopping sea views at every turn, and plenty of trails to stop and hike. On **Trip 30: Cabot Trail**, Celtic and Acadian communities dot the area, and their foot-stompin', crazy-fiddlin' music vibrates through local pubs. Despite the climate and the winter snows, the trail is open throughout the year.

Trip 30

Charlevoix

A pastoral strip of rolling hills northeast of Québec City, the Charlevoix region harvests much of the province's food. Gastronomes road-trip out, knowing that produce from the farms and orchards that flash by will, in true farm-to-table fashion, end up as part of their next meal. Village inns and alehouses serve the distinct, locally made wares. Get your fill on **Trip 25: Around, Over & In the St Lawrence River**.

Trip 25

The Prairies

Driving through the flatlands of Saskatchewan turns up uninterrupted fields of golden wheat that stretch to the horizon. When the wind blows, the wheat sways like waves on the ocean, punctuated by the occasional grain elevator rising up like a tall ship. Big skies mean big storms that drop like an anvil, visible on the skyline for kilometers. Enjoy the serene landscapes on **Trip: 12 Explore Southern Saskatchewan**.

Trips 10 12 13

JAMESLEE999/GETTY IMAGES ©

(left) **The Prairies** Fields of golden wheat in Saskatchewan (p143)

(below) **Vancouver Island** Surfers on Long Beach, Tofino (p74)

CHASE CLAUSEN/SHUTTERSTOCK ©

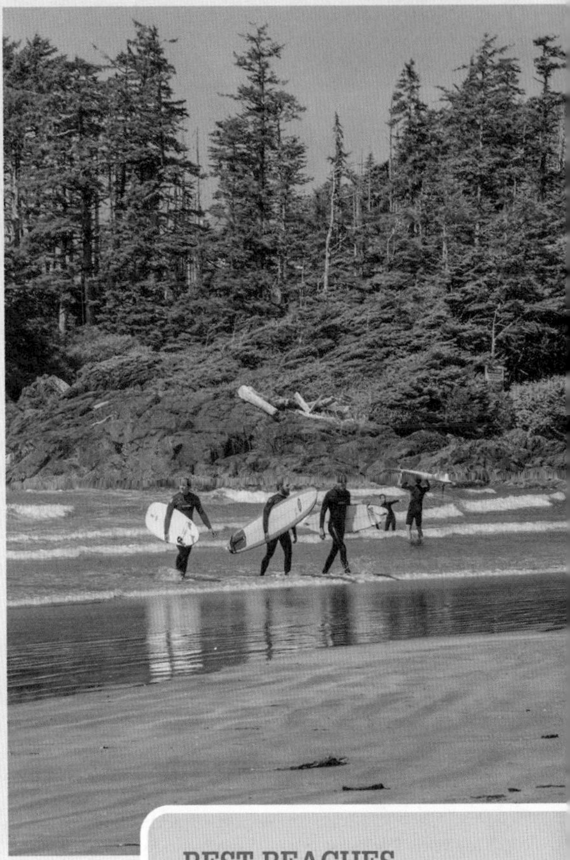

Vancouver Island

Picture-postcard Victoria is the island's heart, beating with bohemian shops, wood-floored coffee bars and a tea-soaked English past. Brooding Pacific Rim National Park Reserve sports the West Coast Trail, where the wind-bashed ocean meets a mist-shrouded wilderness, and surfers line up for Tofino's waves. Then there's colorful Cowichan Bay, with its art studios and local eateries. Take it all in on **Trip 4: Southern Vancouver Island Tour**.

Trips 3 4 5

BEST BEACHES

Long Beach Gorgeous stretch of sandy shore on Vancouver Island. **Trip** 5

Prince Edward Island National Park Walking amid the dunes of this remote shoreline. **Trip** 31

Manitou Beach Take a dip into mineral-rich Dead Sea-like waters. **Trip** 13

Lawrencetown Beach Go surfing off this Nova Scotia beauty. **Trip** 28

Pinery Provincial Park Dunes and emerald waters on Lake Huron. **Trip** 20

The Kawarthas Elk in Kawartha Highlands Provincial Park (p21

Wildlife Watching

On land, in the water and in the air, Canada is teeming with the kind of camera-worthy critters that make visitors wonder if they haven't stepped into a safari park by mistake.

5 **Vancouver Island's Remote North** Look for giants of the land (bears) and sea (orcas) on this nature-filled drive.

11 **Icefields Parkway** Dramatic Rocky Mountains drive lined with jaw-dropping wildlife viewing.

19 **The Kawarthas** Look for the majestic moose (and myriad other creatures) in this wooded wonderland.

30 **The Cabot Trail** Go whale-watching off the coast, then look for bald eagles on the famed Skyline Trail.

Panoramic Views

Canada's roads will take you to some spectacular destinations, where you can linger over the sweep of mountains, forests, lakes and seashore.

2 **Sea to Sky Highway** A stunning array of waterfalls, old-growth forests and lofty lookouts.

15 **Dempster Highway** Take in the vast boreal forests and Northern Lights as you drive into the Arctic Circle.

32 **Icebergs, Vikings & Whales** Photogenic small towns set against the rugged beauty of the Newfoundland coastline.

20 **Southern Ontario Nature Loop** Relishing the quiet beauty of cliffside lookouts, coves and forest-fringed lakes.

Food & Wine

Canada's delectable cuisine varies wildly from region to region. That means fabulous seafood east and west, French-influenced Québécois fare, barbecued steak in Canada's cowboy and craft breweries wherever you roam.

6 **Okanagan Valley Wine Tour** Wineries, orchards and farm-to-table restaurants set the stage for serious indulgence.

23 **Eastern Townships** Visit a chocolate museum, munch on cheese made by monks and sample delicacies at farmers markets.

21 **Thousand Island Parkway** Indulge in Ontario's locavore food scene on this gourmet ramble from Kingston to Ottawa.

31 **Two Islands, Three Provinces** Pairing local craft brews with fresh lobster and other seafood in charming island towns.

Okanagan Valley Glorious vineyard and lake views at Mission Hill Family Estate (p83) winery

Aquatic Adventures

Whether you head east, west or into the center, you'll find some fantastic paddling opportunities, from gliding past ancient forests and totem poles in BC's Gwaii Haanas National Park Reserve, to spotting breaching whales in Newfoundland.

26 **The Saguenay Fjord & Lac St Jean** Go kayaking on the dramatic forest- and cliff-backed fjord.

16 **Lake Superior Coastline** Go swimming off sandy beaches, then take a canoe tour off the Slate Islands.

4 **Southern Vancouver Island Tour** Explore tidal pools, visit an aquarium and look for orcas on this island-hopping wander.

13 **North From Saskatoon** Canoe pristine lakes followed by beachside relaxing.

Hiking

You don't have to be a hiker to hike in Canada. While there are plenty of multiday treks for wilderness junkies, there are also innumerable opportunities for those who prefer a gentle stroll around a lake with a pub at the end.

22 **Up to the Laurentians** Take memorable hikes amid Québec's oldest national park.

8 **Circling the Rockies** Hike past alpine lakes and beneath soaring peaks on this mountain-filled ramble.

2 **Sea to Sky Highway** Walk through old-growth forests to shimmering waterfalls and up to sweeping lookouts.

30 **The Cabot Trail** Enjoy jaw-dropping coastal walks on this fabled Nova Scotia journey.

History

Much of Canada's colorful heritage and geological wonders are accessible to visitors, with hundreds of national historic sites covering everything from forts and battlefields to famous homes and awe-inspiring fossil parks.

10 **Dinosaurs, Hoodoos & the Wild** Walk through a fossil field, see ancient petroglyphs and First Nations sites.

14 **Klondike Highway** Follow the trail blazed by fortune seekers to the gold rush towns of the early 1900s.

17 **People & Culture Loop** Visit a thriving Mennonite village founded in the 1830s, and learn about the Dawn Settlement, a former community of escaped enslaved people.

28 **Central Nova Scotia** Visit 19th-century heritage sites and 300-million-year-old fossil-filled cliffs.

NEED  KNOW

CURRENCY
Canadian dollar ($)

LANGUAGES
English, French

VISAS
Visitors may require a visa to enter Canada. Those exempt require an Electronic Travel Authorization (eTA; $7), with the exception of Americans. See www.cic.gc.ca/english/visit/eta-start.asp.

FUEL
Gas is sold in liters on major highways. Expect to pay around $1.30 to $1.50 per liter, with higher prices in more remote areas.

RENTAL CARS
Be sure to have an international license if you're not from an English- or French-speaking country.

Budget (www.budget.com)

Hertz (www.hertz.com)

Practicar (www.practicar.ca)

Thrifty (www.thriftycanada.ca)

IMPORTANT NUMBERS
Emergency (☎911) Ambulance, police, fire, mountain rescue, coast guard.

Roadside assistance (☎1 800-222-4357)

Climate

When to Go

High Season (Jun–Aug)

» Sunshine and warm weather prevail; far northern regions briefly thaw.

» Accommodation prices peak (up 30% on average).

» December through March is equally busy and expensive in ski resort towns.

Shoulder (May, Sep & Oct)

» Crowds and prices drop off.

» Temperatures are cool but comfortable.

» Attractions keep shorter hours.

» Fall foliage areas (eg Cape Breton Island and Québec) remain busy.

Low Season (Nov–Apr)

» Places outside the big cities and ski resorts close.

» Darkness and cold take over.

» April and November are particularly good for bargains.

Your Daily Budget

Budget: Less than $100

» Dorm bed: $25–40

» Campsite: $25–35

» Self-catered meals from markets and supermarkets: $12–20

Midrange: $100–250

» B&B room: $80–180 ($100–250 in major cities)

» Meal in a good local restaurant: from $20 plus drinks

» Rental car: per day $45–70

Top end: More than $250

» Four-star hotel room: from $180

» Three-course meal in a top restaurant: from $65 plus drinks

» Skiing day pass: $50–90

Eating

Cafes Often serve sandwiches, soups and baked goods, as well as coffee.

Diners Brunches and lunches, sometimes served 24 hours; often family-friendly.

Pubs Home-cooked fish and chips, burgers and salads.

Vegetarians Options are decent outside of rural areas.

The following price ranges are for main dishes.

$	less than $15
$$	$15–$25
$$$	more than $25

Sleeping

B&Bs Purpose-built villas to heritage homes, they are often atmospheric.

Motels Good-value options dotting the highways into town.

Hostels Traveler hangouts, favored by outdoor adventurers in remoter regions.

Camping Campgrounds are plentiful.

The following price ranges refer to a double room with private bathroom in high season, excluding tax (which can be up to 17%).

$	less than $100
$$	$100–$250
$$$	more than $250

Arriving in Canada

Toronto Pearson International Airport Trains (adult/child $12.35/free) run downtown every 15 minutes from 5:30am to 1am; taxis cost around $60 (45 minutes).

Montréal Trudeau International Airport A 24-hour airport shuttle bus ($10) runs downtown. Taxis cost a flat $40 (30 to 60 minutes).

Vancouver International Airport Trains ($7.95 to $10.70) run downtown every six to 20 minutes; taxis cost around $40 (30 minutes).

Land Border Crossings The Canadian Border Services Agency (www.cbsa-asfc.gc.ca/bwt-taf/menu-eng.html) posts wait times (usually 30 minutes).

Cell Phones

Local SIM cards can be used in unlocked GSM 850/1900 compatible phones. Other phones must be set to roaming. Coverage is spotty.

Internet Access

Wi-fi is widely available in hotels, cafes, many restaurants.

Money

ATMs are widely available. Credit cards are accepted in nearly all hotels and restaurants.

Tipping

Tipping is a standard practice. Generally you can expect to tip:

Restaurant waitstaff 15% to 20%

Bar staff $1 per drink

Hotel bellhop $1 to $2 per bag

Hotel room cleaners From $2 per day

Taxis 10% to 15%

Useful Websites

Destination Canada (en.destinationcanada.com) Official tourism site.

Environment Canada Weather (www.weather.gc.ca) Forecasts for any town.

Lonely Planet (www.lonelyplanet.com/canada) Destination information, hotel recommendations and more.

Government of Canada (www.gc.ca) National and regional information.

Parks Canada (www.pc.gc.ca) Lowdown on national parks.

Canadian Broadcasting Corporation (www.cbc.ca) National and provincial news.

For more, see Road Trip Essentials (p360).

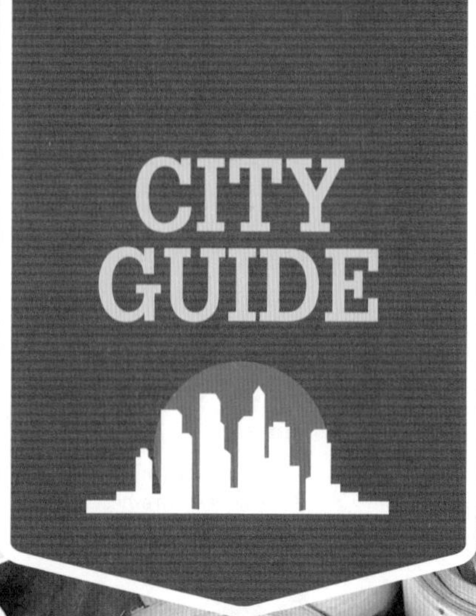

VANCOUVER

Vancouver always lands atop the 'best places to live' lists, and who's to argue? Sea-to-sky beauty surrounds the laid-back, cocktail-lovin' metropolis. With skiable mountains on the outskirts, beaches fringing the core and Stanley Park's thick rainforest just blocks from downtown's glass skyscrapers, it's a harmonic convergence of city and nature.

Chinatown (p114) Dim sum dishes on display

Getting Around

Transit in Vancouver is cheap, extensive and generally efficient. Vancouver's TransLink (www.translink.ca) bus network is extensive. The SkyTrain system is fast but limited to only a few routes.

Parking

There are some free spots on residential side streets but many require permits. Numerous streets have metered parking (up to $6 per hour). Pay-parking lots (typically from $6 per hour) are a better proposition – arrive before 9am at some for early-bird, day-rate discounts. For a map of parking-lot locations, check EasyPark (www.easypark.ca).

Where to Eat

Vancouver has an eye-popping array of generally good-value dine-out options. Gastown has innovative independent dining rooms, while Main Street offers quirky indie restaurants and neighborhood hangouts. Chinatown, not surprisingly, has some top-notch authentic eateries.

Where to Stay

Staying in downtown puts you within walking distance to stores, restaurants, nightlife and some attractions. The West End is near Stanley Park with many midrange restaurants nearby.

Useful Websites

Scout Magazine (www.scoutmagazine.ca) Hip food and bar scene zine.

Tourism Vancouver (www.tourismvancouver.com) Official tourism site.

Lonely Planet (www.lonelyplanet.com/canada/vancouver) Destination information.

Trips Through Vancouver 1

NONG AMORY/SHUTTERSTOCK ©

TOP EXPERIENCES

➡ Exploring Gastown

The brick-paved, heritage-hugging neighborhood where 19th-century Vancouver began has seen a cool wave of bars, restaurants and boutiques opening in recent years. The former skid row 'old town' area is now a picturesque and popular balance of old and new.

➡ Walking the Capilano Suspension Bridge

Arrive early to avoid the summer crowds and you'll have a great time inching over the swaying rope bridge that stretches across a roiling, tree-lined river canyon.

➡ Munching in Granville Island Public Market

From pyramids of glistening fresh fruit to drool-triggering deli counters that inspire a picnicking approach to life, this market is a taste-tripping wander for browsers.

➡ Strolling Stanley Park Seawall

You'll encounter rippling ocean backed by looming mountains on one side and the gentle swish of dense forest and smiling cyclists on the other. It's a sigh-triggering reminder of how great life can be.

➡ Delving into Chinatown

The largest in Canada, Vancouver's Chinatown still has the bustling feel of a vibrant community, from its busy apothecary shops to its steam-shrouded barbecue meat stores.

➡ Sipping and Shopping on Main Street

Vancouver's indie heart is a stroll-worthy feast of quirky stores, unique places to eat and wood-floored coffee shops that invites long afternoons of laid-back exploring among the plaid-shirted locals.

Old Montréal Cobblestone streets and old-world charm

MONTRÉAL

North America's largest francophone city is a blend of French-inspired joie de vivre and cosmopolitan dynamism that has come together to foster a flourishing arts scene, an indie rock explosion, the Plateau's extraordinary cache of swank eateries and a cool Parisian vibe that pervades every *terrasse* (patio) in the Quartier Latin.

Getting Around

Montréal's four metro lines provide speedy efficient service around the city and run from 5am to midnight and until 1:30am on Friday and Saturday nights. The city's popular Bixi bike-sharing system has more than 500 stations around town.

Parking

Street parking in Montréal can run to $4 per hour, while overnight lots charge from $17 to $28 for 24 hours. The lot near Longueuil metro station has better prices (from $8.25 for 24 hours).

Where to Eat

Downtown and Plateau Mont-Royal are a diner's delight, linked by arteries Blvd St-Laurent and Rue St-Denis. Mile End and Outremont have a wide selection of bistros and ethnic eateries, particularly along Ave Laurier, Ave St-Viateur and Rue Bernard.

Where to Stay

Old Montréal is ultra-convenient for many sights, old-world charm and access to Old Port. Nearby downtown is handy for key sights and museums. The atmospheric Plateau Mont-Royal has charming B&Bs within strolling distance of great dining and nightlife.

Useful Websites

MTL Blog (www.mtlblog.com) Opinionated local voices on the latest in dining, drinking, festivals and daily life in the city.

Tourisme Montréal (www.mtl.org) Useful multilingual info, travel ideas and events calendar from the city's modern, official website.

Trips Through Montréal

22 23 24

Toronto (p236) City skyline at twilight

TORONTO

A hyperactive stew of cultures and neighborhoods, Toronto strikes you with sheer urban awe. Will you have dinner in Chinatown or Greektown? Five-star fusion or a peameal bacon sandwich? In Ontario's cool capital, mod-art galleries, theater par excellence, rockin' band rooms and hockey mania add to the megalopolis.

Getting Around

Toronto's subway is the fastest way to get across town; service runs from 6am (8am Sunday) until 1:30am daily

Parking

Parking in Toronto is expensive, usually $3 to $4 per half hour in a private lot; public lots and street parking range from $1.50 to $4 per hour, depending on the neighborhood. Private lots offer reduced-rate parking before 7am and after 6pm.

Where to Eat

The Financial and Entertainment Districts have fine dining and celebrity chefs, while Kensington Market and Chinatown are all about hole-in-the-wall eats and homegrown talent.

Where to Stay

Downtown puts you in the heart of the action, with a good range of lodging for all budgets and easy subway access. For something more atmospheric book at Old Town, Corktown & Distillery District. The latter is a buzzing spot for restaurants, galleries, specialty boutiques and live music.

Useful Websites

Tourism Toronto (www.seetorontonow.com) Official city tourism website with loads of info, including top lists.

blogTO (www.blogto.com) The go to blog, with up-to-date info on local happenings – city wide and by neighborhood.

Toronto Life (https://torontolife.com) Excellent lifestyle magazine with restaurant reviews and event listings.

Trips Through Toronto

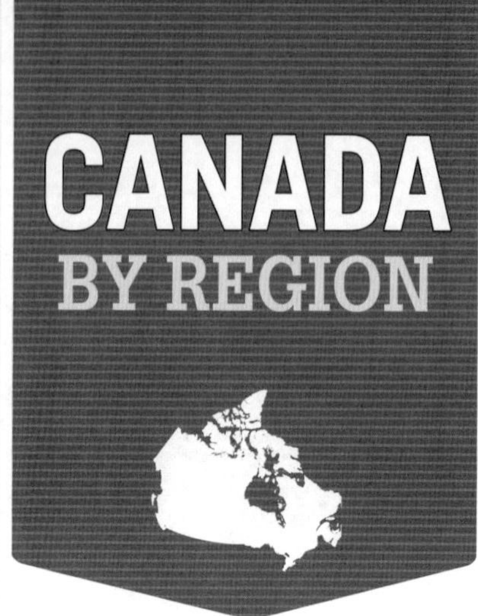

Snow-capped peaks, glacial lakes, rocky islands and soaring old-growth forests are just a few of the attractions awaiting on these grand Canadian road trips. Here's your guide to what each region has to offer.

The Prairie Provinces & the North (p119)

Those rippling oceans of grain have a mesmerizing poetry to their movement, the songbirds and crickets providing accents to the endlessly rustling wind. This is also the gateway to photogenic badlands, vast fossil and the rugged, awe-inspiring wilderness of the great north.

Peer back into the Mesozoic Era on Trip 10

British Columbia (p33)

It's not too hard to wax lyrical about the mighty mountains, deep forested valleys and dramatic shorelines of British Columbia. This province is unbeatable for life-enhancing hiking, kayaking and skiing experiences that can make these trips of a lifetime.

Take in the grandeur of Mother Nature on Trip 8

Québec (p241)

Canada's French-speaking province is packed with natural treasures. The jagged, pine-clad arc of the Laurentians gives way to the captivating beauty of the Saguenay Fjord, while in Charlevoix a patchwork of farms overlooks sweeping bays on the St Lawrence River.

Sample famed Québécois produce on Trip 23

The Atlantic Region (p307)

If you enjoy the rugged and the rough, there are few more beautiful places. Bright houses painted like rainbows spill over the cliffs; menus advertise crowberries; at night, fiddles compete with the howling wind, its chill countered by the warmest locals you'll ever meet.

Immerse yourself in island culture on Trip 32

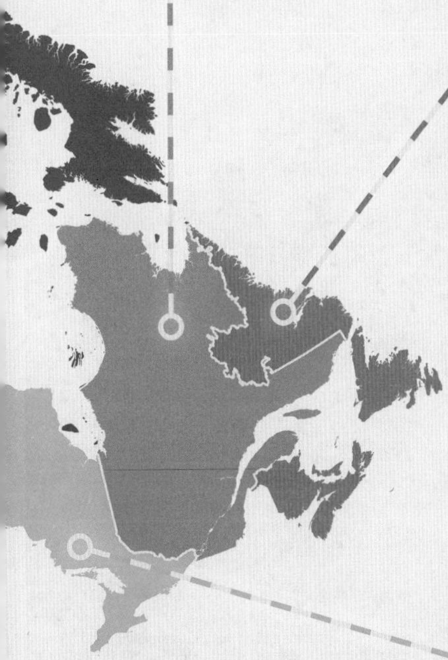

Ontario (p179)

Within easy striking distance of Toronto and Ottawa, Ontario is a four-season playground of vast spruce forests, vineyard-dotted islands and thundering waterfalls. Magnificent scenery aside, Ontario is a cultural showcase of Mennonite villages, vibrant arts-minded towns and First Nations settlements.

Discover the province's fascinating multi-ethnic roots on Trip 17

CANADA

Classic Trips

TODAMO/SHUTTERSTOCK ©

What is a Classic Trip?

All the trips in this book show you the best of Canada, but we've chosen nine as our all-time favorites. These are our Classic Trips – the ones that lead you to the best of the iconic sights, the top activities and the unique Canadian experiences.

Above: Fort Whoop-Up (p130), Alberta
Left: Mt Garibaldi (p51), British Columbia

British Columbia

FOLLOW WINDING ROADS INTO THE DEEP FORESTS OF NORTHERN VANCOUVER ISLAND, where bald eagles patrol and black bears munch dandelions, or point your wheels north toward Whistler, where dramatic glazed mountaintops scrape the sky. Then coast back down to explore dynamic Vancouver or quaint Victoria. Healthy living reaches its zenith in British Columbia (BC). You'll eat well, drink well and play well. From islands to glaciers to world-class vineyards, this region beckons for road trips and doesn't disappoint.

Whistler (p52) Skiing on world-class slopes

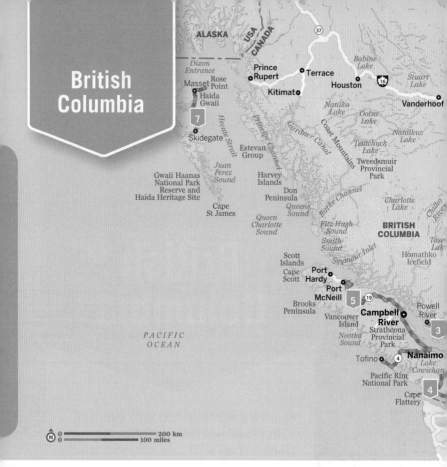

British Columbia

1 **Vancouver & the Fraser Valley 2 Days**
Brave suspension bridges and relive pioneer life in a dramatic mountain valley.

2 **Sea to Sky Highway 1–2 Days**
Go from coastal towns to snowy peaks with classic BC sights and views en route.

3 **A Strait Hop 2–3 Days**
Features some of BC's largest trees, contemporary fishing villages and an awe-inspiring ferry ride.

4 **Southern Vancouver Island Tour 4–5 Days**
Time slows down with mellow island-hopping, artsy villages and dramatic beaches.

5 **Vancouver Island's Remote North 2–3 Days**
Endless sand, old-growth forest, whales, bears and plenty of First Nations culture.

Classic Trip
6 **Okanagan Valley Wine Tour 2 Days**
Overflowing fruit stands, award-winning vineyards and amazing cuisine next to a shimmering lake.

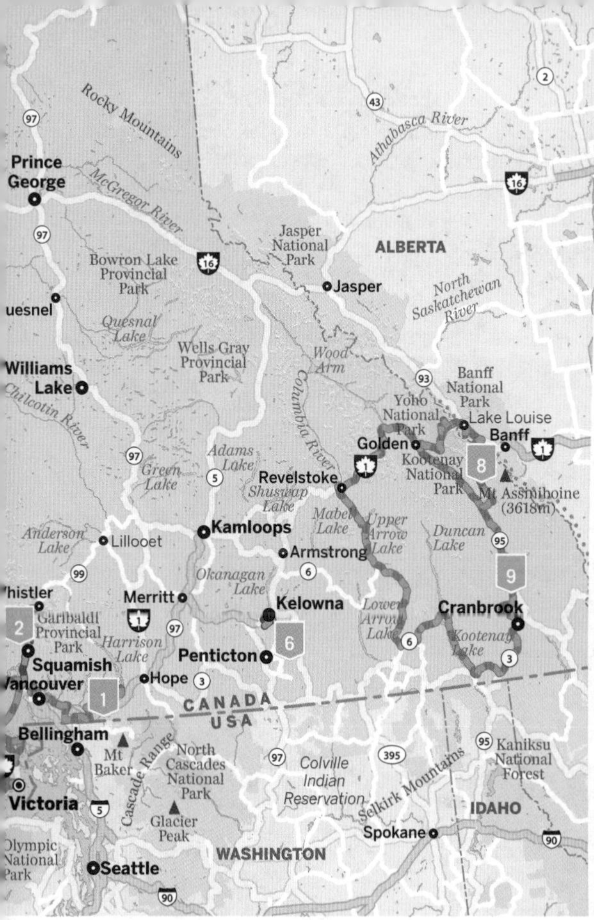

7 **Haida Gwaii Adventure 2 Days**
Experience remote wilderness and fascinating First Nations culture on these edge-of-the-earth islands.

8 **Circling the Rockies 3 Days**
Topaz lakes, snowy peaks, vast canyons and one famous national park form the backdrop to this enchanting alpine journey.

9 **Around the Kootenays 5–6 Days**
Admire alpine meadows and rugged sawtooth ridges, with scenic lakes and nice towns in between.

DON'T MISS

First Nations Culture
With state-of-the-art museums, art galleries, totem poles and modern communities, indigenous culture is accessible on Trips 4 5 7

Local Refreshments
In-house roasted coffee, local breweries, countless wineries and unique cideries will tempt your taste buds on Trips 3 4 6

Dramatic Beaches
Long Beach with its endless sand, remote Botanical Beach and forested China Beach await on Trips 3 4 5

Ancient Forests
Looking up at the towering old-growth trees in Cathedral Grove, Goldstream Provincial Park and Capilano will leave you dizzy on Trips 1 3 5 8

Wildlife
While never a sure bet, you have a chance to spot a bear, a bald eagle or a pod of whales on Trips 4 5 8 9

Vancouver & the Fraser Valley

This tour has something for everyone – parks, beaches, mountains, vineyards, hot springs and a big dollop of history, starting with an exploration of the coveted oceanfront city of Vancouver.

TRIP HIGHLIGHTS

7 km
Capilano Cliffwalk
Exhilarating glass-and-steel walkway that makes tightrope walking seem a cinch

11 km
Grouse Mountain Nature Reserve
Orphaned grizzlies, domesticated wolves, owls, beehives and more

3
2
North Vancouver
1
START
Burnaby
4
Mission
FINISH
Harrison Hot Springs

Stanley Park Seawall
Fresh air and to-die-for views, all on Vancouver's doorstep
0 km

Fort Langley
Step back in time and experience BC at its birth
67 km

2 DAYS
186KM/116 MILES

GREAT FOR...

BEST TIME TO GO

June to September for warm days and ripened fruit.

ESSENTIAL PHOTO

Wobbling over the Capilano Suspension Bridge.

BEST FOR FAMILIES

Fort Langley offers family fun for all ages. And you might strike it rich panning for gold!

Vancouver Walking along the Capilano Suspension Bridge (p39)

1 Vancouver & the Fraser Valley

As you step onto the swinging Capilano Suspension Bridge, get eyed up by a grizzly bear atop Grouse Mountain or watch your children hone their bartering skills over wolverine skins at Fort Langley, you might wonder what happened to the promised pretty valley drive. But don't worry; it's here. With dramatic mountains rising on either side, a tour along the Fraser River is as action-packed as it is scenic.

TRIP HIGHLIGHT

1 Stanley Park

Just steps from downtown Vancouver, which is also worth a walk (p114) around, but seemingly worlds away, **Stanley Park** (www.vancouver.ca/parks; West End; P 👪; 🚌19) is a spectacular urban oasis, covered in a quarter of a million trees that tower up to 80m. Rivalling New York's Central Park, this 1000-acre peninsula is a favorite hangout for locals, who walk, run or

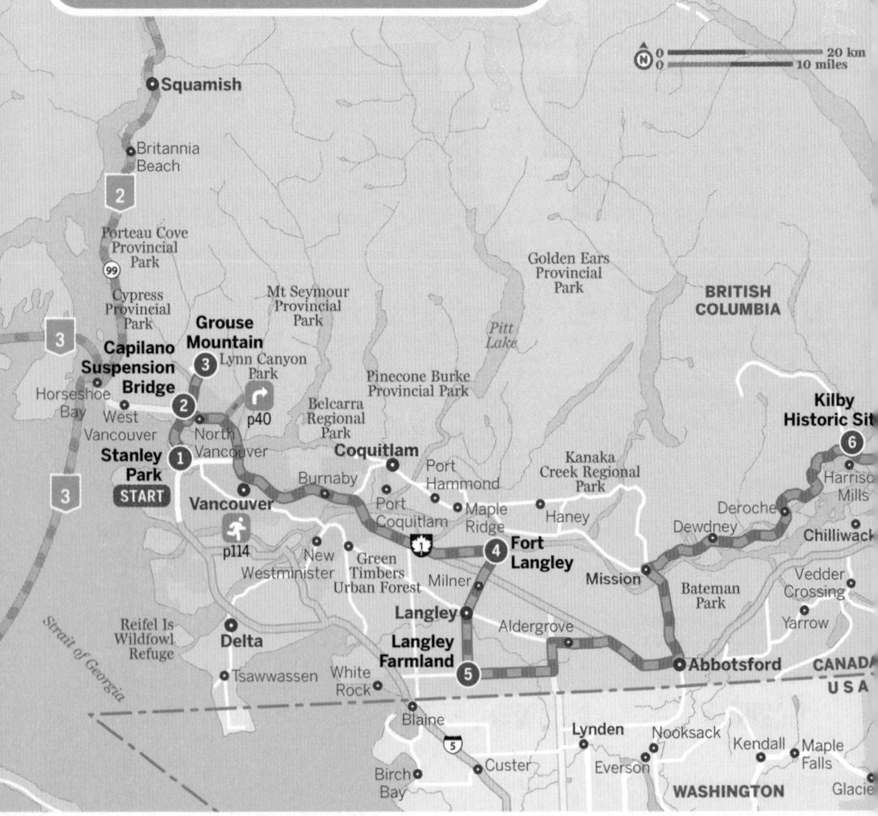

cycle around the 9km super-scenic **seawall** that circles the outer edge of the park. The pathway offers shimmering views of Burrard Inlet and passes impressive **totem poles**, squat **Brockton Point Lighthouse** and log-strewn **Third Beach**, where you can also take a dip. Watch for the dramatic **Siwash Rock**, standing sentry off the western shoreline. Meaning 'he is standing up,' Siwash was named after a traditional First Nations legend that indicates it is a man transformed into stone; the hole in the rock is where he kept his fishing tackle.

Looking out across tree-fringed English Bay, Second Beach has a heated outdoor **swimming pool** (open May to September) that's wildly popular with families. From here, a long sandy beach stretches south along Beach Ave. Looking for some kid-friendly action? The park's eastern shoreline is home to a fantastic **water park** (Lumberman's Arch, Stanley Park; 10am-6pm Jun-Sep;) that will keep your youngsters happily squealing for hours.

Also in the park is the ever-popular **Vancouver Aquarium** (604-659-3400; www.vanaqua.org; 845 Avison Way, Stanley Park; adult/child $38/21; 9:30am-6pm Jul & Aug, 10am-5pm Sep-Jun; ; 19). One of the city's biggest attractions, it's home to penguins, otters and a plethora of BC marine critters.

Yale
Harrison Lake
Choate
Sasquatch Provincial Park
Hope
Harrison Hot Springs
p42
Laidlaw
7 FINISH
Kent
Minter Gardens
Mt Baker-Snoqualmie National Forest

LINK YOUR TRIP

2 Sea to Sky Highway

Head northwest from Vancouver, rather than east, and wind your way up into the mountains.

3 A Strait Hop

Drive onto the ferry at Horseshoe Bay in West Vancouver.

The Drive » Head north on Stanley Park Causeway and cross the beautiful Lions Gate Bridge to North Vancouver. Head east on Marine Dr for a block and turn left onto Capilano Rd, heading north for 2.4km.

p43

TRIP HIGHLIGHT

2 Capilano Suspension Bridge

Not for the faint of heart, **Capilano Suspension Bridge Park** (604-985-7474; www.capbridge.com; 3735 Capilano Rd, North Vancouver; adult/child $47/15; 8am-8pm May-Aug, reduced hours off-season; ; ; 236) is home to one of the world's longest (140m) and highest (70m) pedestrian suspension bridges, swaying gently over the roiling waters of Capilano Canyon. As you gingerly cross, try to remember that the steel cables you are gripping are embedded in huge concrete blocks on either side. This is the region's most popular attraction, hence the summertime crowds. The grounds here include rainforest walks, totem poles and some smaller bridges strung between the trees that offer a lovely squirrel's-eye forest walk. You can also test your bravery on the **Cliffwalk**, a glass-and-steel walkway secured with horizontal bars to a granite cliff face and suspended 90m over the canyon floor. Deep breath...

The Drive » Continue north on Capilano Rd. This turns into Nancy Greene Way, which ends at the next stop.

TRIP HIGHLIGHT

3 Grouse Mountain

One of the region's most popular outdoor hangouts, **Grouse Mountain** (☎604-980-9311; www.grousemountain.com; 6400 Nancy Greene Way, North Vancouver; adult/child $56/29; ⏰9am-10pm; P 👪; 🚌236) rises 4039ft over North Vancouver's skyline. In summer, Skyride gondola tickets to the top include access to lumberjack shows, bird-of-prey displays and alpine hiking trails plus a **nature reserve** that's home to orphaned grizzly bears and timber wolves. You can also brave the two-hour, five-line **zip-line course** ($89, excluding Skyride) or the 'Eye of the Wind' tour, which takes you to the top of a 20-story wind turbine tower for spectacular 360-degree views. In winter, Grouse is a very popular magnet for local and visiting skiers and snowboarders.

The Drive » Return south down Nancy Greene Way and Capilano Rd, taking a left onto Edgemont Blvd, which leads to Hwy 1. Head east, following the highway through Burnaby, crossing the Second Narrows Bridge and then the impressive, 10-lane Port Mann Bridge. Continue on Hwy 1, exiting at 88 Ave East and following signs to Fort Langley. Trips takes round an hour.

DAISUKE KISHI/GETTY IMAGES ©

DETOUR: LYNN CANYON PARK

Start: 2 Capilano Suspension Bridge

For a free alternative to Capilano, divert to **Lynn Canyon Park** (www.lynncanyon.ca; Park Rd, North Vancouver; ⏰10am-5pm Jun-Sep, noon-4pm Oct-May; P 👪; 🚌228 then 227), a temperate rainforest area that's home to its own lofty but slightly smaller suspension bridge. There are also plenty of excellent hiking trails and some great tree-hugging picnic spots here. Check out the park's **Ecology Centre** (☎604-990-3755; www.lynncanyonecologycentre.ca; 3663 Park Rd, North Vancouver; by donation; ⏰10am-5pm Jun-Sep, 10am-5pm Mon-Fri & noon-4pm Sat & Sun Oct-May; 👪; 🚌227) for displays on the region's rich biodiversity. If you're really keen on local flora, drop into a bookstore on your travels and pick-up a copy of the *Vancouver Tree Book* (David Tracey, 2016). It details many of the region's leafy wonders and shows you how to spot them while you're here. To find the park, head east on Hwy 1 from Capilano Rd and turn left on Lynn Valley Rd.

TRIP HIGHLIGHT

4 Fort Langley

Little Fort Langley's tree-lined streets and 19th-century storefronts make it one of the Lower Mainland's most picturesque historic villages. Its main heritage highlight is the evocative **Fort Langley National Historic Site** (☎604-513-4777; www.parkscanada.gc.ca/fortlangley; adult/child $8/4; ⏰10am-5pm; 👪; 🚌562), perhaps the region's most important old-school landmark.

A fortified trading post since 1827, this is where James Douglas

Grouse Mountain Skiers on the slopes

announced the creation of British Columbia in 1858, giving the site a legitimate claim to being the province's birthplace. Chat with costumed re-enactors knitting, working on beaver pelts or sweeping their pioneer homes. Also open to explore are re-created artisan workshops and a **gold-panning area** that's very popular with kids. And when you need a rest, sample baking and lunchtime meals from the 1800s in the **Lelem' Cafe**.

Be sure to check the fort's website before you arrive: there's a wide array of events that bring the past back to life, including a summertime evening campfire program that will take you right back to the pioneer days of the 1800s.

The Drive » Head south out of the village on Glover Rd, crossing Hwy 1 and then taking a slight left so that you're traveling south on 216th St. The next stop is just past 16th Ave.

✕ p43

❺ Langley Farmland

The vine-covered grounds of **Chaberton Estate Winery** (☎604-530-1736; www.chabertonwinery.com; 1064 216 St, Langley; ⏰10am-6pm, to 8pm Thu-Sat, 11am-6pm Sun) is the setting for the Fraser Valley's oldest wine-making operation, here since 1991. The French-influenced, 55-acre vineyard specializes in cool-climate whites: its subtle, Riesling-style Bacchus is dangerously easy to drink. There's also a handy bistro here.

Head south and right on 4th St to the charming **Vista D'oro** (☎604-514-3539; www.vistadoro.com; 346 208th St, Langley; ⏰11am-5pm Thu-Sun Mar-Dec), a working farm and winery where you can load up on fresh pears, plums, apples and stripy heirloom tomatoes. Sample preserves such as piquant mango lime salsa and sweet rhubarb and vanilla jam. Also pick up a bottle of their utterly delicious, port-style walnut wine that's made from nuts grown just outside the shop. It's definitely small batch, so if you see it, buy it.

The Fraser Valley is home to countless farms, producing everything from tulips to cheese. Many accept visitors, give tours and sell their wares in farm shops. If you're keen to visit some more, go to www.circlefarmtour.com for details.

The Drive » Return north up 216th St and turn right on North Bluff Rd. Continue east for four blocks and turn left onto 248th St, which takes you to the Fraser Hwy. Head east toward Abbotsford, and then north on the Abbotsford Mission Hwy over the Fraser River to Hwy 7. Turn right and follow the road along the river. Approximately 1½ hours.

TOP TIP: TRAFFIC REPORTS

Traffic over the Lions Gate Bridge and along Hwy 1 can be heavy enough to bring you to a standstill at times. Check the website of DriveBC (www.drivebc.ca) for traffic, construction and incident reports.

6 Kilby Historic Site

To get to **Kilby Historic Site** (☎604-796-9576; www.kilby.ca; 215 Kilby Rd; adult/child $10/8; ⏰11am-4pm Jul & Aug, reduced hours Sep-Jun), turn right onto School Rd and then right again onto Kilby Rd. The clocks turn back to the 1920s when you enter this site, all that remains of the once thriving Harrison Mills community. Join a tour led by costumed interpreters as you explore the general store, hotel, post office and working farm, complete with friendly farm animals.

The Drive » Return to Hwy 7 and carry on east, passing through farmland and hazelnut orchards. Turn left on Hwy 9, which takes you to Harrison Hot Springs, for a total drive of 21km.

7 Harrison Hot Springs

Set on the edge of Harrison Lake and with views to forest-carpeted mountains, Harrison Hot Springs (www.tourismharrison.com) is a resort town that draws both locals and visitors to its sandy beach, warm lagoon and lakeside promenade. While the lake itself is glacier-fed, two hot springs bubble at the southern end of the lake and the warm water can be enjoyed year-round at the town's upscale resort and the indoor public pool. You should time your Harrison visit with the area's cultural festival. July's multiday Harrison Festival of the Arts (www.harrisonfestival.com) has been running for more than 30 years, bringing live music, gallery shows, workshops and more to the area's beachfront streets.

🛏 p43

DETOUR: HOPE

Start: 7 Harrison Hot Springs

Hope's nickname is the 'Chainsaw Capital' and this rather unusual moniker certainly draws attention. The name was earned by the wooden sculptures peppered throughout the town. Hope is a small community at the eastern edge of the Fraser Valley, set beneath the shadow of the Cascade Mountains. The 70-plus chainsaw sculptures are the products of both local and visiting artists. Most depict wildlife, including the Sasquatch who is believed to live in the nearby woods.

Eating & Sleeping

Stanley Park 1

Sylvia Hotel — Hotel $$

(604-681-9321; www.sylviahotel.com; 1154 Gilford St, West End; d from $199; P @ ; 5) This ivy-covered 1912 charmer enjoys a prime location overlooking English Bay. Generations of guests keep coming back – many requesting the same room every year – for a dollop of old-world ambience, plus a side order of first-name service. The rooms, some with older furnishings, have an array of comfortable configurations; the best are the large suites with kitchens and waterfront views.

Listel Hotel — Boutique Hotel $$$

(604-684-8461; www.thelistelhotel.com; 1300 Robson St, West End; d from $340; P @ ; 5) A lounge-cool sleepover with famously friendly front-deskers. Rooms at the Listel have a relaxed West Coast feel and typically feature striking original artworks. But it's not all about looks; cool features include glass water bottles in the rooms, a daily wine reception (from 5pm) and the free use of loaner e-bikes if you want to explore nearby Stanley Park (p38).

Fort Langley 4

Veggie Bob's Kitchen — Vegan $

(604-888-1223; www.veggiebobs.com; 9044 Glover Rd; mains $8-12; 11am-8pm Tue-Sun; ; 562) A few years ago Veggie Bob's went 100% vegan without having to change the fundamentals of its American heartland meets Mexican menu. Unlikely favorites include a vegan hot dog smeared with mac and cheese, the ever-popular quesadilla with guacamole, and a doorstep-sized apple pie for dessert. Seating is coffee-bar style amid an array of sculpted busts.

Wendel's Bookstore & Cafe — Cafe $

(604-513-2238; www.wendelsonline.com; 9233 Glove Rd; dishes $8-16; 7:30am-10pm; ; 562) It's difficult to work out if Wendel's is a bookshop attached to a cafe or a cafe attached to a bookshop. Both are equally visit-worthy. This is certainly more than a soup-and-sandwich hangout for bibliophiles. You can get baby back ribs here, and the homemade desserts (including caramel and pecan cheesecake) are surely from another sweeter planet.

Harrison Hot Springs 5

Harrison Hot Springs Resort — Hotel $$

(604-796-2244; www.harrisonresort.com; 100 Esplanade Ave; r from $160; P) This fabled resort on the lakefront in Harrison Hot Springs exudes peace. Open since 1886, it has an art-deco flair and offers good service. The hot-spring pools are set in an inner courtyard complete with trees and fairy lights. There is also a divine-smelling spa, numerous restaurants and a concierge who can arrange everything from fishing trips to golf.

Classic Trip

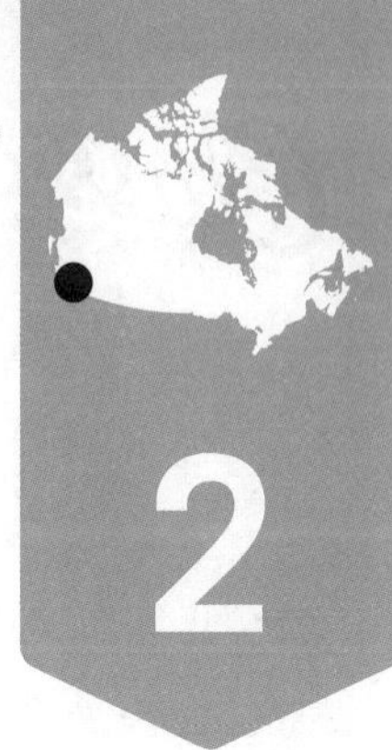

Sea to Sky Highway

The coastal scenery here is magnificent – as are the deep forests, crashing waterfalls and lofty mountains. When you can see it all in a day, it's almost too good to be true.

TRIP HIGHLIGHTS

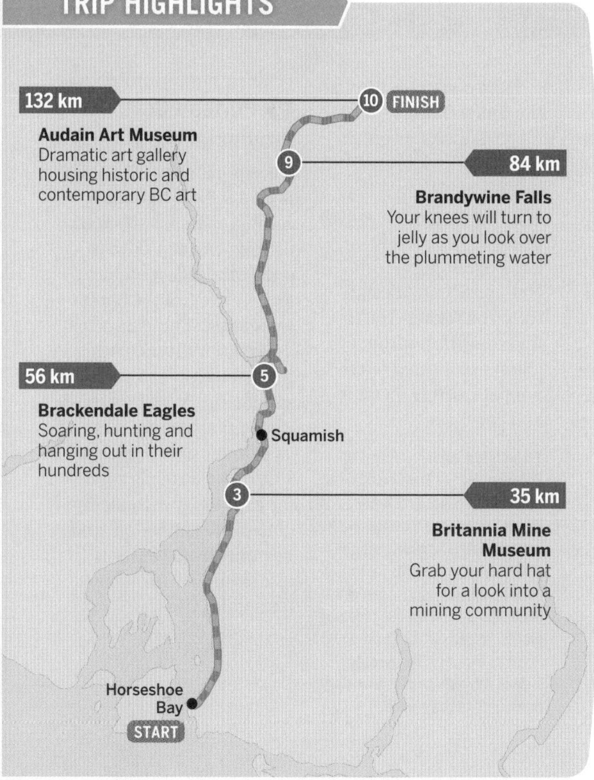

132 km
Audain Art Museum
Dramatic art gallery housing historic and contemporary BC art

10 FINISH

9

84 km
Brandywine Falls
Your knees will turn to jelly as you look over the plummeting water

56 km
Brackendale Eagles
Soaring, hunting and hanging out in their hundreds

5

Squamish

3

35 km
Britannia Mine Museum
Grab your hard hat for a look into a mining community

Horseshoe Bay
START

1–2 DAYS
132KM/82 MILES

GREAT FOR...

BEST TIME TO GO

November to March has the best snow; June to September offers sunny hiking, plus driving without chains.

ESSENTIAL PHOTO

Get the ultimate snowy-peak picture from Tantalus Lookout.

BEST FOR OUTDOORS

Ski Olympic-style down Whistler Mountain.

Tantalus Mountain Range View of the snowy peak from Tantalus Lookout (p49)

Classic Trip

2 Sea to Sky Highway

Drive out of North Vancouver and straight onto the wild west coast. This short excursion reveals the essence of British Columbia's shoreline with majestic sea and mountain vistas, outdoor activity opportunities, wildlife-watching possibilities and a peek into the regional First Nations culture and pioneer history that's woven into the route. There's even freshly roasted, organic coffee along the way. How much more 'BC' can you get?

1 Horseshoe Bay

As clouds and mist drift in across the snowcapped mountains of Howe Sound, standing at the foot of Horseshoe Bay may well make you feel like you've stepped into middle-earth. Green-forested hills tumble down around the village, which has a small-town vibe that doesn't attest to its proximity to Vancouver. Grab a coffee and some fish and chips from one of the many waterfront cafes and watch the bobbling boats from the seaside park. This first stop is all about slowing down and taking it all in.

Have a wander through the **Spirit Gallery** (☎604-921-8972; www.spirit-gallery.com; 6408 Bay St, Horseshoe Bay, West Vancouver; ⏰10am-6pm; 🚌257), which is filled with classic and contemporary First Nations art and design from the region. You'll find everything from eye glasses to animal hand-puppets, prints, pewter and carvings.

The Drive » Head north for 25km on Hwy 99, which curves around the coast and follows Howe Sound. You'll be traveling between steep mountainsides, down which waterfalls plummet, and the often misty ocean where islands are perched like sleeping giants. Watch out for Tunnel Point Lookout on the western side of the highway for a vantage point across the sound.

2 Porteau Cove Provincial Park

Once popular with regional First Nations communities for sturgeon fishing, Porteau Cove is one of the oldest archaeological sites on the northwest coast. These days it's a haven for divers, with a sunken ship and reefs supporting countless species of marine life, such as octopus and wolf eels. The rocky beach is good for exploring, with plenty of logs to clamber on, and in summer the water is just about warm enough for a quick dip.

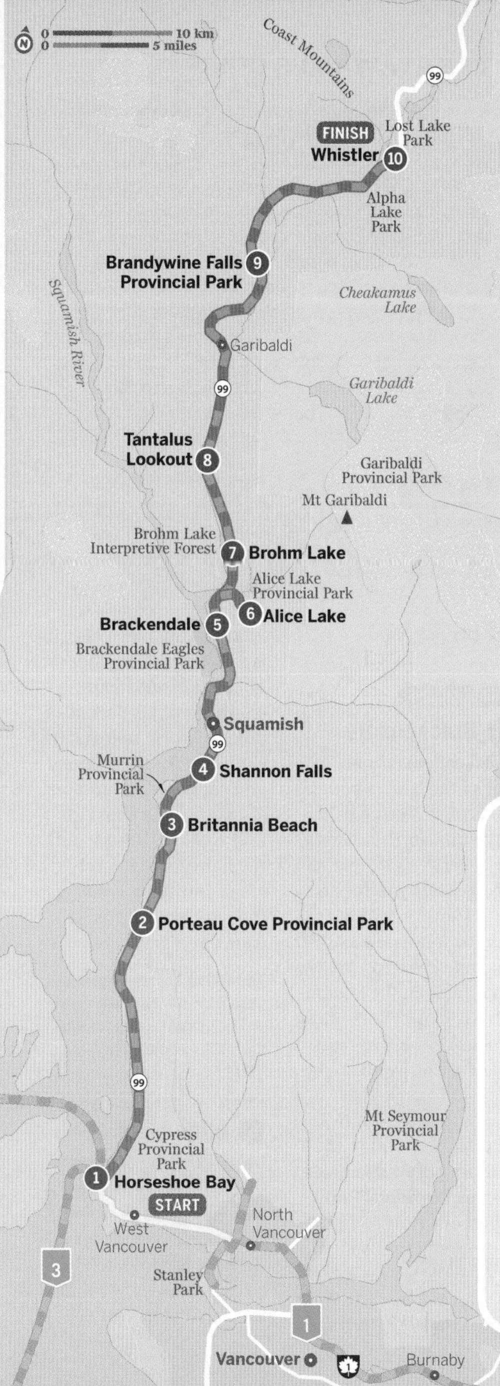

The Drive » From here, the sound narrows and as you continue 8km north on Hwy 99, the mountains from the opposite shore begin to loom over you.

TRIP HIGHLIGHT

3 Britannia Beach

Don a hard hat and hop on a bone-shaking train that trundles you through a floodlit mine tunnel. With hands-on exhibits, gold panning, an engaging film and entry into the dizzying 20-story mill, the **Britannia Mine Museum** (☎604-896-2260; www.britanniaminemuseum.ca; Hwy 99, Britannia Beach; adult/child $30/19; ⏱9am-5pm; 👪) has plenty to keep you (and any kids in tow) busy. Factor in a couple of hours here.

LINK YOUR TRIP

1 Vancouver & the Fraser Valley

Highway 99 begins in North Vancouver where you can divert onto this multifarious exploration of Vancouver and its fertile hinterland.

3 A Strait Hop

A Strait Hop goes through Horseshoe Bay, also the first stop on this shore-tracking tour of Vancouver Island and the Sunshine Coast.

THE STAWAMUS CHIEF

Towering 700m above the waters of Howe Sound like 'The Wall' in *Game of Thrones*, the Chief is the world's second-largest freestanding granite monolith. The three peaks have long been considered a sacred place to the Squamish people; they once came here seeking spiritual renewal. It's also the nesting grounds of peregrine falcons, who are increasingly returning to the area.

The views from the top are unbelievable. The sheer face of the monolith has become a magnet for rock climbers, while hikers can take a steep trail starting from the base station of the **Sea to Sky Gondola** to one or all of the three summits.

The Drive » Continue 7km north on Hwy 99, through the lush green Murrin Provincial Park.

p53

4 Shannon Falls

Torpedoing 335m over the mountaintop, **Shannon Falls** (www.bcparks.ca; Hwy 99, Squamish) is the third largest flume in the province. Historically, the medicine people of the Squamish First Nation trained alongside these falls. A short, picturesque walk through the woods leads to a viewing platform.

You can also hike from here to the peak of the **Stawamus Chief** (two to three hours round-trip) or hop back in your car and continue another minute or two along Hwy 99 to the **Sea to Sky Gondola** (604-892-2551; www.seatoskygondola.com; 36800 Hwy 99, Squamish; adult/child $42/14; 10am-6pm May-Oct, reduced hours Nov-Apr) where a cable car zips you up to a summit lodge at 885m. From here you can walk across a shaky suspension bridge to access a network of above-the-treeline trails.

The Drive » Continue north on Hwy 99, past the Stawamus Chief and through Squamish, where you can stop for gas or sample from a raft of craft breweries and distilleries. Carry on along the highway, taking a left on Depot Rd and then another left onto Government Rd. The next stop is a few minutes up the road on your right.

p53

TRIP HIGHLIGHT

5 Brackendale

Brackendale is home to one of the largest populations of wintering bald eagles in North America. Visit between November and February to see an almost overwhelming number of these massive, magnificent birds feasting on salmon in the Squamish River. A path running alongside the riverbank offers a short walk and plenty of easy eagle-spotting opportunities. Across the river are the tall trees of **Brackendale Eagles Provincial Park**, where the beady-eyed birds perch in the night.

Also in this neighborhood is the historic **West Coast Railway Heritage Park** (604-898-9336; www.wcra.org; 39645 Government Rd, Squamish; adult/child $25/15; 10am-3pm;). This large, mostly outdoor museum is the final resting place of British Columbia's legendary *Royal Hudson* steam engine and has dozens of other historic railcars, including working engines and cabooses, sumptuous sleepers and a cool vintage mail car. Check out the handsome Roundhouse building, housing the park's most precious trains and artifacts.

The Drive » Hwy 99 leaves the Squamish River 5km north of Brackendale and heads into the trees. The next stop is on the right.

6 Alice Lake

Delve into an old-growth hemlock forest for hiking and biking trails as well as lakeside picnic opportunities. Surrounded by a ring of towering mountains and offering two sandy beaches fringed by relatively warm water in summer, **Alice Lake Provincial Park** (www.discovercamping.ca; Hwy 99, Brackendale; campsites $43) is a popular spot for a dip, a walk and an alfresco lunch.

Next stretch your legs on the 6km **Four Lakes Trail**, an easy hike that does a loop around all four lakes in the park, passing through stands of Douglas fir and western red cedar. Keep your eyes (and your ears) peeled for warblers, Steller's jays and chickadees as well as for the box turtles that sometimes sun themselves on the logs at Stump Lake.

Britannia Beach Mine carts at the Britannia Mine Museum (p47)

The Drive » Continue north along Hwy 99 for around 6km to Brohm Lake.

7 Brohm Lake

Less developed than Alice Lake Provincial Park, **Brohm Lake Interpretive Forest** has 10km of walking trails, many of them easy and flat. The lake is warm enough for summer swimming as the sun filters down onto the tree-studded shoreline.

Archaeological digs from this area have unearthed arrowheads and tools from early First Nations communities that date back 10,000 years. The area was later the scene of a logging mill and today is home to **Tenderfoot Fish Hatchery** (☎604-898-3657; 1000 Midnight Way, Brackendale; ⊙8am-3pm), a facility aimed at replenishing depleted chum and chinook salmon stocks, which fell from around 25,000 in the 1960s to around 1500 in the early 1980s. You can visit the hatchery and take a self-guided tour by following a 3km trail from Brohm Lake.

The Drive » Continue up Hwy 99 just over 3km to the next stop.

8 Tantalus Lookout

This viewpoint looks out across the **Tantalus Mountain Range**. Tantalus was a character in Greek mythology who gave us the word 'tantalize'; apparently the mountains were named by an explorer who was tempted to climb the range's snowy peaks, but was stuck on the other side of the turbulent Squamish River. In addition to Mt Tantalus, the Greek hero's entire family is here – his wife Mt Dione, his daughter Mt Niobe, his son Mt Pelops and his grandson Mt Thyestes.

TOP TIP: GAS STATION

There is nowhere to fill your tank between North Vancouver and Squamish, a distance of around 50km. This is mountain driving so make sure you've got at least half a tank when you set out.

Classic Trip

HAILSHADOW/GETTY IMAGES ©

LEONWANG/SHUTTERSTOCK ©

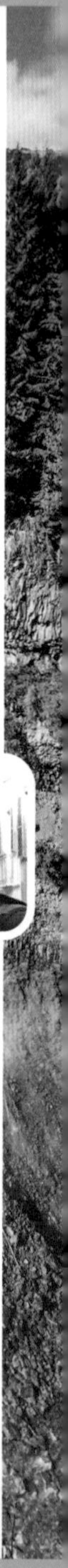

WHY THIS IS A CLASSIC TRIP
BRENDAN SAINSBURY, WRITER

If you live in BC (as I do), this is where you take any visiting friend or relative to instantly impress them. It's BC's greatest hits in one morning (or afternoon) – mountains, water, forests, wildlife, First Nations myths, and a rugged but well-maintained road that never strays far from the wilderness. A stop in Squamish for coffee and a quick 'run' up the Chief is de rigueur.

Above: Hikers on top of Stawamus Chief (p48)
Left: Eagle perched in Brackendale Eagles Provincical Park (p48)
Right: Brandywine Falls

The Squamish people once used this area to train in hunting, and believe that long ago hunters and their dogs were immortalized here, becoming the soaring mountain range. Those stone hunters must be rather tantalized themselves; the forested slopes of the mountains are home to grizzly bears, elk, wolves and cougars.

The Drive » Follow Hwy 99 22km north through the woods, skirting the edge of Daisy Lake before reaching the next stop on your right.

TRIP HIGHLIGHT

9 Brandywine Falls Provincial Park

Surging powerfully over the edge of a volcanic escarpment, **Brandywine Falls** (www.env.gov.bc.ca/bcparks/explore/parkpgs/brandywine_falls; Hwy 99) plunge a dramatic 70m – a straight shot into the pool below. Follow the easy 10-minute trail through the woods and step out onto the viewing platform, directly over the falls.

From here you can also see **Mt Garibaldi**, the most easily recognizable mountain in the Coast Range. Its distinctive jagged top and color has earned it the name Black Tusk. This mountain is of particular significance to local First Nations groups who believe the great Thunderbird landed here. With its supernatural ways, it shot bolts of lightning from its eyes, creating the color and shape of the mountaintop.

A 7km looped trail leads further through the park's dense forest and ancient lava beds to **Cal-Cheak Suspension Bridge**.

The Drive » Continue north for 17km along Hwy 99, passing Creekside Village and carrying on to the main Whistler village entrance (it's well signposted and obvious once you see it).

TRIP HIGHLIGHT

⑩ Whistler

Nestled in the shade of the formidable Whistler and Blackcomb Mountains, Whistler has long been BC's golden child. Popular in winter for its world-class ski slopes and in summer for everything from hiking to one of North America's longest zip-lines, it draws fans from around the world. It was named for the furry marmots that fill the area with their loud whistle, but there are also plenty of berry-snuffling black bears about.

THE STORY BEGINS

As you enter the **Squamish Lil'wat Cultural Centre** (☎604-964-0990; www.slcc.ca; 4584 Blackcomb Way; adult/child $18/5; ⏰10am-5pm daily Apr-Oct, Tues-Sun Nov-Mar) in Whistler, take a look at the carved cedar doors you're passing through. According to the center's guide map, the door on the left shows a grizzly bear – protector of the Lil'wat – with a salmon in its mouth, representing sharing. The carving references a mother bear and cub that walked into the Centre during construction. The door on the right, depicting a human face and hands up, symbolizes the Squamish welcoming all visitors.

The site of many of the outdoor events at the 2010 Winter Olympic and Paralympic Games, Whistler village is well worth a stroll and is filled with an eclectic mix of stores, flash hotels and seemingly countless cafes and restaurants.

Crisscrossed with more than 200 runs, the **Whistler-Blackcomb** (☎604-967-8950; www.whistlerblackcomb.com; day-pass adult/child $178/89) sister mountains are linked by a 4.4km gondola that includes the world's longest unsupported span. Ski season runs from late November to April on Whistler and to June on Blackcomb. **Ziptrek Ecotours** (☎604-935-0001; www.ziptrek.com; 4280 Mountain Sq, Carleton Lodge; adult/child from $119/99; 👪) offers year-round zip-line courses that will have you screaming with gut-quivering pleasure.

While you're here, be sure to take in the wood-beamed Squamish Lil'wat Cultural Centre (p52), built to resemble a traditional longhouse. It's filled with art, images and displays that illuminate the traditional and contemporary cultures of the Squamish and Lil'wat Nations.

A short stroll away, **Audain Art Museum** (☎604-962-0413; www.audainartmuseum.com; 4350 Blackcomb Way; adult/child $18/free; ⏰10am-5pm, to 9pm Fri, closed Tue) is home to an array of paintings from BC icons, including Emily Carr and EJ Hughes, plus a collection of historic and contemporary First Nations works. Allow at least an hour here.

✕ 🛏 p53

Eating & Sleeping

Squamish ❹

✕ Howe Sound Pub & Brewing Company — Pub Food $$

(☎778-654-3358; www.howesound.com; 37801 Cleveland Ave, Squamish; mains $15-26; ⏲11am-midnight, to 1am Fri, from 8am Sat & Sun; 📶) This wood-beamed, ever-popular brewpub has a deck with views of the Chief, where you can get comfortable and partake of some irresistible yam fries and bold Devil's Elbow IPA. Or head inside for handmade pizzas, burgers and sandwiches, and elevated pub classics including mussels in a honey pale ale broth.

🛏 Howe Sound Inn — Inn $$

(☎604-892-2603; www.howesoundinn.com; 37801 Cleveland Ave, Squamish; d $145; 📶) Quality rustic is the approach at this comfortable inn, where the rooms are warm and inviting with plenty of wooden furnishings. Recover from your climbing escapades in the property's popular sauna – or just head to the downstairs brewpub, which serves some of BC's best housemade beers. Inn guests can request free brewery tours.

Even if you're not staying, it's worth stopping in at the restaurant here for great pub grub with a gourmet twist.

Whistler ❿

✕ 21 Steps Kitchen & Bar — Canadian $$

(☎604-966-2121; www.21steps.ca; 4433 Sundial Pl; mains $18-41; ⏲5:30-11pm; 🍷) Offering small plates ($6 to $16) for nibblers and main dishes for starving skiers, the chefs at this casual upstairs spot advertise their work as 'modern comfort food'. Vegetarians will sigh contentedly at the 'vegetable tower' (roasted eggplant, zucchini and squash), pescatarians will relish the pan-seared trout and visiting Aussies will get homesick over the Australian lamb chop in a vermouth reduction.

The loungier Attic is an affiliated upstairs bar usually commandeered by locals imbibing beer and cocktails.

🛏 HI Whistler Hostel — Hostel $

(☎604-962-0025; www.hihostels.ca/whistler; 1035 Legacy Way; dm/r $43/120; @📶) Built as athlete accommodation for the 2010 Winter Olympics, this sparkling hostel is 7km south of the village, near Function Junction. Transit buses to/from town stop right outside. Book ahead for private rooms (with private baths and TVs) or save by staying in a small dorm. Eschewing the sometimes institutionalized HI hostel feel, this one has IKEA-style furnishings, art-lined walls and a licensed cafe.

There's also a great TV room for rainy-day hunkering. If it's fine, hit the nearby biking and hiking trails or barbecue on one of the two mountain-view decks.

🛏 Adara Hotel — Boutique Hotel $$

(☎604-905-4009; www.adarahotel.com; 4122 Village Green; r from $219; 📶🏊🐾) Unlike all those lodges now claiming to be boutique hotels, the sophisticated and blissfully affordable Adara is the real deal. With warm wood furnishings studded with orange exclamation marks, the rooms offer spa-like baths, cool aesthetics and 'floating' fireplaces that look like TVs. Boutique extras include fresh cookies and in-room boot dryers. Prices dip significantly in shoulder season.

Queen of Coquitlam
VICTORIA

A Strait Hop

BC's forested, multi-fjorded coastline stretches for at least 24,000km. But you don't have to drive that far for a taste of the region's salty, character-packed waterfront communities.

3

TRIP HIGHLIGHTS

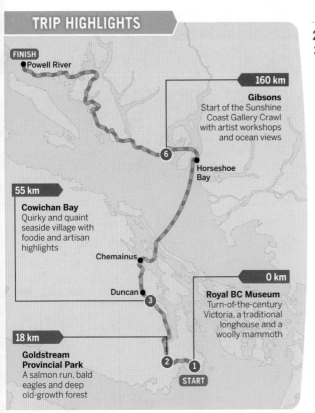

FINISH
Powell River

160 km
Gibsons
Start of the Sunshine Coast Gallery Crawl with artist workshops and ocean views

Horseshoe Bay

55 km
Cowichan Bay
Quirky and quaint seaside village with foodie and artisan highlights

Chemainus

Duncan

0 km
Royal BC Museum
Turn-of-the-century Victoria, a traditional longhouse and a woolly mammoth

18 km
Goldstream Provincial Park
A salmon run, bald eagles and deep old-growth forest

START

2–3 DAYS
351KM/219 MILES

GREAT FOR...

BEST TIME TO GO

June to September offers the most sunshine and least rain.

ESSENTIAL PHOTO

Clouds draped across mountaintops from the deck of a Horseshoe Bay ferry.

BEST FOR FOODIES

Dive into some delightful regional flavors in Cowichan Bay.

Horseshoe Bay (p46) The Queen of Coquitlam ferry arrives in the bay

3 A Strait Hop

Perhaps it's the way sunlight reflects across the ever-shifting ocean, or the forest walks and beachcombing that seem an essential part of coastal life. Whatever the reason, the towns and villages snuggled next to the Pacific draw artistic folk from around the world to settle here and create strong communities and beautiful art. Take this leisurely tour for a slice of life on both the mainland and Vancouver Island.

TRIP HIGHLIGHT

1 Victoria

British Columbia's lovely, walkable (p116) and increasingly bike-friendly capital is dripping with colonial architecture and has enough museums, attractions, hotels and restaurants to keep many visitors enthralled for an extra night or two.

Must-see attractions include the excellent **Royal BC Museum** (☎250-356-7226; www.royalbcmuseum.bc.ca; 675 Belleville St; adult/child $17/11, incl

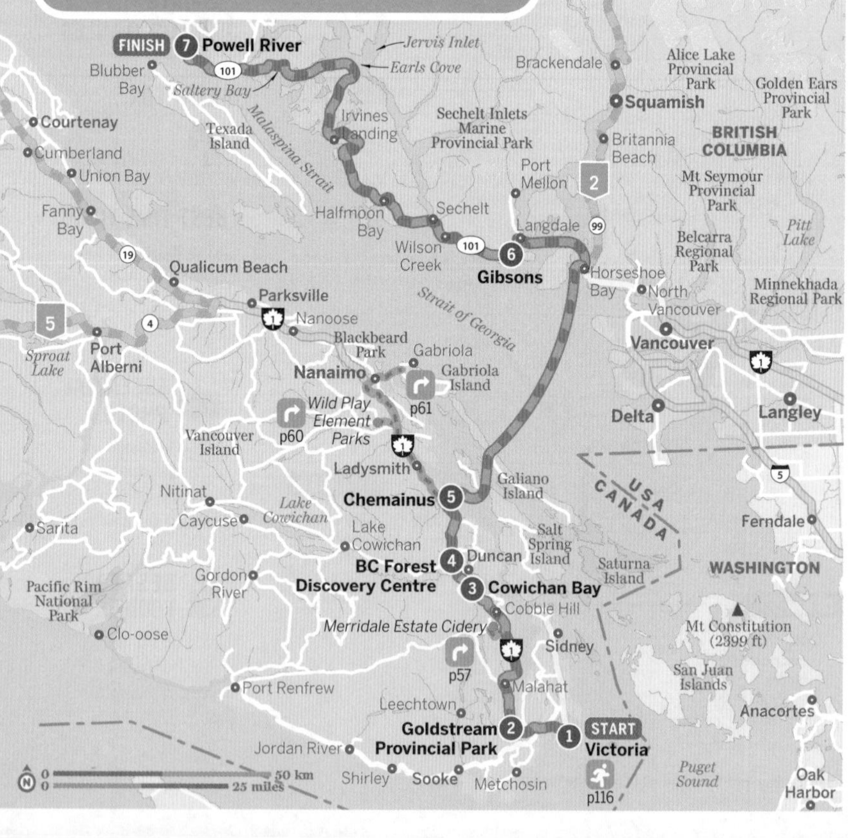

IMAX $26.95/21.25; ⏲10am-5pm daily, to 10pm Fri & Sat mid-May–Sep; 👪; 🚌70). Come eye to beady eye with a woolly mammoth and look out for cougars and grizzlies peeking from behind the trees. Step aboard Captain Vancouver's ship, enter a First Nations cedar longhouse, and explore a re-created early colonial street complete with shops, a movie house and an evocative replica Chinatown. A few minutes' stroll away, you'll also find the hidden gem **Miniature World** (☎250-385-9731; www.miniatureworld.com; 649 Humboldt St; adult/child $16/8; ⏲9am-9pm mid-May–mid-Sep, to 5pm mid-Sep–mid-May; 👪; 🚌70), an immaculate, old-school attraction crammed with 80 diminutive dioramas themed on everything from Arthurian Britain to a futuristic sci-fi realm.

LINK YOUR TRIP

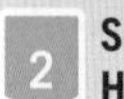

2 Sea to Sky Highway

Join this trip at Horseshoe Bay winding your way up Hwy 99 past the climbing hub of Squamish to the peerless ski-town of Whistler.

5 Vancouver Island's Remote North

From Nanaimo explore the more remote flavor of Vancouver Island by pitching north to Qualicum Beach or west to Tofino.

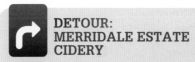

DETOUR: MERRIDALE ESTATE CIDERY

Start: 2 Goldstream

After leaving Goldstream, head west off the highway onto Cobble Hill Rd. This weaves through bucolic farmland and wine-growing country. Watch for asparagus farms, beady-eyed llamas, blueberry stalls and verdant vineyards. Stop in at charming **Merridale Estate Cidery** (☎250-743-4293; www.merridalecider.com; 1230 Merridale Rd, Cobble Hill; ⏲11am-5pm, reduced hours Oct-Mar), an inviting apple-cider producer offering many varieties, as well as artisan gin and vodka. Cobble Hill Rd crosses over the highway and loops east to Cowichan Bay.

Also worth visiting is the **Art Gallery of Greater Victoria** (☎250-384-4171; www.aggv.ca; 1040 Moss St; adult/child $13/2.50; ⏲10am-5pm Tue, Wed, Fri & Sat, to 9pm Thu, noon-5pm Sun; 🚌14), home to one of Canada's best Emily Carr collections. Aside from Carr's swirling nature canvases, you'll find an ever-changing array of temporary exhibitions.

And save time to hop on a not-much-bigger-than-a-bathtub-sized **Victoria Harbour Ferry** (☎250-708-0201; www.victoriaharbourferry.com; fares from $7; ⏲Mar-Oct). This colorful armada of tiny tugboats stop at numerous docks along the waterfront, including the Inner Harbour, Songhees Park and Fisherman's Wharf (where alfresco fish and chips is heartily recommended).

The Drive » Follow Hwy 1 (which begins its cross-country journey in Victoria) 19km west onto the sometimes narrow, heavily forested Malahat Dr section, also known as the Malahat Hwy.

✕ 🛏 p62

TRIP HIGHLIGHT

2 Goldstream Provincial Park

Alongside the Malahat, the abundantly forested **Goldstream Provincial Park** (☎250-478-9414; www.goldstreampark.com; 2930 Trans-Canada Hwy; P) drips with ancient, moss-covered cedar trees and a moist carpet of plant life. The short walk through the woods to the **Freeman King Visitors Centre** (☎250-478-9414; 2390 Trans-Canada Hwy; ⏲9am-4:30pm) is beautiful; once you're there, take in the center's hands-on exhibits about natural history.

The park is known for its chum salmon spawning season (from late October to December), when the water literally bubbles with thousands of struggling fish. Hungry bald eagles also swoop in at this time to feast on the full-grown salmon.

A short 700m trail leads to Niagara Falls, which is a lot narrower but only 4m shorter than it's famous Ontario namesake. Hike beyond the falls and you'll reach an impressive railway trestle (which you're not supposed to walk on).

The Drive » From Goldstream, the Malahat climbs north for 8km to its summit with a number of gorgeous viewpoints over Brentwood Bay. Continue on Hwy 1 for another 28km, following signs east off the highway for Cowichan Bay.

TRIP HIGHLIGHT

3 Cowichan Bay

With a colorful string of wooden buildings perched on stilts over a mountain-shadowed ocean inlet, Cowichan Bay – Cow Bay to locals – is well worth a stop. Wander along the pier of the **Maritime Centre** (250-746-4955; www.classicboats.org; 1761 Cowichan Bay Rd; suggested donation $5; 9am-4pm Wed-Sun) to peruse some salty boat-building exhibits and intricate models and get your camera out to shoot the handsome panoramic views of the harbor. Duck into the galleries and studios lining the waterfront or stretch your legs on a five-minute stroll to the **Cowichan Estuary Nature Centre** (250-597-2288; www.cowichanestuary.ca; 1845 Cowichan Bay Rd; suggested donation $2; noon-4pm;), where area birdlife and marine critters are profiled.

Drop into the **Mud Room** (250-710-7329; www.cowbaymudroom.com; 1725 Cowichan Bay Rd; 9am-6pm Jun-Sep, reduced hours in winter) to see potters at work making usable objects like cups and plates. Look for seaside-themed mugs and the popular yellow-glazed dragonfly motif pieces.

The artisans are also at work in Cow Bay's kitchens. This is a great place to gather the mak-

SUNSHINE COAST GALLERY CRAWL

Along Hwy 101, near Gibsons (p60), keep your eyes peeled for jaunty purple flags fluttering in the breeze. These indicate that an artist is at work on the adjoining property. If your eyesight isn't up to the task (or you're the designated driver), pick up the handy *Sunshine Coast Purple Banner* flyer from visitor centers and galleries in the area to find out exactly where these artists are located. Some are open for drop-in visits while others prefer that you call ahead. The region is studded with arts and crafts creators, working with wood, glass, clay and just about everything else. For further information, check www.suncoastarts.com.

Cowichan Bay Colorful floating houses

ings of a great picnic at True Grain Bread (p62).

The Drive » Return to Hwy 1 and head north a further 12km.

p62

4 BC Forest Discovery Centre

You won't find Winnie-the-Pooh in this 100-acre wood, but if you want to know more about those giants swaying overhead, stop in at the **BC Forest Discovery Centre** (250-715-1113; www.bcforestdiscoverycentre.com; 2892 Drinkwater Rd; adult/child $16/11; 10am-4:30pm Apr-Sep, reduced hours Oct-Mar;). Woodland paths lead you among western yews, Garry oaks and 400-year-old fir trees with nesting bald eagles in their branches. Visit a 1920s sawmill and a 1905 wooden schoolhouse, and climb to the top of a wildfire lookout tower. Hop on a historical train for a ride around the grounds and check out some cool logging trucks from the early 1900s. Visit the indoor exhibits for the lowdown on contemporary forest management.

The Drive » It's a 20km journey to the next stop. Continue north on Hwy 1, turning right onto Henry Rd and then left onto Chemainus Rd.

5 Chemainus

The residents of this tree-ringed settlement – a former resource community that almost became a ghost town – began commissioning **murals** on its walls in the 1980s, part of a forward-thinking revitalization project. The paintings – there are now almost 50 dotted around the community – soon became visitor attractions, stoking the town's rebirth. Among the best are the 17m-long pioneer-town painting of Chemainus c 1891 on Mill St, the 15m-long depiction of First Nations faces and totems on Chemainus Rd, and the evocative Maple St mural showing the waterfront community as it was in 1948.

Pick up a walking tour map of the murals from the **visitor center** next to Waterwheel Park (where there's also a parking lot). In the same building, the town's small **museum** is well stocked with yesteryear reminders of the old town. Be sure to chat with the friendly volunteers; they'll regale you with real-life stories of the area's colorful past.

The lower part of the town is rather quiet but the southern end of Willow St has many cafes, restaurants and boutique galleries to keep you and your wallet occupied.

The impressive **Chemainus Theatre Festival** (☎800-565-7738, 250-246-9820; www.chemainustheatrefestival.ca; 9737 Chemainus Rd; tickets from $25) is also popular, staging shows for much of the year.

The Drive » Head north on Hwy 1 toward Nanaimo. Follow the signs to Departure Bay and catch a BC Ferries vessel to mainland Horseshoe Bay. From there, hop on a second 40-minute ferry ride to Langdale on the Sunshine Coast (there are many restaurants in Horseshoe Bay if you're waiting between ferries). From Langdale, it's a short drive along Hwy 101 to Gibsons.

p62

RULE OF THE ROAD

Bone-shaking automobiles began popping up on the roads of British Columbia in the early years of the 20th century, often the toys of rich playboys with too much time on their hands. But for many years BC had few regulations governing the trundling procession of cars around the region: vehicles could drive on either side of the road in some communities, although the left-hand side (echoing the country's British colonial overlords) gradually became the accepted practice.

Aiming to match driving rules in the US (and in much of the rest of the world) – yet managing to confuse the local issue still further – BC began legislating drivers over to the right-hand side of the road in the early 1920s. One of the last areas to make the switch official was Vancouver Island. During the transition period, some minor accidents were reported around the region as drivers tootled toward each other before veering across at the last minute.

TRIP HIGHLIGHT

6 Gibsons

Gibsons *feels* cozy. If you didn't know better, you'd think you were on an island – such is the strong community and almost isolated feel this town exudes. Head straight for the waterfront area – known as **Gibsons Landing** – where you can take in the many brightly painted clapboard buildings that back onto the water's edge, as well as intriguing artisan stores.

A walk along the town's main wooden jetty leads you past a colorful array of houseboats and floating garden plots. You'll also come to the sun-dappled

DETOUR: WILD PLAY ELEMENT PARKS

Start: 5 Chemainus

Fancy zipping, swinging or jumping from a giant tree? It's an easy 21km drive north on Hwy 1 from Chemainus to **Wild Play Element Parks** (☎250-716-7874; www.wildplay.com; 35 Nanaimo River Rd; 10am-6pm mid-May–Sep, reduced hours Oct–mid-May;) for some woodland thrills involving canopy obstacle courses and a daredevil bungee-jump zone.

gallery of **Sa Boothroyd** (☎604-886-7072; www.saboothroyd.com; Government Wharf; ⊙11am-5pm). The artist is typically on hand to illuminate her browse-worthy and often humorous works. Although her bigger canvases are pricey, there are lots of tempting original trivets, coasters and tea cozies.

Need more culture? Head to the charming **Gibsons Public Art Gallery** (☎604-886-0531; www.gpag.ca; 431 Marine Dr; ⊙11am-4pm Jun-Aug, Thu-Mon only Sep-May), which showcases the work of locals artists and changes its displays every month. Check the website for show openings, always a good time to meet the arty locals.

The Drive » Continue along tree-lined Hwy 101; expect glimpses of sandy coves in the forests on your left. The highway leads through Sechelt (handy for supplies) then on to Earls Cove. Hop on a BC Ferries service across Jervis Inlet to Saltery Bay. This achingly beautiful 50-minute trip threads past islands and forested coastlines. From Saltery Bay, take Hwy 101 to Powell River.

p63

DETOUR: GABRIOLA ISLAND

Start: 5 Chemainus

If you're tempted by those mysterious little islands peeking at you off the coast of Vancouver Island, take the 20-minute BC Ferries (www.bcferries.com) service from Nanaimo's Inner Harbour to **Gabriola Island** (www.gabriolaisland.org). Home to dozens of artists plus a healthy smattering of old hippies, there's a tangible air of quietude to this rustic realm. Pack a picnic and spend the afternoon communing with the natural world.

7 Powell River

Powell River is one of the Sunshine Coast's most vibrant communities. It was founded in the early 1900s when three Minnesota businessmen dammed the river to create a massive hydroelectric power plant. Not long after, a pulp mill was built to take advantage of the surrounding forests and handy deepwater harbor, with the first sheets of paper trundling off its steamy production line in 1912. Within a few years, the mill had become the world's largest producer of newsprint, churning out 275 tonnes daily.

Today there's an active and arty vibe to this waterfront town, including it's historic **Townsite** (☎604-483-3901; www.powellrivertownsite.com; 6211 Walnut Ave, Dr Henderson's House; ⊙noon-4pm Tue-Fri Mar-Oct, 11am-3pm Tue-Fri Nov-Feb) area, which is great for on-foot wandering. Many of Powell River's oldest streets are named after trees and some are still lined with the original mill workers' cottages that kick-started the settlement. The steam-plumed mill is still here, too – although it's shrinking every year and its former grounds are being transformed into parkland. Dip into this history at **Powell River Museum** (☎604-485-2327; www.powellrivermuseum.ca; 4798 Marine Ave; ⊙10am-4pm mid-Jun–Sep, closed Mon Oct–mid-Jun), which covers the area's First Nations heritage and its tough pioneer days.

If you spend the night in town, catch a film at the quaint **Patricia Theatre** (☎604-483-9345; www.patriciatheatre.com; 5848 Ash Ave), Canada's oldest continually operating cinema.

p63

Eating & Sleeping

Victoria 1

Jam Cafe — Breakfast $$

(778-440-4489; http://jamcafes.com; 542 Herald St; breakfast $13-17; 8am-3pm; ; 70) No need to conduct an opinion poll: the perennial lines in the street outside Jam suggest that this is the best breakfast spot in Victoria. The reasons? Tasteful vintage decor (if you'll excuse them the moose's head); fast, discreet service; and the kind of creative breakfast dishes that you'd never have the energy or ingenuity to cook yourself.

Fishhook — Seafood $$

(250-477-0470; www.fishhookvic.com; 805 Fort St; mains $13-24; 11am-9pm; 14) Don't miss the smoky, coconutty chowder at this tiny Indian- and French-influenced seafood restaurant, but make sure you add a tartine open-faced sandwich: it's the house specialty. If you still have room (and you're reluctant to give up your place at the communal table), split a seafood biryani platter with your dining partner. Focused on local and sustainable fish.

Ocean Island Inn — Hostel $

(250-385-1789; www.oceanisland.com; 791 Pandora Ave; dm/d from $36/56; @; 70) The kind of hostel that'll make you want to become a backpacker (again), the Ocean is a fabulous blitz of sharp color accents, global travel memorabilia and more handy extras than a deluxe five-star hotel. Bank on free breakfast (including waffles!), free dinner, a free nightly drink, free bag storage (handy for the West Coast Trail) and free friendly advice.

Hotel Zed — Motel $$

(250-388-4345; www.hotelzed.com; 3110 Douglas St; d from $209; P; 70) If you like accommodations that – in its own words – likes to 'rebel against the ordinary,' then you'll love the Zed, an eccentric motel that has been given a tongue-in-cheek retro makeover, complete with rainbow paintwork and free VW-van rides to downtown (a 20-minute walk away). The rooms are also fun: 1970s phones, bathroom comic books and brightly painted walls.

Cowichan Bay 3

True Grain Bread — Food $

(250-746-7664; www.truegrain.ca; 1725 Cowichan Bay Rd; 8am-6pm, closed Mon Nov-Feb;) Adding the welcome aroma of baking bread to the oily harbor smells, True Grain is part of a three-shop island chain. From sourdough to raisin, the bread is all handcrafted, organic and milled on-site (from BC-farmed grain). Homemade crackers and cookies will add to your picnic hamper – if it's not already too weighed-down with the chocolate buns.

Masthead Restaurant — Northwestern US $$$

(250-748-3714; www.themastheadrestaurant.com; 1705 Cowichan Bay Rd; mains $22-54; 5-10pm) The patio deck of this charming, 1863 heritage-building restaurant is a fine place for a splurge, and the $37 three-course BC-sourced tasting menu is surprisingly good value. Seasonal ingredients form the approach here and there are also some good Cowichan Valley wines to try if you're feeling boozily adventurous.

Dreamweaver — B&B $$

(250-748-7688; www.dreamweaverbedandbreakfast.com; 1682 Botwood Lane; d from $135;) This Victorian-style home welcomes guests with three comfortable, rather floral rooms. It's perched on the edge of the village, just steps away from the restaurants and galleries.

Chemainus 5

Willow Street Cafe — Cafe $

(250-246-2434; www.willowstreetcafe.com; 9749 Willow St; mains $12-15; 8am-5pm;) With a menu founded on wraps, sandwiches and quesadillas, this cafe in a handsome yellow heritage building in the heart of town has a popular summertime patio out front. Save room for a slab of cheesecake before jogging around the town murals.

Gibsons 6

Smitty's Oyster House — Seafood $$

(☎604-886-4665; www.smittysoysterhouse.com; 643 School Rd Wharf; mains $18-29; ⏰noon-late Tue-Sat, to 8pm Sun, reduced hours in winter) The best spot for seafood in Gibsons (especially if you snag a seat at the communal long table alongside the marina boardwalk), Smitty's sparked a renaissance in local dining when it opened a few years back. It's as popular as ever, especially on summer evenings when this is the perfect place to scoff a pile of fresh-shucked bivalves.

Molly's Reach — Breakfast, Burgers $$

(☎604-886-9710; www.mollysreach.ca; 647 School Rd; mains $12-17; ⏰8am-3pm) Any Canadian who was near a TV set in the 1970s and '80s will recognize this sunset-yellow harborside abode as the primary filming location for the long running drama series, *The Beachcombers*.

Drift Cafe & Bistro — Bistro $$$

(☎604-886-5858; www.drift-gibsons.ca; 546 Gibsons Way; mains $19-28; ⏰10am-2pm & 5-9pm Fri-Tue) Residing in a cute little cottage no larger than a two-car garage, Drift (formerly Nova Kitchen) continues to impress, serving everything from egg-and-bacon breakfasts to sweet seared scallops with bacon risotto. On warm days, the deck overlooking the water practically doubles the restaurant's size and is a great spot to enjoy a Persephone beer with your gourmet grub.

Bonniebrook Lodge — Hotel $$

(☎604-886-2887; www.bonniebrook.com; 1532 Ocean Beach Esplanade; d from $249; wi-fi) A handsome, wood-built retreat constructed in 1929 but luxuriously updated, this historic charmer occupies a tranquil waterfront stretch that feels like a million miles from any city. All the rooms are delightfully sumptuous with fireplaces and hot tubs, but if you pay extra for one of the two top-floor penthouse suites, you'll have your own balcony overlooking the ocean.

Powell River 7

Base Camp — Cafe $

(☎604-485-5826; www.basecamp-coffee.com; 4548 Marine Dr; mains $8-16; ⏰7am-5pm; wi-fi) The town's quintessential community coffee hangout has, no doubt, served as base camp for many energetic Sunshine Coast excursions judging by the breakfasts – be it the maple granola parfait or the curried tofu scramble. The communal tables are great for eaves-dropping and the large local map on the wall will help get you oriented while you enjoy the java.

Coastal Cookery — Bistro $$

(☎604-485-5568; www.coastalcookery.com; 4553 Marine Ave; mains $12-28; ⏰11:30am-late) This casual dining favorite has the town's best patio plus a great menu of tweaked classics and seasonal specials – with a strong focus on BC ingredients. If Salt Spring mussels are on the menu, order them immediately or just dive headfirst into the chicken-and-waffle sandwich (especially if you have a marathon to run).

Old Courthouse Inn — Hotel $$

(☎604-483-4000; www.oldcourthouseinn.ca; 6243 Walnut St; s/d from $119/139; wi-fi) A wonderful slice of yesteryear or an old-fashioned over-cluttered inn, depending on your penchant for antiques, this mock-Tudor hotel keeps one foot in the past, reliving its glory days as the town courthouse. The eight rooms retain the feel of the 1940s, but with modern amenities (wi-fi, TVs) thrown in, and a generous hot breakfast is included in the on-site cafe.

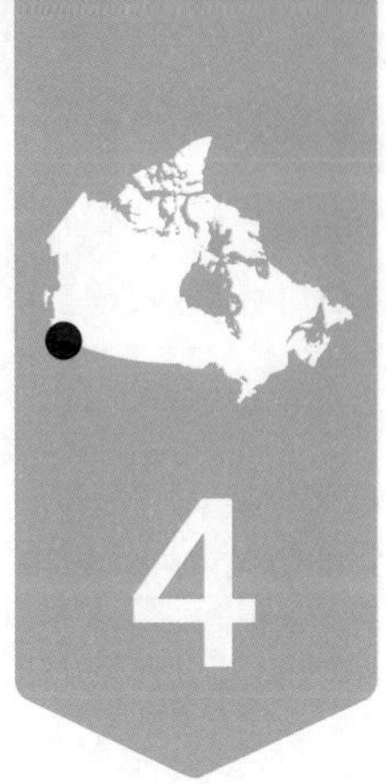

Southern Vancouver Island Tour

Begin on the Gulf Islands among uncommon amounts of creativity and tranquility. Then cross through ancient, fern-lined forests to Vancouver Island's wild west coast.

TRIP HIGHLIGHTS

174 km
Botanical Beach
Explore vibrant tidal pools next to the crashing coastline

24 km
Talisman Books & Gallery
Be inspired by Pender Island's diverse artists

Sidney
START

Jordan River

Victoria
FINISH

China Beach
Delve deep into the forest and emerge onto a huge sandy expanse
213 km

Salt Spring Island Cheese
Experience life on a forested gourmet cheese farm
61 km

4–5 DAYS
290KM/182 MILES

GREAT FOR...

BEST TIME TO GO

June to September for frequent ferries, warm weather and possible whale sightings.

ESSENTIAL PHOTO

Botanical Beach's crashing waves.

BEST FOR OUTDOORS

Salt Spring Island for cycling and hiking, and kayaking in sun-dappled lakes.

Vancouver Island Tidal pools at Botanical Beach (p70)

4 Southern Vancouver Island Tour

Whether you're standing on the deck of a Gulf Islands ferry or on the sandy expanse of China Beach, the untamed ocean is an essential part of life in this part of the world. It seems to foster pods of creativity – small islands where artisans practice crafts from pottery to cheese-making – and it salt-licks the dramatic coastline into shape, with sandy coves fringed by dense, wind-bent woodlands.

❶ Sidney

A short trip north of Victoria, the sunny seaside town of Sidney is ideal for wandering. Along the main street, an almost unseemly number of bookstores jostle for space with boutique shops and cafes. The best for serious bibliophiles is vaguely Dickensian **Haunted Books** (250-656-8805; 9807 3rd St; 10am-5pm). When you reach the water, you'll find the **Seaside Sculpture Walk** – showcasing a dozen or so locally

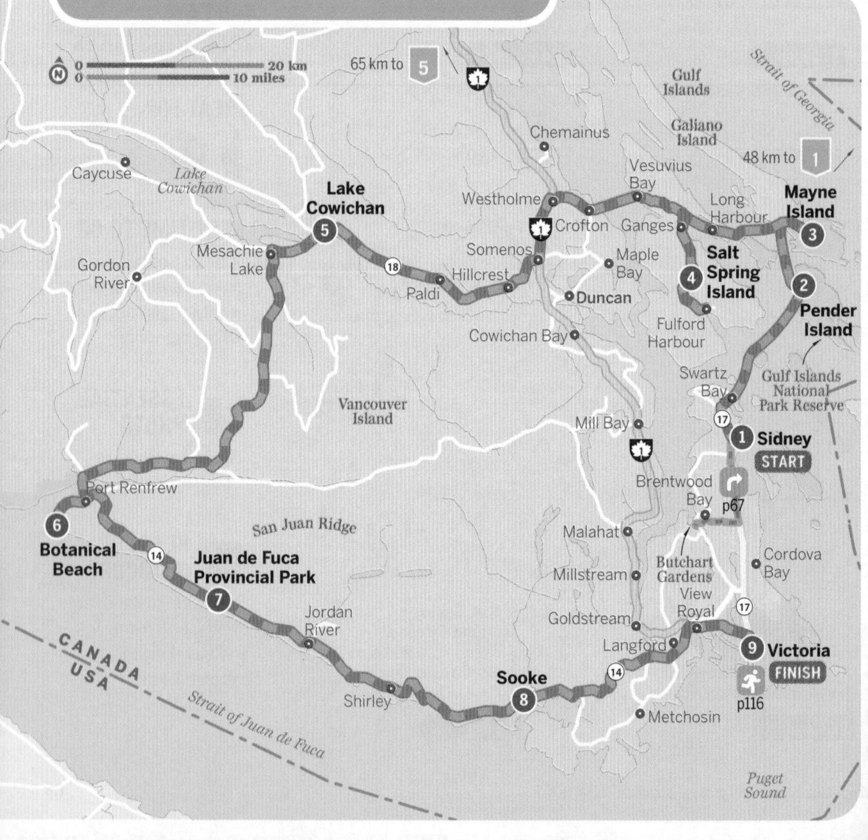

created artworks – plus a picturesque pier with twinkling island vistas.

While you're at the waterfront, visit the compact but brilliant **Shaw Centre for the Salish Sea** (☎250-665-7511; www.salishseacentre.org; 9811 Seaport Pl; adult/child $17.50/12; ⏰10am-4:30pm; 👪). It opens your eyes to the color and diversity in the neighboring Salish Sea with aquariums, touch tanks and plenty of hands-on exhibits. The staff are well-versed and the gift shop is a treasure trove.

The Drive » Follow Hwy 17 (Patricia Bay Hwy) north for 6km to its end at the BC Ferries terminal. Board a boat for a beautiful 40-minute crossing to Pender Island.

p71

DETOUR: BUTCHART GARDENS

Start: 1 Sidney

A 16km drive south of Sidney on Hwy 17, turning west on Keating Cross Rd, brings you to Benvenuto Ave and British Columbia's most famous botanical attraction. The century-old **Butchart Gardens** (☎250-652-5256; www.butchartgardens.com; 800 Benvenuto Ave; adult/teen/child $33.80/16.90/3; ⏰8:45am-10pm Jun-Aug, reduced hours Sep-May; 🚌75), which originated from an attempt to beautify an old cement factory site, has been cleverly planned to ensure there's always something in bloom, no matter what the season. In summer, there are Saturday night fireworks displays and in winter the twinkling seasonal lights are magical. Whatever time of year you arrive, give yourself at least a couple of hours to enjoy the spectacle.

LINK YOUR TRIP

1 Vancouver & the Fraser Valley

From the Gulf Islands, catch a ferry to Tsawwassen to get a closer look at Vancouver and the farm-dotted Fraser River Valley.

5 Vancouver Island's Remote North

When you reach Hwy 1 after leaving Salt Spring Island, you can carry on north for a taste of off-the-beaten-track Vancouver Island.

TRIP HIGHLIGHT

2 Pender Island

Arriving on this small island, you are quickly enveloped in a sense of tangible quietude. Narrow roads wind within deep forests where you'll see countless walking trails, quail crossings and confident deer.

Pender is actually two islands – North and South, joined by a small bridge. **Gowland** and **Tilly Point** on South Pender have beach access; head to Tilly Point for tidal pools and Mt Baker views. Sheltered, sandy **Medicine Beach** on the North Island has lots of clamber-worthy logs. While on the beaches, look out for bald eagles, seals and otters.

Pender is also home to many artists. Pick up a copy of the *Pender Island Artists Guide* on the ferry. A great place to start is **Talisman Books & Gallery** (☎250-629-6944; www.talismanbooks.ca; 4/4605 Bedwell Harbour Rd, Driftwood Centre, North Pender; ⏰10am-5pm, 11am-4pm Sun) in the central Driftwood Centre where you'll also great cakes and coffee.

For locally produced wine, head to **Sea Star Vineyards** (☎250-629-6960; www.seastarvineyards.ca; 6621 Harbour Hill Dr, North Pender; ⏰11am-5pm May-Sep). Using grapes from its own vine-striped hills, Sea Star produces tasty small-batch tipples plus a wide array of fruit, from kiwis to raspberries.

Also worth a look is **Pender Islands Museum** (www.penderislandsmuseum.ca; 2408 South Otter Bay Rd, North Pender; ⏲10am-4pm Sat & Sun Jul & Aug, reduced hours off-season; P), housed in a 1908 farmhouse. Explore the history of the island through its re-created rooms, vintage photos and evocative exhibits.

The Drive » Return to the ferry terminal on North Pender and board a ferry for the 25-minute voyage through the channel to Mayne Island.

 p71

3 Mayne Island

As the boat pulls into Mayne Island, you're greeted with colorful wooden houses, quaint communities and lots of deer. Head to **Georgina Point Lighthouse** for ocean and mountain-filled views across Active Pass. The water literally bubbles here with the strength of the current. This is a popular spot for eagles to fish and you're also likely to see (and hear) sea lions resting on nearby rocks.

For a quiet retreat, visit the **Japanese Garden** (Dinner Point Rd, Dinner Bay Community Park), dedicated to the many Japanese families who settled on the island from 1900 onward. Once constituting a third of the population, they contributed more than half of the island's farming, milling and fish-preservation work. During WWII the government saw them as a national threat and forced their removal. The garden contains traditional Japanese elements within a forest, including shrines and a peace bell.

The Drive » Return to the ferry terminal and board a ferry to Long Harbour on Salt Spring Island. The trip takes around 45 minutes to an hour.

 p71

TRIP HIGHLIGHT

4 Salt Spring Island

When folks from Vancouver talk about quitting their jobs and making jam for a living, they're likely mulling a move to Salt Spring. Once a hippie haven and later a yuppie retreat, it's now home to anyone who craves a quieter life without sacrificing everyday conveniences. The main town of **Ganges** has it all, from grocery stores to galleries. It's a wonderful place to explore.

CNICBC/GETTY IMAGES ©

Salt Spring is also home to many an artisan, from bakers to carvers and winemakers. Stop in at **Waterfront Gallery** (☎250-537-4525; www.waterfrontgallery.ca; 107 Purvis Lane, Ganges; ⏲10am-5pm), which carries the work of many local artists with pottery, glassware, knitwear, candles and even birdhouses prominent. Also

OFF THE FENCE

Going strong for nearly 25 years, Art Off the Fence started as just that – an artist exhibiting her work all over her fence. Each year in mid-July, a dozen or so additional artists hang their work on the fence and in the orchard of a Pender property, creating a weekend-long grassroots outdoor gallery. Look, shop, enjoy the live music and meet the island locals.

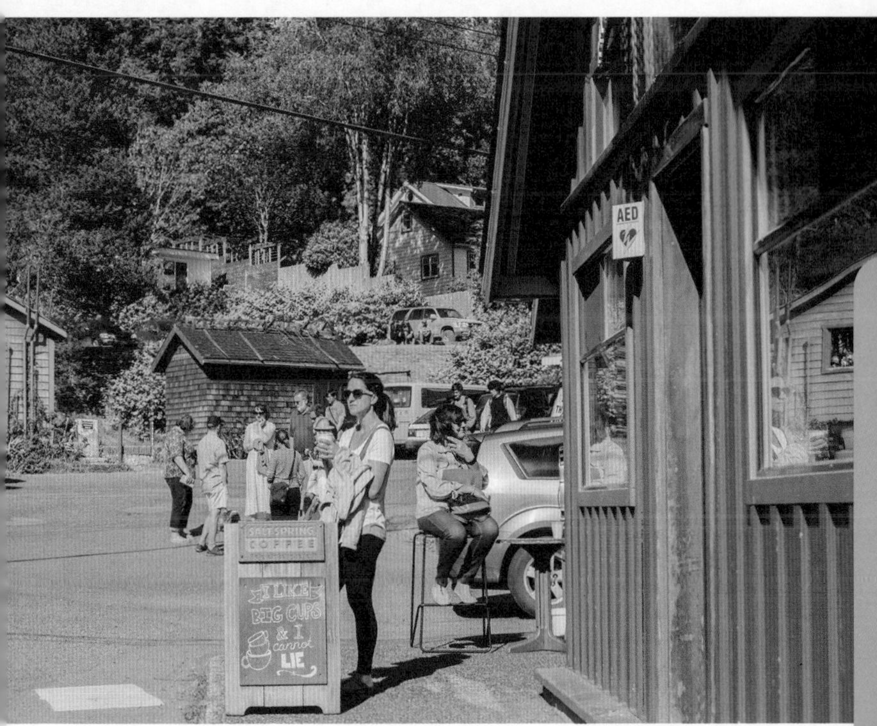

Salt Spring Island Shops at Fulford Harbour

stop in at **Salt Spring Mercantile** (www.saltspring mercantile.com; 2915 Fulford-Ganges Rd, Fulford; ⌚8:30am-6pm), which sells lots of local products, including Salish Sea Chocolates, jars of fresh chutney and flower-petal-packed soaps.

Save time for **Salt Spring Island Cheese** (☎250-653-2300; www.saltspringcheese.com; 285 Reynolds Rd; ⌚11am-5pm, to 4pm Oct-Apr; 👪) on Weston Creek Farm. Meet the goats and sheep that produce milk for the cheese, see it being made, and be awed by the beautiful finale – taste cheeses adorned with lemon slices, flowers and chilies.

Head to **Ruckle Park** for ragged shorelines, gnarly arbutus forests and sun-kissed farmlands. There are trails here for all skill levels as well as great ocean views for a picnic. **Mt Maxwell** offers a steep but worthwhile hike and **Cushion Lake** and **St Mary's Lake** are summertime swimming haunts. Fancy exploring sans car? Visit **Salt Spring Adventure Co** (☎250-537-2764; www.saltspringadventures.com; 125 Rainbow Rd, Ganges; rentals/tours from $40/65; ⌚9am-6pm May-Sep) in Ganges to rent kayaks and join excursions.

The Drive » Head 7km north of Ganges to Vesuvius Bay and take a 25-minute ferry ride to Crofton on Vancouver Island. From the east coast, curve inland for 38km along Hwy 18 and the glassy-calm waters of Lake Cowichan.

✕ 🛏 p71

5 Lake Cowichan

Hop out of the car at Lake Cowichan for some deep breaths at the ultra-clear, tree-fringed lakefront. This is a perfect spot for swimming or setting out for a hike along the lakeside trails.

The Drive » From Lake Cowichan, follow South Shore Rd and then Pacific Marine Rd to Port Renfrew and on to Botanical Beach, 66km from Lake Cowichan.

TRIP HIGHLIGHT

6 Botanical Beach

Feeling like the edge of the earth, it's worth the effort to get to Botanical Beach. Follow the winding road from Port Renfrew and then the sometimes steep pathway down to the beach. The tidal pools here are rich in colorful marine life, including chitons, anemones, gooseneck barnacles, sea palms and purple sea urchins. Surrounded by windblown coastline and crashing waves, this is also a favorite springtime haunt of orcas and gray whales, plus a feeding ground for harbor seals.

The rocks here can be slippery and the waves huge; take care and watch the tide.

The Drive » Head southeast on Hwy 14 for around 40km to nearby Juan de Fuca Provincial Park.

TRIP HIGHLIGHT

7 Juan de Fuca Provincial Park

Welcome to the dramatic coastal wilderness of **Juan de Fuca Provincial Park** (☎250-474-1336; www.env.gov.bc.ca/bcparks/explore/parkpgs/juan_de_fuca; Hwy 14). There are good stop-off points along this rugged stretch, providing memorable views of the rocky, ocean-carved seafront where trees cling for dear life and whales slide past just off the coast. Our favorite is **China Beach**, reached along a fairly gentle, well-maintained trail through dense forest. The prize is a long stretch of windswept sand. **French Beach** is also popular with day-trippers and requires less of a leg-stretch.

The Drive » Continue southeast along Hwy 14, skirting the coastline to Sooke, 74km away.

8 Sooke

Once considered the middle of nowhere, seaside Sooke is gaining popularity thanks in part to the thriving 55km Galloping Goose trail, a cycling and hiking path linking it with Victoria. For an introduction to the area, stop at **Sooke Region Museum** (☎250-642-6351; www.sookeregionmuseum.com; 2070 Phillips Rd; ⏲9am-5pm Tue-Sun), which has intriguing exhibits on the district's pioneer past, including the tiny **Moss Cottage**, one of the island's oldest pioneer homes.

The Drive » From Sooke, follow Hwy 14 (Sooke Rd) east, all the way to Hwy 1. Join the eastbound traffic, which will lead you to nearby Victoria, 40km from Sooke.

🛏 p71

9 Victoria

The provincial capital is vibrant, charming and highly walkable (p116). The boat-filled Inner Harbour, magnetic boutique shopping and belly-thrilling cuisine make it understandably popular. Add an outgoing university crowd plus a strong arts community and you get an interesting, diverse population.

🛏 p71

MARKET DAY

If you arrive on Salt Spring Island on a summer weekend, the best way to dive into the community is at the legendary **Saturday Market** (www.saltspringmarket.com; Centennial Park, Ganges; ⏲9am-4pm Sat Apr-Oct) where you can tuck into luscious island-grown fruit and piquant cheeses while perusing locally produced arts and crafts.

Eating & Sleeping

Sidney ❶

Beacon Cafe — Cafe $

(☎778-426-3663; 2505 Beacon Ave; snacks $6-11; ⏰8am-4pm) A steadfastly local corner cafe with a few regal touches. The chairs owe a nod to the elegant 'Louis Quinze' epoch while the mantlepiece pays ceramic homage to the British royal family with Jubilee mugs and royal wedding plates. Pastries and sandwiches abound, but the place is best enjoyed for its hot smoothies and all-day high tea.

Sidney Pier Hotel & Spa — Hotel $$

(☎250-655-9445; www.sidneypier.com; 9805 Seaport Pl; d/ste $245/275; @ 📶 🐾) This swish waterfront property fuses West Coast lounge cool with beach pastel colors and is a worthy alternative to staying in Victoria. Many rooms have shoreline views, and each has local artworks lining the walls. A spa and large gym add value, plus you're steps from a rather good micro-distillery.

Pender Island ❷

Vanilla Leaf Bakery Cafe — Cafe $

(☎250-629-6453; 17/4605 Bedwell Harbour Rd, Driftwood Centre, North Pender; snacks $3-8; ⏰7am-5pm, from 8am Sun; 📶) Superb pastries both sweet and savory are served here along with organic coffee. Safeguarded behind a glass partition, you can admire pistachio-cream Danish pastries, steak-and-ale pies and the dangerous-looking 'mile-high apple pie.'

Mayne Island ❸

Bennett Bay Bistro — Canadian $$

(☎250-539-3122; www.bennettbaybistro.com; 494 Arbutus Dr; mains $15-28; ⏰11:30am-8:30pm) You don't have to be a guest of the **Mayne Island Resort** to dine at its restaurant, and you'll find a menu combining pubby classics like fish and chips with elevated dinner features like pasta and steaks. Go for the seafood, though.

Salt Spring Island ❹

Tree House Cafe — Canadian $$

(☎250-537-5379; www.treehousecafe.ca; 106 Purvis Lane, Ganges; mains $12-18; ⏰8am-4pm, to 10pm Wed-Sun, reduced hours Sep-Jun) At this magical outdoor dining experience, you'll be sitting in the shade of a large plum tree while choosing from a menu of North American–style pastas, Mexican specialties and gourmet burgers and sandwiches.

The Cottages on Salt Spring Island — Cottage $$$

(☎250-931-7258; www.cottagesonsaltspring.com; 315 Robinson Rd; cottages from $300; P 📶 🐾) A small 'village' of deluxe cottages spread over lakeside grounds 3km northeast of Ganges. The semi-detached cottage units have huge modern interiors (most have three levels) with king-size beds, full kitchens and spectacular bathrooms equipped with tubs and separate showers. There are four different cottage configurations with the largest measuring 150 sq m. All have two bedrooms.

Sooke ❽

Sooke Harbour House — Hotel $$$

(☎250-642-3421; www.sookeharbourhouse.com; 1528 Whiffen Spit Rd; d from $329; 📶 🐾) Whether you opt for the 'Emily Carr' or the 'Blue Heron,' each of the 28 guest rooms here has a decadent tub or steam shower, while most also have wood-burning fireplaces, balconies and expansive sea views. Expect a decanter of blackberry port to be waiting in your room when you arrive; try not to drink it all in one go.

Victoria ❾

Abigail's Hotel — B&B $$$

(☎250-388-5363; www.abigailshotel.com; 906 McClure St; d from $249; P @ 📶; 🚌7) A boutique hotel with the ambience of a B&B, the historic, regal and faintly English Abigail's is Victoria's most Victorian accommodations despite the fact it was only built in 1930 with a mock Tudor facade. Near-perfect rooms come with heavy drapes, shapely furniture and marble bathrooms.

Vancouver Island's Remote North

Throw yourself head-first into Vancouver Island's natural side. Ancient forests, diving orca, wild sandy beaches, quaint villages and a peek into First Nations cultures make it a well-rounded trip.

TRIP HIGHLIGHTS

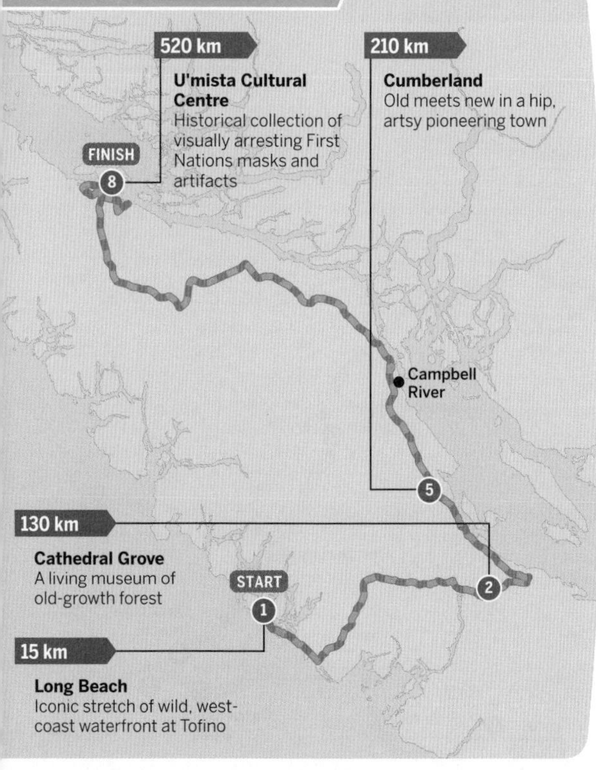

2–3 DAYS
537KM/336 MILES

GREAT FOR...

BEST TIME TO GO

May to September for the most sunshine and the least chance of relentless rain.

ESSENTIAL PHOTO

The forest of totem poles watching over the sea at Alert Bay.

BEST FOR STORM WATCHERS

Watch massive, frothy waves crashing onto Long Beach, especially in winter.

Alert Bay (p78) Totem pole at Namgis Burial Grounds

5 Vancouver Island's Remote North

Following this trip is like following Alice down the rabbit hole – you'll feel you've entered an enchanted land that's beyond the reach of day-to-day life. Ancient, moss-covered trees will leave you feeling tiny, as bald eagles swoop above and around you like pigeons. You'll see bears munching dandelions and watching you inscrutably. And totem poles, standing like forests, will seem to whisper secrets of the past. Go on. Jump in.

TRIP HIGHLIGHT

1 Tofino

Packed with activities and blessed with stunning beaches, former fishing town Tofino sits on Clayoquot (clay-kwot) Sound, where forests rise from roiling waves that continually batter the coastline. Visitors come to surf, whale-watch, kayak, hike and hug trees. For the scoop on what to do, hit the **visitor centre** (☎250-725-3414; www.tourismtofino.com; 1426 Pacific

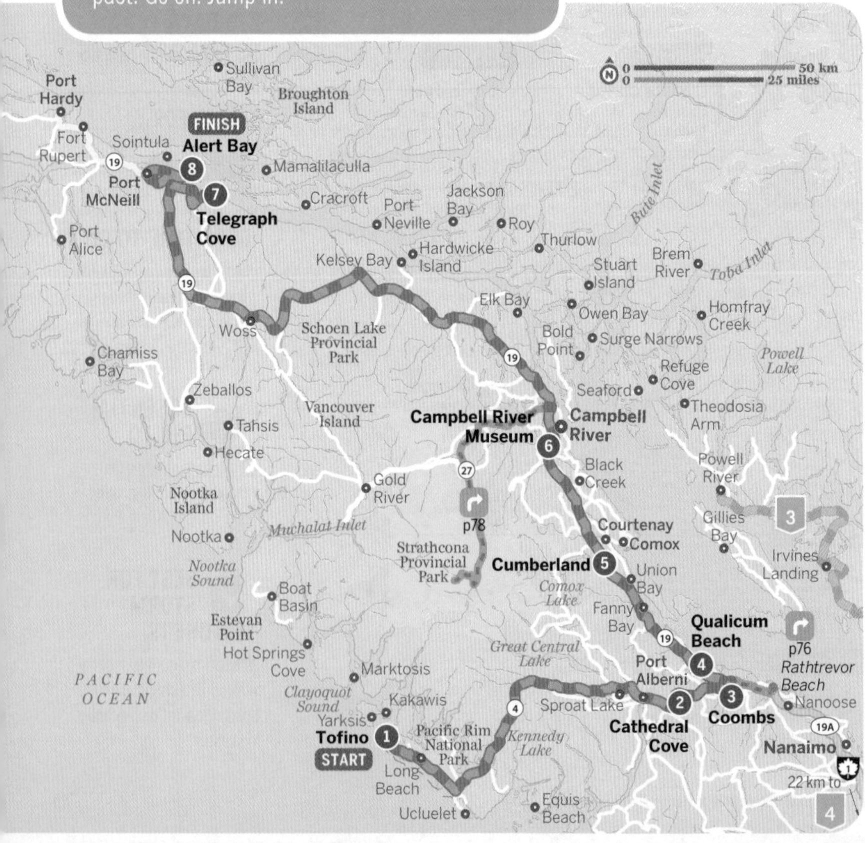

Rim Hwy; ⌚9am-8pm Jun-Aug, reduced hours Sep-May).

The area's biggest draw is **Long Beach**, part of Pacific Rim National Park. Accessible by car along the Pacific Rim Hwy, this wide sandy swath has untamed surf, beachcombing nooks and a living museum of old-growth trees. There are plenty of walking trails; look for swooping eagles and huge banana slugs. Tread carefully over slippery surfaces and never turn your back on the mischievous surf.

Kwisitis Visitor Centre (Wick Rd; ⌚10am-5pm May-Oct, Fri-Sun only Mar, Apr, Nov & Dec) houses exhibits on the region, including a First Nations canoe and a look at what's in the watery depths.

LINK YOUR TRIP

3 A Strait Hop

From Qualicum Beach, travel south on Hwy 19 to Nanaimo, where you can hook up with this water-hugging circuit of the Georgia Strait.

4 Southern Vancouver Island Tour

Drive east from Coombs on Hwy 4A, then south on Hwy 1 for a vision of the Island's more cultivated side.

TOP TIP: VANCOUVER ISLAND NORTH ONLINE

For maps, activities, tide charts and photos to inspire you, visit www.vancouverislandnorth.ca.

While you're in Tofino, don't miss Roy Henry Vickers' **Eagle Aerie Gallery** (☎250-725-3235; www.royhenryvickers.com; 350 Campbell St; ⌚10am-5pm), housed in an atmospheric traditional longhouse. Vickers is one of Canada's most successful and prolific Indigenous artists.

If you're freshly arrived in Tofino and want to know what makes this place so special, head down First Street and join the undulating gravel trail to **Tonquin Beach** (1.2km one-way) where a magical parting of the trees reveals a rock-punctuated swath of sand well-known for its life-affirming sunsets.

The Drive » Follow Pacific Rim Hwy 4 southeast, and then north as it turns into the Mackenzie Range. Mountains rise up on the right as you weave past the unfathomably deep Kennedy Lake. The road carries on along the racing Kennedy River. Continue to the next stop, just past Port Alberni. This longish 140km leg should take a little over two hours.

p79

TRIP HIGHLIGHT

2 Cathedral Grove

To the east of Port Alberni, **Cathedral Grove** (www.bcparks.ca; MacMillan Provincial Park; P) is the spiritual home of tree huggers and the mystical highlight of MacMillan Provincial Park. Look up – way, waaaaay up – and the vertigo-inducing views of the swaying treetops will leave you swooning. Extremely popular in summer, its accessible forest trails wind through dense woodland, offering glimpses of some of British Columbia's oldest trees, including centuries-old Douglas firs more than 3m in diameter. Try hugging that.

The Drive » Continue east for 17km on Hwy 4, past Cameron Lake, with swimming beaches and supposedly a resident monster. From Hwy 4, follow Hwy 4A for 2km into Coombs.

3 Coombs

The mother of all pit stops, **Coombs Old Country Market** (☎250-248-6272; www.oldcountrymarket.com; 2326 Alberni Hwy, Coombs; ⌚9am-6pm Feb-Dec) attracts huge numbers of visitors almost year-round. You'll get inquisitive looks from a herd of goats that spends the summer season on the grassy roof, a tradition here for decades. Nip inside for giant ice-cream cones, heaping pizzas and all the deli makings of a great picnic, then spend an hour or two wandering around the attendant stores, which are filled with unique crafts, clothes and antiques.

The Drive » Continue east for 9km on Hwy 4A, crossing Hwy 19 to Parksville on the coast. Turn left and follow the coastline west past pretty French Creek for 11km and on to Qualicum Beach.

4 Qualicum Beach

A small community of classic seafront motels and a giant beachcomber-friendly bay, Qualicum Beach is a favorite family destination. This coastline is thick with shellfish; many of the scallops, oysters and mussels that restaurants serve up come from here. Wander the beach for shells, and look for sand dollars – they're readily found here.

The Drive » While it's slower than Hwy 19, Hwy 19A is a scenic drive, following the coast north past the Fanny Bay Oyster Farm and Denman Island. After 55km turn left just north of Union Bay to connect with Hwy 19. Turn right, continue north for 5km and take the exit for Cumberland.

p79

TRIP HIGHLIGHT

5 Cumberland

Founded as a coal-mining town in 1888, Cumberland was one of BC's original pioneer settlements, home to workers from Japan, China and the American South. These days, it's officially a 'village' with a main street that's still lined with early-20th-century wood-built stores. But Cumberland has also moved with the times. Instead of blacksmiths and dry-goods shops, you'll find cool boutiques, espresso bars and a local community that's pioneered one of the finest mountain-biking networks in BC in an adjacent forest. You can get kitted out for two-wheeled action at **Dodge City Cycles** (250-336-2200; www.dodgecitycycles.com; 2705 Dunsmuir Ave, Cumberland; bike rentals per 2/24hr $50/120; 9am-6pm Mon-Sat, 10am-2:30pm Sun).

ALL CANADA PHOTOS/ALAMY STOCK PHOTO ©

DETOUR: RATHTREVOR BEACH

Start: 3 Coombs

It's only around 20 minutes from Coombs, but Rathtrevor Beach feels like it's a million miles away. Visit when the tide is out and you'll face a huge expanse of sand. Bring buckets, shovels and the kids, who'll spend hours digging, catching crabs and hunting for shells. The beach is in a provincial park just east of Parksville, and is backed by a forested picnic area. To get there from Coombs, drive east on Hwy 4A, connecting to Hwy 19 northwest and then turning off at Rathtrevor Rd.

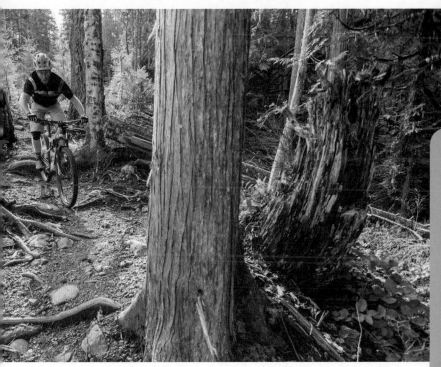

Cumberland Mountain biking through the forest

If you prefer something more sedentary, take time to peruse the very impressive **Cumberland Museum** (☎250-336-2445; www.cumberlandmuseum.ca; 2680 Dunsmuir Ave, Cumberland; adult/child $5/4; ⏰10am-5pm Jun-Aug, closed Mon Sep-May), which explores the area's coal-mining past.

The Drive » Carry on north on Hwy 19, with mountain and island views. Turn right onto Hamm Rd, heading east across farmland and passing a bison farm. Turn left onto Hwy 19A, which skirts Oyster Bay. The next stop is on your left, on the outskirts of Campbell River. Total distance: 55km.

p79

6 Campbell River Museum

Stretch your legs and your curiosity with a wander through the **Museum at Campbell River** (☎250-287-3103; www.crmuseum.ca; 470 Island Hwy; adult/child $8/5; ⏰10am-5pm mid-May–Sep, from noon Tue-Sun Oct–mid-May). Hop behind the wheel of an early logging truck, explore a settler's cabin, see First Nations masks and watch footage of the removal of the legendary, ship-destroying Ripple Rock, which was blasted with thc largest non-nuclear explosion in history.

The Drive » From Campbell River, head northwest on Hwy 19. As you inch into Vancouver Island's north, follow the signs and an increasingly narrow road for 16km to Telegraph Cove. En route, you'll pass Beaver Cove with its flotilla of logs waiting to be hauled away for milling. It's a beautiful drive, but isolated. Fuel up before you head out.

7 Telegraph Cove

Built on stilts over the water in 1912, Telegraph Cove was originally a station for the northern terminus of the island's telegraph. A salmon saltery and sawmill were later added. Extremely popular with summer

DETOUR: STRATHCONA PROVINCIAL PARK

Start: 6 Campbell River Museum

BC's oldest protected area and also Vancouver Island's largest park, **Strathcona** (☎250-474-1336; www.env.gov.bc.ca/bcparks/explore/parkpgs/strath) is a 40km drive west on Hwy 28 from Campbell River. Centered on Mt Golden Hinde, the island's highest point (2200m), it's a pristine wilderness crisscrossed with trail systems that deliver you to waterfalls, alpine meadows, glacial lakes and looming crags. On arrival at the main entrance, get your bearings at **Strathcona Park Lodge & Outdoor Education Centre**. It's a one-stop shop for park activities, including kayaking, guided treks and rock climbing for all ages.

day-trippers, the boardwalk and its many houses have been charmingly restored, with plaques illuminating their original residents. During the season, the waters off the cove are also home to orcas. See (and hear) them on a trip with **Prince of Whales** (☎888-383-4884; www.princeofwhales.com; half-day trip adult/child $130/95). You might also encounter minke and humpback whales as well as dolphins and porpoises.

The Drive » Return to Hwy 19 and carry on for 26km to Port McNeill, from where you can catch a BC Ferries vessel for the 45-minute journey to Alert Bay on Cormorant Island.

p79

TRIP HIGHLIGHT

8 Alert Bay

This spread-out island village has an ancient and mythical appeal underpinned by its strong First Nations culture and community. In some respects, it feels like an open-air museum. On the southern side is an old pioneer fishing settlement and the traditional **Namgis Burial Grounds**, where dozens of gracefully weathering totem poles stand like a forest of ageless art.

Next to the site of the now-demolished St Michael's Residential School is a much more enduring symbol of First Nations community. The must-see **U'mista Cultural Centre** (☎250-974-5403; www.umista.ca; 1 Front St; adult/child $12/5; ⏰9am-5pm Tue-Sat Sep-Jun, daily Jul & Aug) houses ceremonial masks and other items confiscated by the Canadian government in the 1920s and now repatriated from museums around the world.

Continue over the hill to the Big House, where **traditional dance performances** (cnr Wood St & Hill St; ⏰Thu-Sat Jul & Aug) are held for visitors. One of the world's tallest totem poles is also here. Alert Bay is home to many professional carvers and you'll see their work in galleries around the village.

Head to the **visitor center** (☎250-974-5024; www.alertbay.ca; 118 Fir St; ⏰9am-5pm Mon-Fri Jun, Sep & Oct, daily Jul & Aug) for more information.

p79

TOP TIP: PACIFIC RIM PARK PASS

First-timers should drop by the **Pacific Rim Visitors Centre** (☎250-726-4600; www.pacificrimvisitor.ca; 2791 Pacific Rim Hwy, Ucuelet; ⏰10am-4:30pm Tue-Sat) for maps and advice on exploring this spectacular region. If you're stopping in the park, you'll need to pay and display a pass, available here.

Eating & Sleeping

Tofino ❶

Sobo — Canadian $$

(☎250-725-2341; www.sobo.ca; 311 Neill St; mains $17-36; ⏰11:30am-9pm) It's hard not to love a restaurant whose name is short for 'sophisticated bohemian,' a label that might have been invented with Tofino in mind. Once a humble food truck, Sobo is now an ultra-contemporary bricks-and-mortar bistro. The salads are exceptional and the pizzas (especially the exotic mushroom) aren't far behind.

Ecolodge — Hostel $$

(☎250-725-1220; www.tbgf.org; 1084 Pacific Rim Hwy; r incl breakfast from $159; P @ 📶) This quiet, wood-built education center on the grounds of the **botanical gardens** (3-day pass adult/child $12/free; ⏰8am-dusk) is popular with families and groups for its selection of rooms, large kitchen and on-site laundry. There's a bunk room that's around $45 per person per night in summer for groups of four. Rates include garden entry.

Qualicum Beach ❹

Bistro 694 — Canadian $$$

(☎250-752-0301; www.bistro694.com; 694 Memorial Ave, Qualicum Beach; mains $22-32; ⏰4-9pm Thu-Sun) Any local will tell you to cancel your other dinner plans and head straight here. You'll find an intimate, candlelit dining room little bigger than a train carriage and a big-city menu fusing top-notch regional ingredients with knowing international nods. It's worth taking the seafood route, especially if the Balinese prawn curry or highly addictive seafood crepes are available.

Free Spirit Spheres — Cabin $$$

(☎250-757-9445; www.freespiritspheres.com; 420 Horne Lake Rd, Qualicum Beach; spheres from $314) When it comes to extravagantly unconventional accommodations, these three wooden spheres, handmade by owner-inventor Tom Chudleigh and suspended like giant eyes within the forest canopy, score 10 out of 10. Compact two- to three-person spheres have pull-down beds, built-in cabinets and mini-libraries rather than TVs and are a perfect way to commune with BC's giant trees.

Cumberland ❺

Cumberland Brewing — Brewery $$

(☎250-400-2739; www.cumberlandbrewing.com; 2732 Dunsmuir Ave, Cumberland; mains $6-12; ⏰noon-9pm Sun, Tue & Wed, to 10pm Thu-Sat) A microbrewery that's mastered the neighborhood-pub vibe, this tasty spot combines a woodsy little tasting room with a larger outdoor seating area striped with communal tables. Dive into a tasting flight of four beers; make sure it includes the Red Tape Pale Ale.

Telegraph Cove ❼

Telegraph Cove Resort — Resort $$

(☎250-928-3131; www.telegraphcoveresort.com; campsites/cabins/lodge rm from $38/150/220) The dominant business in Telegraph Cove, this well-established heritage resort provides accommodations in forested tent spaces as well as a string of rustic, highly popular cabins on stilts overlooking the marina. A 24-room lodge built from local wood to resemble the nearby **Whale Interpretive Centre** manages to look fabulous without spoiling the fishing-village ambience.

Alert Bay ❽

Alert Bay Cabins — Cabin $$

(☎604-974-5457; www.alertbaycabins.net; 390 Poplar Rd; cabins $145-200) A clutch of well-maintained cabins, each with kitchens or kitchenettes, this is a great retreat-like option if you want to get away from it all. Cabins accommodate four to six people. Call ahead and the staff will even pick you up from the ferry (otherwise it's a 2.5km walk).

Classic Trip

Okanagan Valley Wine Tour

Weave your way between golden hills and the shimmering Okanagan Lake. This route will leave you with a trunkful of first-class wine and, depending on the season, juicy cherries and peaches.

TRIP HIGHLIGHTS

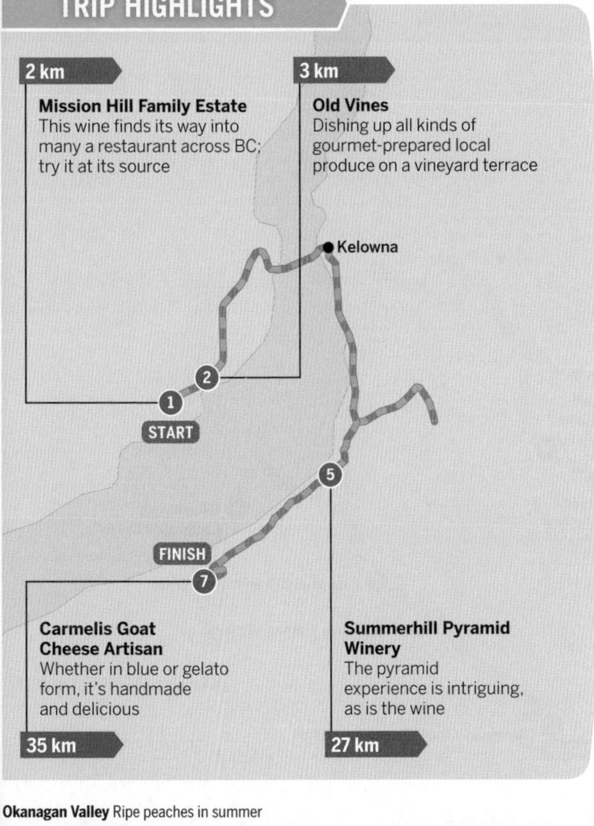

2 km

Mission Hill Family Estate
This wine finds its way into many a restaurant across BC; try it at its source

3 km

Old Vines
Dishing up all kinds of gourmet-prepared local produce on a vineyard terrace

Kelowna

2

1

START

5

FINISH

7

Carmelis Goat Cheese Artisan
Whether in blue or gelato form, it's handmade and delicious

35 km

Summerhill Pyramid Winery
The pyramid experience is intriguing, as is the wine

27 km

2 DAYS
35KM/22 MILES

GREAT FOR...

BEST TIME TO GO

July and September bring hot sunny days – perfect for a slow-paced meander.

ESSENTIAL PHOTO

View from the terrace at Mission Hill Family Estate winery.

BEST FOR FOODIES

Stop for fresh peaches, nectarines, apricots, cherries, raspberries and watermelons in season.

Okanagan Valley Ripe peaches in summer

Classic Trip

6 Okanagan Valley Wine Tour

Filling up on sun-ripened fruit at roadside stalls has long been a highlight of traveling through the Okanagan on a hot summer day. Since the 1980s, the region has widened its embrace of the culinary world by striping its hillsides with grapes. More than 180 vineyards take advantage of the Okanagan's cool winters and long summers. Ice wine, made from grapes frozen on the vine, is a unique take-home tipple. And when you're done soaking up the wine, you can soak up the scenery at the countless beaches along the way.

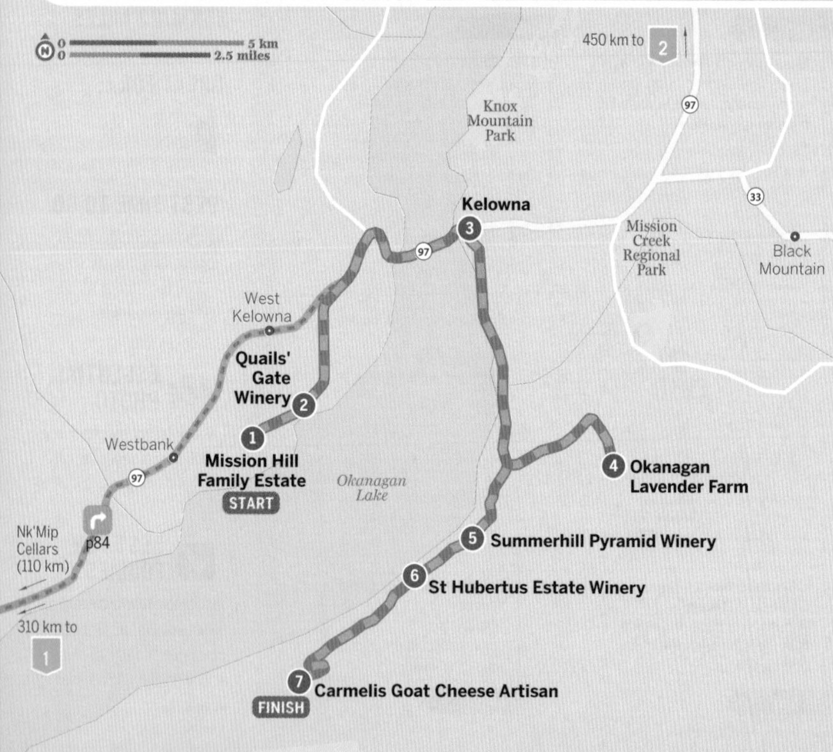

TRIP HIGHLIGHT

1 Mission Hill Family Estate

Begin your leisurely taste-tripping trawl on the western shore of the 100km-long Okanagan Lake, the region's centerpiece. Following Boucherie Rd north, between the lake and Hwy 97, will bring you to Westbank's **Mission Hill Family Estate** (250-768-6400; www.missionhillwinery.com; 1730 Mission Hill Rd, West Kelowna; 10am-7pm; P). The estate is a modernist reinterpretation of mission buildings, reached through imposing gates and dominated by a 26m-high bell-tower. Several tours and tastings are available, including some that include lunch. Aside from checking out vineyards and barrel cellars, you may be lucky enough to see an amazing (and rare) tapestry by French-Russian artist Marc Chagall hanging in one of the rooms.

The winery's Terrace restaurant sits atop a glorious terrace overlooking vineyards and a lake. Its spectacular food matches the setting. Nearby, a grassy amphitheater hosts summer concerts (accompanied by wine, of course). You can also visit the shop for souvenir bottles. Try Oculus, the winery's premium and unique Bordeaux blend.

The Drive » Return to Boucherie Rd and continue 2km north, following the lakeshore.

p88

LINK YOUR TRIP

1 Vancouver & the Fraser Valley

Follow Hwys 3A and 3 from the southern end of Okanagan Lake to Hope and the pastoral Fraser Valley.

2 Sea to Sky Highway

Head northwest from Okanagan Lake on Hwy 97 through Kamloops to Hwy 99 for this spectacular melding of mountains and sea.

TOP TIP: WINE ONLINE

Get the full scoop on the region's 180-plus wineries, events and new releases at www.okanaganwines.ca.

TRIP HIGHLIGHT

2 Quails' Gate Winery

Charming stone and beam architecture reigns at **Quails' Gate Winery** (250-769-4451; www.quailsgate.com; 3303 Boucherie Rd, West Kelowna; 10am-8pm; P). Tours run throughout spring and summer and begin in an on-site pioneer home built in 1873. Tastings are held throughout the day – the rhubarby Chenin Blanc and pleasantly peppery reserve Pinot Noir are recommended. The winery's **Old Vines** restaurant is a foodie favorite, with a menu showcasing seasonal BC ingredients and a commitment to sourcing sustainable seafood. Or you could just chill at vine-side picnic benches.

The Drive » Head 9km northeast on Boucherie Rd before merging with Hwy 97. Cross the lake at the William R Bennett Bridge and head for the 'east coast' town of Kelowna, the Okanagan capital.

p88

3 Kelowna

The wine industry has turned Kelowna into a bit of a boomtown. The population has almost doubled since the early 1990s and property prices have risen accordingly. A wander (especially along Ellis St) will unearth plenty of art galleries and lakeside parks, along with cafes and – delightfully – wine bars.

TOP TIP: WINE FESTIVALS

The Okanagan stages four major multiday seasonal wine festivals (www.thewinefestivals.com) throughout the year. Time your visit right and dip into one of these:

Winter Festival January

Spring Wine Festival May

Summer Wine Festival August

Fall Wine Festival October

Continue your wine education at the **Okanagan Wine and Orchard Museum** (☎778-478-0325; www.kelownamuseums.ca; 1304 Ellis St; by donation; ⏰10am-5pm Mon-Sat, 11am-4pm Sun). Housed in the historic Laurel Packinghouse and expanded to include fruit memorabilia in 2016, the museum offers a look at celebrated bottles, labels and equipment, along with an overview of wine making in the region. There's a separate section on fruit packing.

With vineyards cozied up to Knox Mountain, **Sandhill Wines** (www.sandhillwines.ca; 1125 Richter St; ⏰10am-6pm; P), formerly known as Calona Vineyards, was the Okanagan's first winery, kicking off production in 1932. Its architecturally striking tasting room is an atmospheric spot to try the ever-popular, melon-note Pinot Blanc, along with the port-style dessert wine that makes an ideal cheese buddy. You'll find the winery north of Hwy 97.

The Drive » Head south of Kelowna on Lakeshore Rd, keeping Okanagan Lake on your right. Take a left onto Dehart Rd and follow it to Bedford Rd. Turn right and then right again so that you're heading south on Takla Rd. The 10km drive should take less than 15 minutes.

✖ 🛏 p88

4 Okanagan Lavender Farm

Visiting **Okanagan Lavender Farm** (☎250-764-7795; www.okanaganlavender.com; 4380 Takla Rd;

DETOUR: NK'MIP CELLARS

Start: 2 Quails' Gate

Add a day to your visit and head for this multifarious **cultural center** (☎250-495-7901; www.nkmipdesert.com; 1000 Rancher Creek Rd; adult/child $12/8; ⏰9:30am-4:30pm May-Sep, shorter hours Oct-Apr; P) just east of Osoyoos, part of a First Nations empire that includes a desert golf course, the noted winery **Nk'Mip Cellars**, a resort and more. The architecturally slick cultural center celebrates the Syilx people of the Okanagan nation and the delicate desert ecosystem where they traditionally live. Those with a little reptilian courage can also check out the on-site rattlesnake enclosure.
Save a bit more time to sample one of the region's most distinctive wineries at Nk'Mip Cellars, North America's first indigenous-owned and -operated winery when it opened in 2003. Tastings of five different wines cost $5. The place is known for its ice wines and is open 10am to 6pm in the summer (to 5pm November to March). The two Nk'Mip sites are located about 112km south of Westbank along Hwy 97.

THE OGOPOGO

For centuries, traditional First Nations legends have told of a 15m-long sea serpent living in Okanagan Lake. Called the N'ha-a-itk, or Lake Demon, it was believed to live in a cave near Rattlesnake Island, just offshore from Peachland. People would only enter the waters around the island with an offering, otherwise they believed the monster would raise a storm and claim lives.

Beginning in the mid-1800s, Europeans also began reporting sightings of a creature with a horse-shaped head and serpent-like body. Nicknamed Ogopogo, the serpent has been seen along the length of the 129km lake, but most commonly around Peachland. In 1926, 30 carloads of people all claimed to have seen the monster and film footage from 1968 has been analyzed, concluding that a solid, three-dimensional object was moving through the water.

Cryptozoologist Karl Shuker suggests that the Ogopogo may be a type of primitive whale like the basilosaurus. Keep your eyes peeled, but if you don't have any luck spotting it, you can visit a statue of the Ogopogo at Kelowna's City Park.

tours $5-15; ⏲10am-5pm, tours 10:15am, 11:30am & 2:30pm Jun-Aug; P 👪) is a heady experience. Rows and rows of more than 60 types of lavender waft in the breeze against the backdrop of Okanagan Lake. You can enjoy a guided or self-guided tour of the aromatic acreage and pop into the shop for everything from bath products to lavender lemonade. Your wine-soaked palate will be well and truly cleansed.

The Drive » Retrace your route back to Lakeshore Rd, heading south and then veering left onto Chute Lake Rd after 6.5km.

TRIP HIGHLIGHT

5 Summerhill Pyramid Winery

In the hills along the lake's eastern shore, you'll soon come to one of the Okanagan's most colorful wineries. **Summerhill Pyramid Winery** (☎250-764-8000; www.summerhill.bc.ca; 4870 Chute Lake Rd; ⏲9am-6pm; P) combines a traditional tasting room with a huge pyramid where every Summerhill wine ages in barrels, owing to the belief that sacred geometry has a positive effect on liquids. The winery's vegan-friendly Sunset Organic Bistro is much loved and the Ehrenfelser ice wine is particularly delightful.

The Drive » Return to Lakeside Rd and continue south for 2.5km. The next stop is across from Cedar Creek Park.

p89

6 St Hubertus Estate Winery

Lakeside **St Hubertus Estate Winery** (☎250-764-7888; www.st-hubertus.bc.ca; 5225 Lakeshore Rd, near Kelowna; ⏲10am-5:30pm May-Oct, noon-4pm Mon-Sat Nov-Apr) is another twist on the winery approach. Visiting is like being at a traditional northern European vineyard, complete with Bavarian architectural flourishes.

Despite its emphasis on Germanic wines, including Riesling, St Hubertus isn't conservative: try its floral, somewhat spicy Casselas and the rich Marechal Foch. While there are no formal tours, you can stroll around the vineyard or head to the complimentary tasting room to try four different wines. There's also a shop selling artisan foods and, of course, wine.

The Drive » Continue south on Lakeside for 4km and then take the left turning onto Rimrock Rd. Follow it for 200m to a T-junction and take a right onto Timberline Rd.

p89

Classic Trip

STAN JONES/SHUTTERSTOCK ©

MJ0007/GETTY IMAGES ©: SCULPTOR: PETER SOEHN

WHY THIS IS A CLASSIC TRIP

BRENDAN SAINSBURY, WRITER

Even as a BC resident you still have to sometimes pinch yourself when traveling through the Okanagan to check that you haven't been accidentally teleported over to France or Italy. Not only do the vine-striped hills and glassy water vistas resemble Provence or Lake Garda, the quality and quantity of the wines have also burgeoned to challenge the hegemony of the European stalwarts across the 'pond'.

Above: Vineyard overlooking Okanagan Lake, Kelowna (p83)
Left: Summerhill Pyramid Winery (p85)
Right: Mission Hill Family Estate (p83)

BOB C/SHUTTERSTOCK ©; ARCHITECT: TOM KUNDIG

TRIP HIGHLIGHT

7 Carmelis Goat Cheese Artisan

End your tour by treating your driver to something they can sample at **Carmelis Goat Cheese Artisan** (☎250-764-9033; www.carmelisgoatcheese.com; 170 Timberline Rd; ⏰10am-6pm May-Sep, 11am-5pm Mar, Apr & Oct; P 👪). Call ahead to book a tour of the dairy, milking station and cellar. Even without the tour, you can sample soft-ripened cheeses with names like Moonlight and Heavenly, or the hard-ripened Smoked Carmel or Goatgonzola. For those who prefer something milder, try the super-soft unripened versions like feta and yogurt cheese. The showstopper is the goat's-milk gelato, which comes in 24 different flavors.

Classic Trip

Eating & Sleeping

Mission Hill Family Estate 1

Terrace Restaurant — Modern American $$$

(250-768-6467; www.missionhillwinery.com; 1730 Mission Hill Rd, Mission Hill Family Estate, West Kelowna; mains from $25; noon-8:30pm Jun-Oct) A suitably impressive restaurant to go with a very impressive winery. Terrace (yes, there are views) exemplifies farm-to-table with its fresh and inventive menu.

Blind Angler Grill — Pub Food $

(250-767-9264; www.blindangler.com; 5899a Beach Ave, Peachland; mains from $10; 11am-9pm, from 9.30am Sat & Sun) This shack-like place overlooks Peachland's small marina. What's lost in structural integrity is more than made up for in food quality: breakfasts shine, lobster wraps are a treat, and nighttime ribs and halibut are tops.

Quail's Gate 2

Old Vines Restaurant — Bistro $$$

(250-769-2500; www.quailsgate.com; 3303 Boucherie Rd, Quails' Gate Estate, West Kelowna; mains from $23; 11am-10pm) Using only the freshest ingredients available, this terrace-style restaurant draws crowds. At brunch, try the Dungeness crab cakes with coconut, cilantro and pineapple, and the daikon radish salad. Or dig into smoked quail or prawn risotto at lunch.

A View of the Lake — B&B $$

(250-769-7854; www.aviewofthelake.com; 1877 Horizon Dr, West Kelowna; r from $130; P) Set on the west side of Okanagan Lake, this B&B offers privacy and magnificent views. Book the Grandview Suite for a lake vista that extends even to the air-jet bathtub. Rooms are peaceful, beds are comfy and the three-course breakfast on the deck is gourmet.

Kelowna 3

Little Hobo Soup & Sandwich Shop — Cafe $

(778-478-0411; www.facebook.com/littlehobokelowna; 596 Leon Ave; mains from $7; 8am-2pm Mon-Fri) This unadorned sandwich shop is hugely popular and for good reason: the food is excellent. Custom sandwiches are good, but the daily specials really shine (meatloaf, pasta, pierogi etc) and the variety of soups is simply superb.

Kelowna Farmers Market — Market $

(250-878-5029; www.kelownafarmersandcraftersmarket.com; cnr Springfield Rd & Dilworth Dr; 8am-1pm Wed & Sat Apr-Oct) The farmers market has more than 150 vendors, including many with prepared foods. Local artisans also display their wares. It's east of downtown near the Orchard Park Shopping Centre, off Hwy 97.

RauDZ Regional Table — Fusion $$

(250-868-8805; www.raudz.com; 1560 Water St; mains from $17; 5-10pm) Noted chef Rod Butters has defined the farm-to-table movement with his casual bistro that's a temple to Okanagan produce and wine. The dining room is as airy and open as the kitchen. The seasonal menu takes global inspiration for its Mediterranean-infused dishes, which are good for sharing, and serves steaks and seafood.

BNA Brewing Co & Eatery — Canadian $$

(236-420-0025; www.bnabrewing.com; 1250 Ellis St; mains from $14; 4pm-late) While the beer-tasting room is open from midday to 6pm daily, dining kicks in from 4pm at this welcoming spot in a historic building. There's a good line of tapas-like plates for sharing, as well as a wide range of main courses. If you've come for the beer, try the Don't Lose Your Dinosaur IPA.

Train Station Pub — Pub Food $$

(778-484-5558; www.thetrainstationpub.com; 1177 Ellis St; mains from $12; 9:30am-late) The long-disused 1926 Canadian National train station has been reborn as an upscale pub with an excellent selection of beers. The usual pub-food standards show color and flair; enjoy the wide terrace on balmy days.

Hotel Eldorado — Hotel $$

(250-763-7500; www.hoteleldoradokelowna.com; 500 Cook Rd; r from $180;) This historic lakeshore retreat, south of Pandosy Village, has 19 heritage rooms where you can bask in antique-filled luxury. A modern, low-key wing has 30 more rooms and six opulent waterfront suites. It's classy, artful and funky all at once. Definitely the choice spot for a luxurious getaway.

Hotel Zed — Motel $$

(250-763-7771; www.hotelzed.com; 1627 Abbott St; r from $90;) An old Travelodge has been reborn as this funky throwback to a 1960s that never existed. The rooms come in many shapes and sizes; all are in cheery colors. Extras such as free bike rentals, Ping-Pong, hot tub, comic books in the bathrooms and much more are way cool. It's perfectly located downtown, across from **City Park**.

Lakeshore Bed & Breakfast — B&B $$

(250-764-4375; www.lakeshorebb.ca; 4186 Lakeshore Rd; r from $115;) This bright, two-room B&B has a prime lakefront location, 6km south of the center, complete with its own tiny strip of sand. The larger of the two rooms is a real deal, with broad water views and a private outdoor sitting area. Furnishings are modern and upscale.

Accent Inns Kelowna — Motel $$

(250-862-8888; www.accentinns.com; 1140 Harvey Ave; r from $99;) Best of the chain motels near the center, this three-story property is a 10-minute walk from the lake. The 102 rooms are roomy and have a fridge and microwave. Flowers adorn the walkways, and the staff are charmers. Free breakfast.

Summerhill Pyramid Winery 5

Summerhill Pyramid Bistro — Bistro $$

(250-764-8000; www.summerhill.bc.ca; 4870 Chute Lake Rd, Summerhill Pyramid Winery; mains from $15; 11am-11pm) Acclaimed chef Jeremy Luypen has created excellent locally sourced and organic menus for lunch and dinner. In between, there is an exquisite selection of small dishes, which go well with an afternoon of organic wine tasting.

St Hubertus Estate Winery 6

Home Block at CedarCreek — Bistro $$$

(250-980-4663; www.cedarcreek.bc.ca; 5445 Lakeshore Rd, Cedar Creek Estate; mains from $24; 10am-9pm Jun–mid-Sep) A long list of local suppliers graces the menu at this small winery restaurant. The food is fresh and seasonal; the views are outstanding.

Haida Gwaii Adventure

Far-flung and isolated, the lush Haida Gwaii ('Islands of Beauty') are steeped in superlatives – most stunning scenery, freshest seafood and most accessible First Nations culture.

TRIP HIGHLIGHTS

FINISH

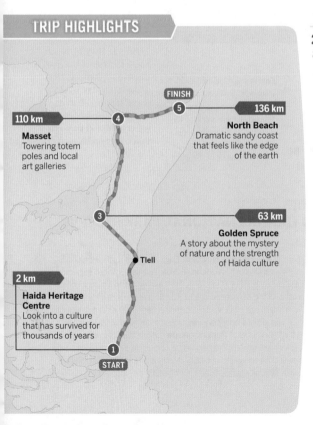

5 — 136 km
North Beach
Dramatic sandy coast that feels like the edge of the earth

4 — 110 km
Masset
Towering totem poles and local art galleries

3 — 63 km
Golden Spruce
A story about the mystery of nature and the strength of Haida culture

Tlell

1 — 2 km
Haida Heritage Centre
Look into a culture that has survived for thousands of years

START

2 DAYS
85 MILES/136KM

GREAT FOR...

BEST TIME TO GO

July and August: more likely sunshine and less vicious wind.

ESSENTIAL PHOTO

Capture the islands' wilderness from Tow Hill's viewpoint.

Gain insight into the resurgence of Haida culture at Haida Heritage Centre.

Haida Gwaii Tow Hill in Naikoon Provincial Park (p96)

7 Haida Gwaii Adventure

You'll be welcomed to what feels like the edge of the earth. Once known as the Queen Charlotte Islands, this rugged northwestern archipelago maintains its independent spirit, evident in its quirky museums, rustic cafes, down-to-earth art and nature-loving locals. You'll feel closer to the natural world than ever before, and some of the Northern Hemisphere's most extraordinary cultural artifacts are found here.

TRIP HIGHLIGHT

❶ Skidegate

If you're not bringing your car, you can rent a car in advance of your **BC Ferries** (☎250-386-3431; www.bcferries.com) arrival in Skidegate on Graham Island (or air arrival in Sandspit). Spend some time perusing the clapboard houses or fueling up at the home-style pub or cafes in nearby Queen Charlotte. Save an hour or two for the unmissable: the **Haida Heritage Centre** (☎250-559-7885 www.haidaheritagecentre.com; Second Beach Rd. Hwy 16, Skidegate; adult/child $16/5; ⏲9am-5pm Jul & Aug, reduced hours Sep-Jun), a striking crescent of totem-fronted cedar longhouses that's arguably British Columbia's best First Nations attraction. Check out ancient carvings and artifacts recalling 10,000 years of Haida history and look for the exquisite artworks of the legendary Bill Reid, such as huge canoes and totem poles.

Hitting Hwy 16, head north to explore the distinctive settlements that make latter-day Haida Gwaii tick. You'll wind along stretches of rustic waterfront and through shadowy woodland areas.

DETOUR: GWAII HAANAS NATIONAL PARK RESERVE

Start: ❶ Skidegate

Famed for its mystical élan, **Gwaii Haanas National Park Reserve** (☎250-559-8818; www.pc.gc.ca/en/pn-np/bc/gwaiihaanas) covers much of Haida Gwaii's southern section, a rugged region only accessible by boat or floatplane. The reserve is the ancient site of Haida homes, burial caves and the derelict village of Ninstints with its seafront totem poles (now a Unesco World Heritage site). Visitors often remark on the area's magical and spiritual qualities, but you should only consider an extended visit if you are well prepared. It is essential that you contact **Parks Canada** (☎250-559-8818; www.pc.gc.ca/en/pn-np/bc/gwaiihaanas; Haida Heritage Centre at Kay Llnagaay, Skidegate; ⏲office 8:30am-noon & 1-4:30pm Mon-Fri) in advance, as access to the park is very limited and most visitors will find it best to work with officially sanctioned tour operators.

600 km to 14
0 20 km
0 10 miles
Dixon Entrance
Rose Point
Wiah Point
FINISH
Rose Spit
North Beach
Old Masset
Masset
Naikoon Provincial Park
Haida Gwaii
Graham Island
Masset Inlet
Port Clements
Tlell
Hecate Strait
Lawnhill
Skidegate
START
Queen Charlotte
Sandspit
Alliford Bay
Moresby Island
40 km to p92
410 km to 5

The Drive » Follow Hwy 16 north along the shoreline. Take a few minutes to walk down to the beach when you see the pullout and signage for Balancing Rock just out of Skidegate. At 22 miles (35.4km) you'll enter the flat, arable land around Tlell River. Turn left at Wiggins Rd when you see signs for Crystal Cabin, then right on Richardson Rd.

2 Tlell

Crystal Cabin (250-557-4383; www.crystalcabingallery.com; 778a Richardson Rd, Tlell; 9am-6pm May-Sep, reduced hours Oct-Apr) features the works of 20 Haida artists at the jewelry workshop of April and Sarah Dutheil, second-generation artisans and sisters who were taught by their father, local legend and authority on island geology, Dutes. April has

LINK YOUR TRIP

5 Vancouver Island's Remote North

After a seven-hour boat ride from Skidegate to Prince Rupert you travel along the inside passage on a 22-hour ferry to Port Hardy. From here drive 25 miles (40km) along Hwy 9 to Port McNeill to pick up this trip.

14 Klondike Highway

Take the ferry from Skidegate to Prince Rupert, then boat north to Skagway, Alaska to reach the iconic Klondike Highway.

written on Haida Gwaii agate collecting and is happy to explain Dutes' Tlell Stone Circle, which is just outside the cabin. There are many forms of art here, including carvings from argillite, a local rock that can only be carved by Haida artisans.

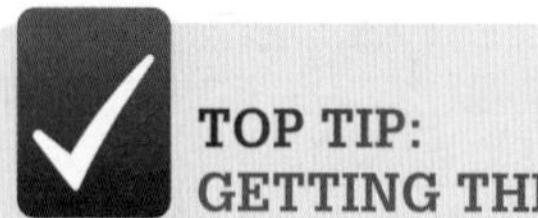

TOP TIP: GETTING THERE

From mainland Prince Rupert in northern BC, take the BC Ferries (p92) service to Skidegate on Graham Island. The crossing usually takes seven to eight hours.

The Drive » Continue 13.5 miles (21.7km) northwest along Hwy 16. This incredibly straight route was a walking trail until 1920 when a road was built by placing wooden planks end-to-end along the ground. Watch for deer by the road and shrub-like shore pines along the now-paved route.

p97

TRIP HIGHLIGHT

3 Port Clements

At Port Clements, head around through town on Bayview Ave until it turns south and becomes a gravel road. Follow this for 2 miles (3.5km) to the **Golden Spruce Trail**. The easy 15-minute (one-way) walk through the forest leads to the banks of the Yakoun River and the site of the legendary Golden Spruce. Tragically cut down in 1997 by a deranged environmentalist, the tree – a 150ft, 300-year-old genetic aberration with luminous yellow needles – was revered by local Haida as the transformed spirit of a little boy. The tree's death was traumatic for many island residents. You can see a seedling taken from a cutting from the felled tree in Millennium Park in Port Clements. For a gripping read, pick up *The Golden Spruce: A True Story of Myth, Madness and Greed* by John Vaillant (2006).

Head back to the village and nip into **Port Clements Museum** (☎250-557-4576; www.portclementsmuseum.ca; 45 Bayview Dr; adult/child $5/free; ⏲10am-4pm Jun–mid-Sep, from 2pm Sat & Sun mid-Sep–May), where you're welcomed by a forest of rusty logging machinery. Learn about early logging prac-

THE STORY OF THE GOLDEN SPRUCE

Long ago a harsh blizzard hit a small village, burying it in snow. Supplies diminished and villagers died of cold and starvation. Eventually only a young boy and his grandfather remained and, with hopes of surviving, they dug themselves out and began trekking.

As they walked in search of a new village, the blizzard ended and spring arrived. The grandfather warned his grandson: 'Don't look back. If you do, you will go into the next world. A world where people can admire you, but will not be able to speak with you. You will be standing in this sacred place until the end of the world.'

Missing his home, the boy stole one last glance in the direction of the village they'd left behind. The boy was rooted to the forest floor. Seeing what had happened, the grandfather said, 'It is okay. Future generations will come and see you and remember your story.' The boy had become the Golden Spruce.

And the grandfather was right. Many did come to marvel at the Golden Spruce, a tree that defied the laws of nature, with needles that should not have been able to absorb the sunlight but thrived among the green trees along the shoreline. It was a tree that stood between this world and the next.

RANPLETT/GETTY IMAGES ©

Masset Haida Gwaii totem pole

tices and check out toys and tools from pioneering days. You'll also encounter a stuffed albino raven, another genetic aberration that was also revered until it electrocuted itself on local power lines.

The Drive » Head north along Hwy 16, which hugs Masset Inlet to the northern coast. Continue north to Masset and Old Masset, 27 miles (43.5km) from Port Clements. Hwy 16 is officially the Yellowhead Hwy and Mile 0 is at Masset. From here Yellowhead Hwy runs to Winnipeg, Manitoba, although you'll have to take the ferry between Haida Gwaii and Prince Rupert.

p97

TRIP HIGHLIGHT

4 Masset

Masset primarily occupies the rather stark, institutional buildings of a disused military base and the adjoining **Old Masset** is a First Nations village where wood-fired homes are fronted by broad, brooding totem poles. There are several stores here where visitors can peruse and buy Haida carvings and paintings.

Also in Masset is the **Dixon Entrance Maritime Museum** (www.massetbc.com/visitors/maritime-museum; 2183 Collinson Ave, Masset; adult/child $3/free; ⌚1-6pm daily Jun-Aug, 2-4pm Sat & Sun Sep-May). Housed in what was once the local hospital, the museum features exhibits on the history of this seafaring community, with displays on shipbuilding, medical pioneers, military history, and nearby clam and crab canneries. Local artists also exhibit their work here.

The Drive » Head east off Hwy 16 along a well-marked road signposted for North Beach and Naikoon Provincial Park. The next stop is 17 miles (27.4km) from Masset.

p97

RETURN OF THE HAIDA

The Haida are one of Canada's First Nations peoples, and had lived here for thousands of years before Europeans turned up in the 18th century. Centered on the islands, these fearsome warriors had no immunity to such diseases as smallpox, measles and tuberculosis that were brought by the newcomers, and their population of tens of thousands was quickly decimated. By the early 20th century, their numbers had fallen to around 600.

Since the 1970s, the Haida population – and its cultural pride – has grown anew, and the Haida now make up about half of the 5000 residents on the islands. In 2009, the Government of British Columbia officially changed the name of the islands from the Queen Charlottes to Haida Gwaii ('Islands of the People') as part of the province's reconciliation process with the Haida.

Historically, the Haida have one of the most vibrant of First Nations cultures, with very strong narratives and oral history. Legends, beliefs, skills and more are passed down from one generation to the next and great importance is placed on the knowledge of past generations. Today the Haida seek to live in harmony with their environment. Traditional laws recognize the stunning nature of the islands and embrace both the past and look to the future.

To learn more about the Haida, visit www.haidanation.ca.

TRIP HIGHLIGHT

 Rose Spit

The region's wild northern tip is home to **Naikoon Provincial Park** (☎250-626-5115; www.env.gov.bc.ca/bcparks; off Hwy 16). This dense, treed park has more than 60 miles (96km) of white-sand beach and is the area's most popular destination for summertime nature fans.

Continue along the tree-lined dirt road until you reach **Tow Hill**, a steep, dense and easily enjoyed short forest walk (0.6 miles/1km each way). Look out for trees where strips of bark have been carefully removed for Haida basket-making over the decades, then catch your breath at the summit while you gaze over the impenetrable coastal forest stretching into the mist.

Finally, head for the park's extreme coastal tip and **North Beach**. Leave the car here and tramp along the wave-smacked sandy expanse, where locals walk in the surf plucking Dungeness crabs for dinner. With the wind watering your eyes, you'll feel closer to nature than you've ever felt before.

p97

Eating & Sleeping

Skidegate ❶

✕ Jags Beanstalk Bistro & Beds — Canadian $

(☎250-559-8826; www.jagsbeanstalk.com; 100 16 Hwy, Skidegate; mains from $10; ⏲7:30am-4pm Mon-Fri, 9am-4pm Sat) Fresh, wholesome food delivered with speedy, friendly service about 1.5km north of the ferry terminal. Great coffee, pizzas, tacos and salads, with an effort to source ingredients locally. It also has cozy guest rooms above the coffee shop.

Tlell ❷

✕ Haida House at Tllaal — Seafood $$

(☎855-557-4600; www.haidahouse.com; 2087 Beitush Rd, Tlell; mains from $20; ⏲5-7:30pm Tue-Sun mid-May–mid-Sep) This Haida-run restaurant next to the river in Tlell at the end of Beitush Rd has excellent, creative seafood and other dishes with island accents, such as Haida favorites with berries. Also rents plush rooms at this magical spot in the forest.

Port Clements ❸

Golden Spruce Motel — Motel $

(☎250-557-4325; www.goldenspruce.ca; 2 Grouse St, Port Clements; r from $90; P) Urs, the owner of this simple yet comfortable motel, gives a warm welcome and has a good breakfast cafe. Some rooms have kitchenette and there are firepits outside for guest use.

Masset ❹

Copper Beech House — B&B $$

(☎250-626-5441; www.copperbeechhouse.com; 1590 Delkatla Rd, Masset; r from $120; P) This legendary B&B in a rambling old 1920s 'character house' on Masset Harbor is owned and managed by writer Susan Musgrave. It has five unique rooms, and there's always something amazing cooking in the kitchen.

Rose Spit ❺

Agate Beach Campground — Campground $

(☎250-557-4390; www.env.gov.bc.ca/bcparks; Tow Hill Rd, North Shore, Naikoon Provincial Park; tent & RV sites $18; P) This stunning, wind-whipped campground is right on the beach on the north shore. Frolic on the sand, hunt for its namesake rocks and see if you can snare some flotsam.

All The Beach You Can Eat — Cabin $$

(☎250-626-9091; www.allthebeachyoucaneat.com; Km 15, Tow Hill Rd, North Shore; cabins from $120; P) On beautiful North Beach, five cabins are perched in the dunes, back from the wide swath of sand that runs for miles east and west. Like other properties with rental cabins out here, there is no electricity; cooking and lighting are fueled by propane. It's off the grid and out of this world.

Generally you can get cell-phone reception on the beach at low-tide.

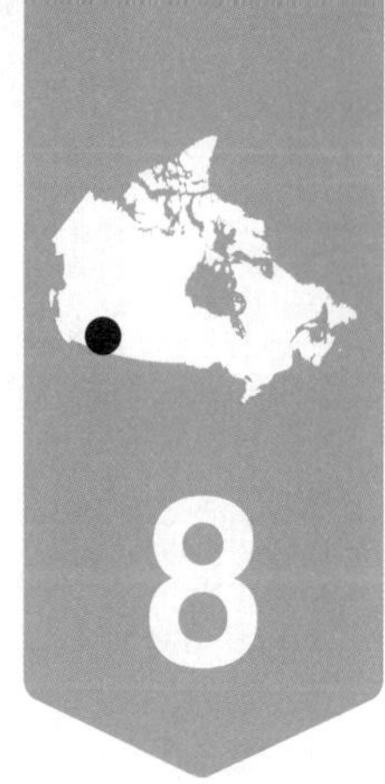

Circling the Rockies

Taking you through Kootenay, Banff and Yoho National Parks and dipping into Alberta, this trip shows off Mother Nature at her best – lofty snowy peaks, deep forests and natural hot springs.

TRIP HIGHLIGHTS

201 km
Takakkaw Falls
Thundering, misty and utterly mesmerizing

161 km
Lake Louise
Unbelievably stunning lake with a backdrop of snowy peaks and a looming glacier

FINISH
Golden

Castle Junction

87 km
Marble Canyon
Teeter above this gorgeous, somewhat dizzying, wonder of nature

0 km
Radium Hot Springs
Soak in the scenery and the curative, bubbling waters

START

3 DAYS 294KM/183 MILES

GREAT FOR...

BEST TIME TO GO

July and August when the snow has melted and all of the roads are open.

ESSENTIAL PHOTO

Mt Temple Viewpoint in Banff National Park for postcard-perfect mountain shots.

BEST FOR WILDLIFE

Watch for bears, elk, big horn sheep and plenty of moose.

Kootenay National Park Big horn sheep

8 Circling the Rockies

This route will give you a new perspective on nature. This is where mountains stretch up to the stars and where bears and moose own the woods (and sometimes the road). Waterfalls, canyons and gem-colored lakes lay deep in the forest, waiting to be discovered. It's impossible not to be awed, not to feel small, and not to wish you had longer to explore.

1 Radium Hot Springs

Set in a valley just inside the southern border of **Kootenay National Park**, the outdoor **Radium Hot Springs** (250-347-9485; www.pc.gc.ca/hotsprings; off Hwy 93; adult/child $7.30/4.95; 9am-11pm) has a hot pool simmering at 102°F (39°C) and a second pool to cool you off at 84°F (29°C). Originally sacred to indigenous groups for the water's curative powers, these springs are uniquely odorless and colorless. The large tiled

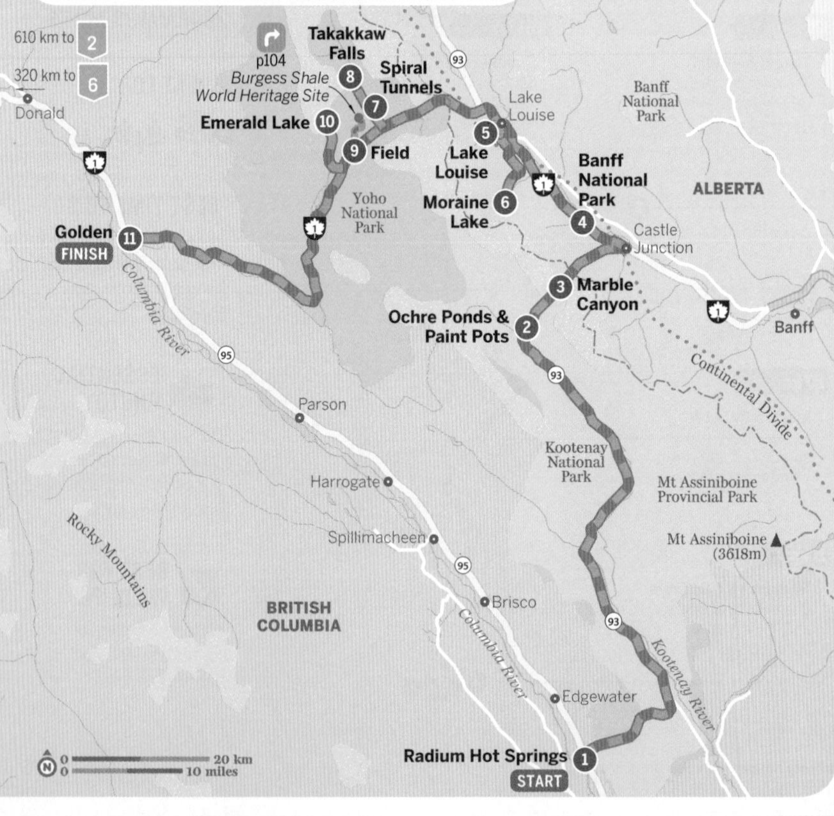

pool can get crowded in summer. You can rent lockers, towels and even swimsuits.

The Drive » From Radium Hot Springs, it's a lovely 52-mile (83km) drive on Hwy 93 through the park to Ochre Ponds & Paint Pots.

TOP TIP: ROAD CONDITIONS

Weather is very changeable in the mountains. Be sure to carry chains outside of the summer months of June, July and August. Check www.drivebc.ca in BC for current road conditions; in Alberta check www.511.alberta.ca or dial 511.

2 Ochre Ponds & Paint Pots

As the road delves down into the woods along Hwy 93, a signpost leads to a short, flat interpretive trail. Follow this to the intriguing red-and-orange Ochre Ponds. Drawing Kootenay indigenous groups for centuries – and later European settlers – this iron-rich earth was collected, mixed with oil and turned into paint. Further along the trail are three stunning crystal-blue springs that are known as the Paint Pots.

The Drive » Continue north along Hwy 93 for 1.9 miles (3km) to the next stop.

LINK YOUR TRIP

Sea to Sky Highway

Mountain-hop to the Coast Mountains by heading west from Golden on Hwy 1 and then taking Hwy 99 southwest to Whistler.

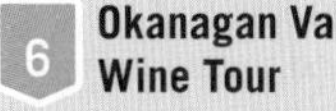

Okanagan Valley Wine Tour

From Golden, a lovely 214-mile (345km) drive along Hwys 1 and 97 will take you to Kelowna in the heart of the Okanagan Valley wine country.

3 Marble Canyon

This jaw-dropping stop is not for the faint-of-heart. An easy 15-minute trail zigzags over Tokumm Creek, giving phenomenal views deeper and deeper into Marble Canyon below. The limestone and dolomite walls have been carved away by the awesome power of the creek, resulting in plunging falls and bizarrely shaped cliff faces. The trail can be slippery. Take sturdy shoes and your camera.

The Drive » Continue north along Hwy 93 and across the provincial border into Alberta to the junction with Hwy 1 (Castle Junction). Head west.

4 Banff National Park

More of a drive than a stop, the stretch of Hwy 1 running from Castle Junction to Lake Louise is one of the most scenic routes through Banff National Park. The highway runs through the Bow Valley, following the weaving Bow River and the route of the Canadian Pacific Railway. The craggy peaks of the giant Sawback and Massive mountain ranges sweep up on either side of the road. The resulting perspective is much wider than on smaller roads with big open vistas.

There are several viewpoint pull-offs where gob-smacked drivers can stop to absorb their surroundings. Watch for the unmissable **Castle Mountain** looming in its crimson glory to the northwest. The Panorama Ridge then rises in the south, after which the enormous **Mt Temple** comes into view, towering at 11,620ft. Stop at the **Mt Temple Viewpoint** for a good gander.

The Drive » The turnoff for Lake Louise Village is 14.9 miles (24km) from Castle Junction.

p105

5 Lake Louise

With stunning emerald-green water and tall, snowy peaks that hoist hefty Victoria Glacier up for all to see, Lake Louise has captured the imaginations of mountaineers, artists and visitors for over a century. You – and the enormous numbers of other visitors – will notice the lake's color appears slightly different from each viewpoint.

Follow the **Lakeshore Trail**, a 2.4-mile (4km) round trip, or head up the gorgeous (though somewhat more difficult) route to **Lake Agnes** and its sun-dappled teahouse, perched 4.4 miles (7km) from Lake Louise's shore. For a more relaxed experience, rent a canoe from **Lake Louise Boathouse** (403-522-3511; www.fairmont.com/lake-louise/promotions/canoeing; canoe rental per 30min/1hr $115/125; 8am-8:30pm Jun-Sep, weather permitting) and paddle yourself through the icy waters.

Drive back downhill and cross over Hwy 1 to reach the **Lake Louise Gondola** (403-522-3555; www.lakelouisegondola.com; 1 Whitehorn Rd; adult/child $38/17; 9am-4pm mid-May–mid-Jun, 8am-5:30pm mid-Jun–Jul, to 6pm Aug, to 5pm Sep–mid-Oct;), which lands you at a lofty 6850ft for a view of the lake and the surrounding glaciers and peaks. En route you'll sail over wildflowers and possibly even a grizzly bear. At the top is the **Wildlife Interpretation Centre**, which hosts regular theater presentations and guided walks.

The Drive » From Lake Louise Dr, head south along Moraine Lake Rd for 8.7 miles (14km).

p105

6 Moraine Lake

You'll be dazzled by the scenery before you even reach Moraine Lake, set in the Valley of the Ten Peaks. En route, the narrow, winding road gives off fabulous views of the imposing **Wenkchemna Peaks**. Look familiar? For years this scene was carried on the back of the Canadian $20 bill. In 1894, explorer Samuel Allen named the peaks with numbers from one to 10 in the Stoney Indian Language (*wenkchemna* means 'ten'); all but two of the mountains have since been renamed. You'll quickly notice the **Tower of Babel**, ascending solidly toward the heavens at the northeastern edge of the range.

Many people prefer the more rugged and remote setting of Moraine Lake to Lake Louise. The turquoise waters are surprisingly clear for a glacial reservoir. Take a look at the surrounding mountains through telescopes secured to the southern shore (free!) or hire a boat and paddle to the middle for a 360-degree view. There are also some great day hikes from here and, to rest your weary legs, a cafe, dining room and lodge. The road to Moraine Lake and its facilities are open from June to early October.

The Drive » Return to Hwy 1 and continue west, across the provincial border and into Yoho National Park.

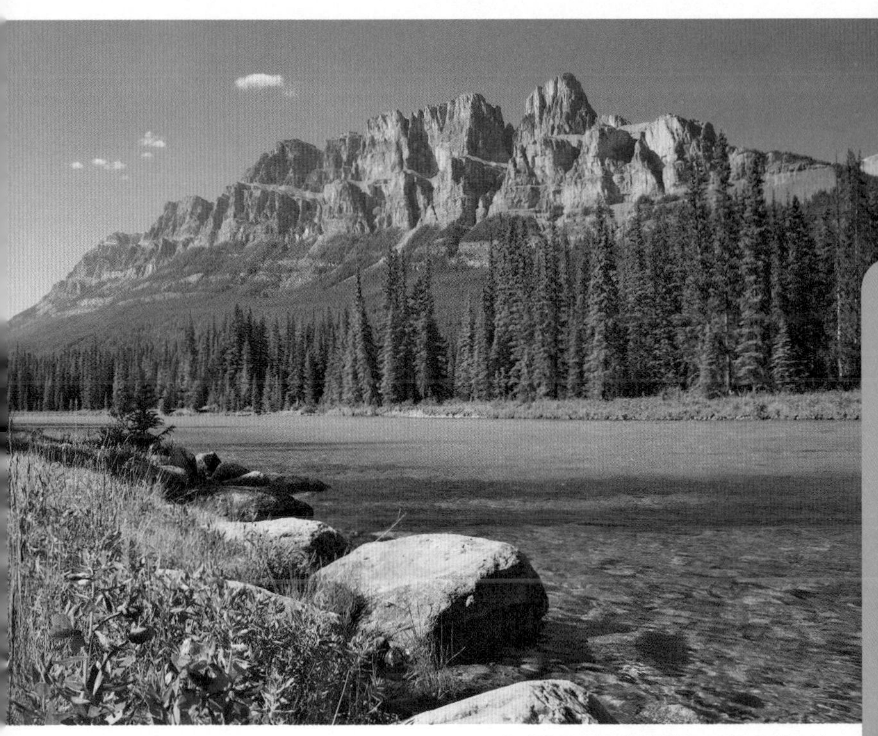

Banff National Park (p101) Views of Castle Mountain

7 Spiral Tunnels

Upon completion of the railway in 1885, trains struggled up the challenging **Kicking Horse Pass**, which you'll cross soon after the Alberta–British Columbia provincial border. This is the steepest railway pass in North America, and wrecks and runaways were common. In 1909 the Spiral Tunnels were carved into Mt Cathedral and Mt Ogden and are still in use today. If you time it right, you can see a train exiting from the top of the tunnel while its final cars are still entering at the bottom. Watch from the main viewing area on the north side of the highway.

The Drive » Continue west on Hwy 1 and then turn north onto Yoho Valley Rd (open late June to October). This road climbs a number of tight switchbacks.

8 Takakkaw Falls

Named 'magnificent' in Cree, Takakkaw Falls is one of the highest waterfalls in Canada (804ft). An impressive torrent of water travels from the Daly Glacier, plunges over the edge of the rock face into a small pool and jets out into a tumbling cloud of mist.

En route to the falls you'll pass a second **Spiral Lookout** and the **Meeting of the Rivers**, where the clear Kicking Horse runs into the milky-colored Yoho.

The Drive » Return to Hwy 1 and continue west to Field.

9 Field

In the midst of Yoho National Park, on the southern side of the Kicking Horse River, lies the quaint village of Field. This historic but unfussy railroad town has a dramatic overlook of the river. While Field may be short on sights, it's a

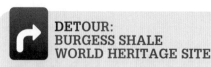

DETOUR: BURGESS SHALE WORLD HERITAGE SITE

Start: 9 Field

In 1909, Burgess Shale was unearthed on Mt Field. The fossil beds are home to perfectly preserved fossils of marine creatures, dated at least 500 million years old and recognized as some of the earliest forms of life. The area is now a World Heritage site and accessible only by guided hikes, led by naturalists from the **Yoho Shale Geoscience Foundation** (800-343-3006; www.burgess-shale.bc.ca; 201 Kicking Horse Ave; tours adult/child from $94.50/65; 9am-4pm Tue-Sat mid-Jun–mid-Sep). Reservations are essential, as is stamina: it's a 12-mile (19.3km) round trip, ascending 2500ft.

beautiful place to wander around.

This is also the place to come if you want to organize an activity in the park – from dog-sledding in winter to canoeing and white-water rafting in summer.

The Drive » Continue west on Hwy 1 and take the first right. Continue north for 6.2 miles (10km).

p105

10 Emerald Lake

Gorgeously green Emerald Lake gains its color from light reflecting off fine glacial rock particles that are deposited into the lake by grinding glaciers. It's a highlight of the park, so the lake attracts visitors year-round, either to simply admire its serenity or to fish, skate, hike or horseback ride. In summer, the water warms up just enough to have a very quick dip.

En route to the lake watch for the impressive **natural bridge** stretching across the Kicking Horse River.

The Drive » Return to Hwy 1 and continue to Golden, 33.5 miles (54km) from the turnoff.

11 Golden

With six national parks in its backyard, little Golden is a popular base. It's also the center for white-water rafting trips on the turbulent Kicking Horse River. Powerful grade III and IV rapids and breathtaking scenery along the sheer walls of Kicking Horse Valley make this rafting experience one of North America's best. Full-day trips on the river are about $159; half-day trips $99. Operators include **Alpine Rafting** (250-344-6521; www.alpinerafting.com; 1509 Lafontaine Rd; raft trips from $89; Jun-Sep;).

More than 60% of the 120 ski runs at **Kicking Horse Mountain Resort** (250-439-5425; www.kickinghorseresort.com; Kicking Horse Trail; 1-day lift ticket adult/child winter $94/38, summer $42/21) are rated advanced or expert. It's 8.7 miles (14km) from Golden on Kicking Horse Trail.

The **Northern Lights Wolf Centre** (250-344-6798; www.northernlightswildlife.com; 1745 Short Rd; adult/child $12/6; 9am-7pm Jul & Aug, 10am-6pm May, Jun & Sep, noon-5pm Oct-Apr; P) is a refuge for this misunderstood animal, which is being hunted to extinction. Meet a resident wolf or two and learn about their routines and survival.

p105

Eating & Sleeping

Banff National Park 4

Baker Creek Bistro European $$$
(403-522-3761; www.bakercreek.com/baker-creek-bistro; Bow Valley Pkwy; mains $30-55; 7am-10pm) This attractive cabin restaurant is located inside the **Baker Creek Chalets** complex and is among the few places to eat on the Bow Valley Pkwy. Good thing it's decent, with such exotic lures as wild-caught Vancouver Island salmon and Alberta beef tenderloin with a three-peppercorn demi-glaze. It also has a cheaper lounge selling burgers and the like, and a breezy patio.

Skoki Lodge Lodge $$
(403-522-3555; www.skoki.com; r per person incl 3 meals & afternoon tea $240-305) Built in 1931 overlooking a glorious high mountain valley, Skoki was one of the Canadian Rockies' earliest backcountry lodges and remains one of the most magical places to stay in the whole national park. The rustic but delightfully cozy lodge is only accessible on foot, horseback or skis via an 11km climb over two high mountain passes from Lake Louise.

Lake Louise 5

Lake Agnes Teahouse Teahouse $
(www.lakeagnesteahouse.com; lunch $7.50-15; 8am-5pm early Jun-early Oct) The 3.4km hike from Lake Louise to Lake Agnes is among the area's most popular – surely because it ends here. This fabulously rustic alpine teahouse perched at 2135m (7005ft) seems to hang in the clouds beside the ethereal lake and its adjacent waterfall. Homemade soup, thick-cut sandwiches and lake-water tea help fuel the jaunt back down. Cash only. Expect queues.

HI Lake Louise Alpine Centre Hostel $
(403-522-2201; www.hihostels.ca; 203 Village Rd, Lake Louise village; dm/d $64/192; P) This is what a hostel should be – clean, friendly and full of interesting travelers – and the rustic, comfortable lodge-style buildings, with plenty of raw timber and stone, are fine examples of Canadian Rockies architecture. Dorm rooms are fairly standard and the small private rooms are a bit overpriced, but this is as close as you'll get to budget in Lake Louise.

Private rooms with lofts are great for families. Don't miss the on-site **Bill Peyto's Café**.

Field 9

Truffle Pigs Lodge Hotel $$
(250-343-6303; www.trufflepigs.com; 100 Centre St; r from $120; Jun-Sep; P) Field's only hotel is a timber building with heritage charm. The 14 rooms are fairly simply decked out, though. Some have small kitchens. The owners run the town's well-known restaurant, **Truffle Pigs bistro** in the same attractive building.

Golden 11

Bacchus Books & Cafe Cafe $
(250-344-5600; www.bacchusbooks.ca; 409 9th Ave N; mains from $8; 9am-5:30pm) This bohemian hideaway at the end of 8th St is a favorite haunt for Golden's artsy crowd. Browse for books (new and secondhand) in the downstairs bookstore, then head upstairs to find a table for tea among the higgledy-piggledy shelves. Sandwiches, salads and cakes are made on the premises, and the coffee is as good as you'll find in Golden.

Kicking Horse Canyon B&B Guesthouse $$
(250-899-0840; www.kickinghorsecanyonbb.com; 644 Lapp Rd; d from $120; P) Hidden away among the hills to the east of Golden, this endearingly offbeat B&B takes you into the bosom of the family the minute you cross the threshold. Run by genial host Jeannie Cook and her husband, Jerry, it's a real alpine home-away-from-home, surrounded by private grassy grounds with views across the mountains.

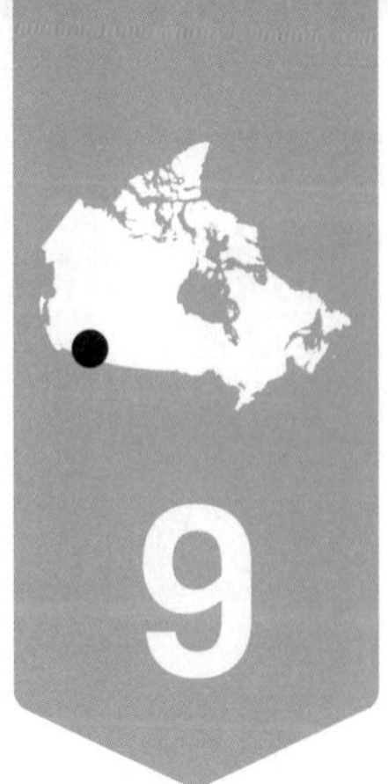
9

Around the Kootenays

Multiple mountain ranges, pockets of mining history and relaxed small towns with idiosyncratic art scenes, BC's Kootenay region is the quiet, unpublicized alternative to the Rocky Mountain national parks.

TRIP HIGHLIGHTS

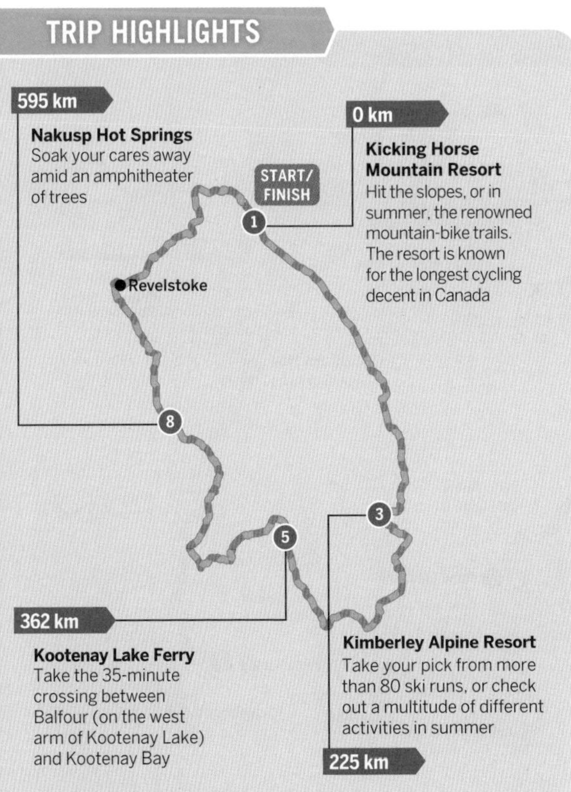
595 km
Nakusp Hot Springs
Soak your cares away amid an amphitheater of trees
0 km
Kicking Horse Mountain Resort
Hit the slopes, or in summer, the renowned mountain-bike trails. The resort is known for the longest cycling decent in Canada
START/ FINISH
1
Revelstoke
8
3
5
362 km
Kootenay Lake Ferry
Take the 35-minute crossing between Balfour (on the west arm of Kootenay Lake) and Kootenay Bay
Kimberley Alpine Resort
Take your pick from more than 80 ski runs, or check out a multitude of different activities in summer
225 km

5–6 DAYS
870KM/543 MILES

GREAT FOR...

BEST TIME TO GO

June to September when roads and trails are snow-free and accessible.

ESSENTIAL PHOTO

Summit of Mt Revelstoke.

BEST FOR OUTDOORS

Biking, hiking, and – best of all – whitewater rafting.

Kootenay National Park Hiking on Stanley Glacier Trail

9 Around the Kootenays

The commanding ranges of the Monashee, Selkirk and Purcell Mountains striate the Kootenays, with the Arrow and Kootenay Lakes adding texture in the middle. This drive allows you to admire their placid alpine meadows and rugged sawtooth ridges while popping into appealing towns such as Revelstoke, Golden, Nelson and Radium Hot Springs in between. Herein lie plenty of launchpads for year-round outdoor adventures.

TRIP HIGHLIGHT

1 Golden

Golden sits at the confluence of two rivers, three mountain ranges and five national parks – all of them less than 90 minutes drive away.

The town is the center for white-water rafting trips on the turbulent and chilly Kicking Horse River. Along with the powerful grade III and IV rapids, the rugged scenery that guards the sheer walls of the Kicking Horse Valley makes this

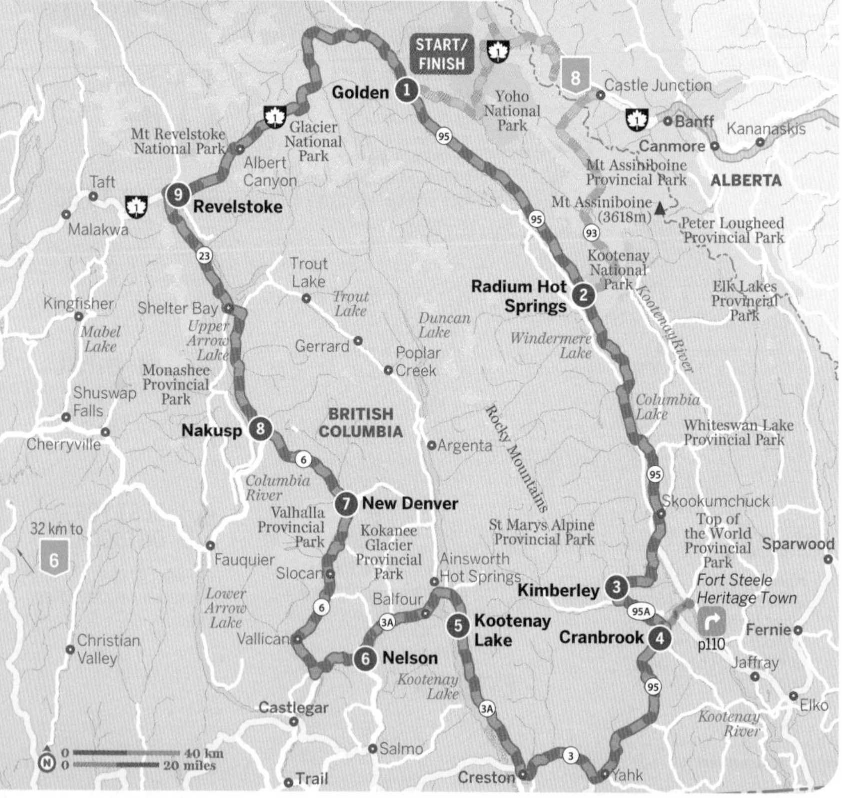

rafting experience one of North America's best.

Indelibly linked to Golden is the **Kicking Horse Mountain Resort** (250-439-5425; www.kickinghorseresort.com; Kicking Horse Trail; 1-day lift ticket adult/child winter $94/38, summer $42/21) 6km to the west – a ski resort that opened in 2000 and is known for its abundance of expert runs. In the summer, the resort and its gondola are handed over to mountain bikers and, more recently, climbers keen to tackle several newly installed via ferrata routes.

The Drive » Head south on Hwy 95 through the Columbia River Wetlands, a hugely important ecological area that's home to 260 species of bird and numerous animals, including grizzly bears. In just over an hour, you will arrive in Radium Hot Springs.

 p113

2 Radium Hot Springs

Lying just outside the southwest corner of Kootenay National Park, Radium Hot Springs is a major gateway to the entire Rocky Mountains national park area.

The town itself isn't much more than a gas and coffee pit-stop. The main attraction is the namesake hot springs, 3km north of town at the jaws of Kootenay National Park (you can hike in via the Sinclair Canyon). One of three hot springs in the Rockies region, Radium is the only one that is odorless. Keeping its water between 37°C and 40°C, the facility is more public baths than fancy spa, although the exposed rock and overhanging trees make for a nice setting.

The Drive » Heading south, Hwy 93/95 follows the wide Columbia River valley between the Purcell and Rocky Mountains. It's not especially interesting, unless you're into the area's industry (ski resort construction), agriculture (golf courses) or wild game (condo buyers). South of Skookumchuck on Hwy 93/95, the road forks. Go right on Hwy 95A and within 30-minutes you'll be in Kimberley.

LINK YOUR TRIP

Okanagan Valley Wine Tour

After completing the tour at Revelstoke, head three hours southwest to the start of this scenic drive among the rolling, vine-covered hills.

Circling the Rockies

At Radium Hot Springs, divert east onto Hwy 93 which will take you into Kootenay National Park on this epic Rockies loop.

TRIP HIGHLIGHT

3 Kimberley

Welcome to Kimberley, a town famous for its erstwhile lead mine, contemporary alpine skiing resort and Canada's largest cuckoo clock.

For well over half a century, Kimberley was home to the world's largest lead-zinc mine, the Sullivan mine, which was finally decommissioned in 2001. Since 2015, the local economy has switched track somewhat and now hosts Canada's largest solar farm.

In the 1970s, Kimberley experimented with a Bavarian theme in the hope of attracting more tourists. Remnants of the Teutonic makeover remain. The central pedestrian zone is named the Platzl and you can still bag plenty of tasty schnitzel and sausages in its restaurants, but these days the town is better known for the **Kimberley Alpine Resort** (250-427-4881; www.skikimberley.com; 301 N Star Blvd; 1-day lift pass adult/child $75/30) with 700 hectares of skiable terrain.

For a historical detour, take a 15km ride on **Kimberley's Underground Mining Railway** (250-427-7365; www.kimberleysundergroundminingrailway.ca; Gerry Sorensen Way; adult/child $25/10; tours 11am, 1pm & 3pm May-Sep, trains to resort 10am Sat & Sun), where a tiny train putters through the steep-walled Mark Creek Valley toward some sweeping mountain vistas.

The Drive » It's a short 30-minute drive southeast out of Kimberley on Hwy 95A to Cranbrook where you'll merge with Hwy 95 just east of the town.

❹ Cranbrook

The region's main commercial center with a population of just under 20,000, Cranbrook is a modest crossroads. Hwy 3/95 bisects the town, which is a charmless array of strip malls.

The main reason for stopping here is to visit the multifarious **Cranbrook History Centre** (☎250-489-3918; www.cranbrookhistorycentre.com; 57 Van Horne St S, Hwy 3/95; adult/child $5/3; ⏲10am-5pm Tue-Sun). Dedicated primarily (though not exclusively) to train and rail travel, the center displays some fine examples of classic Canadian trains, including the luxurious 1929 edition of the Trans-Canada Limited, a legendary train that ran from Montréal to Vancouver. Also on-site is a fabulous model railway, the town museum (with plenty of First Nations and pre-human artifacts), and the elegant Alexandra Hall, part of a grand railway hotel that once stood in Winnipeg but was reconstructed in Cranbrook in 2004.

The Drive » Take Hwy 3 (Crowsnest Hwy) out of Cranbrook. The road is shared with Hwy 95 as far as Yahk, beyond which you pass through the Purcell Mountains to Creston. North of Creston, turn onto Hwy 3A and track alongside the east shore of Kootenay Lake. This leg takes around 2½ hours.

p113

TRIP HIGHLIGHT

❺ Kootenay Lake

Lodged in the middle of Kootenays between the Selkirk and Purcell Mountains, Kootenay Lake is one of the largest bodies of freshwater in BC. It's crossed by a year-round toll-free **ferry** (☎250-229-4215; www2.gov.bc.ca/gov/content/transportation/passenger-travel) that runs between the two small communities of Kootenay Bay on the east bank, and Balfour on the west. The ferry's a worthwhile side trip if traveling between Creston and Nelson for its long lake vistas of blue mountains rising sharply from the water. Ferries run every 50 minutes throughout the day and the crossing takes 35 minutes. On busy summer weekends, you may have to wait in a long line for a sailing or two before you get passage.

The Drive » From where the ferry disembarks in Balfour on the western shore of Kootenay Lake, take Hwy 3A along the north shore of the West Arm for 32km before crossing the bridge into the town of Nelson.

DETOUR: FORT STEELE HERITAGE TOWN

Start ❹ Cranbrook

Fort Steele is an erstwhile gold rush town that fell into decline in the early 1900s when it was bypassed by the railway, which went to Cranbrook instead. In the early 1960s, local authorities elected to save the place from total oblivion by turning it into a **heritage site** (☎250-426-7342; www.fortsteele.ca; 9851 Hwy 93/95; adult/youth $18/12 summer; ⏲10am-5pm mid-Jun–Aug, shorter hours winter) of pioneering mining culture. Buildings were subsequently rescued or completely rebuilt in vintage 19th century style to lure in tourists. The site today consists of old shops, stores and a blacksmith, plus opportunities to partake in gold-panning, go on train rides or see a performance in a working theater.

In summer there are all manner of activities and re-creations, which taper off to nothing in winter, although the site stays open.

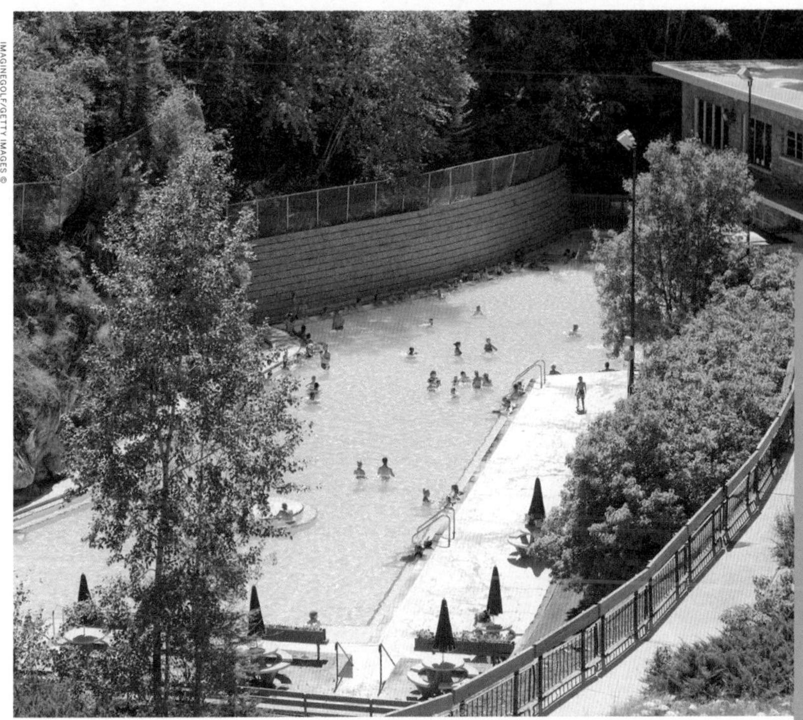

IMAGINEGOLF/GETTY IMAGES ©

Radium Hot Springs (p109) Bathers enjoy the natural hot pool

6 Nelson

Nelson is a great reason to visit the Kootenays and should feature on any itinerary in the region. Tidy brick buildings climb the side of a hill overlooking the west arm of deep-blue Kootenay Lake, and the waterfront is lined with parks and beaches. The thriving cafe, culture and nightlife scene is a bonus. But what really propels Nelson is its personality: a mix of hippies, creative types and rugged individualists (many locals will tell you it's the coolest small town in BC). You can find all these along Baker St, the pedestrian-friendly main drag.

Founded as a mining town in the late 1800s, Nelson embarked on a decades-long heritage-preservation project in 1977. Almost a third of Nelson's historic buildings have been restored to their original architectural splendor. Pick up the superb *Heritage Walking Tour* from the visitor center, which gives details on more than 30 buildings and offers a good lesson in Victorian architecture.

The town is also an excellent base for hiking, skiing, kayaking the nearby lakes, and – in recent years in particular – mountain-biking. Free-riding pedal-heads have plenty of favorite spots in British Columbia and the Rockies, but many particularly enjoy Nelson's unique juxtaposition of top-notch single-track and cool bikey ambience. The surrounding area is striped with great trails, from the epic downhill of **Mountain Station** to the winding **Svoboda Road Trails** in West Arm Provincial Park.

The Drive » Heading north from Nelson to Revelstoke, Hwy 6 threads west for 16km before turning north at South Slocan. The road eventually runs alongside pretty Slocan Lake for about 30km before reaching New Denver, 97km from Nelson.

p113

7 New Denver

With only around 500 residents, New Denver is an historic little gem that slumbers away peacefully right on the clear waters of Slocan Lake. Chapters in its not-so-sleepy history have included silver mining and a stint as a WWII Japanese internment camp. Details of the former can be found at the **Silvery Slocan Museum** (250-358-2201; www.newdenver.ca/silvery-slocan-museum; 202 6th Ave; by donation; 9am-5pm Jul-Aug, Sat & Sun only Sep-Jun), located in an 1897 Bank of Montreal building.

The Drive » It is a relatively straightforward 46km drive from New Denver to Nakusp on Hwy 6 via Summit Lake Provincial Park. Look out for mountain goats on the rocky outcrops.

TRIP HIGHLIGHT

8 Nakusp

Situated right on Upper Arrow Lake, Nakusp was forever changed by BC's orgy of dam building in the 1950s and 1960s. The water level here was raised and the town was relocated to its current spot, which is why it has a 1960s-era look. It has some attractive cafes and a tiny museum. If you missed Radium Hot Springs or just can't get enough of the Rocky Mountains' thermal pleasures, divert to **Nakusp Hot Springs** (250-265-4528; www.nakusphotsprings.com; 8500 Hot Springs Rd; adult/child $10.50/9.50; 9:30am-9:30pm), 12km northeast of town to soak away your cares amid an amphitheater of trees.

The Drive » Head north on Hwy 23 along the east shore of Arrow Lake for 48km. You'll need to cross this lake, too, on a ferry between Galena and Shelter Bay. Hwy 23 continues on the west shore and will take you all the way to Revelstoke, 52km north of Shelter Bay.

9 Revelstoke

Gateway to serious mountains, Revelstoke doesn't need to blow its own trumpet – the ceaseless procession of freight trains through the town center makes more than enough noise. Built as an important point on the Canadian Pacific transcontinental railroad that first linked Eastern and Western Canada, Revelstoke echoes not just with whistles but with history. If you haven't yet been satiated with Canadian railway memorabilia, you can sample a bit more at the **Revelstoke Railway Museum** (250-837-6060; www.railwaymuseum.com; 719 Track St W; adult/child $10/5; 9am-5pm May-Sep, shorter hours Oct-Apr; P).

Revelstoke's compact center is lined with heritage buildings, yet it's more than a museum piece. **Grizzly Plaza**, between Mackenzie and Orton Aves, is a pedestrian precinct and the heart of downtown, where free live-music performances take place every evening in July and August.

Notwithstanding, this place is mainly about the adjacent wilderness and its boundless opportunities for hiking, kayaking and, most of all, skiing. North America's first ski jump was built here in 1915. One year before, Mt Revelstoke became Canada's seventh national park. From the 2223m summit of Mt Revelstoke, the views of the mountains and the Columbia River valley are excellent. To ascend, take the 26km Meadows in the Sky Parkway, 1.6km east of Revelstoke off the Trans-Canada Hwy. Open after the thaw, from mid-May to mid-October, this paved road winds through lush cedar forests and alpine meadows and ends at Balsam Lake, within 2km of the peak. From here, walk to the top or take the free shuttle.

The Drive » Keep your eyes on the road or, better yet, let someone else drive as you traverse the Trans-Canada Hwy (Hwy 1) for 148km between Revelstoke and Golden. Stunning mountain peaks follow one after another as you go.

p113

Eating & Sleeping

Golden 1

Wolf Den Pub Food $$

(250-344-9863; www.thewolfsdengolden.ca; 1105 9th St; dinner mains from $14; 4-10pm) An excellent pub with live music on Sundays. It's hugely popular with locals, who love the burgers and hearty fare, which is way above average. The beer menu includes some of BC's best on tap. It's just south of the river from downtown.

Dreamcatcher Hostel Hostel $

(250-439-1090; www.dreamcatcherhostel.com; 528 9th Ave N; dm/r from $32/90; P) Run by two veteran travelers, this centrally located hostel has everything a budget traveler could hope for. There are three dorm rooms, five private rooms, as well as a vast kitchen and a comfy common room with a stone fireplace. Outside there's a garden and a barbecue.

Cranbrook 4

Retro Cafe French $

(250-428-2726; www.retrocafe.ca; 1431 NW Blvd, Creston; mains from $8; 7am-4pm Mon-Fri, to 3pm Sat) A French mirage in Creston, 'retro' will probably be the last thing on your mind as you scour the hand-scrawled blackboard and tuck into *très délicieux* crepes.

Valley View Motel Motel $

(250-428-2336; www.valleyviewmotel.info; 216 Valley View Dr, Creston; r from $75; P) In motel-ville Creston, this is your best bet. On a view-splayed hillside, it's clean, comfortable and quiet.

Nelson 6

Jackson's Hole & Grill Canadian $$

(250-354-1919; www.jacksonsgrill.ca; 524 Vernon St; dinner mains from $14; 11:30am-9pm Sun-Tue, to 10pm Wed & Thu, to midnight Fri & Sat) In a historic building that has been around since 1897, this place is both lively and friendly. Used as Dixie's Café in the Steve Martin and Darryl Hannah Hollywood classic *Roxanne* in 1986, Jackson's serves soups, salads, sandwiches, wraps, burgers and pastas. Plenty to choose from in a very convivial atmosphere.

Hume Hotel & Spa Hotel $$

(250-352-5331; www.humehotel.com; 422 Vernon St; r incl breakfast from $120; P) This 1898 classic hotel maintains its period grandeur. The 43 rooms vary greatly in shape and size; ask for the huge corner rooms with views of the hills and lake. Rates include a delicious breakfast. It has several appealing nightlife venues.

Revelstoke 9

Modern Bakeshop & Café Cafe $

(250-837-6886; www.themodernbakeshopandcafe.com; 212 Mackenzie Ave; mains from $6; 6:30am-5pm Mon-Sat;) Try a croque monsieur (grilled ham-and-cheese sandwich) or an elaborate pastry for a taste of Europe at this cute art-deco cafe. Many items, such as the muffins, are made with organic ingredients. Discover the baked 'boofy uptrack bar' for a treat. Nice seating outside.

Regent Hotel Hotel $$

(250-837-2107; www.regenthotel.ca; 112 1st St E; r from $110; P) The poshest place in the center is not lavish, but it is comfy. The 42 modern rooms bear no traces of the hotel's 1914 roots and exterior. The restaurant and lounge are justifiably popular. Many guests bob the night away in the outdoor hot tub.

STRETCH YOUR LEGS VANCOUVER

Start/Finish: Gastown

Distance: 10km

Duration: Three to four hours

Wandering around Vancouver, with its visually arresting backdrop of sparkling ocean and snow-dusted mountaintops, you discover there's more to this city than appearances. It's a kaleidoscope of distinctive neighborhoods, strongly artistic and just as hip as it is sophisticated.

Take this walk on Trip

Gastown

Crammed into a dozen, often brick-paved blocks, trendy Gastown is where the city began. Century-old heritage buildings now house cool bars and quirky galleries, with the landmark **steam clock** (cnr Water & Cambie Sts; S Waterfront) whistling to a camera-wielding coterie of onlookers every 15 minutes. Tucked along handsome historic rows, swish boutiques, artisan stores and chatty coffee shops invite leisurely browsing and laid-back java sipping. And when you need a fuel-up, **Brioche** (www.brioche.ca; 401 W Cordova St; mains $10-16; 7am-9pm Mon-Fri, 8am-9pm Sat & Sun; S Waterfront) is a colorful, comfy place to stop for lunch.

The Walk » Follow Water St east, turning right on Carrall St and heading south for three blocks to Pender St and Chinatown.

Chinatown

North America's third-largest Chinatown is a highly wanderable explosion of sight, sound and aromas. Check out the towering **Chinatown Millennium Gate** (cnr W Pender & Taylor Sts; S Stadium-Chinatown) and visit the tranquil **Dr Sun Yat-Sen Classical Chinese Garden** (www.vancouverchinesegarden.com; 578 Carrall St; adult/child $14/10; 9:30am-7pm mid-Jun–Aug, 10am-6pm Sep & May–mid-Jun, 10am-4:30pm Oct-Apr; S Stadium-Chinatown). Save time for the **Chinese Tea Shop** (www.thechineseteashop.com; 101 E Pender St; 1-6pm Wed-Mon; 3), which has all the makings of a perfect cuppa, and slip into colorful apothecary stores for a fascinating eyeful of traditional Chinese medicine.

The Walk » Follow Keefer St and Keefer Pl west, crossing the roundabout at the end and continuing along the footpath to Beatty St. Turn left and walk three blocks to Robson St. Turn right, crossing Granville St, and continue along Robson to Hornby St.

Vancouver Art Gallery

A palatial former courthouse building, the grand home of the **Vancouver Art Gallery** (www.vanartgallery.bc.ca; 750 Hornby

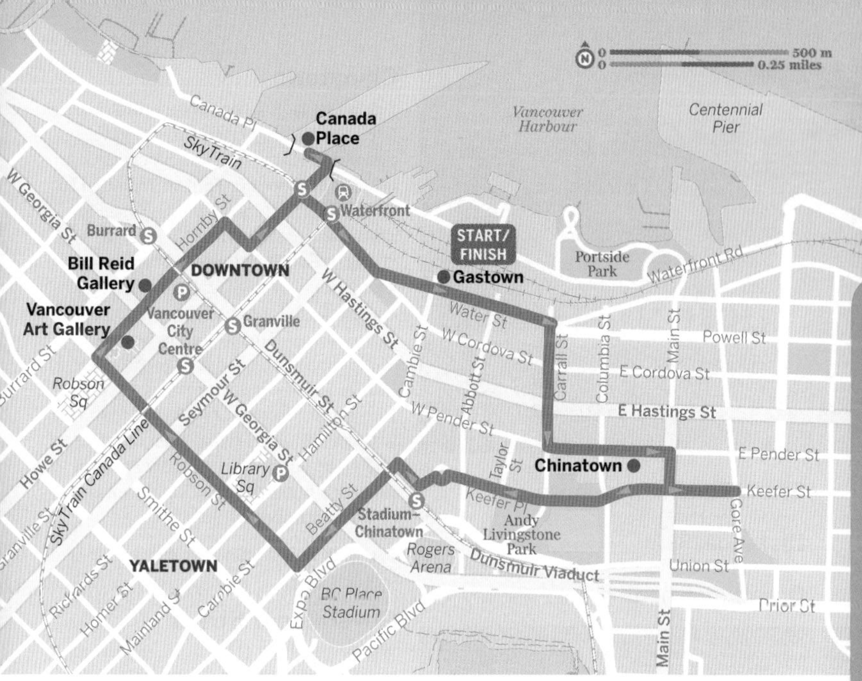

St, Downtown; adult/child $24/6.50; ⏲10am-5pm Wed-Mon, to 9pm Tue; 🚌5) showcases contemporary exhibitions, work by time-honored masters, and blockbuster international traveling shows. Check out **FUSE** (www.vanartgallery.bc.ca/fuse; $29; ⏲8pm-midnight), a regular late-night party event where you can hang out with the city's young creatives over wine and live music. Check ahead for regular gallery talks and tours and, if you're travelling on a tight budget, consider postponing your visit to a Tuesday when entry is by donation after 5pm.

The Walk » Exit the gallery on the Hornby St side and walk two blocks northeast along Hornby.

Bill Reid Gallery

The **Bill Reid Gallery of Northwest Coast Art** (www.billreidgallery.ca; 639 Hornby St, Downtown; adult/youth/child $13/6/free; ⏲10am-5pm May-Sep, 11am-5pm Wed-Sun Oct-Apr; Ⓢ Burrard) showcases carvings, paintings and jewelry from Canada's most revered Haida artist as well as his fellow First Nations creators. This is one of the city's must-visit art galleries if you're interested in the region's rich First Nations heritage. Give yourself plenty of time for a full-on cultural immersion here.

The Walk » Continue up Hornby St to Pender St. Turn right and then left onto Howe St. Follow this towards the water.

Canada Place

Shaped like a series of sails jutting into the sky over the harbor, **Canada Place** (www.canadaplace.ca; 999 Canada Place Way, Downtown; Ⓟ 👪; Ⓢ Waterfront) is a cruise-ship terminal, convention center and pier where you can stroll the waterfront and enjoy handsome views of the grand North Shore mountains. Save time to snap photos of the floatplanes landing and taking off alongside, framed by Stanley Park in the background. Next door, check out the grass-roofed convention-center expansion and the tripod-like **Olympic Cauldron**, a permanent reminder of the 2010 Games.

The Walk » Backtrack up Howe St for one block and turn left onto W Cordova St. After three blocks, edge left onto Water St and back into Gastown.

STRETCH YOUR LEGS VICTORIA

Start/Finish: Chinatown

Distance: 6km

Duration: 5 hours

It's not sugar coating – the seaside provincial capital really is as charming and beautiful as it first appears. Filled with funky boutiques, excellent museums, unique neighborhoods and a jewel of a park, Victoria makes for a blissful wander.

Take this walk on Trips

Chinatown

Settled in 1858, Chinatown announces itself with a bright, traditional gate, and stretches two packed blocks along Fisgard St. Pop into **Fantan Trading Ltd** (250-381-8882; 551 Fisgard St; 11am-5pm; 70) for a maze of made-in-China goods or **Fan Tan Home & Style** (www.fantanvictoria.com; 541 Fisgard St; 9:30am-5:30pm; 70) for beautiful wooden and woven items. Dine at **Venus Sophia** (www.venussophia.com; 540 Fisgard St; afternoon tea $14-30; 10am-6pm Jul & Aug, from 11am Wed-Sun Sep-Jun; ; 70), a tearoom with a vegetarian twist, then breathe in and slide along super-narrow **Fan Tan Alley**. It's home to many small boutiques and vintage shops.

The Walk » At Chinatown's gate, turn right onto Government St.

Government Street

With everything from book emporiums to ice-cream parlors, Government St is a great stretch of pavement to pound. Visit **Silk Road** (https://silkroadteastore.com; 1624 Government St; 10am-5:30pm Mon-Sat, 11am-5pm Sun; 70) for heavenly teas, and detour onto Johnson St for quirky independent stores. Hungry? Continue along Government St, turn left onto Fort St and then around the corner onto Broad St for the phenomenal **Pagliacci's** (www.pagliaccis.ca; 110 Broad St; mains $17-29; 11:30am-10pm, Sun-Thu, to 11pm Fri & Sat; 70), a pasta place.

The Walk » Continue eight blocks south on Government St.

The Inner Harbour

Watched over by the grand Empress Hotel, the handsome **Parliament Buildings** (www.leg.bc.ca; 501 Belleville St; tours 9am-5pm mid-May–Aug, from 8:30am Mon-Fri Sep–mid-May; 70) and the brilliantly educational Royal BC Museum (p56), the Inner Harbour is Victoria's most photogenic location. On lazy summer afternoons, walk down along the waterfront promenade to check out the boats

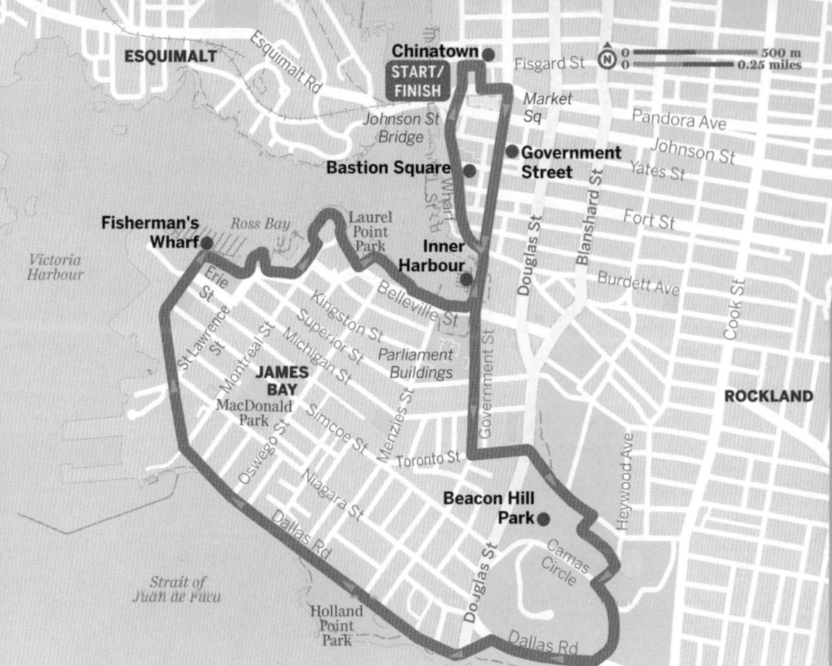

bobbling like candy-colored corks and enjoy a full roster of artisan market stalls and top-notch street performers.

The Walk » Continue south on Government St to Toronto St. Turn left and follow this east for three blocks to Beacon Hill Park.

Beacon Hill Park

An idyllic fusion of planted gardens and wild and woody sections, Beacon Hill Park is naturally popular. There's a playground, an excellent petting zoo and a heron-nesting zone worth cricking your neck to see. Head south and you'll find one of North America's tallest totem poles and eventually Dallas Rd, a breeze-licked oceanside walk where whale sightings aren't uncommon.

The Walk » Follow Dallas Rd to its end.

Fisherman's Wharf

At **Fisherman's Wharf** (www.fishermanswharfvictoria.com; P; bus 30), fishing boats share dock space with a floating community of eclectic, colorful houseboats. Wander along the sun-dappled boardwalks and visit the galleries – then add a hunger-busting pit stop. **Barb's** (www.barbsfishandchips.com; 1 Dallas Rd; meals $10-23; hours 11am-dusk mid-Mar–Oct; bus 30) is hard to resist for fish and chips, and kids' eyes will pop at the counter of **Jackson's Ice-Cream**.

The Walk » Follow the shoreline footpath east along the water from Fisherman's Wharf, all the way back to the Inner Harbour. Alternatively, jump on one of the cute harbour ferries. From the Inner Harbour, follow Wharf St north.

Bastion Square

Historic **Bastion Square** hosts a popular seasonal **artisan market** along with cafes and buskers. This is also a great area to come to for dinner. **ReBar** (50 Bastion Sq; mains $16-18; hours 11:30am-9pm Mon-Fri, from 10am Sat, 10am-8pm Sun; vegetarian; bus 70) is a favorite among Victorians for good reason. Popular with vegetarians, it also serves up chicken and fish dishes to keep the carnivores happy.

The Walk » Carry on up Wharf St to Fisgard St to complete the loop.

The Prairie Provinces & the North

A SETTING FOR LIMITLESS ADVENTURES, THIS REGION IS HOME TO FABLED NATIONAL PARKS, archaeological wonders and the peaceful grasslands where bison still roam. The road trips here offer abundant allure for adventurers: hiking, kayaking, camping and just enjoying the views of lakes, mountains and forests.

This is also a land of fascinating relics from the past – dinosaur bones and fossil fields, First Nations historical parks, Wild West towns and old gold-mining sites once packed with 19th-century dreamers. The southern reaches have long and flat stretches of highway, but offer their own quiet and subtle beauty. The further north you go, the plains are replaced by lakes, vast boreal forest and wilderness until you run out of road and any form of population. It's the gateway to adventure – and a place where being well prepared are essential.

Horseshoe Canyon (p125) Visitors admire the multicolored hills

The Prairie Provinces & the North

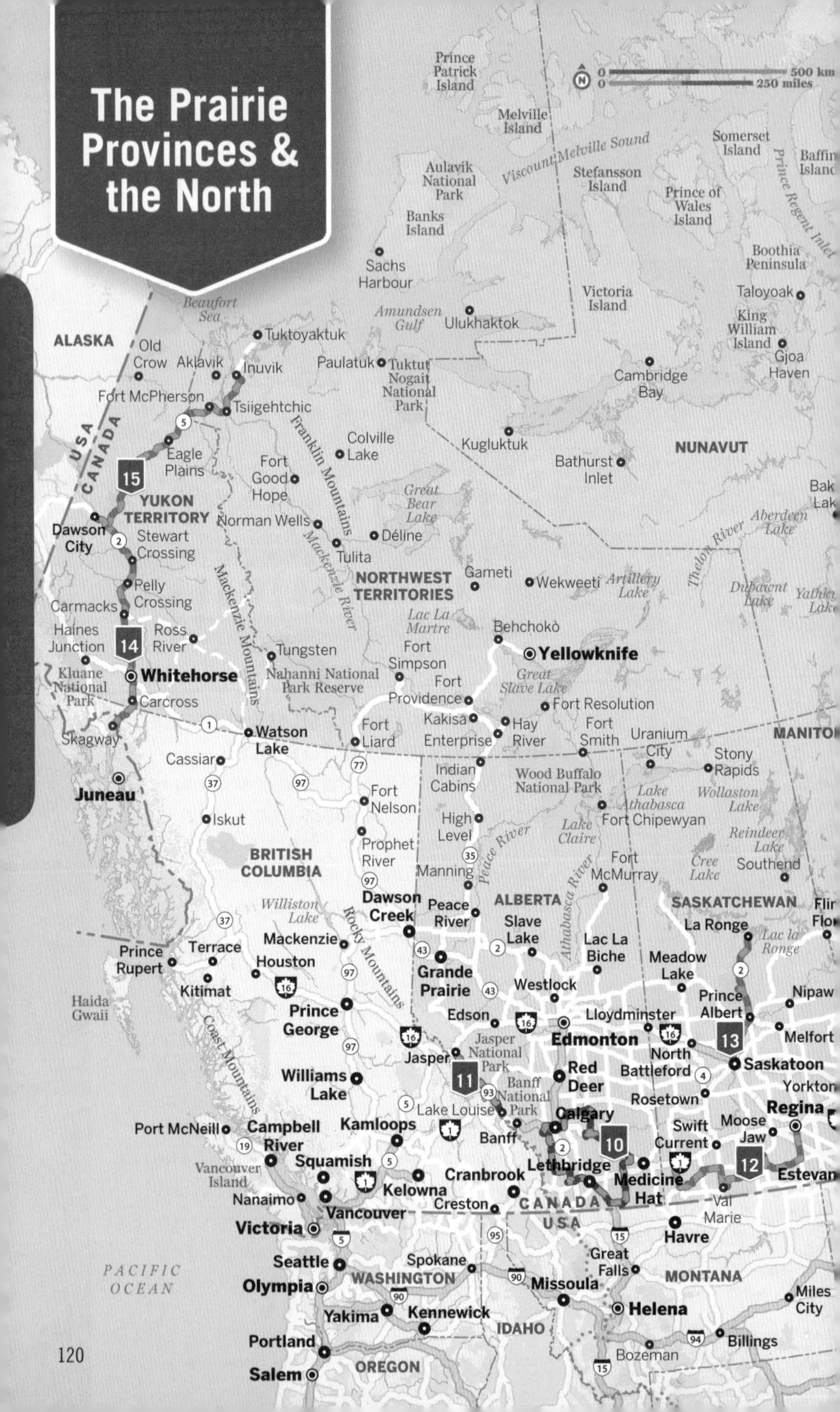

Dawson City (p164) Atmospheric shopfront

Dinosaurs, Hoodoos & the Wild West 2–3 Days
Set off from Calgary into a realm of big skies, indigenous sites and awe-inspiring fossil fields.

Icefields Parkway 2 Days
Revel in Canada's majestic wilderness, complete with soaring mountains, glacial lakes and thundering waterfalls.

Explore Southern Saskatchewan 3–4 Days
Serene grasslands set the stage for discovering creatures great and small: from a towering T. Rex to petite prairie dogs.

North from Saskatoon 3–4 Days
Get off the beaten path amid lakes, forests and one delightfully surprising town (Saskatoon!).

Klondike Highway 4–5 Days
Journey though historic gold rush towns and into rugged mountain wilderness as you go from Alaska into the Yukon.

15 **Dempster Highway 6–7 Days**
Reconnect with mother nature on this unforgettable trip through stark mountains, emerald valleys and huge tracts of tundra.

DON'T MISS

Prince Albert National Park
Canoeing clear waters or hiking the verdant forests of this family-friendly and blissfully crowd-free park. Go there on Trip 13

T-rex Discovery Centre
Learn about the famously terrible dinosaur unearthed in its entirety in southwest Saskatchewan. See it on Trip 12

Dawson City
Walk in the footsteps of 19th-century gold prospectors in this remote riverfront town. Get there on Trip 14

Lake Louise
Walk the trails around this breathtakingly beautiful mountain-fringed lake, one of the great wonders of Banff National Park. Lace up your boots on Trip 11

Arctic Circle
Earn bragging rights as you cross into Earth's northernmost region, while making the most of your long summer days (or endless winter nights). Go there on Trip 15

FORMATION

Classic Trip

Dinosaurs, Hoodoos & the Wild West

This gorgeous drive takes you to dinosaur-fossil-studded hills and great museums, to petroglyph-marked canyons, to Unesco-preserved Blackfoot heritage sites and to the land of the cowboy.

TRIP HIGHLIGHTS

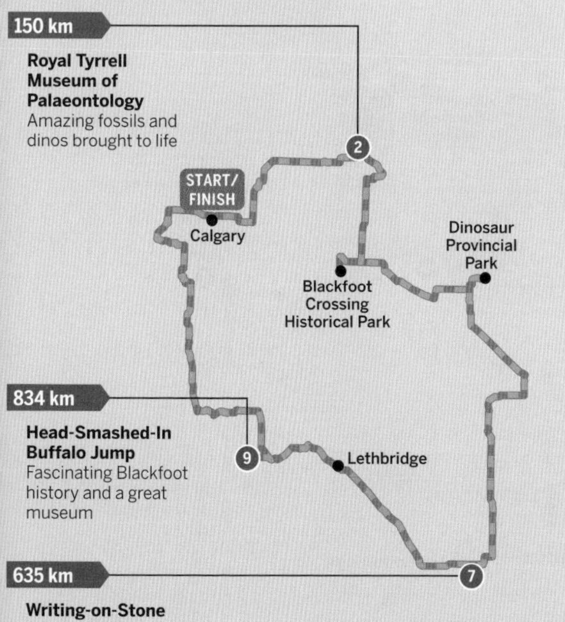

2–3 DAYS
1020KM/634 MILES

GREAT FOR...

BEST TIME TO GO

Best driven between June and August.

ESSENTIAL PHOTO

The painted, eerie, fossil-strewn hills of the Badlands.

BEST FOR FAMILIES

Visiting the Royal Tyrrell Museum of Palaeontology.

rumheller The World's Largest Dinosaur (p125) statue marks the entrance to the town's visitor center

Classic Trip

10 Dinosaurs, Hoodoos & the Wild West

This road trip has a lot of driving but the payoff is seeing some of the most stunning historical sites Canada has to offer. However, we'd be remiss if we didn't point out that you also get to climb the wazoo of the world's biggest dinosaur and stare out at the town of Drumheller from between its fearsome, gaping jaws.

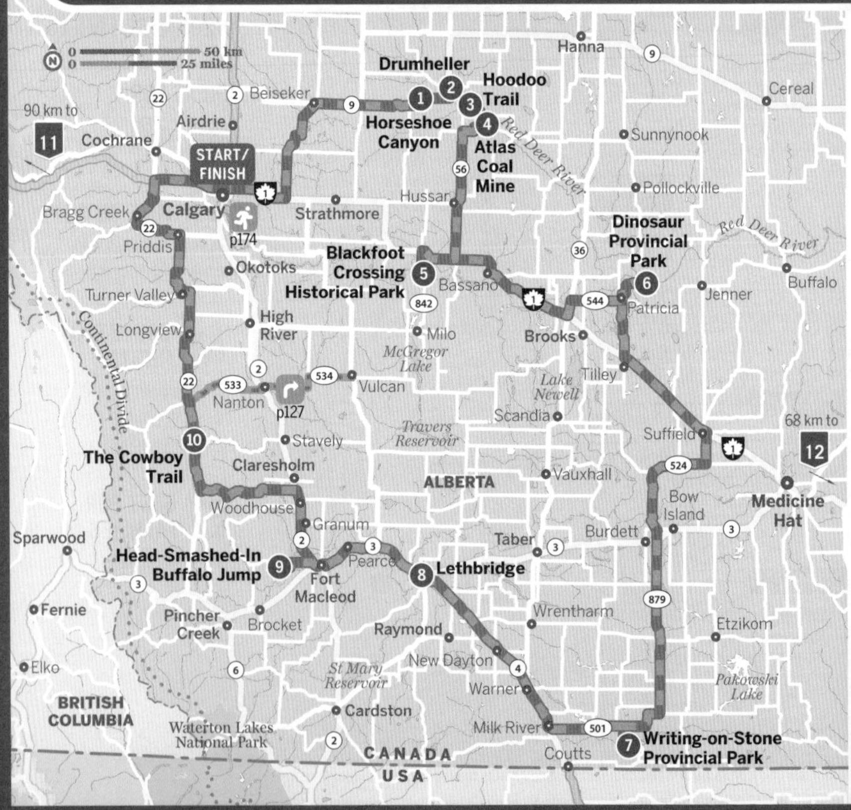

❶ Horseshoe Canyon

Head east! Leave Calgary behind and almost immediately you'll feel like time's slowing down. It's all flat farmland out here, with rolling hills and big, big sky. The placid monotony is what makes the Badlands so impressive. The multicolored hills descend into beautiful **Horseshoe Canyon** (Hwy 9), where there are well-maintained hiking trails, restrooms and even a **helicopter viewing option** (☎403-334-4354; http://mvheli.com; from $55; ⏲9am-4pm mid-Jun–Aug). Whether you stretch your legs a bit or jump into the helicopter for a bird's-eye view, it's a nice introduction to the landscape in these parts that will only get better as you continue the drive.

The Drive » Back in the car, drive just 18km more and you'll be in Drumheller. It's essentially a straight shot on Rte 9 all the way; just be sure to turn left (east) when you leave the canyon.

LINK YOUR TRIP

11 Icefields Parkway

After reaching the Cowboy Trail (stop 10), it's another three hours west northwest to stunning Lake Louise and the beginning of this outdoors-loving road trip.

12 Explore Southern Saskatchewan

From Lethbridge (stop 8), drive three hours east to Maple Creek and the start of this grasslands and forest journey.

❷ Drumheller

This tiny town is big on just one thing: dinosaurs. Head straight to the **Royal Tyrrell Museum of Palaeontology** (☎403-823-7707; www.tyrrellmuseum.com; 1500 North Dinosaur Trail, Midlands Provincial Park; adult/child/family $19/10/48; ⏲9am-9pm mid-May–Aug, 10am-5pm Sep, 10am-5pm Tue-Sun Oct–mid-May; 👪) and plan on spending at least three hours here, more if you have kids who want to make a fossil cast or participate in other activities. Take your time wandering around this incredible museum, filled with some of the world's best examples of the dinosaur age.

At the **World's Largest Dinosaur** (60 1st Ave W; adult/family $4/10.50; ⏲10am-5:30pm; 👪), just a few minutes down the road in the center of town, you can climb in near the tail, ahem, and ascend until you're looking out through the mouth. It's good ole hokey fun at its best.

If you're hungry, swing by Café Olé (p131) and grab some soup, a sandwich, a smoothie or some coffee for the road, then hit the trail again.

The Drive » The Hoodoo Trail, mainly Rte 56, runs for about 25km along the Red Deer River. Just head south out of Drumheller rather than back the way you came.

✖ 🛏 p131

❸ Hoodoo Trail

You'll see instantly why this stretch of road is called the Hoodoo Trail: like something from a Dr Seuss book, hoodoos rise up on either side of the river – majestic, strange shapes created by erosion of the substrate around a flat rock. This gives them the shape of a king oyster mushroom: a wide cap at the top, a narrower, smooth, even delicate neck below, which gradually gets broader as it joins the riverbed or cliffs.

The **Rosedale Suspension Bridge** (Hwy 56, Rosedale) is a lovely excuse to get out of the car, bringing you over the river to a hillside (that's often slippery!) with some walking trails and viewpoints.

The Drive » Keep going on Rte 56 for now. In a few kilometers you'll see the town of East Coulee on your right. A little past that, on the right and across the river, is the weird shape of the Atlas Coal Mine's tipple, seeming too rickety to even stand.

4 Atlas Coal Mine

At the **Atlas Coal Mine** (☎403-822-2220; https://atlascoalmine.ab.ca; East Coulee; adult/family $12/35, tours $14-27; ⏲9:45am-5pm Sep-Jun, to 6:30pm Jul & Aug), you can tour the mine shaft and tipple, and even ride an above ground coal train for a bit, learning about the history and the workers here. For adults there's an 'Unmentionables' tour, discussing the more sordid side of Atlas's history. Plan on spending an hour here if you want to do a tour, though you can just peek at the gift shop or marvel at the tipple for free from the parking lot.

If history's your thing, you'll also want to stop at the **East Coulee School Museum** (☎403-822-3970; http://ecsmuseum.ca; 359 2nd Ave, East Coulee; $7; ⏲10am-5pm May-Sep). The museum has fascinating historical details about a real school that's been preserved and the lives of people in the town; there's a good cafe inside (if you didn't eat in Drumheller).

The Drive » Don't cross back over the river, but head up the coulee on Rte 569, saying goodbye to the hoodoos (for now). At the church in Dalum, turn left onto Rte 56 S. Follow it for 52km until you hit Hwy 1. Turn right, then after 16km jog left onto Rte 842. Expect to see prairie dogs and many hawks.

5 Blackfoot Crossing Historical Park

Sitting on the top of a lovely hill that extends down into a valley, **Blackfoot Crossing Historical Park** (☎403-734-5171; www.blackfootcrossing.ca; Hwy 842; adult/child $15/10; ⏲9am-6pm Jul & Aug, to 5pm Mon-Fri Mar-Jun, Sep & Oct, 10am-3pm Mon-Fri Nov-Feb) is worth the $5 per person admission fee to wander around outside, even if you don't see the museum. There are hiking trails, a tipi village, and bear sightings from time to time, but the real gem is the visitor center and museum, built with great care to make it blend into not just the landscape,

LOCAL KNOWLEDGE: COMMON ANIMALS OF THE PRAIRIES

You won't be able to miss the prairie dogs, and we may mean that literally – some of them seem hell bent on diving underneath your vehicle. Slow down though, and it's not just prairie dogs you'll see. There's a host of other cool animals to look for as well.

» Ducks, grebes, herons and avocets line the edges of nearly every pasture pond.

» Horned larks, a common bird in the area, so named for the two prominent 'horns' (feather tufts, really) that stick up on either side of their ears.

» Hawks, vultures and even eagles soar overhead – look for the characteristic 'v' of a vulture's wings to tell it from its raptor cousins.

» Coyotes and foxes are shy but not uncommon. Look for them slinking around near fences or across fields, especially at dawn or dusk.

» Pronghorn antelope, the fastest land animal in North America, which can run faster than 97 km/h (60 mph). Spy them in the middle of fields. At a distance they have a much pinker color than deer or elk.

» Another ungulate, the moose, is unmistakable – the dark chocolate coat, the large rack on males and the beard are all distinctive.

DETOUR: VULCAN

Start: ⑩ The Cowboy Trail

You've been driving back through time this whole trip, so why not detour and head into the future for a bit? The town of Vulcan, a short detour from the Bar U Ranch, will let you do just that. Though the town's name had absolutely nothing to do with *Star Trek* (it was named for the Roman god of fire), that didn't stop the town of fewer than 2000 residents rebranding it the 'Official Star Trek Capital of Canada.'

Now, with a statue of the *Starship Enterprise* for folks to take selfies in front of, a tourism center shaped like a spacecraft, and even the streetlights made to look like the *Enterprise*, it's pretty clear they're in deep on the theme. It's hokey, sure, but it's also a fun diversion, and you can even don costumes and have your photo taken, then have the image digitally placed onto *Star Trek*–themed backgrounds. Ever wanted to sit in Kirk's chair? Voilà! You just did!

And it's become evermore popular with die-hard Trekkies. Leonard Nimoy himself came here in 2010. In addition to the ship, there's a bust of Spock, and the town hosts a Vul-Con convention each year. Vul-Con...get it?

From Rte 2 take Rte 533 and Rte 534. Vulcan is about a 30-minute drive.

but also the culture of the Blackfoot people.

Inside, part of it is shaped like a tipi. There's a wall of windows that look over the valley, and you feel almost hawk-like staring outside. The entryway has a shade made from giant feathers – invoking the feathered headdresses that First Nations peoples wore. Inside, the history of what these people had, and what they lost, as settlers actively or passively took their land and culture away, is very poignant, staying with you long after you leave.

The Drive » Head north on Rte 842, turn right onto Hwy 1 E, then zip through prairies and small towns until you hit Rte 36 N. Turn left and drive for 6km before turning right onto Rte 544 E. This merges with Rte 876, which you should follow when it veers left (north). There are signs from there (you're only a few minutes away).

---

❻ Dinosaur Provincial Park

This Badlands area is a jaw-dropping collection of hills and valleys that contain the highest concentration of dinosaur fossils in the world. In the *world*. It's so easy to find fossils that you'll likely find some yourself if you take a guided tour. Set this up at the **Dinosaur Visitors Centre** (☎403-378-4342; http://albertaparks.ca; gallery admission adult/child $6/3; ⏰9am-4pm Mon-Fri, from 10am Sat & Sun Apr–mid-May, 9am-5pm Sun-Thu, to 7pm Fri & Sat mid-May–Aug, 9am-4pm Sun-Thu, 10am-5pm Fri & Sat Sep–mid-Oct, 9am-4pm Mon-Fri mid-Oct–Mar). You can also see videos explaining the area and (if it's been a full day) camp (p131).

The finds and history of this area can't be understated: some of the world's best preserved, most complete dinosaur skeletons were here. So many, in fact, that scientists decided to stop excavating certain ones, leaving them in the ground undisturbed.

The Drive » Get back on Hwy 1 and continue east to Suffield. Turn right, take Range Rd 93 to Rte 524 W, turn right again, and then go left (south) onto Rte 879. Follow that for almost 100km, at which point you'll see signs as you turn right onto Rte 501. Drive 20km and turn left onto Rte 500 S...and you're there.

🛏 p131

Classic Trip

DAVID BUTLER/GETTY IMAGES ©

JEWHYTE/GETTY IMAGES ©

WHY THIS IS A CLASSIC TRIP

RAY BARTLETT, WRITER

This trip is what I think of when I say 'I love Alberta.' You simply can't get more classic, wonderful, majestic or amazing than what you'll see on this giant loop, which takes in nearly 1000km of Canada's most impressive natural wonders: dinosaurs, fossils, haunting indigenous legacies, the iconic Wild West that still exists today as it has for centuries. It's all here.

Above: Hoodoos in the Badlands
Left: Atlas Coal Mine (p126)
Right: Rosedale Suspension Bridge (p125)

DAVID J. MITCHELL/SHUTTERSTOCK ©

7 Writing-on-Stone Provincial Park

At **Writing-on-Stone Provincial Park** (☎403-647-2364; www.albertaparks.ca) you'll say hello to hoodoos again. There's a great self-guided hike that brings you past some of the best petroglyphs and the indescribable hoodoos, and along a riverbank. You can take a guided tour to some of the best (and protected) glyphs, and the **visitor centre** (☎403-647-2364; https://albertaparks.ca; 9:30am-4:30pm Sun-Thu, to 7pm Fri & Sat mid-May–Jun, 9:30am-4:30pm Sun-Wed, to 7pm Thu-Sat Jul & Aug, 9:30am-4pm Sep, by appointment Mon-Fri Oct–mid-May) has lots of information about the area, the people who may have made the glyphs and more.

There's a **campground** (☎403-647-2877; https://albertaparks.ca; campsites/RV sites from $26/33) here as well, but nothing to eat, so it's better to push on for another 1½ hours to Lethbridge.

The Drive » Heading in a general northwest direction, you'll go another 128km. Rte 500 takes you back to Rte 501, where you'll turn left and follow it west for 32km until it intersects with Rte 4. Turn right (there's a small jog at Railway Rd) and follow Rte 4 all the way to Lethbridge, about 78km away.

8 Lethbridge

Plan to overnight in Lethbridge, Alberta's third-largest city, which still feels like a tiny rural town. When you're ready, head to **Fort Whoop-Up** (☎403-320-3777; https://fort.galtmuseum.com; 200 Indian Battle Park Rd; adult/child $10/5; ⌚May-Sep) and get a feel for what Wild West living was like. There are wagon rides, exhibits, and a gift store with minerals and raccoon-skin hats and the like. Also stop by the **Helen Schuler Nature Centre & Lethbridge Nature Reserve** (☎403-320-3064; www.lethbridge.ca/nature; Indian Battle Rd; by donation; ⌚10am-4pm Tue-Sun Apr, May, Sep & Oct, 10am-6pm Jun-Aug, 1-4pm Tue-Sun Nov-Mar), meandering the paved walking trails looking for porcupines, deer and other denizens of the riparian woods.

The Drive » Head west for about half an hour, returning to seemingly endless prairies and canola fields. Hop on Rte 3 for 45km, then get on Rte 2 N at Fort Macleod. After just 2km, turn left onto Rte 785 and follow it until you see signs on the right for the Head-Smashed-In Buffalo Jump parking area.

p131

9 Head-Smashed-In Buffalo Jump World Heritage Site

The **museum and visitor center** (☎403-553-2731; https://headsmashedin.ca; Secondary Hwy 785; adult/child $15/10; ⌚10am-5pm) here are so well blended into the landscape that you could easily drive past without noticing them, were it not for the large Head-Smashed-In Buffalo Jump signage. Inside, you'll find a stunning depiction of all aspects of Blackfoot culture, including the buffalo jump, which involved – when conditions were just right – herding the bison to stampede over cliffs, fatally injuring themselves by the hundreds or thousands. Start by taking a walk out to the 'kill site,' where the buffalo plummeted. Then go back inside, and level by level, you'll see the complete picture of Blackfoot life, culture, religion and the rituals around the sacred buffalo jump.

The Drive » Heading north now, retrace your steps to Rte 2 N, then use any of the rural side roads to get to Rte 22, which parallels Rte 2. Route 22, aka the Cowboy Trail, was an old wagon route, now known for its tourist sites and scenic beauty.

10 The Cowboy Trail

Only an hour's drive from Calgary, the **Bar U Ranch** (☎403-395-3044; www.parkscanada.gc.ca/baru; Hwy 22, Longview; adult $7.80; ⌚10am-5pm mid-May–Sep) is one of the key reasons this stretch of Rte 22 is known as the Cowboy Trail. It's a preserved historic site, one of the only parks that commemorates the vital importance of ranching in Alberta's history.

This spot is a unique combination of part living-history museum, part gallery, part exhibition, and a stop will bring all kinds of Western ranch life and livelihood into clear detail. See cabins and other buildings that have been meticulously preserved.

It's a taste of the West that once was the norm for this area; now, like the dinosaurs, the petroglyphs and the buffalo jumps, it has become a cherished, revered part of the past.

The Drive » Hop in the car, set your sights on Calgary and hit the gas. You're only an hour away. The prettiest way back is also the easiest – stay on Rte 22 all the way to Hwy 1, passing through Turner Valley, Priddis and Bragg Creek. Turn right onto Hwy 1 and you'll be back in Calgary in no time.

p131

Eating & Sleeping

Drumheller 2

Café Olé Cafe $

(403-800-2090; www.facebook.com/cafeoledrum; 11 Railway Ave; sandwiches $8-13; 8am-5pm Sun-Thu, to 7pm Fri & Sat;) This quiet, darkly lit cafe serves up soups, sandwiches, coffees, teas and desserts that would hold their own in New York City. Flavorful and fresh, mains pair perfectly with a London Fog chai or a fruit smoothie. The waitstaff are kind, helpful and attentive, though in a busy moment things can be slow – but worth the wait, for sure.

Rosedeer Hotel Historic Hotel $

(403-823-9189; http://visitlastchancesaloon.com; 555 Jewel St, Wayne; camping $20, r $65-80; P) If you've wondered what it's like to stay in a ghost town (or in what's rumored to be a haunted hotel!), this is your chance to find out. The Rosedeer is much like it was in yesteryear: small rooms, simple furnishings and a rip-roaring Wild West saloon downstairs. Don't come expecting frills and fanciness, and reserve ahead (it fills fast).

Dinosaur Provincial Park 6

Dinosaur Campground Campground $

(403-378-4342; https://albertaparks.ca; campsites/RV sites $26/33, comfort camping $105-130, reservation fee $12; year-round; P) The campground at **Dinosaur Provincial Park** (p127) sits in a hollow by a small creek; the ample tree cover is a welcome reprieve from the volcanic sun. Laundry facilities and hot showers are available, as are a small shop and cafe. This is a popular place, especially with the RV set, so phone ahead. With reservations ($12 extra), you can also opt for 'comfort camping' – a riverside, furnished, prospector-style tent on a raised floor.

Lethbridge 8

Telegraph Tap House Pub Food $$

(403-942-4136; https://taphouse.pub; 310 6th Street S; mains $15-23; 11am-11pm Mon-Thu, to 1am Fri, 9am-1am Sat, 9am-10:30pm Sun) So this is where cool Lethbridgians go. Park yourself at the bar with a craft brew and pulled-pork sliders or chili-cheese fries. Was the stack of antique suitcases left behind by those who dared try the Baked Ultimate Poutine and didn't make it out the door?

Sandman Signature Lethbridge Lodge Hotel $$

(403-328-1123; www.sandmanhotels.com; 320 Scenic Dr S; r from $139; P @) Rooms here are clean and bright, if a little unmemorable; the atrium, on the other hand, is something else, making this a great deal. All of the rooms look down into the fake-foliage-filled tropical interior, complete with winding brick pathways, a kidney-shaped pool and water features.

The Cowboy Trail 10

Chuck Wagon Cafe Diner $$

(403-933-0003; 105 Sunset Blvd, Turner Valley; mains $9-20; 8am-2:30pm Mon-Fri, to 3:30pm Sat & Sun) Housed in a tiny red barn, the legendary Chuck Wagon Cafe feels much like the homestead kitchen it is – it draws hungry diners from miles around. The enormous, all-day breakfast of smoked hash, triple-A steak and eggs Benedict will have you shouting 'Yeehaw!' This is ranch cooking at its best.

Icefields Parkway

Winding through the wilds of Banff and Jasper National Parks for 230km, the Icefields Parkway offers mesmerizing front-row perspectives on some of North America's most spectacular scenery and wildlife.

TRIP HIGHLIGHTS

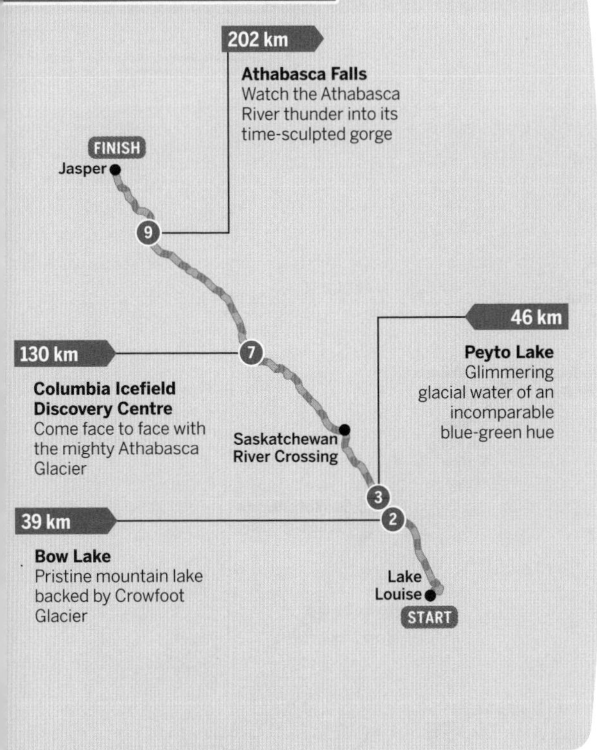

FINISH
Jasper

202 km
Athabasca Falls
Watch the Athabasca River thunder into its time-sculpted gorge

130 km
Columbia Icefield Discovery Centre
Come face to face with the mighty Athabasca Glacier

Saskatchewan River Crossing

46 km
Peyto Lake
Glimmering glacial water of an incomparable blue-green hue

39 km
Bow Lake
Pristine mountain lake backed by Crowfoot Glacier

Lake Louise
START

2 DAYS
230KM/143 MILES

GREAT FOR

BEST TIME TO GO

June through September for best weather and road conditions

The glacial blue-green surface of Peyto Lake

Walking on the ice at Athabasca Glacier

Banff National Park Scenic view of Peyto Lake (p135)

Classic Trip

11 Icefields Parkway

No North American road trip compares to the Icefields Parkway. Smack along the Continental Divide, this 230km odyssey leads you through one of the least developed stretches of Canada's magnificent Rocky Mountain wilderness. Along the way you'll pass jewel-hued glacial lakes, roaring waterfalls, unbroken virgin forest and a relentless succession of shapely mountain crags, culminating in the awe-inspiring Columbia Icefield. At every turn, spontaneous wildlife sightings are a distinct possibility.

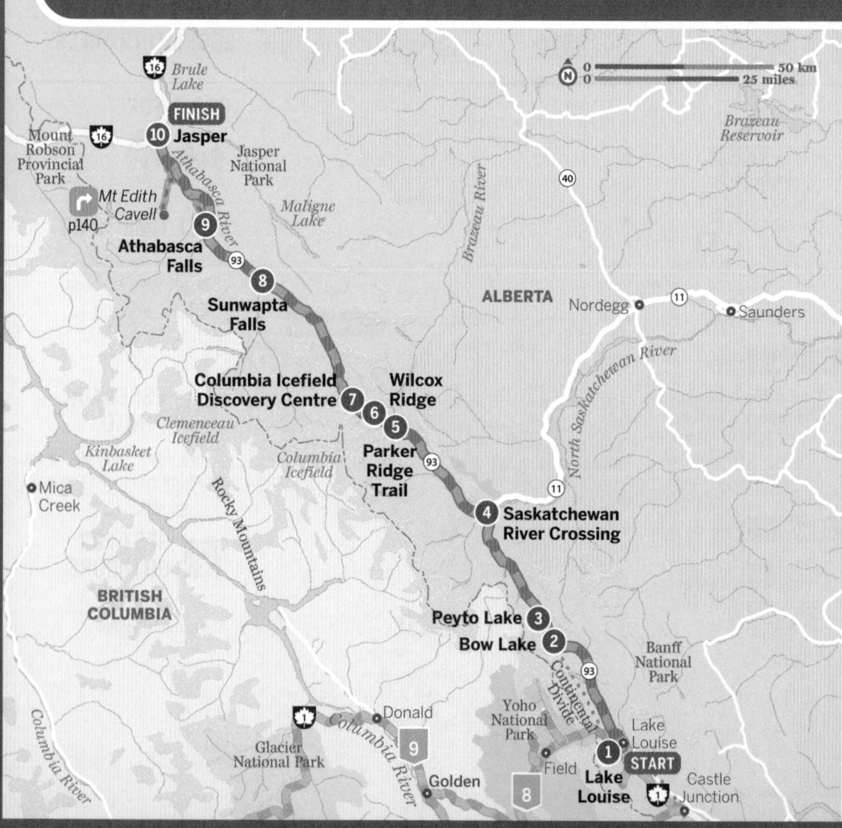

❶ Lake Louise

Considered by many the crown jewel of Banff National Park, Lake Louise is nearly impossible to describe without resorting to shameless clichés. This serene, implausibly turquoise lake spreads out elegantly below a stately amphitheater of finely sculpted mountains, with Victoria Glacier gleaming high above it all on the opposite shore.

You could easily spend an entire morning gazing at the lake, but anyone with a penchant for hiking should head off to explore the surrounding trails. The most famous leads 4km uphill to the historic **Lake Agnes teahouse** (www.lakeagnesteahouse.com; lunch $7.50-15; ⌚8am-5pm early Jun-early Oct), where you can rejuvenate with scones and hot tea before continuing up to the top of the Big Beehive for spellbinding views back down over blue-green Lake Louise.

The Drive » Lake Louise sits a stone's throw from the southern entrance to the Icefields Pkwy. Follow the Trans-Canada Hwy a mere 2km west, then take the first exit, purchase (or display) your park entrance pass at the Icefields Pkwy entrance booth, and begin your northward journey into the majestic Rockies, turning left after 37km at the parking lot for Num-Ti-Jah Lodge.

p141

LINK YOUR TRIP

8 Circling the Rockies

Continue exploring Canada's national parks on this scenic ramble through Banff, Kootenay and Yoho. Join the route in Lake Louise.

9 Around the Kootenays

Get off-the-beaten-track amid the small towns and lakes of British Columbia's Monashee, Selkirk and Purcell Mountains. Start in Golden, 84km west of Lake Louise.

❷ Bow Lake

Ringed by massive peaks and tucked beneath the imposing **Crowfoot Glacier**, Bow Lake is one of the prettiest sights in the Canadian Rockies. Early Banff entrepreneur and wilderness outfitter Jimmy Simpson built his pioneering Num-Ti-Jah Lodge here in 1923 – 12 years before the Icefields Pkwy itself – and it still stands today, its carved-wood interior full to the brim with backcountry nostalgia, animal heads and photos from the golden age.

The hotel's rustic yet elegant **Elkhorn Dining Room** (☎403-522-2167; www.num-ti-jah.com; breakfast buffet cold/hot $14/22, dinner mains $30-50; ⌚8-10am & 6:30-9pm mid-May–mid-Oct) lets you step back in time to Simpson's world, complete with stone fireplace and majestic views. At the time of research, the hotel and restaurant were temporarily closed, but with plans to reopen soon. Usually, non-hotel guests can stop in here for breakfast or return at night to dine on elk burgers or crispy steelhead trout beneath the watchful eye of moose, wolverines and other hunting trophies. Guests get seating priority; reserve ahead.

The Drive » Your next stop is just a short 7km up the hill. Get back on the Icefields Pkwy and climb north to Bow Summit. Here, follow the signs on the left for Peyto Lake and park in the first (lower) parking lot.

🛏 p141

❸ Peyto Lake

You'll have already seen the indescribably vibrant blue color of Peyto Lake in a thousand publicity shots, but there's nothing like gazing at the real thing – especially since the viewing point for this lake is from a lofty vantage point several hundred feet above the water. The lake gets its extraordinary color from sunlight hitting fine particles of glacial sediment suspended in the water. The lake is best visited in the early morning, between the time the sun first illuminates the water and the first tour bus arrives.

From the bottom of the lake parking lot, follow a paved trail for 15 minutes up a steady gradual incline to the wooden platform overlooking the lake. From here you can return to the parking lot or continue uphill for more fine views from the Bow Summit Lookout trail.

The Drive » Head north on the Icefields Pkwy and enter the Mistaya Valley watershed. After 16km, pass Waterfowl Lakes on your left, a good place to stretch your legs and soak up more views. Another 19km north, just before Saskatchewan River Crossing, pause on the bridge over the North Saskatchewan River for dramatic views of the river meandering out towards the prairies.

4 Saskatchewan River Crossing

This junction of Hwy 93 (the Icefields Pkwy) and Hwy 11 (the David Thompson Hwy) marks the site where 19th-century fur trappers crossed the North Saskatchewan River on their way through the Rockies to British Columbia. Today, just west of the junction you'll find interpretive historical displays, along with a **motel** (☎403-761-7000; www.thecrossingresort.com; cnr Hwy 11 & Icefields Pkwy; d $229-299; ⏰mid-Apr–mid-Oct; P 📶), restaurant and gas station – the only facilities between Lake Louise and the Columbia Icefield.

The Drive » Follow the parkway north along the North Saskatchewan River valley towards an imposing mountain wall. Near the 30km mark, a huge hairpin bend signals the beginning of the ascent to Sunwapta Pass. Stop at the Bridal Veil Falls parking area for fine views back down the valley you're leaving behind. After 38km you'll reach Parker Ridge parking area.

5 Parker Ridge Trail

If you only do one hike along the Icefields Pkwy, make it Parker Ridge Trail. It's short enough to crack in an afternoon, but leads to one of the most impressive lookouts of any of Banff's day hikes, with a grandstand view of Mt Saskatchewan, Mt Athabasca and the gargantuan Saskatchewan Glacier. From the parking lot the trail runs through a narrow wood before emerging on the hillside and entering a long series of switchbacks. Crest the ridge at the 2km (1.2-mile) mark, to be greeted by a blast of arctic wind and an explosive panorama of peaks and glaciers.

To the west loom Mts Athabasca and Andromeda, and just to their south is the gleaming bulk of the Saskatchewan Glacier, which lurks at the end of a deep valley. At almost 13km (8 miles) long, the glacier is one of the longest in the Rockies, but it's actually just a spur from the massive 230-sq-km (88-sq-mile) Columbia Icefield that lies to the north. For the best views, follow the trail southeast along the edge of the ridge.

The Drive » A short drive northwest on the Icefields Pkwy brings you to your next stop. Shortly after crossing Sunwapta Pass and passing from Banff National Park into Jasper National Park, look for signs for Wilcox Campground on your right and park at the Wilcox Ridge trailhead.

TOP TIP: SPOTTING WILDLIFE

To increase your odds of seeing wildlife, travel the Icefields Pkwy in the early morning or late afternoon. Top areas for wildlife spotting include Tangle Falls (137km north of Lake Louise) and the Goats & Glaciers Viewpoint (195km north of Lake Louise).

❻ Wilcox Ridge

One of Jasper's most accessible high country walks is this 9km out-and-back jaunt to Wilcox Ridge. From the trailhead, the path climbs rapidly above the treeline, reaching a pair of red chairs after 30 minutes, where you can sit and enjoy fine Athabasca Glacier views.

If you've had enough climbing, you can simply return from here to the parking lot. Otherwise continue ascending, gazing down over a river canyon on your left as you traverse wide-open meadows to reach Wilcox Pass (2370m) at the 3.2km mark. Here you'll turn left, following the undulating trail another 1.3km to reach the Wilcox Ridge viewpoint. Up top, dramatic, near-aerial views of the Athabasca Glacier unfold across the valley. To return to the parking lot simply retrace your steps downhill.

The Drive » Drive 2.5km west along the Icefields Pkwy to the Columbia Icefield Discovery Centre.

ESTIVILLML/GETTY IMAGES ©

Wilcox Ridge View of the Athabasca Glacier

❼ Columbia Icefield Discovery Centre

The massive green-roofed **Columbia Icefield Discovery Centre** (Icefields Pkwy) marks your arrival at the Icefield Pkwy's star attraction, **the Athabasca Glacier**.

The glacier has retreated about 2km since 1844, when it reached the rock moraine on the north side of the road. To reach its toe (bottom edge), walk from the Icefield Centre along the 1.8km Forefield Trail, then join the 1km Toe of the Glacier Trail. You can also park at the start of the latter trail. Visitors are allowed to stand on a small roped section of the ice, should not attempt to cross the warning tape – the glacier is riddled with crevasses.

To walk safely on the Columbia Icefield, you'll need to enlist the help of **Athabasca Glacier Icewalks** (☎780-852-5595; www.icewalks.com; Icefield Centre; 3hr tour adult/child $110/60, 6hr tour $175/90; ⏲late May–Sep), which supplies all the gear you'll need and a guide to show you the ropes. Its basic tour is three hours; there's a six-hour option for those wanting to venture further out onto the glacier.

The other, far easier (and more popular) way to get on the glacier is via the **Columbia Icefield Adventure** (www.banffjaspercollection.com/attractions/columbia-icefield; adult/child $114/57; ⏲9am-6pm Apr-Oct) tour. A giant all-terrain vehicle known as the Ice Explorer grinds a track onto the ice, where it stops to allow you to go for a 25-minute wander on the glacier. Dress warmly, wear good shoes and bring a water bottle so you can try some freshly melted glacial water. Tickets can be bought at the Icefield Centre or online; tours depart every 15 to 30 minutes.

Snacks and meals are available at the **Columbia Icefield Discovery**

Classic Trip

WHY THIS IS A CLASSIC TRIP

GREGOR CLARK, WRITER

When I first hitchhiked down the Icefields Parkway on a snowy May morning three days after my 20th birthday, I felt like I had landed on another planet. The endless succession of massive mountains stratified into bands of black rock and white ice filled me with a mixture of awe, joy and terror. Years later, I still react the same way: dwarfed and amazed in the presence of all-powerful, primordial nature.

Above: Parker Ridge Trail (p136)
Left: Athabasca Glacier (p137)
Right: Sunwapta Falls

Centre dining room (www.banffjaspercollection.com; Columbia Icefield Discovery Centre; breakfast/lunch buffet $26/33, dinner mains $24-45; ⏲cafeteria 9am-6pm, restaurant 7:30-9:30am, 10:45am-2:45pm & 6-9pm May-Oct), a rather humdrum mall-like affair catering to bus tourists.

The Drive » Begin your long descent down the Athabasca River valley, following the parkway north. Soon after leaving the Columbia Icefield Discovery Centre, watch for Tangle Falls on your right. Bighorn sheep are commonly sighted here. At the 49km mark, follow signs left off the main highway to the Sunwapta Falls parking lot.

p141

8 Sunwapta Falls

Meaning 'turbulent water' in the language of the Stoney First Nations, the 18m Sunwapta Falls formed when the glacial meltwaters of the Sunwapta River began falling from a hanging valley into the deeper U-shaped Athabasca Valley. The falls are a magnificent sight as they tumble into a deep narrow gorge; stand on the bridge above for the best views. Afterwards you can stop in for a snack, a meal or an overnight stay at the **Sunwapta Falls Rocky Mountain Lodge** (☎780-852-4852; www.sunwapta.com/restaurant; Icefields Pkwy; breakfast $12-18, dinner mains $25-43; ⏲7-11am & 6-9pm May-Nov).

The Drive » Return to the main highway and drive 24km north. Turn left onto Hwy 93A, following signs for the Athabasca Falls parking area.

9 Athabasca Falls

Despite being only 23m high, Athabasca Falls is Jasper's most dramatic and voluminous waterfall, a deafening combination of sound, spray and water. The thunderous Athabasca River has cut deeply into the soft limestone rock, carving potholes, canyons and water channels. Interpretive signs explain the basics of the local geology. Visitors crowd the large parking lot and short access trail. It's at its most ferocious during summer.

The Drive » You're on the home stretch. A mere 30km jaunt north takes you to Jasper townsite. About 6km before town, you'll cross the Athabasca River and bid farewell to the Icefields Pkwy.

10 Jasper

With a long and fascinating history that has included fur trappers, explorers, railway workers and some of the Canadian Rockies' earliest tourists, Jasper is the hub town for Jasper National Park. Less than 5000 residents live here year-round, but it feels like a major metropolis after the long journey through the Canadian wilderness. Celebrate with dinner at one of Jasper's diverse selection of eateries: lamb shank or coconut seafood at Raven Bistro, Greek food at **Something Else** (780-852-3850; www.somethingelserestaurant.com; 621 Patricia St, Jasper Town; mains $16-40; 11am-11pm), a vegan 'dragon bowl' at **Olive Bistro** (780-852-5222; www.olivebistro.ca; Pyramid Lake Rd, Jasper Town; mains $14-35; 4-10pm May-Oct, 5-9pm Nov-Apr;), a slow-cooked barbecue at **Maligne Canyon Wilderness Kitchen** (844-762-6713; www.banffjaspercollection.com; Maligne Canyon Rd; lunch mains $16-26, dinner $55; 8am-10pm May-Sep, 9am-4pm Sun-Fri, to 10pm Sat Oct-Apr) or burgers and microbrews at **Jasper Brewing Co** (780-852-4111; www.jasperbrewingco.ca; 624 Connaught Dr, Jasper Town; 11:30am-1am). Afterwards, settle in for the night at one of the many local cabins or bungalows.

p141

DETOUR: MT EDITH CAVELL

Start: 9 Athabasca Falls

Rising like a snowy sentinel west of the Icefields Pkwy, Mt Edith Cavell (3363m) is one of Jasper National Park's most distinctive and physically arresting peaks. What it lacks in height it makes up for in stark, ethereal beauty. The mountain is famous for its flowery meadows and wing-shaped Angel Glacier.

It was named in honor of a humanitarian British nurse, who was executed by a German firing squad during WWI after helping to smuggle more than 200 wounded Allied soldiers into neutral Holland.

To get here, leave the Icefields Pkwy at the Athabasca Falls turnoff and follow Hwy 93A north 18km, then turn left onto sinuous Edith Cavell Rd, following it until it dead ends at a parking lot. To return to the main route, retrace your steps north on Edith Cavell Rd, then turn left onto Hwy 93A for 5km to its junction with the Icefields Pkwy.

Eating & Sleeping

Lake Louise 1

Lake Louise Station Restaurant — Canadian $$$

(403-522-2600; www.lakelouisestation.com; 200 Sentinel Rd, Lake Louise village; mains lunch $16-26, dinner $20-48; 11:30am-4pm & 5-9pm daily Jun-Sep, noon-4pm & 5-8:30pm Wed-Sun Oct-May) Lake Louise's historic train station is the most atmospheric place in town for a meal. Details like stacks of turn-of-the-century luggage, the stationmaster's desk and the original dining cars out back transport you back to 1910, when the elegant edifice was first built. Dig into maple-glazed salmon, *Wiener schnitzel* or slow-braised bison ribs and soak up the vintage vibe. Reservations recommended.

HI Lake Louise Alpine Centre — Hostel $

(403-522-2201; www.hihostels.ca; 203 Village Rd, Lake Louise village; dm/d $64/192; P) This is what a hostel should be – clean, friendly and full of interesting travelers – and the rustic, comfortable lodge-style buildings, with plenty of raw timber and stone, are fine examples of Canadian Rockies architecture. Dorm rooms are fairly standard and the small private rooms are a bit overpriced, but this is as close as you'll get to budget in Lake Louise.

Bow Lake 2

Num-Ti-Jah Lodge — Inn $$$

(403-522-2167; www.num-ti-jah.com; d with mountain/lake view $375/425; mid-May–mid-Oct; P) On the edge of Bow Lake, the historic Num-Ti-Jah Lodge is full to the brim with backcountry nostalgia. Built by pioneer Jimmy Simpson in 1923 (12 years before the highway), the carved-wood interior displays animal heads and photos from the golden age. The 16 rooms have big views, but show their age with worn furniture, dated decor and tiny bathrooms.

Columbia Icefield Discovery Centre 7

Glacier View Lodge — Hotel $$$

(888-770-6914; www.banffjaspercollection.com; Icefield Centre, Icefields Pkwy; d with mountain/glacier view $489/519; mid-Apr–mid-Oct; P) The panoramic perspectives over the glacier are unbelievable at this revamped hotel on the top floor of the Icefield Centre. Rooms have been given a total makeover, with loads of Scandinavian-style blonde wood, while the lobby area sports plush chairs and a telescope for admiring spectacular views through the floor-to-ceiling windows.

Jasper 10

Raven Bistro — Mediterranean $$$

(780-852-5151; www.theravenbistro.com; 504 Patricia St, Jasper Town; lunch mains $16-27, dinner mains $28-46; 11:30am-11pm;) This cozy, tastefully designed bistro offers vegetarian dishes, encourages shared plates and earns a loyal clientele with sublime offerings like Kaffir lime–coconut seafood pot or lamb shank glazed with fresh mint, horseradish, honey and Dijon mustard. Not in a lunch-dinner mood? Try the 'late riser' breakfast skillet, or come for happy hour (3pm to 5:30pm daily).

Athabasca Hotel — Hotel $$

(780-852-3386; www.athabascahotel.com; 510 Patricia St, Jasper Town; r with/without bath $239/139, 1-/2-bedroom ste $425/395; P @) Around since 1929, the Atha-B (as it's known) is the best budget hotel in town. A taxidermist's dream, with animal heads crowding the lobby, it has small, clean rooms with wooden-and-brass furnishings and thick, wine-colored carpets. Less expensive rooms share a bathroom. Dated but not worn, it feels like you're staying at Grandma's (if Grandma liked to hunt).

Explore Southern Saskatchewan

Don't just blow on through southern Saskatchewan on the Trans-Canada Hwy. Take time to savor the prairies; meet Scotty the T. rex, plains bison and prairie dogs on your way to Regina.

TRIP HIGHLIGHTS

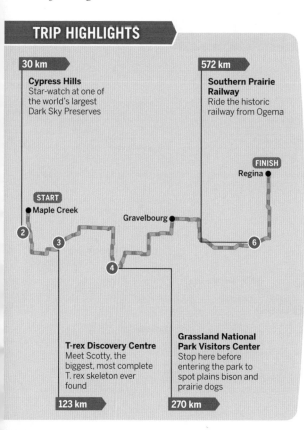

30 km
Cypress Hills
Star-watch at one of the world's largest Dark Sky Preserves

572 km
Southern Prairie Railway
Ride the historic railway from Ogema

FINISH
Regina

START
Maple Creek

Gravelbourg

2 3 4 6

T-rex Discovery Centre
Meet Scotty, the biggest, most complete T. rex skeleton ever found
123 km

Grassland National Park Visitors Center
Stop here before entering the park to spot plains bison and prairie dogs
270 km

3–4 DAYS
688KM/428 MILES

GREAT FOR...

BEST TIME TO GO

June to August when things are up and running

ESSENTIAL PHOTO

Scotty the T.rex at the T-rex Discovery Centre

BEST FOR CULTURE

Gravelbourg, a touch of Europe on the Prairies

Gravelbourg Our Lady of the Assumption Co-Cathedral (p147)

12 Explore Southern Saskatchewan

The province's south is often regarded as boring flat prairies to be raced through as fast as possible, but the backroads to Regina offer up some spirited little communities with surprisingly interesting things going on. Give yourself a few days from the Alberta border and go on a voyage of discovery through the small towns, parks and historic sites on your way to the provincial capital.

1 Maple Creek

If you've come from Calgary or points west on the Trans-Canada Hwy (Hwy 1), about 30km east of the Alberta border, head 8km south on Hwy 21 to find the town of Maple Creek. Founded in 1883, this small town is on the railroad main line and makes a good stop. Jasper St, the town's main shopping street, is a nice stroll. Maple Creek is a gateway to Cypress Hills Interprovincial Park, south of town. The

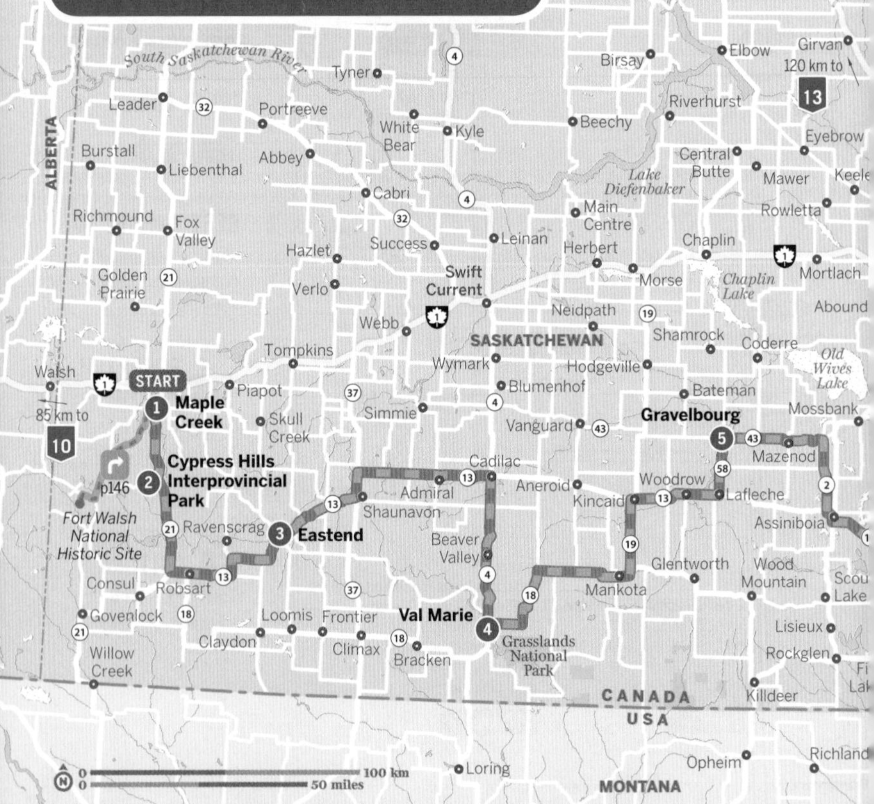

park has two large blocks of land separated by about 20km. The Western Block, half of which is in neighboring Alberta, is hard to access, with few facilities apart from Fort Walsh, while the Central Block has year-round access and plenty of man-made fun. Eat in town at the **Rockin' Horse Cookhouse & Bar** (306-662-2430; www.thehorse.ca; 103 Maple St; 11am-11pm Tue-Fri, 4pm-2am Sat) and if you're looking for a good coffee, head to Shop Bakery & Deli (p149).

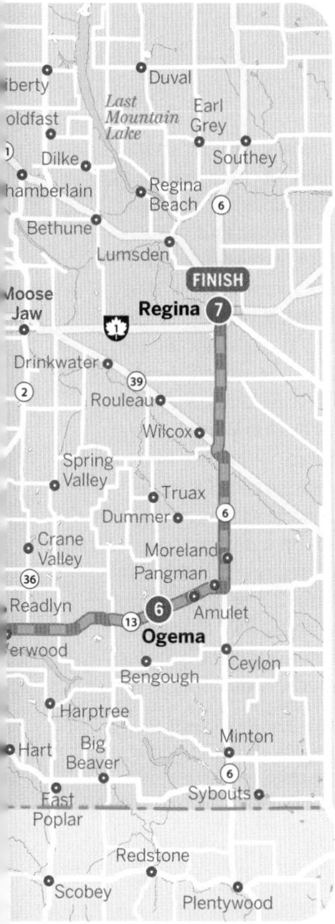

The Drive » Drive south on Hwy 21 for about 20 minutes (40km), trying to avoid countless gophers on the sealed road, to get to the Cypress Hills Interprovincial Park Central Block turnoff. It's 5km from there on Hwy 221 to the park entrance.

p149

2 Cypress Hills Interprovincial Park

The Central Block of the interprovincial park is fully developed with year-round facilities, much easier to access than the Western Block and perfect for families, with lots of things to do. There are places to stay like Resort at Cypress Hills (p149) and at **campgrounds** (Centre Block reservations 855-737-7275; www.cypresshills.com; tent & RV sites $16-36; P), plus a plethora of activities such as a swimming pool, zip-line, golf, Segway, canoeing and paddle-boats. There's a park visitor center next to Loch Leven, a general store, restaurants and one of the largest Dark Sky Preserves in the world for star-watching.

The Drive » Back out on Hwy 21, head south until you hit Hwy 13 at a T-junction. The flat prairie road may seem endless, but eventually you'll hit the junction. Turn left and follow Hwy 13 east to Eastend. All up, the distance is 186km on good sealed roads.

p149

3 Eastend

Isolated in southwest Saskatchewan, Eastend would be tumbleweed quiet if not for the discovery of Scotty, the biggest T. rex ever to be found. Scotty was stumbled upon nearby in 1991 and the Royal Saskatchewan Museum's glitzy working lab **T-rex Discovery Centre** (306-295-4009; www.royalsaskmuseum.ca/trex; T-Rex Dr; by donation; 10am-6pm Jun-Aug; P) has put Eastend on the tourist map. The Discovery Centre, carved into a hillside above town, has Scotty's massive skeleton, a variety of tours, a documentary film on Scotty's dig, plenty of other dinosaur discovery info and a gift shop. You can even see what the on-site paleontologists are up to.

LINK YOUR TRIP

10 Dinosaurs, Hoodoos & the Wild West

Drive the Southern Saskatchewan itinerary in reverse, then continue from Maple Creek west to Lethbridge (stop 8) for the last part of this fossil and Wild West road trip.

13 North from Saskatoon

Head north after exploring the south by driving from Regina to Saskatoon.

DETOUR: FORT WALSH NATIONAL HISTORIC SITE

Start: 1 Maple Creek

Established in 1875 and operational for eight years, the **Fort Walsh outpost** (www.parkscanada.ca/fortwalsh; off Hwy 271, Cypress Hills Interprovincial Park; adult/child $10/5; 9:30am-5:30pm daily Jul & Aug, 9:30am-5:30pm Tue-Sat Jun & Sep; P) had a small yet significant role in the history of the west. It was originally built to curb the illegal whiskey trade, protect Canada's nearby border with the United States, and aid with indigenous policy. It was built after the Cypress Hills Massacre of 1873 in which 21 people were killed in a battle among American bison hunters, wolf hunters, whiskey traders and Assiniboine people – that brought about the establishment of the North-West Mounted Police (NWMP). Then, after the Battle of the Little Big Horn, also known as Custer's Last Stand, Chief Sitting Bull and 5000 of his followers arrived in the area. The local mounties maintained peaceful relations with the Sioux while they remained in Canada. Though the fort was closed and dismantled in 1883, it was reconstructed in the 1940s to breed horses for the Royal Canadian Mounted Police.

Located 55km southwest of Maple Creek on sealed Hwy 271, Fort Walsh sits amid rolling prairies across two sections: the Western and the Central Block. Gap Rd, an unpaved, frequently boggy track links the two, but if you make the effort to go to Fort Walsh, you'd be best to return to Maple Creek before driving south on Hwy 21 to go to the Central Block.

Down in town, the **Eastend Historical Museum** (www.eastendhistoricalmuseum.com; 306 Red Coat Dr; adult/child $5/free; 10am-5:30pm May-Sep) has interesting fossils and bones, while its Machine Shed has all sorts of old transportation.

The Drive » From Eastend, carry on driving on Hwy 13 to Shaunavon township, where the road turns north, then east to Cadillac. It's all Hwy 13 to here. At Cadillac, turn south on Hwy 4 to Val Marie. All up it's 128km of good, sealed roads from Eastend to Val Marie.

p149

4 Val Marie

You've come to the tiny town of Val Marie, originally populated by French settlers, to visit Grasslands National Park. This is a unique opportunity to try to spot plains bison, re-introduced to the park after a 120-year absence, and to see black-footed prairie dogs in the wild. Make the most of your visit and follow the Ecotour Scenic Drive through the park. Be sure to visit the **Grassland National Park Visitors Center** (306-298-2257; www.pc.gc.ca/en/pn-np/sk/grasslands; cnr Hwy 4 & Centre St; 9am-5pm daily Jul & Aug, 9am-5pm Thu-Mon mid-May–Jun & Sep–mid-Oct) in Val Marie before heading out.

Val Marie is also home to Convent Inn (p149), offering a holier than thou sleeping experience with beds amid classic brickwork and beautiful hardwood floors in a convent built in 1939. In what was the brick Val Marie schoolhouse (1927–85), the Friends of Grasslands, known as **Prairie Wind & Silver Sage** (306-298-4910; www.pwss.org; Centre St; 9am-midday & 1-5pm), have set up a museum, gallery, bookstore, gift shop and cafe. It's beautifully done, with free wi-fi, brewed coffees and daily home-made treats.

The Drive » From Val Marie, take Hwy 18 to past Mankota, then turn north on Hwy 19 to Kincaid. At Kincaid, turn east on

DOPEYDEN/GETTY IMAGES ©

Plains bison

Hwy 13 to La Fleche, then north again on Hwy 58 to Gravelbourg. All up, it's 155km to Gravelbourg.

p149

5 Gravelbourg

Delightful Gravelbourg is one of the last places you'd expect to find a taste of France, adrift on a vast sea of prairie. Lavish buildings designed to lure French settlers date to the early 1900s. Palatial buildings and houses are scattered along 1st Ave. The undisputed centerpiece of this *très jolie* little town is the disproportionately large and beautiful **Our Lady of the Assumption Co-Cathedral** (La Co-Cathédrale Notre Dame de l'Assomption; 306-648-3322; www.gravelbourgcocathedral.com; 1st Ave; P), built in 1919 in a Romanesque and Italianate style. It was designated a national historic site in 1995. Next door, the handsome yellow-brick former **Bishop's Residence** (888-648-2321; www.bishopsresidencebandb.com; 112 1st Ave W; r incl breakfast from $70; P) has been turned into a unique B&B with nine rooms. Take a look at individual rooms online before you book them. On the main street, pop in to see the friendly folk at the **Café de Paris** (306-648-2223; www.facebook.com/CafeParisGravelbourg; 306 Main St; mains from $8; 8am-7pm Mon-Fri, 9am-5pm Sat) for a light lunch and a delicious milkshake. It's right downtown; vintage details include a pressed-tin ceiling.

The Drive » Head east out of Gravelbourg on Hwy 43, before turning south when you hit Hwy 2. At Assiniboia, turn east on

THE DISCOVERY OF 'SCOTTY'

Scotty is the biggest, most complete *Tyrannosaurus rex* skeleton ever found. The 67-million-year-old specimen, estimated to have weighed 8800kg, was found in August 1991 by Robert Gebhardt, a local high school principal. Gebhardt was with paleontologists Tim Tokaryk and John Storer on an exploratory expedition in the Frenchman River Valley when he stumbled across a T. rex tail vertebra on a cattle trail. The group later found a piece of dinosaur jaw, with teeth still attached, sticking out of the side of a hill. Scotty was duly named after the celebratory bottle of scotch used to toast the discovery.

SCENIC DRIVE: GRASSLANDS NATIONAL PARK

A top way to see Grasslands National Park is to do the well-organized self-guided Ecotour Scenic Drive. An explanation brochure, a map and good advice are all available at the **Grassland National Park Visitors Center** (p146) in Val Marie, so be sure to go there first. From Val Marie, head east on Hwy 18 for 15km, then drive 5km south on a gravel road to reach the entrance to the park.

There are seven points of interest and two short walks on the ecotour. All the points of interest have full explanation boards. Do the full 80km drive through the park and back to Val Marie as a big loop in a couple of hours, or drive into Frenchman Valley campground and back (34km return from the park entrance).

A highlight is Top Dogtown (stop two), where prairie dogs line the side of the gravel road and yap at visitors. This is the only place in Canada where colonies of black-tailed prairie dogs still exist in their native habitat. There is also the possibility of spotting bison, with the herd now numbering more than 400 after plains bison were re-introduced to the park in 2005, after a 120-year absence. While there were more than 60-million bison roaming the Great Plains of North America before European contact, there were only a few hundred left by 1880. The bison live in a large territory, so count yourself lucky if you see one. This is also rattlesnake country, so keep your wits about you and watch where you step!

Hwy 13 and follow it all the way to Ogema. All up, it's 150km on sealed roads.

6 Ogema

You've come to tiny Ogema to ride the historic **Southern Prairie Railway** (☎306-459-7808; www.southernprairierailway.com; 401 Railway Ave; tours adult/child from $49/32; ⊙Sat & Sun Jun-Sep), which has been turning heads since its maiden voyage for the town's centenary in 2012. The informative 1½- to three-hour tours chug across the prairie to explore an abandoned grain elevator and some even get robbed by train bandits. Special tours are held throughout the year including the occasional stargazing expedition. To make the most of your explorations in southern Saskatchewan, get your dates sorted out to be in Ogema on a day when the Southern Prairie Railway is operating. In general, this is on Fridays, Saturdays and Sundays, but it also runs special events.

Also in Ogema, the **Deep South Pioneer Museum** (☎306-459-7909; www.ogema.ca; 510 Government Rd; adult/child $5/3; ⊙10am-5pm Sat & Sun May-Sep) is an astounding collection of more than 30 preserved buildings, along with farming equipment, scores of vehicles and a huge volume of historic artifacts.

The Drive ›› From Ogema, continue east on Hwy 13, then turn north when you hit Hwy 6. Head straight up this major highway to the provincial capital, Regina. All up, it's 116km to Regina.

p149

7 Regina

With a population of 230,000, Regina is definitely the 'big smoke' of southern Saskatchewan. It's the province's capital and boasts a bustling central city, heritage buildings, a beautiful park and lake area, and a plentiful choice of restaurants and pubs. Head to Tourism Regina at the Wascana Centre in Wascana Park for recommendations and walking tours.

p149

Eating & Sleeping

Maple Creek 1

Shop Bakery & Deli — Bakery $

(☎306-662-2253; www.theshopmc.com; 113 Harder St; bread from $4.50; ⊙6am-6pm Mon-Fri) Lovingly run by Chef Jordyn, this place will meet all your bread, bakery, pastry and coffee needs during the day in the middle of Maple Creek. The cheese-platter bento box with French baguette ($14.99) makes a filling lunch. Good outdoor seating.

Cobble Creek Lodge — Lodge $$

(☎306-662-5100; www.cobblecreeklodge.com; 201 SK-21; r incl breakfast from $135; P ⊖ ❄ ☎) Locally owned and run, Cobble Creek offers 36 well-appointed rooms, including standard queens right up to luxury suites. Rates include wi-fi and continental breakfast.

Cypress Hills Interprovincial Park 2

Resort at Cypress Hills — Resort $$

(☎306-662-4477; www.resortatcypresshills.ca; 5 Pine Ave; r from $125; P ⊖ ❄ ☎) Surrounded by a dense thicket of cypress, this sprawling woody resort has a bunch of comfortable motel rooms, cabins (great value) and town houses. There's an on-site restaurant and a plethora of fun activities to enjoy within the park.

Eastend 3

Cypress Hotel — Hotel $

(☎306-295-3505; www.dinocountry.com; 343 Red Coat Dr; r from $60; ⊖ ☎) The Cypress Hotel could well be your one-stop shop in Eastend as it includes functional rooms, a cafe (The Loft) and a bar. Built in 1914, it is hard to miss – it's the brick cube on the town's main street.

Val Marie 4

Convent Inn — B&B $

(☎306-298-4515; www.convent.ca; Hwy 4; r incl breakfast from $85; P ⊖ ☎) For a holier than thou sleeping experience, the Convent offers beds amid classic brickwork and beautiful hardwood floors. Built in 1939, this former residential school has nine beautifully restored rooms, a labyrinth of staircases and even a confessional (in case you break a vow or two during the night). It has lovely patios for chilling with a view.

Ogema 6

Solo Italia — Italian $$

(☎306-459-7747; www.soloitalia.ca; 202 Main St; pizzas from $14; ⊙9am-6:30pm Tue-Sat) Specializing in pizza, pasta and espresso, Solo Italia is run by an Italian family passionate about *la cucina italiana* (Italian cuisine). This is a unique opportunity to taste authentic, homemade Italian specialties on the Saskatchewan prairies.

Regina 7

Willow on Wascana — Canadian $$

(☎306-585-3663; www.barwillow.ca; 3000 Wascana Dr; mains lunch from $12, dinner from $15; ⊙11:30am-11pm Mon-Thu, to 1am Fri-Sun) Views over Wascana Lake are one of Regina's upscale pleasures. The menu here changes seasonally and is a classic example of farm-to-table creativity. Dishes are kept simple to let the flavors come through. Sample the kitchen's best with a four-course tasting menu, and there's a long wine list.

Hotel Saskatchewan — Historic Hotel $$

(☎306-522-7691; www.marriott.com; 2125 Victoria Ave; r from $160; P ⊖ ❄ ☎) Overlooking Victoria Park, this 1927 former grand dame of the Canadian National Railroad maintains a lofty presence. There's a degree of wow factor upon entry. The 224 rooms come in sizes from compact to grand and feature luxe, period decor. It's affiliated with Marriott.

North from Saskatoon

Two-thirds of Saskatchewan sits to the north of Saskatoon, relatively undiscovered by travelers. Take your time to delve into this intriguing part of Canada and see what few get to see.

TRIP HIGHLIGHTS

448 km — 8 FINISH

La Ronge
It's all wilderness from here at this frontier-like town

270 km — 7

Prince Albert National Park
Plenty of things to do in Saskatchewan's northern national park

181 km — 6

Prince Albert
Check out PA and its interesting historical museum

Petrofka Orchard

Rosthern

0 km — START 1

Saskatoon
Enjoy Saskatchewan's lively biggest city, its restaurants and nightlife

3–4 DAYS
448 KM/278 MILES

GREAT FOR...

BEST TIME TO GO

June to August when the days are long and warm

ESSENTIAL PHOTO

Reflections on a Prince Albert National Park lake

BEST FOR WILDLIFE

Keep your eyes open in Prince Albert National Park

Prince Albert National Park (p156) Waskesiu Lake and surrounding boreal forest

13 North from Saskatoon

This trip is for explorers, those who are willing to get off the beaten track and see what rural Saskatchewan and the north of the province has to offer. This is the land of the immigrants, and the further north you go, the more you'll feel like you are 'out there.' Prairies and flat farmland give way to the vast boreal forest, lakes and wilderness of the north.

1 Saskatoon

Saskatoon, Saskatchewan's biggest city, with 270,000 people, is full of hidden treasures. Head into the downtown core and inner neighborhoods to get a sense of this vibrant city. The majestic South Saskatchewan River winds through downtown, offering beautiful, natural diversions. Leafy parks and rambling riverside walks help you make the most out of long, sunny summer days, and there are plenty of great spots to stop for a refreshing drink and a chat with locals.

Saskatoon knows how to heat up cold winter days and short summer nights, with a proud heritage of local rock and country music and a vibrant live-music scene. Local girl Joni Mitchell made good and there are plenty hoping to follow.

Before you head out on your northern sojourn, take a walking tour of the city to see what it really has to offer – Stretch Your Legs: Saskatoon (p176).

The Drive ›› Head north out of Saskatoon on Hwy 11 until it splits with Hwy 12. Take Hwy 12 directly north past Martensville. About 30km north of Saskatoon, you'll find signage for Sunnyside Dairy Creamery on the right side of Hwy 12.

p157

2 Summerlands Creamery

This is a great opportunity to check out a Saskatchewan dairy farm and try fresh milk. Bas and Martha Froese-Kooijenga run 30 cows, individually named, on the farm that Martha's parents raised 12 children. At **Sunnyside Dairy Creamery** (306-242-8949; www.sunnysidedairyfarm.com; Hwy 12, north of Martensville; 10am-6pm Tue-Fri, noon-6pm Mon, 8am-5pm Sat), as well as selling dairy products the Farmyard Market has *perogies* (filled dumplings) and pies, eggs and veggies. *Perogies* are extremely popular throughout Saskatchewan. Try the freshest of milk for $2.50 per liter and chat with Martha and locals who buy produce here. The market also sells produce sourced from local farmers.

The Drive ›› Continue north on Hwy 12, staying on 12 when it splits with Rte 312. Immediately after crossing the North Saskatchewan River on the Petrofka Bridge, you'll find Petrofka Orchards signposted on the right. It's around 30km from Summerlands Creamery.

3 Petrofka Orchard

Petrofka Orchard (306-497-2234; www.petrofkaorchard.com; Hwy 12, just past Petrofka Bridge; 10am-7pm Jun-Oct) is a working orchard in an area settled by Doukhobor

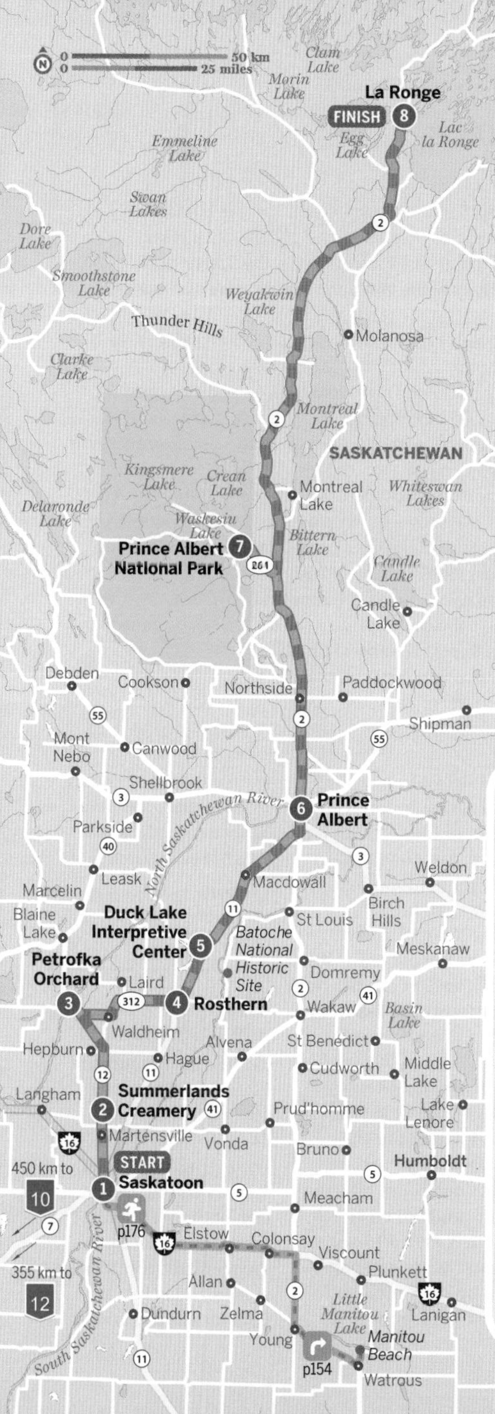

immigrants from eastern Europe in 1899 (Petrofka is a Doukhobor name). The orchard shop offers apple products including cider and vinegar, plus local jams, honey, condiments and other food. Enjoy homemade baking and meals at the on-site Prairie Sensation Cafe, walk maintained trails or picnic down by the river. Try Perogy Buns and clay oven Doukhobor bread at the orchard store.

The Drive » Head back the way you came on Hwy 12, crossing back over the river. After about 4km, turn left at the sign that reads 'Waldheim 10km'. This road is sealed and easy to drive. Continue through tiny Waldheim, then turn left on Rte 312 to Rosthern. All up, it's about 30km from Petrofka Orchard.

LINK YOUR TRIP

10 Dinosaurs, Hoodoos & the Wild West

From Saskatoon, drive five hours southwest to Horseshoe Canyon where you can pick up this road trip replete with history and raw natural beauty.

12 Explore Southern Saskatchewan

Head to the province's south after exploring the north by driving to Maple Creek, near the Alberta border in southern Saskatchewan.

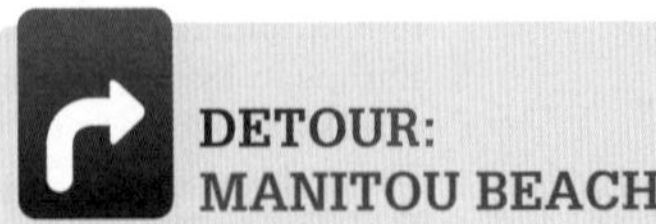

DETOUR: MANITOU BEACH

Start: ❶ Saskatoon

Near the town of Watrous, Manitou Lake is a hidden gem. The lake is one of only three places in the world with Dead Sea–like waters full of minerals and salt, meaning that you can't sink! The others are Karlovy Vary in the Czech Republic and the Dead Sea itself. If the cool waters of the lake don't appeal, there's an indoor heated pool option in town too.

Right on the water, the village feels like a throwback to a simpler time. In the 1920s and '30s it was extremely popular, with thousands coming to enjoy the mineral waters and beach during summer. There were three large dance halls, two indoor bathhouses, restaurants, cafes and apparently bootleggers and a brothel too. Things went downhill during the Great Depression, but today there's a new energy in Manitou Beach to return to the glory days.

Today, you can browse the artwork of over 100 Saskatchewan artists at the **Little Manitou Art Gallery** (306-759-7889; www.littlemanitouartgallery.com; 204 Elizabeth Ave; 9am-5pm). You can stop in for a meal at the waterfront **Oda Coffee & Wine Bar** (306-952-5493; 305 MacLachlan Ave; mains from $15; 4-9pm Mon-Wed, from 11am Thu & Fri, from 9am Sat & Sun), and join the dance crowd at **Danceland** (800-267-5037; www.danceland.ca; 511 Lake Ave; Jun-Oct). You can also overnight (or soak in the famed waters) at the **Manitou Springs Resort & Mineral Spa** (306-946-2233; www.manitousprings.ca; 302 McLachlan Ave; pool day pass adult/child $21/16).

Manitou Beach is 120km southeast of Saskatoon, via Hwys 16 and 2.

❹ Rosthern

Tiny Rosthern (pop 1700) is a good place to get a feel for rural northern Saskatchewan. Be sure to visit the **Mennonite Heritage Museum** (306-232-4437; www.historicplaces.ca; 7010 5th St, Rosthern; by donation; 10am-4:30pm Thu-Sat). The first Mennonite settlers arrived in Rosthern in 1891 and this lovingly cared for little museum tells the story of the Mennonite community's commitment to the preservation of its identity. The building was the German-English Academy until 1963, established to provide instruction in English, to preserve the German language, and to maintain the Mennonite religion and way of life.

On the main street, stop at the old train station. Here, at the **Station Arts Centre & Tea Room** (306-232-5332; www.stationarts.com; 701 Railway Ave, Rosthern; 9am-4pm Tue-Sat), is a beautiful gallery showing the works of local artists, plus a tea room offering lunch and baked snacks. There is also a 160-seat theater with a strong line-up of events, and a small museum in a train caboose (donated by Canadian National Railway) on the tracks side of the station.

The Drive » It's 19km direct from Rosthern to Duck Lake on Hwy 11.

❺ Duck Lake Interpretive Center

This excellent **museum** (www.ducklakemuseum.com; Hwy 11; adult/child $4.50/2.50; 10am-5:30pm Mon-Fri), just off Hwy 11, focuses on the preservation of the Willow Cree First Nation, Métis and Pioneer cultures through stories and artifacts. A circular path around the

HENRYK SADURA/GETTY IMAGES ©

Saskatoon (p152) Skyline views at dusk

gallery, looks at the various groups, their religion, their education, the political period of upheaval around the rebellion of 1885 and the development of economic life. A stairway to the top of the museum's distinctive 24m tower reveals sweeping views.

The Drive » From Duck Lake, Hwy 11 north will connect with Hwy 2 just short of Prince Albert. Hwy 2 then runs straight through Prince Albert. All up it's 44km to PA.

6 Prince Albert

Prince Albert (PA), Saskatchewan's third biggest city, has a dilapidated yet evocative old brick downtown in a pretty location beside the North Saskatchewan River. Established in 1776 as a fur-trading post, PA was later named after Queen Victoria's husband, Prince Albert of Saxe-Coburg-Gotha, who died in 1861. Prince Albert became the capital of the District of Saskatchewan, a regional administrative division of what then constituted the Northwest Territories, and there were hopes for a great future. This ended in 1905 when Saskatchewan became a full province and Regina was chosen as the new provincial capital. PA's plans for greatness was based on the hope that the Transcontinental Railway would pass through the city, but the Canadian Pacific Railway chose a more southerly route.

Make sure to visit the **Prince Albert Historical Museum** (☎306-764-2992; www.historypa.com; 10 River St; adult/child $4/2; ⏰9am-5pm). This packed little museum is in what was the Central Firehall from 1912 until 1975, right on the banks of the North Saskatchewan River. It takes in many aspects of the town's long history.

A great place to stay here is **Keyhole Castle B&B** (☎306-763-3321; www.keyholecastle.com; 1925 1 Ave E; r from $159; P ⊖ ❄ 📶). This is an opportunity to stay in an extraordinary 'castle', built during Prince Albert's boom times of the early 1900s. In the East Hill neighborhood, it's a designated national historic site.

The Drive » From Prince Albert, cross the river on the bridge (the only bridge for miles in each direction) and head directly north on Hwy 2 for 60km to Rte 264, the turnoff for Waskesiu in Prince Albert National Park. The park entry is about 5km off Hwy 2 and it's another 5km to Waskesiu Lake and township.

🛏 p157

7 Prince Albert National Park

Prince Albert National Park is a jewel in the wild. Just when you thought the vast prairie would never end, the trees begin, signaling the start of the vast boreal forest. This national park is one of those special places that will give you the feeling that you are truly on the edge of the known world. A forested sanctuary of lakes, untouched land and wildlife, this park puts the 'wild' back into 'wilderness.' Outdoor activities such as canoeing, hiking and camping are at their shining best here. There is a multitude of potential adventures to be had, whether it be the unforgettable 20km trek to Grey Owl's Cabin, a canoe trip or even just chilling out on a beach.

The quaint little resort village of Waskesiu Lake is your base for exploration within the park. Make sure you drop in at the **Prince Albert National Park Visitor Center** (306-663-4522; www.pc.gc.ca; 969 Lakeview Dr, Waskesiu Lake; 7am-8pm Jun-Aug) for everything you need to know about the park. There are campgrounds, and in Waskesiu, **Hawood Inn** (306-663-5911; www.hawood.com; 188 Waskesiu Lake, Waskesiu Lake; r from $140; P) is a top place to stay. This family-run lodge right on the waterfront is a good spot to relax. There's a decent dining room and lounge, rooftop hot tubs, and nearby shops, restaurants and activities.

The Drive » Back out on Hwy 2, you've got 180km of driving virtually straight north to what feels like the end of the line at La Ronge.

p157

8 La Ronge

La Ronge is the southern hub of the far north – your last chance for supplies before heading off the grid. It's a rough, basic town, popular with anglers, hunters and folks on the run. **Lac La Ronge Provincial Park** (www.tourismsaskatchewan.com; Hwy 2; May-Sep) surrounds huge, island-filled Lac La Ronge and feels all-encompassing. It's great for fishing, canoeing and hikes among stubby pines. There are at least a 100 more lakes and more than 1000 islands. The park has five year-round campgrounds and endless backcountry camping. Before you head out, the legendary **Robertson's Trading Post** (306-425-2080; 308 La Ronge Ave, La Ronge; 8am-6pm Mon-Sat) is the place to go if you're in the market for a bear trap, wolf hide or case of baked beans. If you need a place to stay, **Waterbase Inn** (306-425-5550; www.waterbaseinn.ca; La Ronge Ave, La Ronge; r from $95; P) is a decent option, while Cravings Late Night Food (p157) will make sure you won't go hungry.

It's hard to believe that almost half of Saskatchewan still lies further north of here. This is frontier territory, the end of the paved road. If you're not skittish about extreme isolation and you're outfitted appropriately, then this is it! Self sufficiency here is key: make sure you maintain your vehicle, have plenty of fuel, gear and supplies, and keep your head together.

p157

Eating & Sleeping

Saskatoon 1

Cathedral Social Hall — Pub Food $$

(☎306-668-1011; www.cathedralsocialhall.com; 608 Spadina Cres E; mains from $14; 11am-midnight) CSH focuses on local Saskatchewan fare and beer, including gluten-free and vegetarian options. Try the Beer Soup ($8) or the Social Hall Burger ($15) out on the front terrace, along with your choice from the 30 taps.

Ayden Kitchen and Bar — Canadian $$$

(☎306-954-2590; www.aydenkitchenandbar.com; 265 3rd Ave S; mains from $22; 5:30-9pm Mon-Sat) Saskatoon's restaurant-of-the-moment works magic with local produce and other seasonal specialties. Chef Dale MacKay is a star on the Canadian food scene. You never know what surprises he has in store at this unpretentious downtown bistro. Book ahead.

James Hotel — Boutique Hotel $$

(☎306-244-6446; www.thejameshotel.ca; 620 Spadina Cres E; r from $160; P) Attentive service at the James begins with your welcome to the property. From the minimalist yet sumptuous rooms featuring marble bathrooms, balconies and top-notch bedding to the stylish cocktail bar, the James gets it right. It's close to the riverfront parks; try for a room with a view.

Hotel Senator — Historic Hotel $$

(☎306-244-6141; www.hotelsenator.ca; 243 21st St E; r from $99; P) Dating from 1908, this well-maintained and updated hotel is creaky but cool. You can get a sense of the ornate past in the lobby. The pub is a good place to while away the night, and you can't beat the location – everything is a short walk away.

Prince Albert 6

Prince Albert Inn — Hotel $$

(☎306-922-5000; www.painn.com; 3680 2 Ave W; r from $119; P) Nothing exceptional here, but the rooms are clean with all the expected hotel amenities; there's an on-site restaurant and bar, plus a good-sized indoor pool. PA Inn is connected by a skywalk to the Northern Lights Casino next door.

Prince Albert National Park 7

Pete's Terrace Restaurant and Bar — Cafe $$

(☎306-663-5530; www.facebook.com/petesterrace; Lakeview Dr, Waskesiu Lake; pizzas from $20; 11am-10pm) Indulge in pizzas, burgers and beer at Pete's, overlooking the lake waterfront in Waskesiu. Time it right for live music in summer – check out the Facebook page.

Flora Bora Forest Lodging — Yurt $$

(☎306-961-9554; www.florabora.ca; off Hwy 263, Emma Lake; yurts from $190; P) Yurt it up in the delightful Flora Bora Forest Lodging, between Emma and Christopher Lakes. These wilderness huts have decks and are removed from the parking area.

La Ronge 8

Cravings Late Night Food — Canadian $$

(☎306-425-2769; www.facebook.com/airronge; 317 Husky Ave; mains from $12; 11am-11pm Tue-Fri, from 2pm Sat & Sun) This place gets the nod in La Ronge for decent home-style food, prices and quirkiness. You definitely won't go away hungry. Try The Wild One (wild rice burger) for $13.25 or The Trump (loaded burger) for $12.25. Take-out is available too.

Co.
KLONDIKE
KLONDIKE
MASTER
11
12

Klondike Highway

14

Follow the same basic route as the gold-crazed prospectors of 1898 to Bonanza Creek near Dawson City, only they didn't have a nice sealed highway and a car to drive.

TRIP HIGHLIGHTS

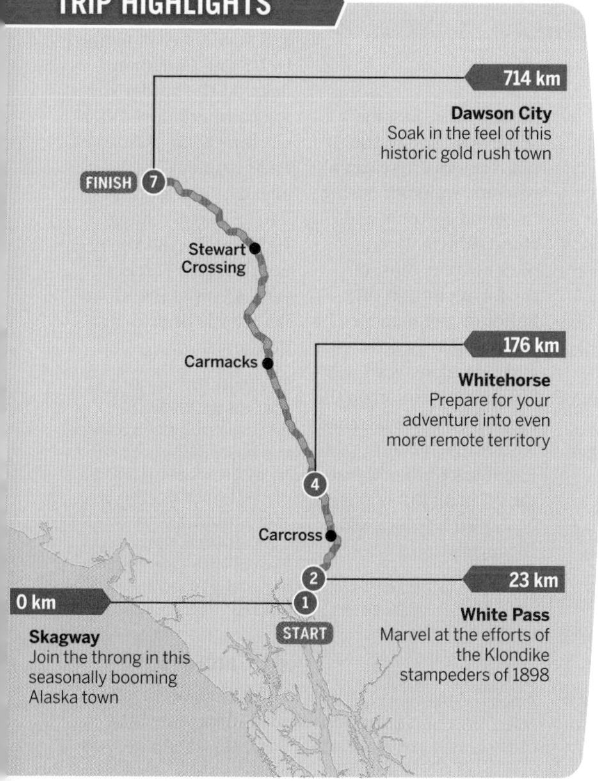

714 km
Dawson City
Soak in the feel of this historic gold rush town

FINISH 7

Stewart Crossing

Carmacks

176 km
Whitehorse
Prepare for your adventure into even more remote territory

4

Carcross

2

23 km
White Pass
Marvel at the efforts of the Klondike stampeders of 1898

1

START

0 km
Skagway
Join the throng in this seasonally booming Alaska town

4–5 DAYS
714KM/443 MILES

GREAT FOR...

BEST TIME TO GO

June to August when the days are long and warm

ESSENTIAL PHOTO

SS Klondike National Historic Site in Whitehorse

BEST FOR OUTDOORS

Camping along the way

'**hitehorse** SS Klondike National Historic Site (p162)

14 Klondike Highway

Virtually the whole trip on the Klondike Hwy from Skagway, Alaska, through 56km of British Columbia, then through the Yukon Territory to Dawson City, is wonderful wilderness. These days it's an easy drive, but you'll still need to be prepared and to keep your eyes open and your wits about you – you never know what might pop out of the forest to cross the road.

1 Skagway

At first sight, Skagway appears to be solely an amusement park for cruise-ship day-trippers, a million of whom disgorge onto its sunny boardwalks every summer. But, haunted by Klondike ghosts and beautified by a tight grid of handsome false-fronted buildings, this is no northern Vegas. Skagway's history is very real.

During the 1898 gold rush, some 40,000 stampeders passed through; they were a sometimes-unsavory cast of characters who lived against a backdrop of brothels, gunfights and debauched entertainment wilder than the Wild West. Today, the main actors are seasonal workers, waitstaff posing in period costume and storytelling national-park rangers. Most of the town's important buildings are managed by the National Park Service and this, along with Skagway's location on the cusp of a burly wilderness with trails (including the legendary Chilkoot) leading off in all directions, has saved it from overt Disneyfication.

The Drive » The first 23km of the drive is a steady climb on what is Hwy 98 on the Alaska side of the border. You're climbing from sea level in Skagway to 1003m at the pass. At the 11km mark you'll pass the US Customs Station, where all travelers entering the US must stop. You're heading out so just drive on through.

p165

2 White Pass

The White Pass mountain summit and Summit Lake area more closely resembles a moonscape than any earthly landscape, with twisted trees, small lakes, and barren foliage that create truly unique scenery. Take your time and stop at one of the many pullouts off the road to savor the scenery. The national border is just past the pass – spot the signage and small obelisk flanked by US and Canadian flags. At the border you are passing into a different time zone – Canada Pacific time is one hour ahead of Alaska time – don't forget to change your watch. And you're not in Yukon Territory yet – 56km of the Klondike Hwy is in British Columbia.

The Drive » Continuing on what is now Canadian Hwy 2, the Canadian Customs Station is at Fraser, British Columbia; it's open 24 hours and all vehicles must stop for inspection. Bring your passport. You'll be in BC for a further 44km, with gorgeous views of Tutshi Lake. At 105km from Skagway, you'll arrive in Carcross.

3 Carcross

Long a forgotten gold-rush town, cute little Carcross (the name was shortened from Caribou Crossing in 1902) is an evocative stop. There's a growing artisan community, old buildings are being restored and the site on Lake Bennett is superb – although Klondike prospectors who had to build boats here to cross the lake and head on to Dawson City didn't think so. The old train station has good displays on local history.

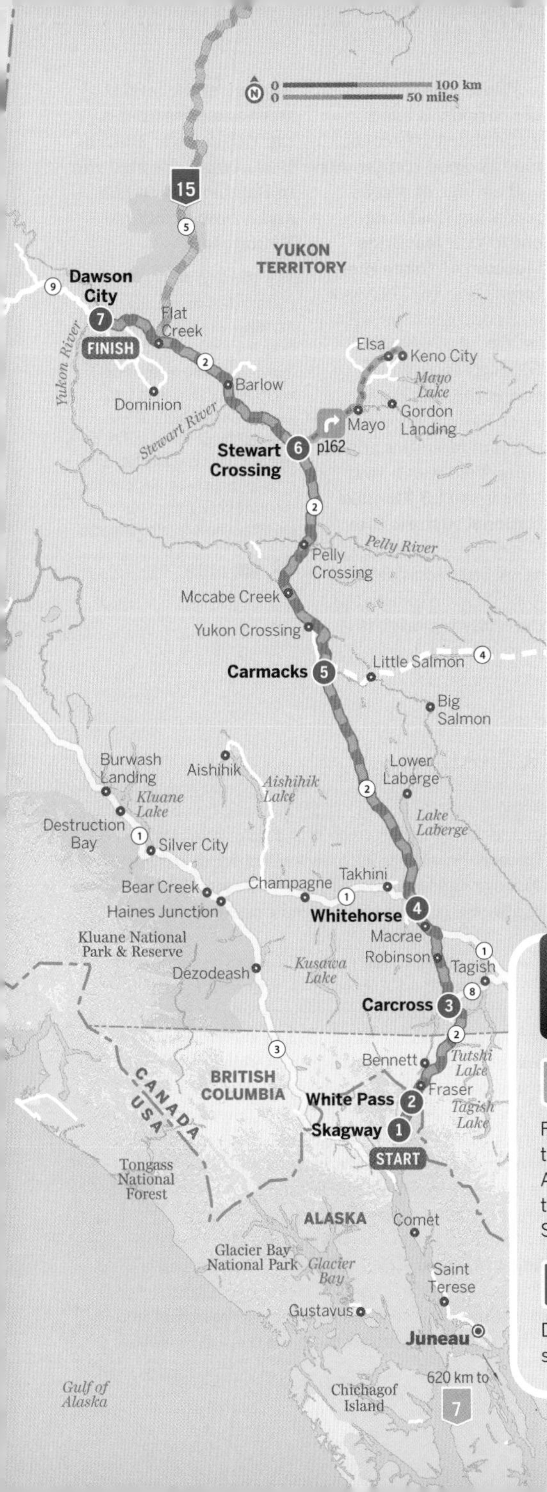

Just north of town, on the highway, is the Carcross Desert, proudly claimed as the world's smallest desert, covering less than 260 hectares. It's actually the remains of the sandy bottom of a glacial lake left after the last ice age. A dry climate and strong winds created the sand dunes and allow little vegetation to grow.

The Drive » At 12km north of Carcross, pull off for a view of lovely Emerald Lake. At 53km from Carcross, the Klondike Hwy

LINK YOUR TRIP

7 Haida Gwaii Adventure

Ferry from Skagway, Alaska to Prince Rupert, BC, by the Alaska Marine Hwy system, then by BC Ferries to Skidegate on Haida Gwaii.

15 Dempster Highway

The start of the Dempster Highway is 40km southeast of Dawson City.

runs into the Alaska Hwy and joins it for 34km. You're about to hit the 'big smoke' of the Yukon – Whitehorse is 176km from Skagway and 71km from Carcross.

---

4 Whitehorse

The capital city of the Yukon Territory since 1953, to the continuing regret of much smaller and isolated Dawson City, Whitehorse is a hub for transportation. It was a terminus for the White Pass & Yukon Route railway from Skagway in the early 1900s, and during WWII a major center for work on the Alaska Hwy.

Whitehorse rewards the curious. It has a well-funded arts community, good restaurants and a range of accommodation. Take time out to visit **MacBride Museum of Yukon History** (867-667-2709; www.macbridemuseum.com; 1124 Front St; adult/child $10/5; 9:30am-5pm), which covers the gold rush, First Nations people, intrepid Mounties and more. Well worth your time is the **SS Klondike National Historic Site** (867-667-4511; www.pc.gc.ca; cnr South Access Rd & 2nd Ave; 9:30am-5pm May-Aug). Carefully restored, this was one of the largest stern-wheelers used on the Yukon River. Built in 1937, it made its final run to Dawson City in 1955 and is now a National Historic Site.

The Drive » Around 12km north of Whitehorse, the Klondike Hwy (Hwy 2) splits from the Alaska Hwy (Hwy 1) and heads more or less due north. About 7km from the junction, a well-signposted side road heads west to Takhini Hot Springs. Consider taking time for a dip here. Back on the Klondike Hwy, 166km from the junction, you'll reach Carmacks.

p165

DETOUR: THE SILVER TRAIL

Start: 6 Stewart Crossing

As prospectors found it harder and harder to become rich and stake gold claims around Bonanza Creek near Dawson City after 1898, others searched further afield and by 1920, silver had been found at Keno Hill, 200km to the east, and 600 claims staked. A town built up, named after the gambling game Keno, popular in mining camps at that time.

Transporting the heavy ore was a problem though and horse-drawn sleighs were used to haul it to the Stewart River, where it was picked up by specially designed sternwheeler paddle-steamers and shipped out, initially downriver to Dawson City, then all the way down the Yukon River and out to the Bering Sea, then to a smelter in San Francisco. The small town of Mayo built up as a transportation center on the Stewart River where supplies were dropped off and the silver ore was picked up.

To see these mining communities, take the dead end Silver Trail (Hwy 11) northeast from Stewart Crossing. **Mayo** (population 450; www.villageofmayo.ca), formerly known as Mayo Landing, is 51km up paved Hwy 11 and is getting a new lease on life. It is the largest community in the region and has become a staging point for backcountry wilderness trips, canoeing, hiking, big-game hunting, fly-in fishing and more.

A further 61km up the now gravel Hwy 11 you'll find **Keno City**, site of the silver mine camp, the **Keno City Mining Museum** (867-995-3103; www.yukonmuseums.ca; Main St, Keno City; 10am-6pm Jun-Sep), which houses a collection of artifacts, memorabilia and photographs that provide a snapshot of Keno's colorful past, and these days, about 20 people. The only way out is back down the road you came on.

Carcross (p160) Old steam locomotive

5 Carmacks

This small village sits right on the Yukon River and is named for one of the discoverers of gold in 1896, George Washington Carmack. A rogue seaman wandering the Yukon, it was almost by luck that Carmack (with Robert Henderson, Tagish Charlie and Keish – aka Skookum Jim Mason) made their claim on Bonanza Creek. Considering the life of debauchery that followed, it's fitting that Carmack be honored by this uninspired collection of gas stations, stores and places to stay. Like elsewhere in the territory, residents here are keenly attuned to the land, which supplies them with game and fish throughout the year.

The Drive » Continue north through constant wilderness on the Klondike Hwy for a further 180km.

p165

6 Stewart Crossing

Stewart Crossing is on the Stewart River, a tributary of the Yukon River, but there's not much to get excited about. Little more than a petrol station and store, the village is also at the junction of the Klondike Hwy and the Silver Trail, which makes a 224km round-trip northeast to the village of Mayo and the mining town of Keno City.

The Drive » Continue northwest for 180km to Dawson City. Around 24km from Stewart Crossing is Moose Creek Lodge, a top place to stay with comfy little cabins set back from the highway in the forest. About 40km short of Dawson City, you'll run into the Dempster Highway, one to consider for your next adventure.

LOCAL KNOWLEDGE: DO THE LOOP

The Klondike Hwy is an amazing drive, but most people end up going to Dawson City and then driving back down the same road to Whitehorse. For the adventurous, an exciting loop awaits to take you back to Yukon Territory's capital via Alaska (you'll need your passport).

From Dawson City, the George Black free car ferry crosses the Yukon River from the end of Front St to the scenic **Top of the World Hwy** (Hwy 9). Only open in summer, the mostly gravel 107km-long road to the US border has superb vistas across the region.

You'll continue to feel on top of the world as you cross at the most northerly US–Canada border crossing at **Poker Creek**. On the US side, the first 19km connection to the intersection with the **Taylor Hwy** (Hwy 5) is newly sealed and gives the impression that the easy roads may last forever.

It's time to go back to the gravel though! Some further 48km south from the intersection with the Taylor Hwy, over unsealed roads, you encounter **Chicken**. The little place was going to be called Ptarmigan, but locals didn't trust their spelling and pronunciation skills so went for Chicken instead.

Another 119km south, now on sealed roading, and you reach the Alaska Hwy at **Tetlin Junction**, where a turn east takes you back to the Yukon. Just a tick west, **Tok** has services and motels. The only place between Dawson City and the Alaska Hwy to get fuel or food is in Chicken, so prepare well.

If you're heading east, back to Whitehorse, there are motels and eating places in **Beaver Creek**, just over the Alaska–Canada border and 156km away on the Alaska Hwy. From Beaver Creek, it's 292km to **Haines Junction** and 445km to **Whitehorse**.

7 Dawson City

If you didn't know its history, Dawson City would be an atmospheric place in which to pause for a while, with a seductive, funky vibe. That it's one of the most historic and evocative towns in Canada is like gold dust on a cake: unnecessary but damn nice.

Set on a narrow shelf at the confluence of the Yukon and Klondike Rivers, Dawson was the destination for Klondike Gold Rush prospectors. Today, you can wander the dirt streets of town, passing old buildings with dubious permafrost foundations, and discover Dawson's rich cultural life. While you're there, be sure to visit the **Bonanza Creek Discovery Site** (Bonanza Creek Rd). Who knows what you may stumble over?

p165

Eating & Sleeping

Skagway 1

Woadie's South East Seafood — Seafood $$

(☎907-983-3133; State St & 4th Ave; mains $14-19; ⏰11:30am-7pm Mon-Thu, noon-6pm Fri & Sat) A food cart with its own deck and awning, equipped with picnic tables, delivers the town's best fish at a lightning pace. Report to the window and place your order for fresh oysters, crab or halibut. It allows BYO booze.

Morning Wood Hotel — Hotel $

(☎907-983-3200; www.skagwayhotelandrestaurant.com/morning-wood-hotel; 444 4th Ave; r with/without bath $175/99; 📶) A buoyant hotel with a handsome, if typical, false-fronted wooden exterior. Inside, the rooms (located at the rear) aren't fancy, but at least they come with deluxe bathroom accessories and sharp color accents. There's an affiliated restaurant and bar.

Whitehorse 4

Klondike Rib & Salmon — Canadian $$

(☎867-667-7554; www.klondikerib.com; 2116 2nd Ave; mains from $14; ⏰11am-9pm May-Sep) The food is superb at this sprawling casual half-tent restaurant in a place originally opened as a tent-frame bakery in 1900. Besides the namesakes (the salmon skewers and smoked pork ribs are tops), there are other local faves. Great place to try bison steak ($34) or Yukon arctic char ($28). It's half-tent, so closed when winter temperatures turn up.

Historical Guest House — B&B $$

(☎867-668-3907; www.historicalguesthouse.com; 5128 5th Ave; r from $105; 🚭📶) A classic wooden home from 1907 with three guest rooms. Top-floor options have individual bathrooms one floor down and angled ceilings. A larger unit has a huge kitchen. Rooms have high-speed internet, and there's a nice garden. A good option with character.

Carmacks 5

Tatchun Centre General Store — Food

(☎867-863-6171; 35607 Klondike Hwy; ⏰7:30am-10pm) This is the biggest store between Whitehorse and Dawson City and offers the opportunity to purchase grocery and food items, drinks, gifts and souvenirs. There are also gas pumps outside.

Hotel & RV Park Carmacks — Hotel $$

(☎867-863-5221; www.hotelcarmacks.com; 35607 Klondike Hwy N; tent & RV sites/cabins/r from $40/95/179; P 🚭 ❄ 📶) It's all here 177km north of Whitehorse with the largest accommodation place on the Klondike Hwy between Whitehorse and Dawson City. Hotel Carmacks offers a good standard of rooms and also features the Gold Panner Restaurant and Gold Dust Lounge. The RV Park offers campsites, power and internet. Nothing like this further north.

Dawson City 7

Drunken Goat Taverna — Greek $$

(☎867-993-5800; 2nd Ave; mains from $14; ⏰5pm-late) Follow your eyes to the flowers, your ears to the Aegean music and your nose to the excellent Greek food, served year-round by the legendary Tony Dovas. A terrace out back is a fine place to while away an evening.

Farmers Market — Market $

(Front St; ⏰11am-5pm Sat May-Sep) A farmers market thrives by the iconic waterfront gazebo. The sweet-as-candy carrots are the product of very cold nights. Try some birch syrup.

Klondike Kate's Cabins — Lodge $$

(☎867-993-6527; www.klondikekates.ca; cnr King St & 3rd Ave; cabins from $175; ⏰Apr-Sep; P 🚭📶) The 15 cabins behind the excellent restaurant of the same name are rustic without the rusticisms. Some units have microwaves and fridges. All have porches, perfect for decompressing.

ARCTIC CIRCLE
LAT 66° 33'N

The Arctic Circle...
Did You Know...

Dempster Highway

On this remote, rugged, challenging route you'll experience pristine wilderness: boundless boreal forest, glacial rivers, snow-tipped hills and desolate tundra.

TRIP HIGHLIGHTS

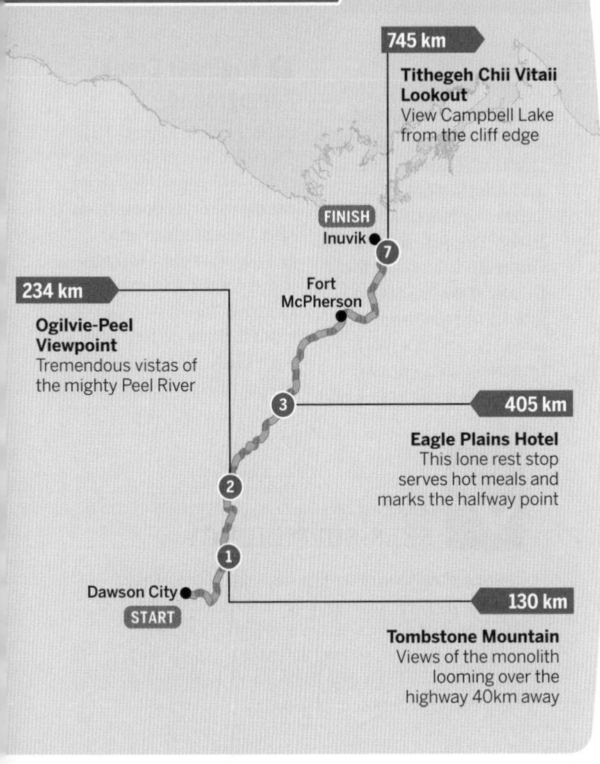

745 km
Tithegeh Chii Vitaii Lookout
View Campbell Lake from the cliff edge

FINISH
Inuvik

Fort McPherson

234 km
Ogilvie-Peel Viewpoint
Tremendous vistas of the mighty Peel River

405 km
Eagle Plains Hotel
This lone rest stop serves hot meals and marks the halfway point

Dawson City
START

130 km
Tombstone Mountain
Views of the monolith looming over the highway 40km away

6–7 DAYS
773KM/480 MILES

GREAT FOR...

BEST TIME TO GO

June to September, when the road conditions are best.

ESSENTIAL PHOTO

Standing next to the Arctic Circle sign at Km 403.

BEST FOR OUTDOORS

Admiring the varied northern landscape of boreal forest, glacial rivers, snow-capped hills and endless tundra.

Dempster Highway Arctic Circle sign (p170)

15 Dempster Highway

Pristine Arctic scenery accompanies you on your journey to Inuvik, the largest northernmost settlement in the Northwest Territories. The only public highway to cross the Arctic Circle, the Dempster starts some 40km east of Dawson City, Yukon. Its name is uttered with awe by drivers in the know; this trip requires preplanning and is not to be taken lightly. One-way rental car drop-off fees are extortionate; prepare for a round trip.

1 Tombstone Territorial Park

Some 130km from the start of the journey in Dawson City and accessed via an eponymous campground at Km 72, this 2200 sq km park consists of a wilderness of rugged peaks, boreal forest and abundant wildlife, including grizzly bears, caribou and wolverine. You need to be wilderness-savvy and self-sufficient, and if you're looking to do full-day hikes here, you need to be prepared for the rough terrain and changeable weather.

At the campground there's an interpretive center that offers free guided walks from May to September, a wheelchair-accessible interpretive trail, short loop train and another one that skirts the North Klondike River. The full-service campsite is a good place to stay if you've set off late in the day from Dawson City, and it's worth lingering a day or two. There are also three basic backcountry campsites in the park, reachable on foot only and requiring advance reservations from late June to mid-September. In winter, the park is a popular day-trip destination from Dawson City for snowshoeing, skiing, snowmobiling and wildlife-spotting.

The Drive » From Tombstone, it's 122km of gently winding road to Engineer Creek Campground. At Km 82, you cross the North Fork Pass (1289m), the highest point of elevation on the Dempster Hwy and the first crossing of the Continental Divide. Spot the plaque at Km 117 that commemorates WJB Dempster, a sergeant of the Royal Mounted Police whose name the highway bears.

2 Engineer Creek Campground

Sitting below Sapper Hill – a collection of dolomite cliffs – this small serviced campground is open from May to September and is a popular day stop for those wanting to explore the rock 'forests' of the eroded ridge on foot and with birdwatchers keen to spot the peregrine

TOP TIP: SELF-SUFFICIENCY

There is no phone reception for most of the drive, and few passing motorists, so be sure to take a satellite phone. The Dempster is also known as 'Puncture Central', so take at least two spare tires and know how to change them. Food, water and a sleeping bag are essential supplies.

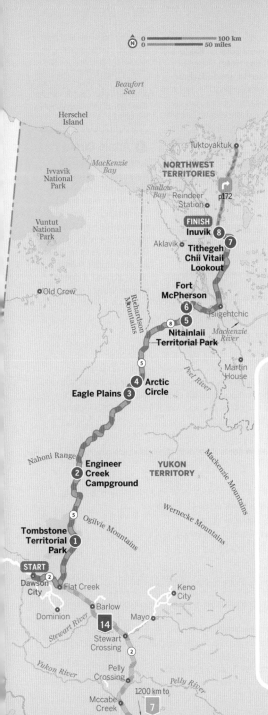

falcons and golden eagles that nest on the cliffs.

The Gwich'in name for Sapper Hill is Chü Akan (Beaver House Mountain). It's a reference to millennia past, when giant beavers roamed the land. 'Sapper' is the nickname for army engineers, and the hill is named for the Third Royal Canadian Army Engineers who constructed the Ogilvie Bridge.

The Drive » The 175km-drive from Engineer Creek winds its way through boreal forest, followed by rolling plains. It's worth stopping at the Ogilvie Ridge at Km 259 for far-reaching views of the Peel River, meandering tundra and bare, rocky hills in the distance.

LINK YOUR TRIP

Haida Gwaii Adventure

From Dawson City, drive eight hours southeast to Skagway, Alaska and take the ferry to Prince Rupert, BC, via the Alaska Marine Hwy system. Then take a BC Ferry to Skidegate on Haida Gwaii.

14 Klondike Highway

Combining your road trip with a drive through the Yukon's gold rush country is easy; the Dempster meets the Klondike Highway near Dawson City and continues south to the Yukon's capital, Whitehorse.

3 Eagle Plains

Congratulations: you've reached the halfway point! Like a beacon of light, Eagle Plains beckons weary travelers. Literally in the middle of nowhere, it consists of a motel-style hotel, open year-round, as well as a full service garage with a mechanic and RV park and campground. Odds are that you'll have already suffered a puncture along the Dempster due to its mix of shale and gravel, so get your tires patched up here and fill up on gas – there isn't another gas station for almost 200km. **Eagle Plains Hotel** is a good place to unwind, chow down on poutine, burgers and other Canadian classics at the cafeteria-style restaurant, and admire the Gwich'in crafts on display in the common areas. There's usually a lively gaggle of other travelers here, their RVs parked outside, so go ahead and trade travel tips, as it's the most people you'll see for most of your drive up.

The Drive » From Eagle Plains, the road winds its way for 36km to the Arctic Circle sign through a landscape of boreal forest. If it has been raining, be very careful just north of Eagle Plains, where a stretch of mostly dirt road turns into a mud slide, and if you're not careful, you can slide right off the steep side of the road.

4 Arctic Circle

A prominent sign off the side of the highway, and display boards on local flora, fauna and the northern lights, announce your arrival at the Arctic Circle. Beyond this point, the sun doesn't set at summer solstice (June 21) and it doesn't rise on winter solstice

HOW TO DRIVE THE DEMPSTER

When to Go

From summer to early fall, driving conditions are easiest – though wildfires can be an issue in July and August, and September brings cooler weather. In the fall, you're likely to spot herds of migrating caribou. Avoid the spring thaw (late April to mid-June), since the route includes two car ferries, and winter freeze-up (mid-October to mid-December), when the highway is closed.

What to Bring

» **Two spare tires, jack and other tools** Parts of the Dempster are covered in shale that's hard on your wheels.

» **Sleeping bag**

» **Tent** For taking advantage of the numerous, beautifully situated campgrounds.

» **Plenty of food and water** Enough for at least three days.

» **Warm clothing** For travelling any time of year.

» **Bug repellent and head net** A must in summer.

» **Satellite phone**

Do's and Don'ts

» **Do** allow yourself at least six days for a round-trip drive up the Dempster. You can get from Dawson City to Inuvik in one day, but it's more relaxing and rewarding to camp and go hiking in various protected areas en route. For current road conditions, see www.dot.gov.nt.ca.

» **Don't** abandon your vehicle if you break down.

» **Do** be mindful of wildlife, such as grizzlies, and keep a safe distance. Stay in the car if you see one.

» **Do** take all your trash with you, particularly if you camp.

PETER CHIGMAROFF/ALAMY STOCK PHOTO ©

Fort McPherson St Mathew's Anglican Church

(December 21). By this point, the endless boreal forest of northern Yukon has given way to low-growing dwarf trees and scrubland-covered hills. Between the Arctic Circle and Nitainlaii Territorial Park, your next stop, you'll cross the boundary between the Yukon and the Northwest Territories at Km 465. The time zone changes here; set your watch to one hour ahead.

The Drive » From the Arctic Circle, the road winds its way for 141km through snow-topped hills and tundra. At Km 447, Rock River Campground sits in a steep gorge of the Richardson Mountains. Wright Pass Summit at Km 464 marks the Dempster's northernmost high point, while Midway Lake at Km 209 hosts an August music festival. At Km 539, board the free Peel River Ferry (9am to 12:30am) to cross the river and make the final 2km drive to Nitainlaii Territorial Park.

5 Nitainlaii Territorial Park

Surrounded by white birch and spruce trees and perched on a bluff overlooking the slow-flowing waters of the Peel River, Nitainlaii Territorial Park is a good place to break your journey. To get here, you will have passed through some of the Dempster's most dramatic scenery of scrubland-covered, craggy hills and a myriad small lakes dotting the tundra.

For an engaging glimpse of the life of the Gwich'in Dene people, stop by the visitor center and peruse the displays on history, language and culture. There are 23 non-powered campsites here, plus washrooms, drinking water, a kitchen shelter and picnic area, and helpful staff.

The Drive » It's a very short drive of just 9km through stunted boreal forest from Nitainlaii Territorial Park to Fort McPherson, the only settlement of any size before you finally reach Inuvik at the end of the Dempster.

6 Fort McPherson

This Tetl'it Gwich'in settlement that was originally founded in 1849 as a fur trading post by a Hudson's Bay Company exporter is a chilled out place to spend an hour or two. It's worth stopping by St Mathew's Anglican Church, just off the main street, and the graveyard where you'll find the graves of the Lost Patrol, the four Mounties who set off for Dawson City in the winter of 1911 but never made it. Visit also the Chii Tsal Dik Gwizheh Tourist & Heritage Center that introduces visitors to Gwich'in

DETOUR: TUKTOYAKTUK

Start: 8 Inuvik

The Inuvik–Tuktoyaktuk Hwy was first planned in the 1960s, and was finally completed and opened to the public in 2017. Since then there's been a steady stream of adventurers continuing the journey from the end of the Dempster Hwy at Inuvik all the way to the Arctic Ocean, some 144km north. Before the highway was completed, the Inuvialuit community of Tuk was relatively isolated, accessible either by flights over the tundra or an ice road in winter. Now, it's far easier for visitors to experience relatively traditional Inuit life through **Arctic Ocean Tuk Tours** (☎867-977-2406; eileenjacobson@hotmail.com) and **Ookpik Tours** (☎867-678-5116; https://ookpiktours.ca; 239 Mangilaluk Rd), staying overnight in one of several B&Bs and checking out traditional sod houses and the icehouse where local hunters keep their catch. The drive out there is wonderful, too, passing through tundra covered in stunted tree growth and myriad small lakes, and skirting an impressive pingo (earth-covered ice hill) near the entrance to Tuk.

culture by organizing traditional dance demonstrations, walking tours, fish-cutting demos and more. Inside you can peruse the Gwich'in-English dictionary and Gwich'in story books.

Fill up on gas here, as it's cheaper than in Inuvik or Eagle Plains.

Sometimes the water levels of the Peel River or the Mackenzie are too high for the car ferries, in which case you have to overnight at the Peel River Inn.

The Drive » From Fort McPherson, a 58km stretch of road winds its way through the tundra to the banks of the mighty Mackenzie River, where you have to take a free car ferry (9am to 12:30am June to mid-October). Alternatively, you can detour by ferry to the hunting, fishing and trapping Gwich'in settlement of Tsiigehtchic, across the river tributary from the highway, before crossing the Mackenzie. Continue for 103km to reach Tithegeh Chii Vitaii Lookout.

🛏 p173

7 Tithegeh Chii Vitaii Lookout

Part of Gwich'in Territorial Park that encompasses 880 sq km of natural wonders of the Mackenzie Delta – rare Arctic ecosystems, limestone cliffs and a reversing river delta, this lookout sits at the edge of the cliffs overlooking **Campbell Lake**, an important bird and wood-frog habitat.

The Drive » The last 33km stretch of your journey passes through a stretch of stunted dwarf boreal forest – dwarf birch and arctic willow. You'll drive by the Gwich'in Territorial Campground (Km 705), the Ehjuu Njik Wayside Park (Km 714), popular for Arctic grayling fishing, and the Jak Park Campsite (Km 731) – a favorite berrying spot for Inuvik residents.

8 Inuvik

A veritable metropolis by comparison to the one or two Gwich'in settlements you've passed through to get here, Inuvik welcomes visitors with its northern charm, its igloo church and a grand choice of places to stay, from the homey Andre's Place and Arctic Chalet to the business-like Nova Inn. And since you're probably hankering after a hot meal, it's worth heading to Alestine's for some hearty home cooking or, if you're lucky enough to be staying at Andre's, you'll be treated to a gourmet, French-inspired meal. Inuvik is also the place to organize any manner of outdoor adventures, from husky sledding to boating on the Mackenzie Delta, to visiting remote northern national parks or driving the winter ice road to a remote Inuit community.

✕ 🛏 p173

Eating & Sleeping

Fort McPherson 6

Peel River Inn — Hotel $$

(867-952-2417; www.peelriverinn.com; Tetlit Gwich'In Rd; r $219;) The only hotel in town, halfway along the main street. The en suite rooms are clean, carpeted and comfortable, and the wi-fi is reliable, but the place is expensive for what it is. Kitchen facilities are a boon.

Inuvik 8

Alestine's — Canadian $$

(867-777-3702; www.facebook.com/alestines; 48 Franklin Rd; mains $13-25; noon-2pm & 5-8pm Tue-Sat) This fantastic mom-and-pop place has single-handedly elevated Inuvik's dining scene. The menu is succinct and makes the most of fresh local produce. Feast on whitefish tacos, grilled salmon and reindeer chili on the upstairs deck or inside the cube-like interior, decked out with local prints. Your meals are cooked in an old school bus.

Andre's Place — French $$$

(867-777-3177; 55 Wolverine Rd; 4-course menu $75; 6:30pm Wed & Fri) Andre is a classically trained chef who learned his craft in Paris. Expect fine dining in an intimate setting; the menu changes weekly (see the updated menu at the visitor center), but may include the likes of rack of lamb with Provençal sauce and tarte tatin. Advance reservations essential.

Arctic Chalet — Guesthouse $$

(867-777-3535; www.arcticchalet.com; 25 Carn St; s/d/tr from $135/140/145, cabins $200-250;) In a boreal glade 3km from town, the main house showcases local fauna in the form of animal skins and piles of antlers. Satellite cabins, sleeping up to four, have simple kitchens. Some of the wood-paneled rooms are en suite. The affable owners rent canoes, kayaks and cars, run dogsledding and other tours and are a good source of local info.

Capital Suites — Business Hotel $$

(867-678-6300; www.capitalsuites.ca; 198 Mackenzie Rd; ste $185-255;) Inuvik's swishest option is unlikely to feature in your social-media posts, though its suites are all spacious, spotless and come with seriously good beds, kitchenettes, cable TV and bathtubs. Popular with business travelers. The lobby gift shop sells carvings, birch-bark artifacts and beadwork by local artisans.

Tuktoyaktuk

Grandma's Kitchen — Canadian $$

(867-678-5226; www.facebook.com/GrandmasKitchenTuk; 330 Ocean View Rd; mains from $15; noon-midnight, to 10pm Sat, 1-9pm Sun) The only place to eat in town, this family-run restaurant serves musk ox burgers, platters of local delicacies and cinnamon buns, with a side order of ocean views.

Hunter's B&B — B&B $$$

(867-977-2558; www.huntersbbtuk.ca; Oceanview Dr; s/d $200/400;) Friendly, knowledgeable Maureen and Patsy are happy to fill guests in on the settlement's history and they run a tight ship: their spotless little B&B overlooks an Arctic beach and the rooms come with down comforters, local art and access to a well-equipped guest kitchen.

STRETCH YOUR LEGS CALGARY

Start/Finish: Fort Calgary

Distance: 3.2km

Duration: 4 hours

Calgary has tons of walking options, but this trip takes you through the Inglewood area, where shopping, great eats and pretty scenery all combine. Its duration really depends on how much time you spend at each stop.

Take this walk on Trip

Fort Calgary

Park your car here and fill the meter with enough for you to spend a few hours inside. **Fort Calgary** (☎403-290-1875; www.fortcalgary.com; 750 9th Ave SE; adult/child $12/7; ⏰9am-5pm) is undergoing expansion, but there's a lot to see inside – exhibits of ranching and Western life, indigenous cultures and plenty more. There are ever-rotating exhibits and events as well, so give yourself plenty of time to check out what's here.

The Walk » Refill your parking meter before heading out east, then turn left onto the Riverwalk.

Riverwalk

This is just a **path**, but it's a pretty one, and it runs along the river. You can walk as long or as little as you like, with cyclists, walkers, families, dogs and kids. This one's essentially up to you.

The Walk » When you're ready to keep going, return to the Inglewood Bridge and cross over on 9th Ave SE. Go a couple of blocks and you'll see Bite on your right.

Bite

Part-grocery, part-deli, part-restaurant, **Bite** (☎403-263-3966; http://biteyyc.com; 1023 9th Ave SE; mains $8-16; ⏰8am-8pm Mon-Fri, to 6:30pm Sat & Sun) is a one-stop-fits-all place to have a nice brunch, a late snack or a cool refreshing beverage – whatever you're in the mood for. Find a table, grab something takeout and sit outside, or order from the menu. The daily specials are fantastic.

The Walk » Bite is on the other side of the same block as Esker, with an indoor connector. Or you can go outside, turn back on 9th Ave SE toward Fort Calgary, and you'll see Esker on your left before the block is done.

Esker Foundation Contemporary Art Gallery

The **Esker Foundation Contemporary Art Gallery** (https://eskerfoundation.com; 1011 9th Ave SE, Inglewood; ⏰11am-6pm Sun, Tue & Wed, to 8pm Thu & Fri) is a great spot

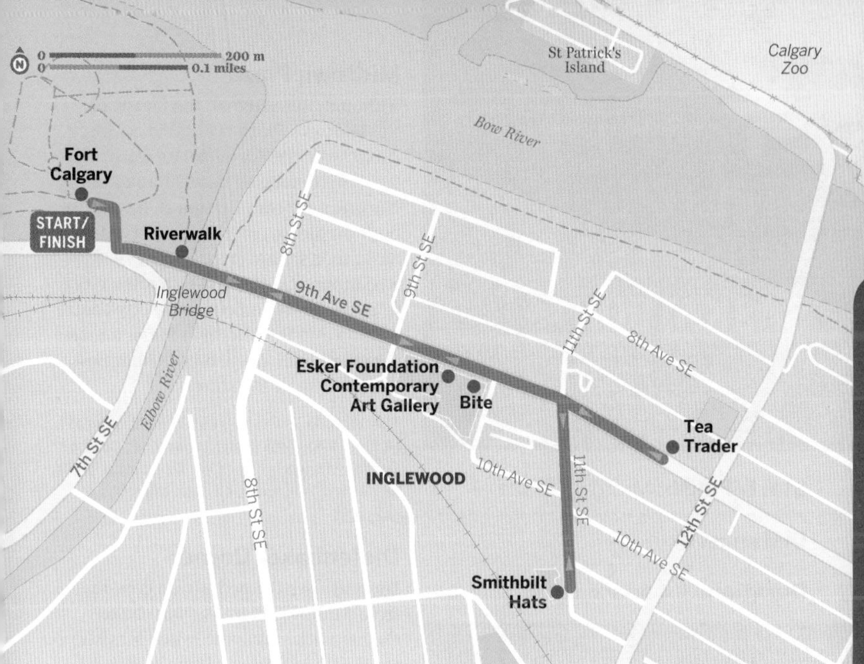

to duck into and enjoy the cool air con while you see the even cooler art that's on display. Thought-provoking, provocative, or just plain weird, there's always something to see here.

The Walk » From Esker, go back on 9th Ave SE and turn right onto 11th St. Smithbilt is a few blocks up on your right.

Smithbilt Hats

Smithbilt Hats (☎403-244-9131; https://smithbilthats.com; 1015 11th St SE; ⏲9am-5pm Mon-Wed & Fri, to 7pm Thu, 10am-4pm Sat) is the place to buy a hat. They run from 'cheap' (about $400) to jaw-dropping-what-the-hey prices (think $1300 or more!), but even if you just look, it's fascinating. The hats are pressed and cut to size right here. You can also see other styles (like top hats even Slash would envy!) and chat with the owners about anything hat you can think of.

The Walk » Exit and follow 11th St SE to 9th Ave, then turn right. The Tea Trader will be on the left, a small shop across from Dragon Pearl restaurant. It's easy to miss if you're not looking closely.

Tea Trader

This lovely little **shop** (☎403-264-0728; www.teatrader.com; 1228a 9th Ave SE, Inglewood; ⏲10am-5pm Tue-Sat, noon-4pm Sun) has a delightful assortment of teas from around the world; while there's no tasting bar set up, you'll still 'taste' the magical aroma as you walk up the stairs. The staff are very friendly, and can guide you to your particular tea needs or to something fun and surprising you might not have tried before.

The Walk » Leave the shop, turn right and follow 9th Ave SE over Inglewood Bridge and back to your car at the parking lot.

STRETCH YOUR LEGS SASKATOON

Start/Finish: Midtown Plaza

Distance: 4km

Duration: 3-4 hours

A wander around Saskatoon offers the opportunity to see what this surprisingly interesting city has on show. The historic buildings along 21st Street, the riverside park, Broadway (where Joni Mitchell played her first gig) and River Landing are all captivating.

Take this walk on Trip

Midtown Plaza

Although not original, the facade of the **Midtown Plaza** (www.midtownplaza.ca; 201 1st Ave S; 9:30am-7pm Mon-Sat, 11am-6pm Sun) is modeled on the Canadian Northern Railway Station that was built on the site in 1910 and served as Saskatoon's main station until 1938. Saskatoon was the first Canadian city to move its station out of the city centre in 1964 and the Midtown Plaza, a major shopping mall, opened in 1970. It now has more than 150 stores.

The Walk » As you pass out the front doors of Midtown Plaza, look straight down 21st St at the 'castle' at the end of the street, 400m away. Cross 1st Ave and head towards it down the right side of 21st St.

Diefenbaker Corner

Directly over the pedestrian crossing from Midtown Plaza is Diefenbaker Corner with statues of Prime Minister Sir Wilfred Laurier talking to local paperboy John Diefenbaker on a visit to Saskatoon in 1910, when he laid the cornerstone for the University of Saskatchewan. After a lengthy conversation, the paperboy famously quipped 'Well Mr Prime Minister, I can't waste any more time, I have to deliver my papers.' The young Diefenbaker went on to become Canada's 13th prime minister (1957–63).

The Walk » Carry on down the right side of 21st St, passing the Mahatma Gandhi statue and historic buildings such as the Hotel Senator of 1908, the Land Titles Building of 1909, and the Saskatoon Club of 1907. Opposite is the Odd Fellows Temple of 1912.

Delta Bessborough

The 'castle' you could see from Midtown Plaza is the wonderful Canadian National Railway hotel of 1935, known as 'the castle on the river'. When it opened as the **Bessborough**, it was considered the most modern and luxurious hotel in Canada with automatic elevators and a telephone, bath and shower in every room. These days it is the **Delta Bessborough** (306-244-5521; www.marriott.com; 601 Spadina Cres E; r from $150;

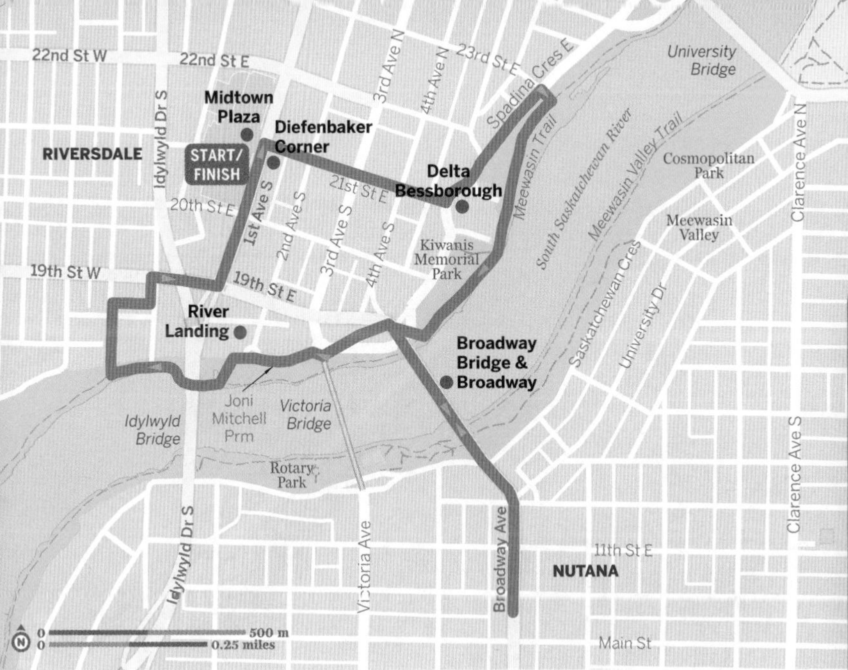

) by Marriott and is a major landmark in Saskatoon that can be seen from all over the city.

The Walk » Head down to the left of 'the castle' to the Meewasin Valley park that lines the South Saskatchewan River. At the Kiwanis WWII Memorial Fountain turn right and wander the trail next to the river. At the Vimy Memorial Bandstand, head up to the Broadway Bridge.

Broadway Bridge & Broadway

This lovely old bridge was built as a 'make-work' project in 1932 during the Great Depression. It links downtown Saskatoon with Broadway, a lively and evocative street of shops, restaurants, theaters and bars a short walk over the bridge. Take a break for a beer at **The Hose & Hydrant Brew Pub** (www.hoseandhydrant.com; 612 11th St E; 11am-late) in the old Firehall building of 1912 or go shopping at **Wanuskewin First Nations Gift Store** (810 Broadway Ave; 10am-5:30pm Mon-Sat). Local Joni Mitchell played her first professional singing gig in Broadway in 1962.

The Walk » Wander back over Broadway Bridge and turn left. Admire the Gabriel Dumont frontiersman statue, the Saskatoon Founders statue of Chief Whitecap and John Lake; carry on along Joni Mitchell Promenade to River Landing.

River Landing

This riverfront redevelopment program has produced a lovely promenade, a play area for families, a rest area with cafe, the **Remai Modern art gallery** (306-975-7610; www.remaimodern.org; 102 Spadina Cres E; adult/child $12/10; 10am-5pm Tue-Sun), **Persephone Theatre** (306-384-7727; www.persephonetheatre.org; 100 Spadina Cres E) and ongoing development through to the **Saskatoon Farmers Market** (306-384-6262; www.saskatoonfarmersmarket.com; 414 Ave B S; market 10am-3pm Wed & Sun, 8am-2pm Sat, cafes 10am-3pm Tue-Sun) on the far side of Idylwyld Dr. The Farmers Market has cafes open even on non-market days.

The Walk » Walk back up 1st Ave to get back to Midtown Plaza.

Ontario

THE BREATHTAKING FOUR-SEASONAL PALETTE OF ONTARIO'S VAST WILDERNESS, endless forests and abundant wildlife awaits. Ontario is larger than France and Spain combined, and its scenic roads and byways wind past more than 250,000 lakes, including the Great Lakes bordering the US that contain a fifth of the planet's fresh water.

Whether you want to reconnect with nature or lose yourself in the excitement of the most multiculturally diverse and socially cohesive region on earth, you've come to the right place. Let Ontario surprise you with the beauty of her scenery and welcome you with the warmth of her people. The joy of Canada, and Ontario particularly, is in how easy it is to leave the city behind and and find yourself surrounded by nature.

Point Pelee National Park (p224) Marsh boardwalk

Ontario

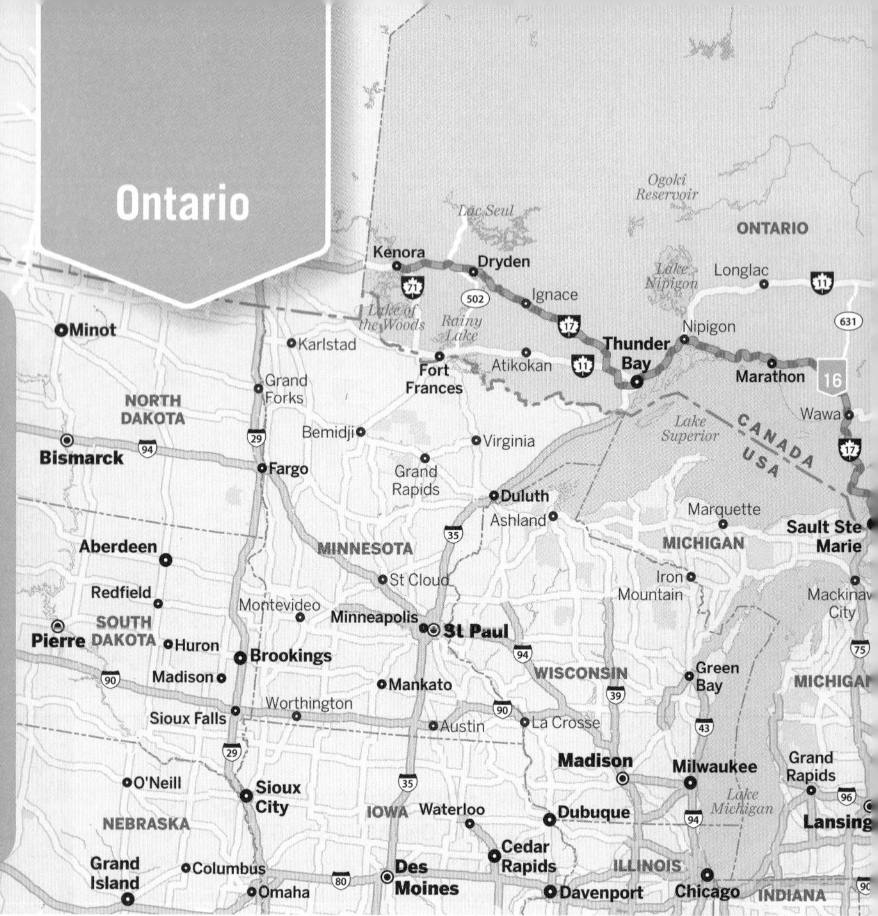

16 **Lake Superior Coastline 7 Days**
Islands, forested reserves and sandy beaches on a photogenic lakeside drive.

17 **People & Culture Loop 4–5 Days**
A cultural showcase complete with Mennonite markets, First Nations museums and a world-class theater.

Classic Trip 18 **The Niagara Peninsula 3 Days**
Vineyards, botanical gardens and one awe-inspiring set of waterfalls.

19 **The Kawarthas 5 Days**
Hiking, canoeing and relaxing amid the region's myriad lakes.

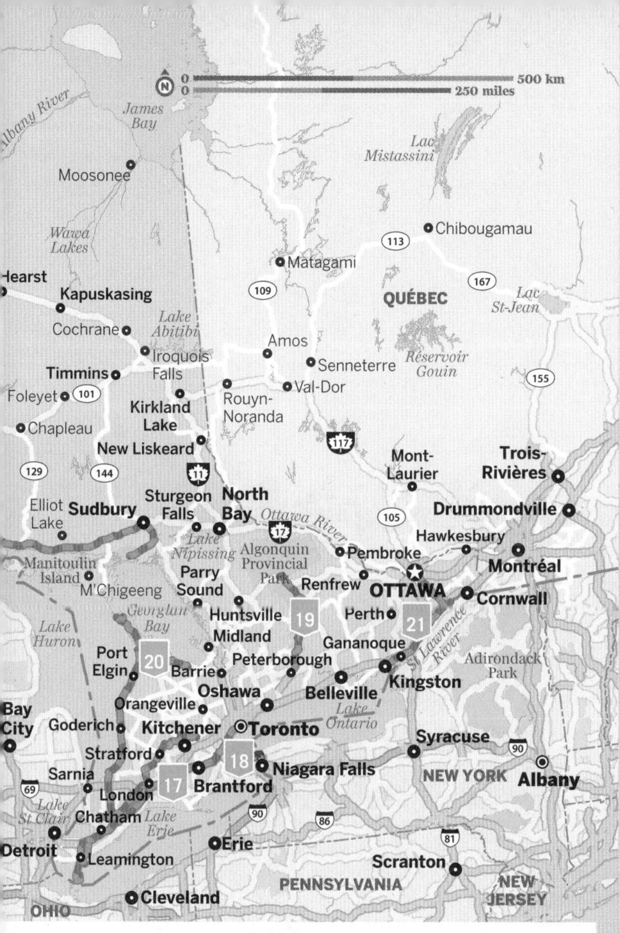

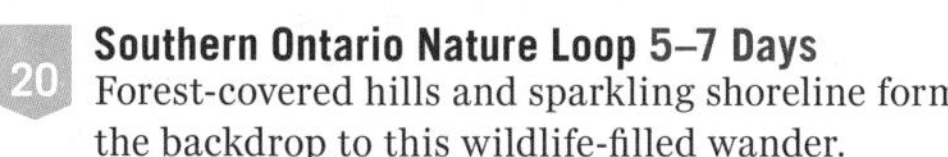

20 Southern Ontario Nature Loop 5–7 Days
Forest-covered hills and sparkling shoreline form the backdrop to this wildlife-filled wander.

21 Thousand Island Parkway 7 Days
Charming villages and great dining accompany the captivating lake-and-island scenery.

DON'T MISS

Table Rock

Admire the magnificent views of thundering Horseshoe Falls from this lofty lookout. Feel the mist on Trip 18

Slate Islands

Spotting herds of caribou and wild geological formations while paddling the shoreline of this archipelago formed by meteorites. See it on Trip 16

St Jacobs

Munching on baked goods, browsing craft shops and filling up the picnic basket at a massive farmers market in this serene Mennonite village. Go there on Trip 17

Algonquin Provincial Park

Looking for moose among the evergreen forests, crystal-clear streams and sparkling lakes of this 7600-sq-km reserve. Hit the trail on Trip 19

Pelee Island

Relishing the quiet beauty of this bucolic island with its wooded trails, swimming beaches and vineyards. Catch the ferry there on Trip 20

Lake Superior Coastline

On this drive packed with forest and coastlines, you'll experience friendly locals, stunning scenery and abundant wildlife.

TRIP HIGHLIGHTS

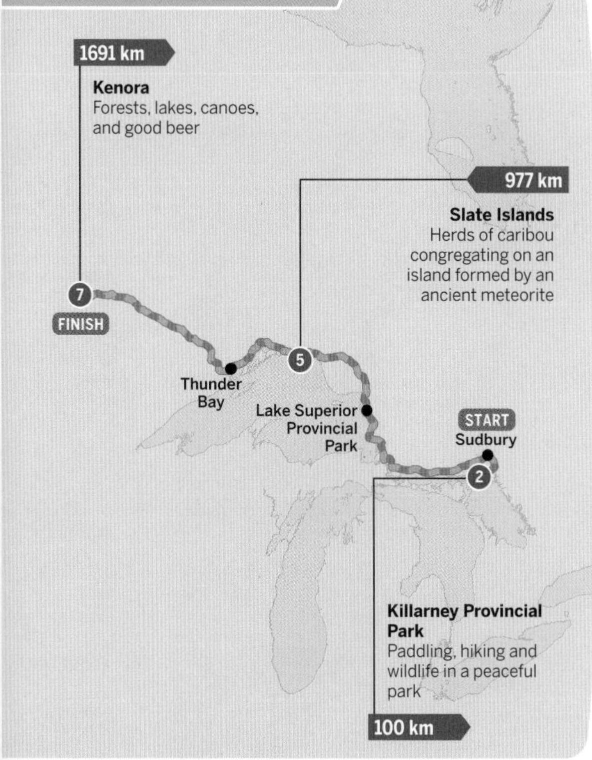

1691 km
Kenora
Forests, lakes, canoes, and good beer

977 km
Slate Islands
Herds of caribou congregating on an island formed by an ancient meteorite

7 FINISH

Thunder Bay

5

Lake Superior Provincial Park

START Sudbury

2

Killarney Provincial Park
Paddling, hiking and wildlife in a peaceful park
100 km

7 DAYS 1691KM/ 1051 MILES

GREAT FOR...

BEST TIME TO GO

June to September for sunny weather and lack of snow on the roads.

ESSENTIAL PHOTO

In front of the lighthouse on Slate Island.

BEST FOR OUTDOORS

Canoeing in Killarney Provincial Park.

Killarney Provincial Park (p185) Exploring the park by canoe

16 Lake Superior Coastline

There will be times on this route when you won't see another car for hours. And that's part of the appeal – enjoy the solitude while cruising alongside Lake Superior, keeping an eye out for moose.

1 Sudbury

While Sudbury is not the most idyllic town in northwestern Ontario, it is an important stop to understand what makes this part of the province tick: mining. Most towns in the region started as mining towns and Sudbury's **Dynamic Earth** (☎705-522-3701; www.dynamicearth.ca; 122 Big Nickel Rd; adult/child $22/18, parking $6 in summer; ⏰9am-6pm Apr-Oct) museum is a great intro to nickel mining and the area's history. Be sure to get your picture

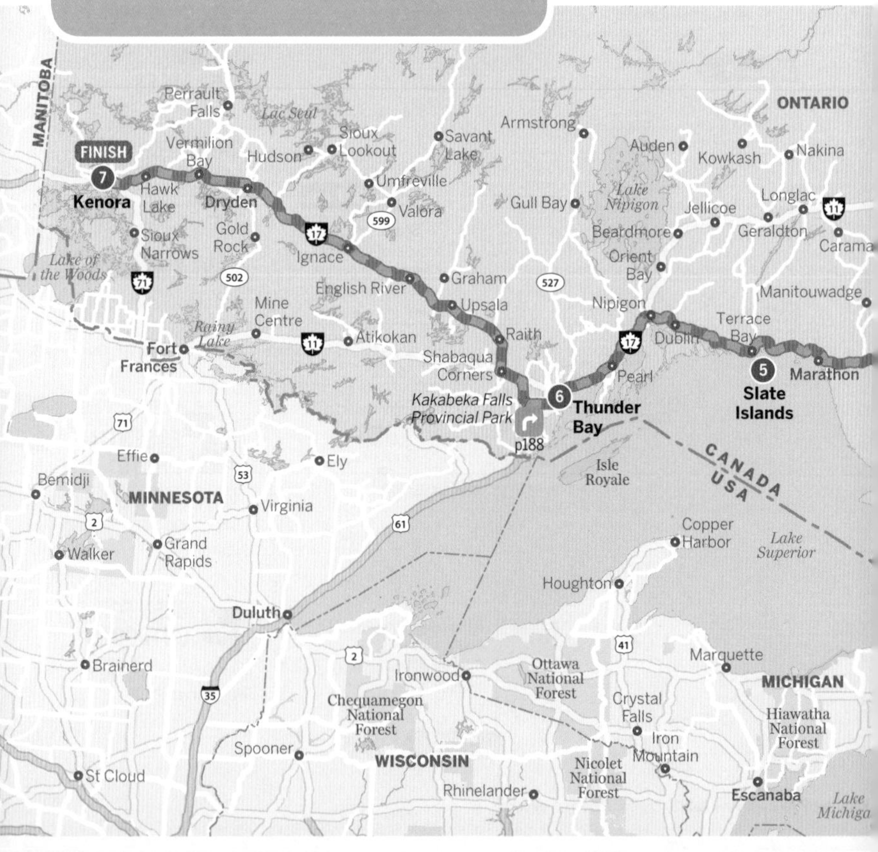

in front of the Big Nickel, a 9m-high stainless steel replica of a 1951 Canadian nickel ($0.05).

If geology is not your thing, Sudbury has a burgeoning food scene. It's easy to while away the rest of the day at **46 North Brewing Corp** (705-586-1870; www.46north.ca; 1275 Kelly Lake rd; 11am-7pm Tue-Sat) followed by dinner at the **Respect is Burning** (705-675-5777; www.ribsupperclub.com; 82 Durham St; mains $19-35; 5-10pm Mon-Thu, to 1am Fri & Sat;) supper club.

The Drive » Be on the lookout for moose and other wildlife on the 100km drive to Killarney Provincial Park, particularly after turning onto Hwy 637 from the Trans-Canada Hwy. The road is quite simple to follow; just keep driving until you reach the park gate.

p189

2 Killarney Provincial Park

Killarney Provincial Park (705-287-2900; www.ontarioparks.com/park/killarney; Hwy 637; day use per vehicle $13, campsite $37-53, backcountry camping adult/child under 18yr $12.50/6, yurt $98, cabin $142; year-round) is an outdoor lovers' dream with 645 sq km of nature. There is a variety of hikes, from the 80km La Cloche Silhouette Trail for experienced hikers to a short 2km loop on the Granite Ridge Trail. This trail also offers great views of the La Cloche mountains and climbs to a lookout point on a ridge overlooking the park.

Those looking to really get away from it all can rent a canoe from **Killarney Kanoes** (888-461-4446, toll-free 705-287-2197; www.killarneykanoes.com; 1611 Bell Lake Rd; canoe rental per day $27-43; 8am-8pm May-Oct) and explore the many lakes in the park. Most people canoe around Bell Lake, but you can also rent canoes at George Lake, Carlyle Lake and Johnny Lake access

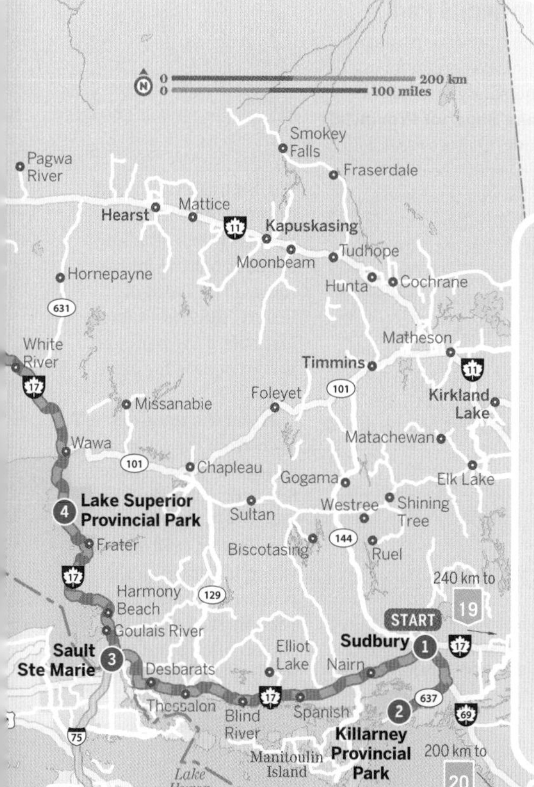

LINK YOUR TRIP

19 The Kawarthas

Extend your return journey south by picking up this lakes region trip at Algonquin Provincial Park, a 250km drive east of Sudbury along Hwy 11/17.

20 Southern Ontario Nature Loop

From Sudbury, drive 3½ hours south to the start of this scenic nature ramble that takes in mountains, beaches, islands and lush nature reserves.

points. Spend the night at Killarney Mountain Lodge (p189), unwinding in the sauna after your day in nature.

The Drive » It's next to impossible to get lost driving in northwestern Ontario as there's only one main route. To get to Sault Ste Marie, follow Hwy 637 for 65km until you reach the Trans-Canada Hwy, turn right and follow Hwy 17 for around 350km to reach 'the Soo'.

p189

3 Sault Ste Marie

A stopover in Sault Ste Marie is like a rite of passage for northern Ontario road trippers. It's not the prettiest city, but it is a friendly place with loads of character. Stay over at the Water Tower Inn (p189) where the kids can play in the pools and the parents can head to the pub. There isn't much nightlife here, but that's a good thing because you'll need to get up early the following day if you're keen to make a day trip through the Lake Superior forest on the **Agawa Canyon Tour Train** (ACR; 855-768-4171, reservations 800-461-6020; www.agawatrain.com; 129 Bay St; adult/child $101/55; late Jun–mid-Oct). It departs at 8am and returns at 6pm and is a must-do in autumn as the foliage turns to magnificent shades of red and orange.

The Drive » The 120km drive to Lake Superior Provincial Park is where you really start to get a feel for the region. Follow Hwy 17 as it hugs the coast, offering fleeting glimpses of the sparkling lake through the forest. Stop in at Harmony Beach if the sun is shining to stretch your legs.

p189

4 Lake Superior Provincial Park

The fjord-like passages, thick evergreen forest and sandy beaches of **Lake Superior Provincial Park** (park office 705-856-2284, visitors centre 705-882-2026; www.ontarioparks.com/park/lakesuperior; Hwy 17; day use per vehicle $14.50/5.25/7.50, campsites $42-47, backcountry camping adult/child $10.17/5.09; Agawa Bay Visitors Centre 9am-8pm Jun-Sep, to 5pm late May & early Oct) are straight out of a postcard.

DARYL BENSON/GETTY IMAGES ©; DESIGNER: TED SZILVA

The highway runs right through the park, but it's well worth stopping to check out the hiking routes. The Twilight Resort (p189) is situated just before the park and is a great base for exploration.

If you can drag yourself away from the resort and its idyllic views of Lake Superior, enter the park and head to the Agawa Bay Visitors Centre, which is 9km from the southern boundary. The friendly staff can advise you on hiking and take you out to the Agawa Rock Pictographs. The ochre-red drawings are

TOP TIP: GAS STATIONS

Hwy 17 is fairly well serviced, but it's still a long route. Be sure to fill up whenever you fall below the half-way point to make sure you don't get stuck. Gas is also much cheaper on indigenous reserves, of which there are many in northern Ontario.

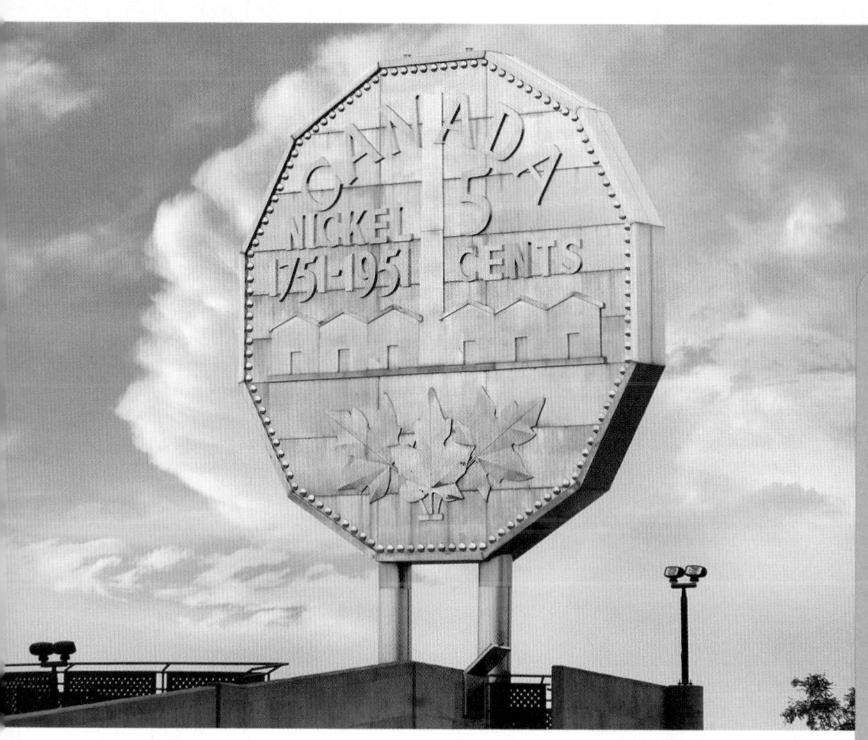

Sudbury (p184) The Big Nickel

a spiritual site for the Ojibwe and are reported to be between 150 and 400 years old.

The Drive » One of the most picturesque drives in Ontario, the 360km drive to Terrace Bay cuts through Lake Superior Provincial Park. The road forks after the park – keep left to stay on Hwy 17 instead of heading into Wawa on Hwy 101. You'll head into the Ontario countryside before veering west again to the next stop, Terrace Bay.

p189

5 Slate Islands

Formed by an ancient meteorite, inhabited by herds of woodland caribou and featuring pristine paddling opportunities... Need we say more? The **Slate Islands** (807-825-3403; www.ontarioparks.com/park/slateislands), located 13km south of Terrace Bay, is one of the top places in the region for a unique experience. Either grab a ferry, or sign up for a paddling tour with **Naturally Superior Adventures** (800-203-9092, 705-856-2939; www.naturallysuperior.com; 10 Government Dock Rd, Lake Superior; courses from $50, day trips from $137). Don't forget your camera as caribou sightings are virtually guaranteed, and you'll no doubt want a selfie in front of the 100-year-old lighthouse. Geology buffs will also love the 'shatter cones', conical shapes in the rocks formed by the impact of a meteorite 400-800 million years ago.

The Drive » You can get to Slate Islands from Terrace Bay either by ferry or your own paddling steam. Once back from the islands, the trip to the next stop is fairly straightforward – follow Hwy 17 for 220km until you reach Thunder Bay.

6 Thunder Bay

For a long time, Thunder Bay was referred to by road trippers as 'a wonderful place to drive

DETOUR: KAKABEKA FALLS PROVINCIAL PARK

Start: 6 Thunder Bay

Kakabeka Falls Provincial Park (807-473-9231; www.ontarioparks.com/park/kakabekafalls; Hwy 11-17; day use per vehicle $11.25) is a very short, but worthwhile detour on your trip from Thunder Bay to Kenora. The 40m-high waterfall is one of Ontario's highest and is quite stunning to view in early spring during the thaw, but also amazing to observe in winter when the falls are encrusted in thick ice. There are also hiking trails in the park, including parts of the 1.3km hike that were historically used by the first Europeans in Canada to portage around the falls.

The falls are also important in Ojibwe folklore. Legend has it that Green Mantle, an Ojibwe princess, pretended to be lost in the region to fool the rival Sioux, which was preparing for an attack, and then led them to their deaths over the falls to prevent the massacre. It's said that you can see Princess Green Mantle when looking into the mist of the falls.

From Thunder Bay, drive along Hwy 11/17 on the way to Kenora for 29km until you see a turnoff to the left towards the falls. To rejoin the main trip, just exit the park and turn left – you'll be back on the main highway and heading towards Kenora.

through.' Until recently, there were few reasons to stop in the city other than to sleep. But a food culture has emerged in this isolated city. **Tomlin** (www.tomlinrestaurant.com; 202 Red River Rd; mains $16-28, cocktails $10-14; 5-10pm Tue-Sat) serves some of the best food this side of Toronto, and the **Sleeping Giant Brewing Co.** (www.sleepinggiantbrewing.ca; 712 Macdonell St; 11am-10pm Mon-Sat, from noon Sun;) makes great ales and lagers, which you'll find all around town. On top of being an ideal base for exploring the vast forests and lakes in northern Ontario, Thunder Bay also offers local hiking up **Mt McKay** (www.fwfn.com; Mission Rd; per vehicle $5; 9am-10pm mid-May–early Oct). You can also learn more about the region's history at **Fort William Historical Park** (www.fwhp.ca; 1350 King Rd; adult/child $14/10; 10am-5pm mid-May–mid-Sep, tours every 45min).

The Drive » Take Hwy 17 out of Thunder Bay, which is called Hwy 11/17 for close to 500km until you reach Kenora. There will be one major split in the road, where Hwy 11 veers off towards Atikokan – stay right.

7 Kenora

Our final stop brings you to the end of northern Ontario before you either head back or on to Winnipeg, Manitoba. It's a quaint little town known for its cottages, lakes and hunting. On the drive, be sure to stop at **Busters Barbeque** (www.bustersbbq.com; Fort Vermillion, Hwy 17, Vermilion Bay; mains $10-16; 11am-8pm May-Sep; P) in Vermilion Bay for a good ol' Canadian BBQ lunch (about 100km before Kenora) and then adjourn for the day by the lake or at **Lake of the Woods Brewing Company** (807-468-2337; www.lowbrewco.com; 350 Second St, Kenora; 11am-12am Mon-Wed, to 1am Thu-Fri May-Sep, 11am-11pm Oct-Apr;) for some beers and more BBQ (you won't go hungry in this part of Ontario). If you don't feel like paddling yourself around the many small lakes and inlets, take a sunset dinner cruise on the **MS Kenora** (www.mskenora.com; Off Bernier Dr; adult/child 3-10yr $31/17; May-Sep) to explore a fraction of the 14,500 islands that dot the Lake of the Woods.

Eating & Sleeping

Sudbury ❶

Motley Kitchen Cafe **$**

(705-222-6685; www.themotleykitchen.com; 70 Young St; mains $14; 11am-3pm Tue-Fri, 10am-2pm Sat & Sun) Sudbury's most popular brunch spot serves unlikely dishes such as breakfast burritos, Welsh rarebit, Croatian crêpes, and French toast stuffed with bananas and Nutella or strawberries and yogurt. Plates are garnished with home fries and fresh fruit, and weekday lunches of tacos, sandwiches and salads are served. The only drawback is that its popularity can mean the food arrives slowly.

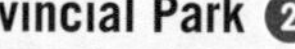

Killarney Provincial Park ❷

Killarney Mountain Lodge Lodge **$$**

(705-287-2242, toll-free 800-461-1117; www.killarney.com; 3 Commissioner St, Killarney; d/ste incl breakfast from $200/269; May-Oct;) In Killarney village, this wooden compound with waterfront accommodations is run by canoeing, kayaking and hiking buffs **Killarney Outfitters** (705-287-2828, toll-free 888-222-3410; www.killarneyoutfitters.com). The beautiful pine rooms, cabins, suites and chalets all provide a luxurious experience of the wilderness, with views of George Island across the Killarney Channel. There's a restaurant and a sauna for unwinding after a long day in the park.

Sault Ste Marie ❸

Arturo's Ristorante Italian **$$$**

(705-253-0002; www.arturoristorante.com; 515 Queen St E; mains $24-45; 5-10pm Tue-Thu, to 10:30pm Fri & Sat) In A shimmering jewel in a dismal downtown strip, decades-old Arturo's is the kind of place you remember after your vacation has ended. Atmospheric but unpretentious with soft lighting, starched white tablecloths and European scenes on the walls, the Italian mains such as veal marsala and chicken piccata (with lemon and capers) are tender and succulent, the sauces rich, and wines appropriately paired.

Water Tower Inn Hotel **$$**

(705-949-8111, toll-free 888-461-7077; www.watertowerinn.com; 360 Great Northern Rd; d from $139; P) Offering a resort for the price of a room, the Water Tower continues to stand out from the rest with its indoor and outdoor pools, grill-house bar-restaurant, pizza-slinging pub and treatment spa. The variety of room types includes family rooms and suites. It's just off Hwy 17, 3.5km northeast of downtown; shuttles to town and the airport are available.

Lake Superior Provincial Park ❹

Voyageurs' Cookhouse Canadian **$**

(705-882-2504; www.voyageurslodge.com; Hwy 17, Batchawana Bay; mains $10-15; 7am to 9pm Apr-late Oct) The restaurant at **Voyageurs' Lodge** serves Lake Superior trout or whitefish with chips, mammoth homemade burgers and the best tastin' gravy for miles. The folksy wood-clad dining room, replete with snowshoes, paddles, hockey shirts and canoe bill holders, makes a pleasant pit stop.

Twilight Resort Campground **$**

(705-882-2183; www.facebook.com/twilighttesort; Hwy 17, Montreal River Harbour; tent sites $30-42, cabins from $100; May-Oct) This wonderfully isolated spot, just south of the entrance to Lake Superior Provincial Park, was once a camp for Mennonite war objectors sent to work on the Trans-Canada Hwy. Today, it's a no-frills, back-in-time holiday spot with eight fishing cabins and plenty of campsites, all facing due west for jaw-dropping sunsets over Lake Superior.

crocs

People & Culture Loop

A country drive showcasing the diversity of Ontario's cultural and historical landscape – from First Nations and Old Order Mennonite communities, to world-class theater festivals and small-town shindigs.

TRIP HIGHLIGHTS

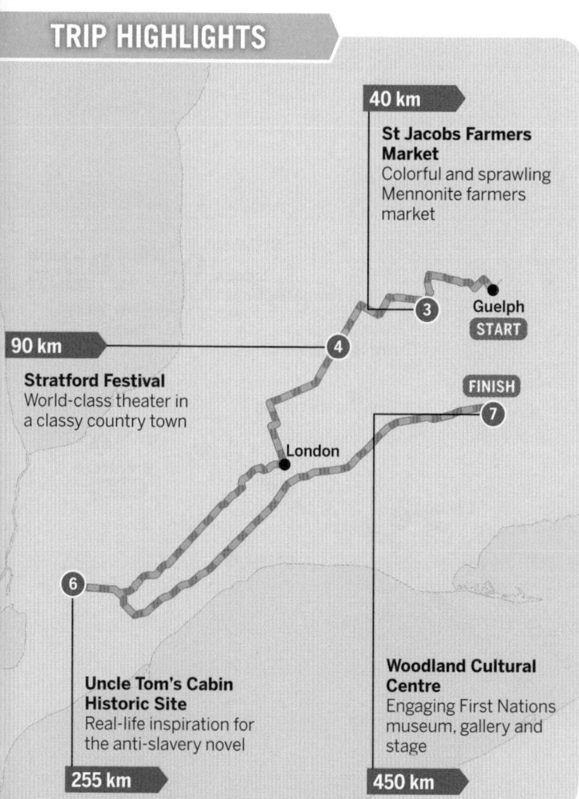

4–5 DAYS
450KM/280 MILES

GREAT FOR...

BEST TIME TO GO

June to August for gardens in bloom and festivals of all kinds.

ESSENTIAL PHOTO

Standing in St Jacobs Farmers Market, a sea of colors and cultures meeting all around.

Exploring the unique amalgam of southern Ontario's cultures.

t Jacobs Mennonite woman selling fresh produce at the Farmers Market (p193)

17 People & Culture Loop

Ontario's small communities fit the classic farm-town mold, with country roads lined with corn fields and dairy farms. They also bubble with ethnic histories and cultural traditions. You'll see the signs: horse-drawn buggies, festivals alive with the sound of bagpipes and deerskin drums, swans floating past theater-bound locals. Stop and explore these unexpected treasures, each a little different, all imbued with Canada's famous charm.

1 Guelph

A walkabout through the vibrant university town of Guelph, just one hour west of Toronto, is worth every step. Start at the **Art Gallery of Guelph** (519-837-0010; http://artgalleryofguelph.ca; 358 Gordon St; suggested donation $5; noon-5pm Tue-Sun; P), a stark, Edwardian-era building housing a remarkable collection of Canadian art, especially Inuit artists. Outside, meander through its **Sculpture Garden**, Canada's largest, with

39 works of contemporary art dotting its manicured grounds. Stroll north on Gordon St, passing the Speed River and a lovely wooden pedestrian bridge, kayakers paddling underneath. At MacDonnell St, look west to the **Basilica of Our Lady Immaculate** (☎519-824-3951; www.churchofourlady.com; 28 Norfolk St; ⏰7am-4:30pm Mon-Fri, 6-9pm Thu, to 6:30pm Sat, 8:30am-1pm Sun; P), a Gothic-Revival–style church, whose twin spires have towered over the city since 1888. Turn right and stop for a pint at the **Brothers Brewing Co**, one of five local breweries serving up delicious craft brews; in the summertime, jump on the free **Guelph Beer Bus** (www.guelph.beer; 15 Wyndham St N; ⏰May-Aug) to visit the others. Walk north on Wyndham St, Guelph's bustling main drag, to **Bookshelf** (☎519-821-3311; www.bookshelf.ca; 41 Québec St; ⏰bar 5pm-midnight Tue-Thu, to 2am Fri & Sat, bookstore 9:30am-9pm Mon-Sat, 11am-7pm Sun), a bookstore and cultural hub hosting indie films, poetry slams, live music and more.

The Drive » Take Hwy 6 north from downtown Guelph into farm country for 6.2km. At Regional Rd 30, turn west, doglegging onto Waterloo Regional Rd 86 west, where horse-drawn buggies begin sharing the road. In Elmira, turn left onto Regional Rd 21. At the roundabout 6.6km later, take the first exit onto Regional Rd 17, eventually turning left on King St.

p198

2 St Jacobs: Town

The heart of Mennonite country since the 1830s, the quaint village of St Jacobs provides a window on this tight-knit community. Just a few blocks long, it's lined with shops, boutiques and the **Stone Crock Bakery** (☎519-664-3612; www.stonecrock.ca; 1402 King St N, St Jacobs; items from $2; ⏰6:30am-6pm Mon-Sat, 11am-5:30pm Sun) – one of the most visited bakeries in the region, known for its homestyle pies, tarts and breads. Stop by **The Mennonite Story** (☎519-664-3518; https://stjacobs.com; suggested donation $5; ⏰11am-5pm Mon-Sat, from 1:30pm Sun Apr-Dec, weekends only Jan-Mar), an interpretive center, to dive deep into the Mennonite history, religion and culture, including the reasons behind their simple dress and resistance to modern-day conveniences like motorized vehicles and radios. Afterwards, walk a couple blocks to the **Maple Syrup Museum** (☎800-265-3353; www.stjacobs.com; 1441 King St N, St Jacobs; ⏰10am-6pm Mon-Sat, noon-5pm Sun; P), located in a repurposed mill. A dated but fascinating museum, it has exhibits about the process of making this sweet treat, from pre-colonial times to the present, including antique buckets, taps and tanks.

The Drive » Head 3.5km south on King St, passing expansive farms using horse-pulled machinery. Look out for slower-moving carriages driven by men in straw hats and dark coats, often carrying entire Mennonite families.

3 St Jacobs: Market

The largest year-round market in Canada, **St Jacobs Farmers Market** (☎519-747-1830; http://stjacobsmarket.com; 878 Weber St N, St Jacobs; ⏰7:30am-3:30pm Thu & Sat year-round, also 8am-3pm Tue Jun-Aug; P) is open every Thursday and Saturday (plus Tuesday in the summer). Head to the biggest barn-like building, which houses

LINK YOUR TRIP

18 The Niagara Peninsula

From Brantford, it's just 24km to Hamilton, where the QEW highway whisks you through wine country and the area around Niagara Falls.

20 Southern Ontario Nature Loop

Join this spectacular route encompassing craggy cliffs and turquoise waters, birding and beach time from Hwy 6 in Guelph or Hwy 401 in London.

two floors of vendors – mostly Mennonite women in long, simple dresses and bonnets. Nosh your way through the first floor, where farm-fresh produce, homemade jams and maple syrup, all sorts of cheeses, smoked meats and freshly baked breads are sold. Upstairs, handcrafted items like wooden toys, quilts, soaps and baby clothes are available – perfect for mementos. In the warmer months, the market spills outside, buggies parked behind each stall. Two additional buildings on-site house a modern flea market and quick-eats food stalls serving up international dishes and sweet treats – an intersection of cultures.

The Drive » Take Lobsinger Line Rd west towards St Clements village, continuing until it ends in Regional Rd 5, about 16km away. Turn left, passing corn fields and Mennonite homes with signs advertising homemade goods such as jams and quilts. Continue for 15.5km as the road becomes Regional Rd 7. Turn left on Perth Country Rd 119, straight to Stratford 17km away.

4 Stratford

A country town turned cultural star, Stratford is internationally acclaimed for its **Stratford Festival** (519-273-1600; www.stratfordfestival.ca; 55 Queen St; Apr-Nov), a theater extravaganza of plays and musicals, including Shakespeare's works, on four distinct stages. Shows often sell out so buy tickets early if you can. If not, head straight to the main box office at the Festival Theatre for a chance at rush tickets. Afterwards, take a leisurely stroll west along the verdant banks of the **Avon River**, as swans float past. Along the way, peruse the works of local artists and craftspeople at **Art in the Park** (http://artintheparkstratford.ca; Lakeside Dr btwn Front St and North St; 10am-5pm Wed, Sat & Sun May-Sep), a juried showcase during the summer. Continue west along the river to the Shakespearean Gardens, a brilliant display of parterre gardens, flowering trees and stone bridges. From here, head east along bustling Ontario St to Downie St and the historic Stratford Market Square with its high-end boutiques and restaurants. Pop into the **Stratford Tourism Alliance** (519-271-5140, 800-561-7926; www.visitstratford.ca; 47 Downie St; 10am-6pm Jun-Aug, reduced hours rest of year) for a 'Bieber-iffic' map, a self-guided tour of hometown pop star Justin Bieber's old haunts.

The Drive » Take Hwy 7 west for 35km, through the countryside, past corn fields and dairy farms. Take a left on Country Rd 23 near the town of Granton, zigzagging onto

TOP TIP: TORONTO TOLL ROAD

Though Hwys 401, 403 and QEW lead directly into Toronto, they are often overloaded with vehicles. Consider taking Hwy 407 – a toll road that cuts around the congestion. It can be expensive ($8 to $10, depending on the day and time), but can be worth the time and aggravation saved.

Stratford Shakespearean Gardens

Country Rd 41 until arriving in London, 26km away.

p198

5 London

A pleasant city with leafy parks and a river running through it, London has a burgeoning arts and music scene. Start at Victoria Park, which has manicured gardens and crisscrossing paths, and is the site of summer festivals and outdoor concerts. The most renowned is **Sunfest** (519-672-1522; www.sunfest.on.ca; Victoria Park, 580 Clarence St; Jul), a world music and jazz fest attracting performers from around the world and more than 225,000 festival-goers from across Canada. Afterwards, cut west on Kent St to Harris Park, a riverside expanse where **Rock the Park** (www.rockthepark.ca; Harris Park, 531 Ridout St N; Jul), a thumping rock and rap fest, brings major headliners to town. Walk south along the verdant banks of the river to **Museum London** (519-661-0333; www.museumlondon.ca; 421 Ridout St N; by donation; noon-5pm Tue, Wed & Fri-Sun, to 9pm Thu; P), a sleek museum showcasing the intersection between art and history with its collection of more than 20,000 artworks and artifacts. From here, head east on Dundas St, which is lined with Victorian-era buildings, to see what's on at the **TAP Centre for Creativity** (519-642-2767; www.tapcreativity.org; 203 Dundas St; noon-5pm Tue-Sat), a vibrant arts center focused on emerging players in the visual- and performing arts.

The Drive » Head west on Riverside Dr as it winds through suburbia for 8.5km. Turn left on Oxford St, feeding onto Country Rd 3, cutting through corn fields for 11.5km. In Delaware, take

Country Rd 2 west for 62km, driving through dairy country. At Thamesville, take Country Rd 21 north to Country Rd 15, which leads to the turnoff, 19km west.

✕ 🛏 p199

6 Uncle Tom's Cabin Historic Site

Sitting on a quiet country road outside of Dresden, the fascinating **Uncle Tom's Cabin Historic Site** (☎519-683-2978; www.uncletomscabin.org; 29251 Uncle Tom's Rd, Dresden; adult/child $7/4.50; ⏲10am-4pm Mon-Sat, noon-4pm Sun May-Oct; P) honors Father Josiah Henson, the inspiration behind the title character in Harriet Beecher Stowe's famous novel. An escapee enslaved person, Henson found freedom here with his wife and four children in 1830. Visit their modest clapboard house and learn about the family's day-to-day life as well as Henson's work on the Underground Railroad, leading 118 people to freedom through a network of secret routes and safe houses. As you explore the site, you'll also come across a historic sawmill, smokehouse and church, all belonging to the Dawn Settlement, a black Canadian community that Henson founded in 1841. End your visit at the Josiah Henson Interpretive Centre, which has loads of multimedia exhibits and artifacts related to Henson, the history of enslaved people in the US and their search for freedom in Canada.

The Drive » Head east on Country Rd 17 for 29km, passing through farmlands and the small town of Thamesville. Take the three-lane Hwy 401

LOCAL KNOWLEDGE: REGIONAL FESTIVALS

Towns that travelers might otherwise overlook often have terrific local festivals dedicated to a particular feature of that area.

Kazoo! Fest (https://kazookazoo.ca; ⏲Apr) is a wonderfully irreverent romp through independent music, and a source of great local pride for this university town. Over 40 acts play at locations around town, ranging from indigenous hip-hop duos to coffee-house electronica. Organizers all but promise you'll leave with a new band-crush.

Fergus Scottish Festival & Highland Games (www.fergusscottishfestival.com; Centre Wellington Community Sportsplex , 550 Belsyde Av E, Fergus; adult/child daily pass from $20/free; weekend pass from $60/free; ⏲mid-Aug; 👪) Many Canadians can trace their roots to Scottish immigrants. The Scottish Festival and Highlands Games are Fergus's celebration of that culture, with all its idiosyncrasies, plus a dose of serious competition. Crowd favorites include flipping a log end over end, 'pipe band' showdowns, and something called 'sheaf tossing': hucking a bag of hay over a high bar using a pitchfork.

Oktoberfest (www.oktoberfest.ca; King St btwn Young & Queen Sts, Kitchener; ⏲Oct) is all about the beer. So it's no surprise there's a ceremonial keg-tapping to kick off this long-running event, and that organizers got into trouble, back in 1970, for a poster depicting stein-toting women – it was frowned upon for 'promoting drinking.' The festival features outstanding German brews, fun events and competitions.

Elmira Maple Syrup Festival (www.elmiramaplesyrup.com; 👪) Hundreds of thousands of pancakes, a Guinness world record ('Largest Single-Day Maple Syrup Festival'), even odes to the joys of turning sap into syrup. Early April is indeed Maple Syrup Festival time in the town of Elmira; just be sure to come hungry.

FIRST NATIONS POET

Emily Pauline Johnson, also known by her indigenous name Tekahionwake, was born in 1861 on the **Six Nations of the Grand River** reservation near Brantford, to a revered Mohawk chief and a British mother. Steeped in both cultures, Johnson was a poet, fiction writer and performer, whose work often examined her mixed-race heritage. She toured for 17 years all over Canada, the US and England, giving dramatic readings of her poems and stories. Her live shows became wildly popular; she often wore indigenous clothing for the first half and a western gown for the second. Johnson's first book, *The White Wampum*, was published during the height of her fame; she published two more volumes of poetry and a book of First Nations stories before her death, and another two collections of short stories were published posthumously. After her death, as sensibilities changed, Johnson's work was criticized as racially insensitive. But recently, there's growing recognition that Johnson's poems, despite their flaws, contain sophisticated and heartfelt renderings of her experience as a First Nations woman, and of the plight of impoverished indigenous families. Part of her poem, 'Autumn's Orchestra', was read during the opening of the Vancouver Olympic winter games in 2010, evoking the sublime magic of an autumn forest.

Johnson's birthplace, now the **Chiefswood National Historic Site** (http://chiefswoodnhs.ca; 1037 Brant County Hwy 54, Ohsweken; self-guided/guided tour $7/10; ⌚10am-3pm Tue-Sun May-Oct; P), offers an insight into this First Nations poet. Open for tours, the grounds are also used for powwows and other community events.

east for 125km, a quick ride, cutting through the center of southwestern Ontario. After Woodstock, merge onto Hwy 403. Take Exit 33, heading south on Brant Av for 7km through Brantford; it eventually becomes Mohawk Av.

7 Brantford

In southern Brantford near the **Six Nations of the Grand River** (www.sixnations.ca) reservation, **Woodland Cultural Centre** (☎519-759-2650; http://woodlandculturalcentre.ca; 184 Mohawk St; adult/child $7/5; ⌚9am-4pm Mon-Fri, 10am-5pm Sat; P) is a remarkable nonprofit dedicated to protecting and promoting the voice of First Nations people. Explore the main building, which houses a gallery with rotating exhibits of contemporary indigenous art; an excellent museum examining the history of the Iroquois and Algonquin peoples; and a stage for performance art, concerts and talks. Next door, peek into the looming Mohawk Institute Residential School, once a government-sanctioned boarding school used to force assimilation upon First Nations children from 1828 to 1970. Afterwards, head 650m west to **Her Majesty's Chapel of the Mohawks** (http://mohawkchapel.ca; 291 Mohawk St; $7; ⌚10am-3pm Tue-Sun May-Oct; P), the oldest Protestant church in Ontario (established in 1785), gifted to the Mohawk people by the British crown for their assistance during the American Revolution. It's a simple, white, clapboard church – don't miss the eight stained-glass windows depicting historical events from the Iroquois people's past.

The Drive » Follow Mohawk Av east around the forested edges of town for 2.5km. Turn right onto Colborne St E and left onto Garden Av, a quiet residential street 1.2km away. Continue for about 3km as it becomes a larger thoroughfare, passing farms and factories. This leads straight to the three-lane Hwy 403 and directly to Toronto, 95km away.

Eating & Sleeping

Guelph 1

Crafty Ramen — Ramen $

(☎519-824-8330; https://craftyramen.com; 17 Macdonell St; ramen $14-18; ⊙11:30am-9pm Mon-Sat;) A tiny, bustling, diner-style eatery serving steaming bowls of ramen packed with ingredients like pork *chashu*, charred corn and lotus chips. Noodles are made in-house and many ingredients are locally sourced. For several years, the owners both lived, traveled and studied everything ramen in Japan before setting up shop in Guelph. Cold ramen as well as vegan 'adaptabowls' are created too.

Artisanale — French $$

(☎519-821-3359; www.artisanale.ca; 214 Woolwich St; mains $15-36; ⊙11:30am-3pm & 5-9pm Wed-Fri, 5-9pm Sat, 10am-2pm Sun) With an emphasis on fresh seasonal local produce, this French country kitchen has a wonderfully simple lunch menu and is popular for its Wednesday and Thursday $35 prix-fixe dinners. Or create your own unfixed selection from irresistible hors d'oeuvres and sides, and hearty mains such as duck confit with crispy potatoes.

Bollywood Bistro — Indian $$

(☎519-821-3999; www.thebollywoodbistro.com; 51 Cork St E; mains $12-20; ⊙11:30am-2:30pm & 5-9pm Mon-Fri, noon-2:30pm & 5-10pm Sat, 5-9pm only Sun) Guelph's favorite Indian restaurant uses a traditional tandoor oven to create well-known dishes with a contemporary twist, with influences from Nepal, Delhi and Mumbai. The creamy butter chicken is one of the best around, and there's a $10 lunch special on weekdays too..

Norfolk Guest House — B&B $$

(☎519-767-1095; www.norfolkguesthouse.ca; 102 Eramosa Rd; r incl breakfast $139-279;) A central location and sumptuously furnished, themed bedrooms, most with en suite Jacuzzi, make the Norfolk – a delightfully restored Victorian home – the logical choice for luxury B&B accommodations in downtown Guelph.

Comfort Inn — Motel $$

(☎519-763-1900; www.choicehotels.ca; 480 Silvercreek Pkwy; d incl breakfast from $130;) Tastefully renovated, this well-maintained motel offers great-value, contemporary-style rooms including a self-serve breakfast. Located about 5km north of the town center.

Stratford 4

Sirkel Foods — Cafe $

(☎519-273-7084; https://sirkelfoodsstratford.com; 40 Wellington St; mains $6-13; ⊙8am-3pm Mon-Sat;) A hopping cafe in the central square, Sirkel is a go-to for locals and visitors in the know. Breakfast is traditional, while lunch brings creative salads and sandwiches made with homemade bread and items like house-cured salmon and fancy cheeses. Arrive early to avoid a wait or just take your meal to go.

The Red Rabbit — Bistro $$$

(☎519-305-6464; www.redrabbitresto.com; 64 Wellington St; mains $16-26, prix-fixe $56-62; ⊙11:30am–2:30pm daily, 5-7pm Tue & Wed, 5-9pm Thu-Sat;) Inventive dishes, global influences and a cool, laid-back vibe are what drive the experience at Stratford's 'it' restaurant. Order à la carte for lunch and after-theater service – the chicken and waffles dish is unreal – or double down for the prix-fixe dinner, with a seasonally changing menu that features dishes like kung pao sweetbreads, and bacon and foie-gras pâté.

Three Houses Bed & Breakfast Inn — B&B $$$

(☎519-272-0722; www.thethreehouses.com; 100 Brunswick St; ste incl breakfast $225-695;) Two Edwardian town houses, a garden carriage house and an 1870s Italianate house make up this meticulous, almost over-the-top 18-room inn. No detail has been spared in decorating these light-filled spaces – even the luggage racks match the quirky individual room designs. A saltwater pool and secret oasis garden add relaxing touches.

The Parlour Inn — Hotel $$

(877-728-4036; www.theparlour.ca; 101 Wellington St; d from $169;) This handsome hotel occupies a heritage building in the center of town, near the Avon Theatre, and has been fully refitted to a high standard – most rooms are spacious and light filled. There's a pub downstairs with a lovely patio, but it doesn't get too rowdy.

London 5

Covent Garden Market — Market $

(519-439-3921; www.coventmarket.com; 130 King St; items from $2; 8am-7pm Mon-Sat, 11am-5pm Sun;) This humongous, chapel-shaped market will whet and satisfy any appetite. There's a permanent collection of delis, bakeries, chocolate shops, fresh-produce stalls and world-cuisine eateries, plus seasonal and pop-up vendors. Check out the sunny, busker-fueled buzz on the patio on Thursday and Saturday mornings (May to December only). Free on-site parking on weekends (2 hours) and weekdays (30 minutes).

The Root Cellar — Cafe $$

(519-719-7675; http://rootcellarorganic.ca; 623 Dundas St; mains $12-19; 11am–9pm Tue-Wed, to 10pm Thu & Fri, 9am-10pm Sat; ; 2, 20) It's all about local and organic food at this boho-chic cafe, with from-scratch creations like free-range water buffalo burgers, kale salad with hemp hearts and quinoa, and vegan pizza. There are lots of gluten-free options too. Located in the up-and-coming Adelaide neighborhood.

Zen Gardens — Vegetarian $$

(519-433-6688; www.zengardenslondon.com; 344 Dundas St; mains $11-18; 11:30am-2:30pm Tue-Sat, 5-9pm Tue-Sun;) This Asian vegetarian restaurant downtown will impress vegetarians and their most hardened carnivorous mates alike. Tofu, mushrooms, and sauced-up soy-and-gluten meat feature heavily. Combinations, served in Japanese bento boxes and costing the same as a main, offer the best value.

Hotel Metro — Boutique Hotel $$

(519-518-9000; www.hotelmetro.ca; 32 Covent Market Pl; d from $169;) Rooms in this oh-so-cool boutique hotel in the heart of downtown have hardwood floors, exposed-brick walls, rainfall showers, deep soaker tubs and plenty of interesting design elements to keep you entertained. Book online for discounted rates.

Fanshawe Conservation Area Campground — Campground $

(519-451-2800; www.fanshaweconservationarea.ca; 1424 Clarke Rd; campsites $39-49, reservations $13;) Convenient camping within the city limits is possible in this 1200-hectare conservation area complete with hiking and biking trails, fishing, kayaking, and even a pool. Located across from Fanshawe Pioneer Village. Kayak and canoe rentals (from $35 per four hours) are available.

Classic Trip

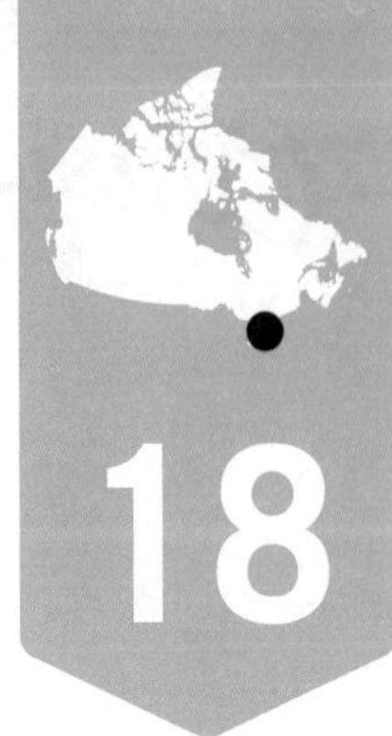

The Niagara Peninsula

A trip through the Niagara Peninsula will offer majestic views, historic sights, vineyards and even a casino – perfect for a short getaway or a side trip from Toronto.

TRIP HIGHLIGHTS

62 km

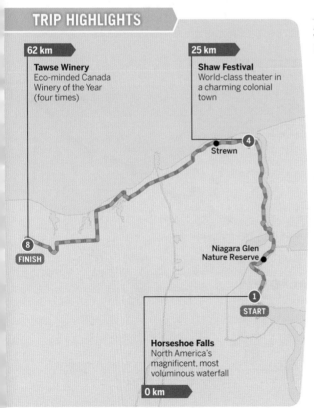

Tawse Winery
Eco-minded Canada Winery of the Year (four times)

25 km

Shaw Festival
World-class theater in a charming colonial town

4
Strewn

8
FINISH

Niagara Glen Nature Reserve

1
START

Horseshoe Falls
North America's magnificent, most voluminous waterfall

0 km

3 DAYS
62KM/39 MILES

GREAT FOR...

BEST TIME TO GO

June to September for warm days and the grape-harvest season

ESSENTIAL PHOTO

On the thundering edge of Horseshoe Falls, from Table Rock viewpoint.

BEST FOR WATERFALLS

Powerful and awe-inspiring, Niagara Falls are a must-see.

Horseshoe Falls (p203) View of the falls from Table Rock

Classic Trip

18 The Niagara Peninsula

The Niagara Peninsula is a feast for the senses. The thunder of water as it cascades over a towering cliff; the delicate brush of mist during a catamaran trip along the falls; the sight of a colonial-era soldier prepping a musket for battle; the cheers and applause at Ontario's most celebrated stages; and the sweet, viscous flavors of ice wine, grown in vineyards stretching as far as the eye can see.

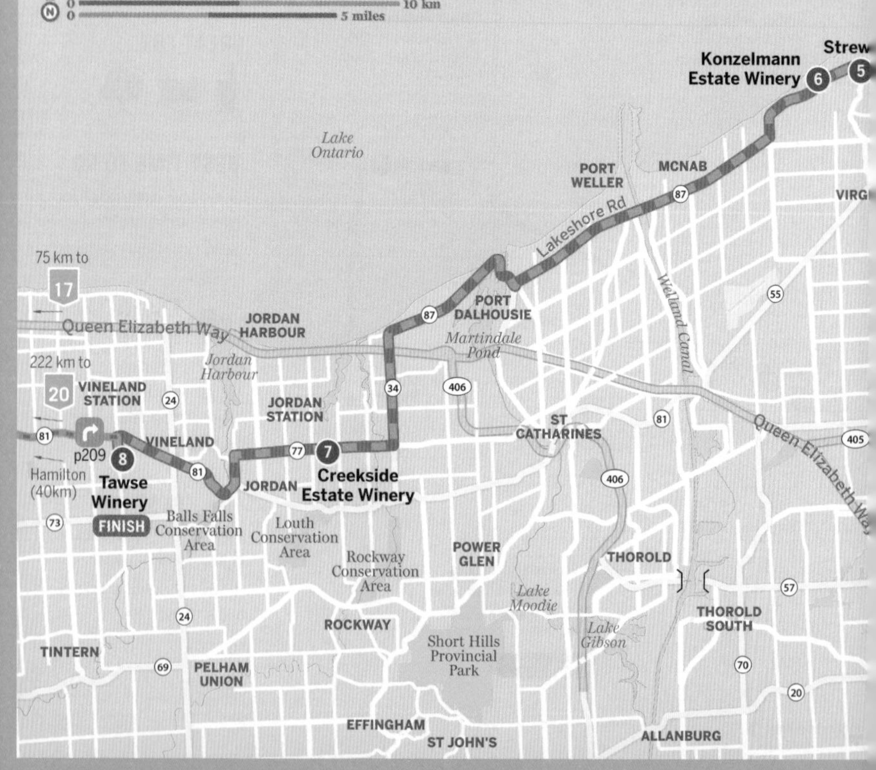

1 Niagara Falls

Horseshoe Falls is the shining star of the town of Niagara Falls – a 670m-wide, U-shaped waterfall, North America's highest-volume cascade, moving 8500 bathtubs worth of water per second over its ridges to the frothing Maid of the Mist Pool below. Enjoy the magnificent views and the falls' cooling mist from **Table Rock** viewpoint. Afterwards, walk north for 1km along the curving Niagara Parkway, taking in the views of the smaller but still impressive **American Falls** and **Bridal Veil Falls**, to the **Hornblower Niagara Cruise** (www.niagaracruises.com; 5920 Niagara Pkwy; adult/child $26/16, fireworks cruise $40; ⏲8:30am-8:30pm May-Sep, to 5:30pm Oct) port. Here, a 20-minute catamaran ride gets you up-close-and-personal with all three of Niagara Falls' cascades; prepare to don a poncho and somehow still get drenched. After this, dry off as you walk up the hill to the 158m **Skylon Tower** (☎905-356-2651; www.skylon.com; 5200 Robinson St; adult/child $16.25/10.50; ⏲9am-10pm Mon-Thu, to 11pm Fri-Sun; P), with its jaw-dropping views of the falls and, on a clear day, Toronto. For some grown-up fun, try your luck at **Niagara Fallsview Casino** (☎888-325-5788; www.fallsviewcasinoresort.com; 6380 Fallsview Blvd; ⏲24hr) across the street. Jackpots won, head to the **Niagara Falls History Museum** (☎905-358-5082; https://niagarafallsmuseums.ca; 5810 Ferry St; adult/child $5/4, Thu 5-9pm free; ⏲10am-5pm Tue, Wed & Fri-Sun, to 9pm Thu; P 👪), 1.5km northwest on Ferry St. A well-curated museum, it has excellent multimedia exhibits on the transformation of the area from an indigenous settlement to a modern-day tourist zone; stories of daredevils and coverage of the War of 1812 are especially engaging. End your visit in famously kitschy **Clifton Hill**, 1.5 km east, a street filled with wax museums, creepy fun houses and arcades.

The Drive » Follow Niagara Parkway north for 8km, winding along the verdant road that Winston Churchill once described as 'the prettiest Sunday afternoon drive in the world.' On one side, you'll see souvenir shops eventually give way to Victorian-era homes; on the other, the grassy cliffs above the Niagara River and the Niagara River Recreation Trail that runs alongside it.

✕ 🛏 p210

LINK YOUR TRIP

17 People & Culture Loop

Add on a country drive through Ontario, exploring its charming towns and fascinating cultures; pick up this tour at Brantford, just 55km west of the QEW.

20 Southern Ontario Nature Loop

After making the final stop at Tawse winery, drive 2½ hours north to the start of this serene around the stunning Bruce Peninsula.

TOP TIP: PARKING IN NIAGARA FALLS

Parking is limited and expensive in Niagara Falls. Before handing over a bucket of cash at a random lot, swing by the **Niagara IMAX Theatre** (☎905-358-3611; www.imaxniagara.com; 6170 Fallsview Blvd; IMAX adult/child $13/9.50, Daredevil Exhibit adult/child $8/6.50, combo adult/child $15.50/13; ⏲9am-9pm; P 👪). It has an open-air lot next to the Skylon, and its parking rates are typically a steal – around $10 per day – and the location is tops.

2 Niagara Glen Nature Reserve

The **Niagara Glen Nature Reserve** (☎905-354-6678; www.niagaraparks.com; 3050 Niagara Pkwy; ⏲Reserve dawn-dusk, Nature Centre 10am-5pm Apr-Nov; P 👪) is a local hikers' fave with 4km of trails leading through the Carolinian forest, down the gorge to the fast-moving Niagara River. Start at the **Nature Center**, to get a trail map and to learn about the terrain, flora and fauna. Then take the 17m-high steel staircase to the start of the trail system. At the bottom, turn north (left) on the limestone-lined **Cliffside Trail** to **Terrace Trail**, a short but steep hike with massive boulders and stone steps that lead to **River Trail**. Head south (right) along the relatively flat trail to take in the beech and tulip trees, the white-capped river, and the towering gorge walls. Finally, dog-leg on **Eddy Trail** to take the challenging **Whirlpool Trail** (expect boulders and uneven terrain) to the fast and furious, cyclone-like whirlpool in the river – look for the gondola over it – or just loop back to the Cliffside Trail, to head back.

The Drive » Continue 650m north along Niagara Pkwy.

3 Botanical Gardens & Butterfly Conservatory

Forty hectares of beautifully landscaped gardens filled with thousands of perennials, sculpted shrubs and towering trees make the **Botanical Gardens** (☎905-356-8119; www.niagaraparks.com; 2565 Niagara Pkwy; butterfly conservatory adult/child $16/10.25, gardens free; ⏲10am-4pm Mon-Fri, to 5pm Sat & Sun Sep-Jun, 10am-7pm Sun-Wed, to 8pm Thu-Sat Jul & Aug; P 👪) a visually inspiring and soothing stop. Meander along the leafy paths, passing the parterre garden and the must-see Victorian rose garden with more than 2400 roses – a popular photo op. In the central part of the gardens sits the Butterfly Conservatory, a high-glass-domed building with a rainforest-like setting – plants, waterfalls, heat and all – with more than 2000 delicate butterflies flitting about, often landing on visitors. Of the 45 species of butterflies living here, 60% are from Costa Rica, El Salvador and the Philippines; the rest are raised in an on-site greenhouse.

TOP TIP: HORSESHOE FALLS PHOTO OP

A little-known but great spot to take a photo of Horseshoe Falls is inside the **Table Rock Visitor Centre**. Head to the 2nd floor and you'll find a bank of floor-to-ceiling windows high enough to overlook the falls and the crowds in front of it. It's a magazine-worthy vista!

NIAGARA FALLS & HYDROELECTRIC POWER

Though nowhere near the tallest waterfalls in the world (that honor goes to 979m Angel Falls in Venezuela), Niagara Falls is one of the world's most voluminous, with more than 168,000 cubic meters of water going over its crest lines every minute. At least, that is, from 8am to 10pm during the peak tourist season, April to September.

In fact, the water making it over the falls – Horseshoe, American and Bridal Veil – only accounts for 25 to 50% of their capacity. The rest is diverted into hydroelectric plants on both sides of the border, depending on the time of day and year: Sir Andrew Beck Station Stations #1 and #2 in Ontario and Robert Moses Hydro Electric Plant in New York. Built across from each other, the hydroelectric plants divert water from the Niagara River using a system of gates located 2.6km before the falls. The water is run through hydro tunnels on both sides of the border to turbines that generate electricity; the water is eventually returned to the Niagara River, just above Lake Ontario. The entire process is governed under the 1950 Niagara Treaty, an international agreement that assures water levels and a fair division of electricity (Ontario actually gets a little more). Power generated from the Niagara River accounts for 25% of all electricity used in Ontario and New York State – a remarkable figure, especially considering Toronto and New York City are included.

For visitors to Niagara Falls this means that, depending on the time of day and year, the falls may appear more or less voluminous. The highest volume any time of year is from April 1 to October 31, during daylight hours. The rest of the year, or at night, the falls look remarkably smaller but the street lights, somehow, seem to shine a little brighter.

The Drive » Continue 15km north on the leisurely Niagara Parkway, passing the Floral Clock, a popular pit stop for photos. As you travel north, the houses become grander, the parkway less crowded and vineyards begin to dot the landscape. Eventually, Niagara Parkway becomes Queen's Parade.

❹ Niagara-on-the-Lake

As you enter the pretty colonial town of Niagara-on-the-Lake, the spiked walls of **Fort George** (www.pc.gc.ca/fortgeorge; 51 Queens Pde; adult/child $11.70/free; ⏲10am-5pm May-Oct, noon-4pm Sat & Sun only Nov-Apr; P 🚻) appear on your right. Dating to 1797, it was the site of several bloody battles during the War of 1812. Wander among well-restored buildings, watch musket demonstrations and learn about the daily life here from chipper staff in historic dress. Just north on Queen's Parade sits the main theater of the **Shaw Festival** (www.shawfest.com; 10 Queens Pde; ⏲Apr-Dec, box office 9am-9pm). A highly respected and popular theater company, it's named after the playwright George Bernard Shaw, whose plays were showcased during the company's first season in 1962. Today, the festival stages plays and musicals from the Victorian era to the modern day in three theaters around town. Splurge on tickets, if you can. From here, head two blocks north on Queen's St (aka Queen's Parade) to the **clock tower**, a WWI memorial. This marks the center of town, an area with flower-lined streets, 19th-century-storefront boutiques and colonial-era homes. Window shop and explore!

The Drive » Head northwest on Mary St, a road that runs parallel to Queen St, five blocks away. Stay on the small road – which becomes Lakeshore Dr – for 5km, as it winds through verdant countryside, passing modest homes and vineyards.

✕ 🛏 p210

Classic Trip

LANZELLOTTO ANTONELLO/AGF/UNIVERSAL IMAGES GROUP VIA GETTY IMAGES ©

ANJELIKAGR/SHUTTERSTOCK ©

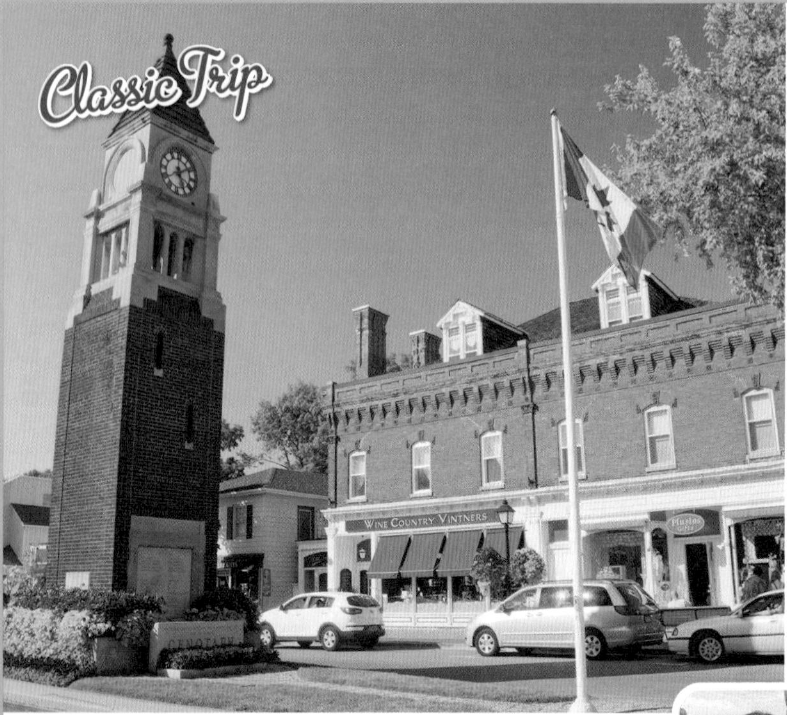

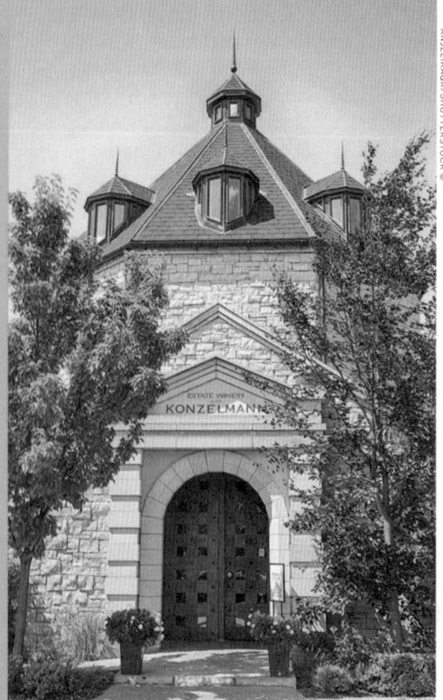

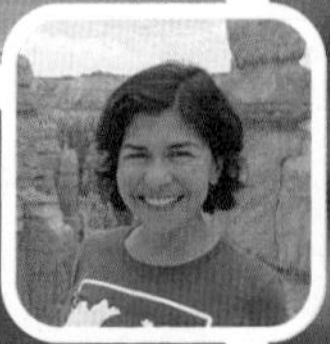

WHY THIS IS A CLASSIC TRIP
LIZA PRADO, WRITER

This trip takes you to one of Canada's most iconic sites: Niagara Falls, a thundering, awe-inspiring set of cascades. Few people realize you can experience them on land, water, and even from high above. But the Niagara Peninsula offers more than the falls – including an exploration of leafy trails and botanical gardens, a beautiful colonial town and a landscape of vineyards.

Above: Niagara-on-the-Lake (p205)
Left: Konzelmann Estate Winery
Right: Botanical Gardens & Butterfly Conservatory (p204)

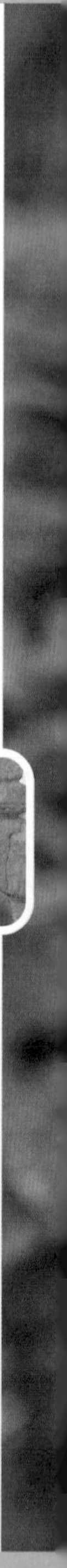

VICTOR KORCHENKO/GETTY IMAGES ©

5 Niagara-on-the-Lake Wine Country: Strewn

Tucked into the west side of Lakeshore Dr is **Strewn** (☎905-468-1229; www.strewnwinery.com; 1339 Lakeshore Rd; tastings $10-15; ⏰10am-6pm). The building itself isn't particularly charming – a modernized and expanded canning facility – but the wines are award-winning and the staff welcoming. Pop in for a wine tasting – its oaky Terroir Chardonnay and sweet Gewurztraminer are the ones you can't miss. In the summer, consider booking a class at its modern **Wine Country Cooking School** (☎905-468-8304; www.winecountrycooking.com; 1339 Lakeshore Rd; classes from $225; ⏰10am-3pm or 4-9pm Sat) to hone your cooking skills or to learn new dishes that pair well with wines.

The Drive » Continue northwest on Lakeshore Dr for 1km.

6 Niagara-on-the-Lake Wine Country: Konzelmann Estate Winery

On the east side of Lakeshore Dr sits **Konzelmann Estate Winery** (☎905-935-2866; www.konzelmann.ca; 1096 Lakeshore Rd; tours $10-35; ⏰10am-6pm, tours May-Sep), one of the oldest vineyards in the region

(established 1984) and the only one set on Lake Ontario. The views over its vineyards to Toronto's skyline are spectacular. Tours of its facilities, including tastings in its elegant, chateau-like building, are a treat. The late-harvest vidal and ice wines are the ticket here.

The Drive » Continue on Lakeshore Dr for 17km, passing over the Welland Canal and through the town of Port Dalhousie until it meets Rte 34. Turn left and continue for 3.4km, passing over Queen Elizabeth Way (QEW) highway, vineyards and orchards of Twenty Valley Wine Country dotting the landscape. At Rte 77, a quiet country road, turn right and drive for 2km.

7 Twenty Valley Wine Country: Creekside Estate Winery

A modest entrance belies the spunky and entrepreneurial spirit of **Creekside Estate Winery** (☎905-562-0035; www.creeksidewine.com; 2170 4th Ave, Jordan Station; tastings from $10, tours $12; ⏲10am-6pm May-Nov, 11am-5pm Dec-Apr, tours at 2pm May-Oct). Come here for a down-and-dirty tour of the cellars and vineyards (really, bring boots) or an afternoon on the patio with live music and a glass of wine in hand. It can also provide picnic lunches to enjoy in the vineyards, including a blanket and wine. Try the Sauvignon Blanc and Syrah, the focus of Creekside's experimental wine portfolio.

The Drive » Turn left on Rte 77, continuing until 19th St. Turn left, passing through the charming village of Jordan; immediately after Jordan House, turn right on King St. Stay on King St for about 4.5km as it curves through farmland and over creeks, eventually passing the outskirts of Vineland. Turn left on Cherry Av, staying on it for just 0.6km.

p211

LOCAL KNOWLEDGE: WINE FESTIVALS

Niagara Peninsula is home to several wine-related festivals (www.niagarawinefestival.com and www.twentyvalley.ca) throughout the year. Time your visit to be able to attend one of these locals' faves in the wine country of Niagara-on-the-Lake and its neighbor Twenty Valley:

Niagara Homegrown Wine Festival (June) Kicks off Niagara's summer wine-tasting season with two weekends of wine-and-food-pairing events; typically more than 30 wineries participate.

Niagara Grape and Wine Festival (September) Celebrates the harvest season with two weeks of wine tastings and concerts around the region as well as two parades in St Catherines.

Niagara Icewine Festival (January) Showcases Ontario's stickiest, sweetest ice wines during a 16-day winter festival, including winery tours, street festivals and a gala party at the **Niagara Fallsview Casino** (p203).

Twenty Valley Winter WineFest (January) Celebrates Twenty Valley wines in Jordan Village during one weekend of tastings, live music and outdoor events like ice wine puck shoot-outs and barrel-rolling competitions.

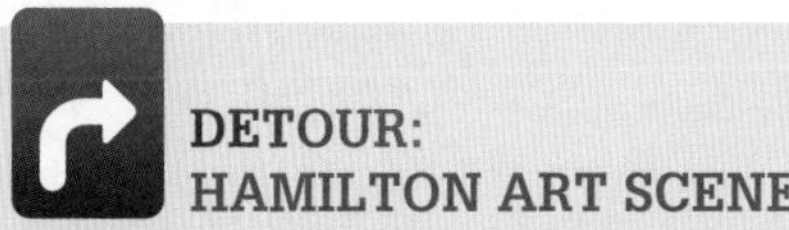

DETOUR: HAMILTON ART SCENE

Start: 8 Twenty Valley Wine Country: Tawse Winery

Once a gritty steel-industry hub, downtown Hamilton today has a welcoming air and a burgeoning arts scene. James St N is a good place to explore, with its independent galleries, quirky boutiques and hipster eateries. On the second Friday of each month, James St hosts **Hamilton Art Crawl** (https://tourismhamilton.com; James St N; 7-10pm, 2nd Fri of every month), a veritable party zone when crowds of locals and visitors meander among galleries and shops that are open late, art studios with open doors and street performers doing their thing. If quiet art appreciation is more your style, pop into the **Art Gallery of Hamilton** (AGH; 905-527-6610; www.artgalleryofhamilton.com; 123 King St W; special exhibitions adult/child $13.25/8.85, free 1st Fri of month; 11am-6pm Wed & Fri, to 8pm Thu, noon-5pm Sat-Sun, to 8pm first Fri of month; P) instead. A sleek affair in the heart of downtown, the collection focuses on modern and 19th-century Canadian art. The gallery offers free tours, led by knowledgeable docents, covering the highlights and hidden gems of the collection; offered at 1pm on Wednesdays and on weekends, the tours are highly recommended if you can swing it. Afterwards, stop for lunch at the nearby **Hamilton's Farmers Market** (905-546-2096; https://hamiltonfarmersmarket.ca; 35 York Blvd; 8am-6pm Tue, Thu & Fri, 7am-5pm Sat; P). You'll find vendors selling fresh and local produce, meat and bread of all sorts at this 180-year-old market; head to the ground level for a remarkable variety of international fast-food eateries, a snapshot of the diversity of this town.

A stop in Hamilton is best done at the beginning or end of your Niagara Peninsula tour. Located just off the QEW, it's a quick jaunt to **Tawse**, just 43km away.

8 Twenty Valley Wine Country: Tawse Winery

A four-time Canada Winery of the Year winner, **Tawse** (905-562-9500; www.tawsewinery.ca; 3955 Cherry Ave, Vineland; tastings $8, tours $15; 10am-6pm May-Oct, to 5pm Nov-Apr) is a must-stop. Sitting on a rise, its elegant tasting room opens to fields of grapes. Known for its organic wines – the chardonnay is over-the-top delicious – Tawse uses a biodynamic approach to farming, utilising the land's natural cycles and animals like sheep and chickens that feed on leaves and bugs to keep its soil and vines healthy. A tour of the facilities, including tastings, is interesting and worthwhile.

Eating & Sleeping

Niagara Falls 1

✕ Queen Charlotte Tea Room — British $

(☎905-371-1350; www.thequeencharlottetearoom.com; 5689 Main St; mains $8-17, high tea $25; ⊙11am-7pm Wed-Thu, Sat & Sun, to 8pm Fri) Expats craving a decent or even fancy cuppa, cucumber sandwiches, steak and kidney or fish and chips with mushy peas should head straight to this quaint establishment on Main St, near the intersection with Lundy's Lane, for a spot of tiffin! Reservations required for high tea; gluten-free options available.

✕ Napoli Ristorante Pizzeria — Italian $$

(☎905-356-3345; www.napoliristorante.ca; 5545 Ferry St; mains $16-36; ⊙4:30-10pm) Head to Napoli for the best Italian in town, hands down. Delicious pizza, rich pasta, creamy risotto and veal parmigiana all feature on the familiar menu.

✕ AG — Canadian $$$

(☎289-292-0005; www.agcuisine.com; 5195 Magdalen St; mains $18-38; ⊙6-9:30pm Tue-Sun) Fine dining isn't something you find easily at the falls, which makes this fine restaurant at the **Sterling Inn & Spa** so refreshing. Service, decor, presentation and especially the quality of the food all rate highly. It has a seasonal menu featuring dishes like fennel-pollen pickerel, coffee-roasted venison and crispy-skinned trout, sourced locally.

Cadillac Motel — Motel $$

(☎905-356-0830; www.cadillacmotelniagara.com; 5342 Ferry St; r $199; P ❄ ≋) A retro motel just west of the kitsch on Clifton Hill, with rooms that are are modern and chic and have great beds and luxe linens. Each has an classic caddy theme – mostly, a photo mural of vintage Cadillacs or models like the pink Fleetwood convertible made famous by Elvis. Outside, Adirondack chairs add to the throw-back feel. Reservations recommended in the summer.

Park Place Bed & Breakfast — B&B $$

(☎905-358-0279; www.parkplaceniagara.ca; 4851 River Rd; r from $150; P ⊖ ❄ ≋) A gorgeous Queen Anne Revival–style house with a wrap-around verandah and lush gardens is the setting for this B&B. There are just two rooms and a carriage house, each unique in style and layout – one has a Jacuzzi, another a working fireplace – but equally upscale. A full breakfast, prepared to order, is offered each morning. The affable owners are a font of regional information.

Niagara-on-the-Lake 4

✕ Pieza Pizzeria — Pizza $$

(☎289-868-9191; www.piezapizzeria.com; 188 Victoria St; pizzas $17-22; ⊙noon-9pm Tue-Sun; ✐ 👪) A cute turn-of-the-century house repurposed into an even cuter pizzeria with simple, streamlined decor. It's the pizza that speaks loudest here: dough made from imported Italian flour, hand-crushed tomatoes, fresh mozzarella, gourmet toppings and a *pizzaiuolu* (pizza maker) born and raised in Naples. An impressive 2268kg wood-burning oven sits, like a sumo wrestler, in the open kitchen.

✕ Irish Harp Pub — Pub Food $$

(☎905-468-4443; www.theirishharppub.com; 245 King St; mains $14-18; ⊙11am-1am) Loved by locals throughout the Niagara region for its hearty pub meals (think Irish hot pot and corned beef and cabbage), some come just for the Irish 'craic' (fun and conversation) and, of course, beer! There are 23 taps, including Guinness and Irish Harp lager, brewed locally from a traditional recipe. All told, plenty to wet your whistle and fill your tum.

Charles Hotel Hotel $$$

(905-800-474-0632; www.niagarasfinest.com/charles; 209 Queen St; d from $295; P ⊖ ❄ ☏) This lovable, romantic little hotel (c 1832) has a sweeping verandah overlooking the golf course and Lake Ontario. Rooms of varying sizes are sumptuously decorated in a diverse range of styles. Each is wonderfully comfortable – there's even a pillow menu.

Prince of Wales Hotel Hotel $$$

(905-468-3246; www.vintage-hotels.com; 6 Picton St; d/ste from $370/510; P ⊖ ❄ ☏ ≋) Prince of N-o-t-L, an elegant Victorian hotel, was knocked into shape around 1864 and retains much of its period primp: vaulted ceilings, timber-inlay floors and red-waistcoated bellhops. Frills and floral prints seem angled toward the elderly and honeymooners, but it's the perfect spot for anyone looking to splash out in a colonial British sort of way.

Twenty Valley Wine Country: Creekside Estate Winery 7

Peach Country Farm Market Market $

(905-562-5602; www.peachcountryfarmmarket.com; 4490 Victoria Ave, Vineland Station; items from $3; 9am-8pm Jun-Aug, to 6pm Sep & Oct) A country market selling fresh fruit, jams, ice cream and fruit pies, all grown, picked and baked on-site by fourth-generation farmers – a roadside gem!

Bonnybank Bed & Breakfast B&B $$

(905-562-3746; www.bonnybank.ca; 4119 21st St, Vineland Station; r incl breakfast $125-154; P ⊖ ❄ ☏) A stately Tudor-meets-Grimsby-sandstone house in an owl-filled wilderness setting. It's a little off the beaten track but makes for a quiet, comfortable stay. Cash only.

Jordan House Inn $$

(905-562-9591; https://jordanhouse.ca; 3751 Main St, Jordan Station; r from $122; P ❄ ☏) A contemporary inn offering pleasant rooms with comfortable beds and mini-fridges. It's attached to a historic tavern, a popular meeting place with occasional live music – a good place for a bite or beer. On weekends, be sure to ask for a room on the far side of the building.

Inn on the Twenty Hotel $$$

(905-562-5336; https://innonthetwenty.com; 3845 Main St, Jordan; r $219, ste $249-279; P ⊖ ❄ ☏) Inn on the Twenty is an elegant hotel in the charming village of Jordan. Guests enjoy spacious, sunny rooms, each decorated in a modern colonial style with a fireplace and soaker tub. An on-site spa and gourmet restaurant lend it a resort-like feel, but also make it easy to unwind. A perfect getaway. Look for online specials and packages.

The Kawarthas

19

A nature- and water-lover's dream, this trip takes you through Ontario cottage country into the oldest park in the province.

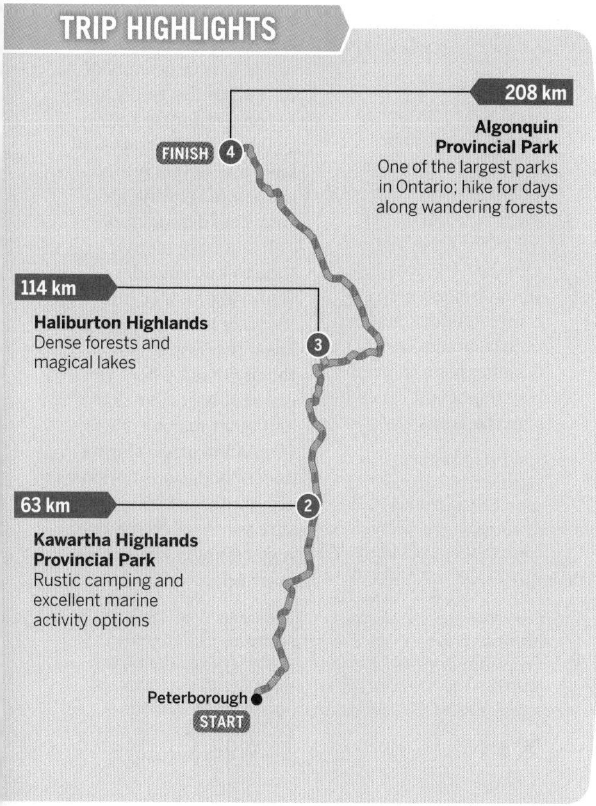

TRIP HIGHLIGHTS

208 km

Algonquin Provincial Park
One of the largest parks in Ontario; hike for days along wandering forests

FINISH 4

114 km

Haliburton Highlands
Dense forests and magical lakes

3

63 km

Kawartha Highlands Provincial Park
Rustic camping and excellent marine activity options

2

Peterborough START

5 DAYS
208KM/129 MILES

GREAT FOR...

BEST TIME TO GO

In September/October as the leaves begin to change color or May/June when the weather is warmer but the summer crowds are less.

ESSENTIAL PHOTO

Swimming or jet-skiing in one of the many lakes

BEST FOR OUTDOORS

Hiking in the Algonquin Provincial Park.

Algonquin Provincial Park (p216) Hikers enjoying the park's autumnal colors

19 The Kawarthas

This is a trip for outdoor and nature lovers who may be short on time. It's a short drive from either Toronto or Ottawa and could work for a long-weekend road trip. While the hiking and activities en route are top notch, the real star here is the drive – a laid-back jaunt through the Kawartha's dense forests, shimmering lakes and small-town vibes.

1 Peterborough

Peterborough has been described as the heart of the Kawarthas, but don't let the fact that it is the biggest city in the area put you off – this is also cabin country and the best accommodations, like Lake Edge Cottages (p217), are on the water's edge. The **Trent-Severn Waterway** (705-750-4900; www.pc.gc.ca/en/lhn-nhs/on/trentsevern; May-Oct), which connects the Kawarthas with Lake Ontario, runs right through Peterborough and offers great canoeing opportunities. Canoeing is so important to the area that the **Canadian Canoe Museum** (866-342-2663; www.canoemuseum.ca; 910 Monaghan Rd, Peterborough; adult/child $12/9.50, 5-8pm Thu free; 10am-5pm Mon-Wed, Fri & Sat, to 8pm Thu, from noon Sun;) is situated here and is undergoing a massive refurbishment in order to better explain to people how important caneoing is to the area's history.

The Drive » Exit Peterborough on Parkhill Rd and drive for 11km until County Rd 28. Follow this road north for 50km, over several small bridges including Young's Point and Burleigh Falls, until you see the turn-off (left) for the Kawartha Highlands Provincial Park. The road, Anstruther Park Rd, forks after 2km – turn right for the access road to Loon Call Lake.

p217

2 Kawartha Highlands Provincial Park

The **Kawartha Highlands Provincial Park** (ext. 261 613-332-3940; https://ontarioparks.com/park/kawarthahighlands; 106 Monck Street, Bancroft; backcountry camping adult/child $13/6) is the second largest in southern Ontario, after Algonquin, but is much more rustic with fewer facilities. Don't expect expensive lodges here, though campsites usually have a loo and picnic tables unless you are backcountry camping. You'll also need your own canoe to access many of the campsites, so it's best to come in for the day, swim in nearby **Loon Call Lake** and have a bite to eat before heading for your next destination.

If you have more time to kill, consider venturing further into the park to **Anstruther Lake**, the largest lake in the park, and where you can rent boats, jet-skis and other marine craft from **Anstruther Marina**. Accommodations options are limited, so make sure you've packed a tent if you plan on staying overnight.

The Drive » Backtrack down Anstruther Park Rd until you reach Hwy 28 and turn left. Travel 21km then turn left onto Country Rd 48. Turn right at the T-Junction and then onto Loop Rd after 2km. Look for a right turn onto S Baptiste Lake Rd after 10km, after which it is a 3km drive to Clarke Rd into the forest.

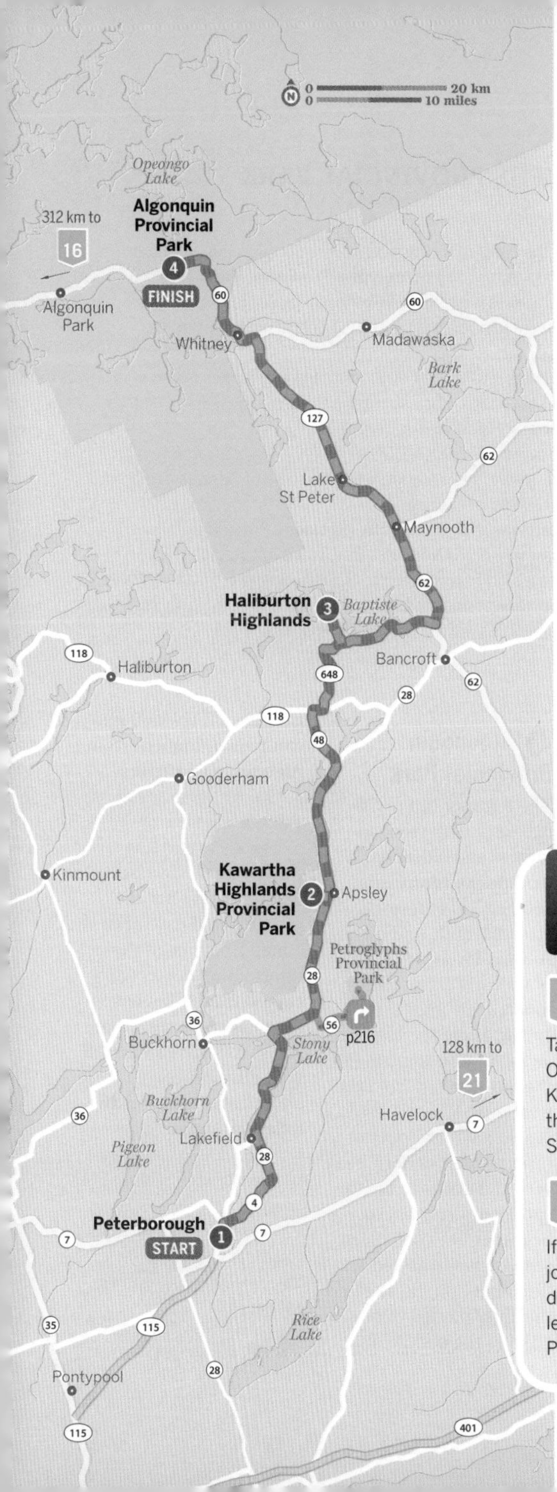

3 Haliburton Highlands

Geologically, the Haliburton Highlands are a southern extension of the Algonquin Provincial Park, with 300 sq km of dense forests and shimmering lakes. Legally, they are not because much of the area is privately owned, including **Haliburton Forest** (☎705-754-2198, 800-631-2198; www.haliburtonforest.com; 1095 Redkenn Rd, Haliburton; day use spring, summer & fall $16, winter $49; ⏰main office 8am-5pm), where you can hike and mountain bike in the summer and snowmobile and dogsled in the winter. There is

LINK YOUR TRIP

16 Lake Superior Coastline

Take your trip further into Ontario's nature up to Kenora. Follow Hwy 11/17 through North Bay and to Sudbury.

21 Thousand Island Parkway

If coming from Ottawa, join up with this trip by driving north before turning left onto Hwy 7 to hit Peterborough 180km away.

DETOUR: PETROGLYPHS PROVINCIAL PARK

Start: ❶ Peterborough

If you leave Peterborough in the early morning, you have more than enough time to take the one-hour round-trip detour to **Petroglyphs Provincial Park** (705-877-2552; www.ontarioparks.com/park/petroglyphs; 2249 Northey's Bay Rd, Woodview; $12.25; 10am-5pm mid-May–mid-Oct), not including time at the park, to view the largest-known concentration of indigenous rock carvings in Canada.

The sacred site, which features carvings of birds, humans and turtles is known as 'The Teaching Rocks' and you can learn more about the Ojibwe carvings and history at the super educational Learning Place Visitor Centre.

The carvings date back to around CE 900–1100 and were not discovered by non-indigenous people until 1954. Today, it is a National Historic Site of Canada and an important link to Canada's precolonial history.

From Peterborough, on your way to the Kawartha Highlands Provincial Park, exit Hwy 28 after 40km onto Regional Rd 56/Northeys Bay Rd. Follow Regional Rd 56 for roughly 11km until you see a sign to turn left into the Petroglyphs Provincial Park. After viewing the paintings, retrace your path back to Hwy 28 and turn right; there is only another 10km until you reach Kawartha Highlands Provincial Park.

also a canopy tour for the adventure-inclined or a canoe lake-crossing tour, which includes entry to the Haliburton Wolf Center on the other side of the lakes. Accommodations are available as well as serviced campsites, so there is an option for different budgets.

The Drive » Retrace your drive until you reach the T-junction and head east for 15km until Hwy 62, where you turn north for Algonquin Park. After 16km you'll reach a junction – keep straight onto Hwy 127, which is signposted for Bancroft. Drive for roughly 38km, and take a left onto Hwy 60, which brings you to the East Gate 9km away.

p217

❹ Algonquin Provincial Park

The Algonquin Provincial Park is the second-largest and oldest park in Ontario, comprising 7600 sq km of forests, streams, cliffs and lakes. Animal lovers are also practically guaranteed moose sightings in the spring along the highway as the moose come to lick the leftover salt from the winter de-icing. There is also a wide variety of birds as well as deer, beavers and otters to try to spot. Paddlers, whether beginner or experienced, are also well-catered for. Beginners should start on the aptly named Canoe Lake in the middle of the park off Hwy 60 and can rent equipment from **Algonquin Outfitters** (800-469-4948; www.algonquinoutfitters.com; canoes per day from $30, 2-day guided trips from $145). Finally, hikers are the most catered for – grab a map from one of the information centers and choose from hikes covering 140km of trail. Once you've exhausted yourself with adventure, splurge a bit and stay at the idyllic **Killarney Lodge** (866-473-5551, 705-633-5551; www.killarneylodge.com; Lake of Two Rivers, turnoff at Km 33 on Hwy 60; cabins per person with full board from $319; mid-May–mid-Oct;) – you've earned it.

p217

Eating & Sleeping

Peterborough 1

Kawartha Dairy — Ice Cream $

(705-745-6437; www.kawarthadairy.com; Park Lane Plaza, 815 High St, Peterborough; small cone $5.20; 9am-9pm) This ice-cream parlor and drive-through sells flavors, including the recommended Moose Tracks, in cones, waffle cones, cups, milkshakes, smoothies and even choc-chip cookie sandwiches. The air-conditioned interior is welcome on a steamy summer day.

Peterborough Farmers Market — Market $

(705-742-3276; www.peterboroughfarmersmarket.com; Peterborough Memorial Centre, 151 Lansdowne St W, Peterborough; 7am-1pm Sat) This community market is a great place to grab a coffee and stop at the C'est Chaud wood-fired pizza stand. It's mostly geared toward tasting and buying local produce, but stands sell bites such as vegan salads, Russian dishes and French toast. In summer, there's also a Wednesday morning outdoor market on Charlotte St between George and Aylmer Sts N.

Lake Edge Cottages — Resort $$$

(705-652-9080; www.lakeedge.com; 45 Lake Edge Rd, Lakefield; cottages from $260;) This outdoorsy resort offers one- and two-bedroom rustic, but well-appointed lakefront cottages with deck and kitchen, on a secluded woody property. There's a wonderful swimming pool, while the cottages have barbecues and electric or gas fireplaces and most have a private hot tub.

Haliburton Highlands 3

Arlington Hotel & Pub — Hostel $

(613-338-2080; www.thearlington.ca; 32990 Hwy 62, Maynooth; HI members dm/s/d/tr/q, without bathroom $25/40/63/85/108, nonmembers $28/45/70/95/120; pub 7pm-1am Fri & Sat;) There's something about this towering century-old monster that makes you just want to disappear into it. In tiny Maynooth, the Arlington is a great place for artists, writers and lonely wanderers who want to escape into their craft for a while: there's nothing here but a rocking pub downstairs.

Algonquin Provincial Park 4

Algonquin Lunch Bar & Restaurant — Diner $

(613-637-2670; 29553 Hwy 60, Whitney; mains $14; 8am-8pm Jun-Sep, 9am-3pm Mon-Thu, to 7pm Fri & Sat, 10am-3pm Sun Oct-May) Attached to Whitney's gas station and shop, this village hub is a good place to insulate yourself with some tea or soup before driving into the woods. Burgers, wraps and more substantial dishes are on the menu.

Wolf Den Nature Retreat — Hostel $

(705-635-9336, 866-271-9336; www.wolfdenbunkhouse.com; 4568 Hwy 60, Oxtongue Lake; dm/s/d without bathroom from $31/48/69) Located 10km outside the West Gate, this outdoorsy hostel-cum-resort offers lodging from dorms to gorgeous eco-cabins accommodating up to six. Guests can also choose between rustic '50s cabins, A-frame bunkhouses, and hostel rooms with shared bathrooms in the cozy central lodge, with its huge kitchen, stunning 2nd-floor lounge and cedar log sauna nearby.

Riverside Motel — Motel $

(705-635-9021; www.riversidemoteldwight.com; Hwy 60, Dwight; r from $135;) Few roadside motels can claim a riverside plot with their own waterfall and swimming hole. Water gurgles under the footbridge leading to the small, neat 11-room motel, where picnic tables set among ponds on the expansive lawn complete the package.

Southern Ontario Nature Loop

Southern Ontario is a region of contrasts, sure to surprise and enthrall, with craggy cliffs and turquoise waters, curving beaches and shipwrecks galore, downhill skiing and some of the country's best birding.

TRIP HIGHLIGHTS

160 km
The Grotto
Beautiful 'sea' cave with green-blue waters

187 km
Flowerpot Island
Tiny island with fascinating limestone formations

Blue Mountain
START

448 km
Pinery Provincial Park
Gorgeous 10km beach fronting Lake Huron

FINISH
Toronto

Pelee Island

634 km
Point Pelee National Park
Birders' paradise plus migrating monarch butterflies in the fall

5–7 DAYS
1075KM/668 MILES

GREAT FOR...

BEST TIME TO GO

March to July for skiing in the earlier months plus good hiking and kayaking conditions for the entire period.

ESSENTIAL PHOTO

On the cliff's edge, overlooking The Grotto and its impossibly turquoise waters.

BEST TWO DAYS

Exploring the Bruce Peninsula's national parks, on land and water.

Bruce Peninsula Park The Grotto (p222), surrounded by crystal-clear turquoise water

20 Southern Ontario Nature Loop

You're standing at the edge of a 'sea' cave. The aquamarine tide surging beneath, the towering cliffs above, the massive expanse of water stretching into the distance – the whole scene screams seashore, yet the sea is a thousand kilometers away. This is Bruce Peninsula, a huge tract of spectacular scenery and rugged pine-clad terrain jutting into Lake Huron, and just one of many jaw-dropping, mind-bending natural treasures in Southern Ontario.

1 Blue Mountain

Ontario's biggest ski resort, **Blue Mountain** (☎833-583-2583; www.bluemountain.ca; 108 Jozo Weider Blvd, Blue Mountains; day lift tickets adult/child from \$74/59, night lift tickets adult/child \$49/44; ⏰9am-9pm) sits just two hours north of Toronto. Spread across 364 acres of Niagara Escarpment, it has breathtaking views over Georgian Bay. In the winter and spring, it boasts **43 ski trails**, ranging from beginner to double black diamond, many of them open at night. The best of the lot are the blue runs, most of them cruisers, some with steeper pitches; the longest, **Butternut** (1.6km), runs alongside the **Badlands Terrain Park**, with expert-level jumps and rails. At the top of the hill, don't miss the scenic **Woodview Mountaintop Skating Trail**, a 1.1km trail of ice, looping through a forest thick with trees. At night, tiki torches light the way, and a fire pit and hot cocoa await you at the start. In summer and fall, the highlights here are leafy **trails**, open to hikers and mountain bikers and accessible by **gondola**, though the more ambitious take steep paths from the base to the trailheads.

The Drive » Take Grey County Rd 19 north to Rte 26, 4km away. Turn left on Rte 26 W, the road running parallel to Georgian Bay, its blue waters occasionally peeking out between the fir trees, which eventually give way to farm country. After 52 km, in Owen Sound, pick up Hwy 6, headed north to Bruce Peninsula National Park, 102km away.

p226

2 Bruce Peninsula National Park: Indian Head Cove & The Grotto

A spectacular 156-sq-km park, **Bruce Peninsula National Park** (519-596-2233; www.pc.gc.ca/brucepeninsula; adult/child $5/free, vehicle US$12; May-Oct; P) is filled with ancient cedar trees, craggy limestone cliffs, rare orchids and stunning turquoise waters. Though there are various entrances, start at **Cypress Lake**. After winding your way through the dense forest to the

LINK YOUR TRIP

17 People & Culture Loop

From Pinery Provincial Park it's just 70km to London, a good place to pick up this tour of Ontario's diverse cultures and rich history.

18 Niagara Peninsula

Tagging on a visit to iconic Niagara Falls is easy. Near Hamilton, take Hwy 403 to QEW highway, which leads straight there.

trailhead, set out on foot along the **Georgian Bay Trail** (1.6km). A wide, flat trail, it leads through the forest, over a creek and past Horse Lake to the shoreline. Once there, the waters seem to glow from between the trees. Eventually you'll hit **Indian Head Cove**, a small, white-boulder beach with huge, flat limestone rocks, and cliffs all around. To the left, high above, is a **natural stone arch**. Continue north along the trail where, steps away, you'll look down and see **the Grotto**, a sea cave surrounded by cliffs, aquamarine water flowing in and an underwater tunnel leading out to Georgian Bay. A rocky tunnel along the cliff allows visitors to corkscrew down – use caution! After exploring, continue north until hitting the **Marr Lake Trail**. This is a more challenging trail – the terrain is uneven and has little signage. If in doubt, look for the impressive **Boulder Beach**, with its seemingly endless number of perfectly round, small white rocks, and turn towards the north side of small Lake Marr, a favorite for water birds. The trail eventually joins the Georgian Bay Trail, which you can follow back to the start.

The Drive » From the Cypress Lake entrance, dogleg on Hwy 6 to Dorcas Bay Rd. Turn left and continue for 1.2km on the small country road.

p226

3 Bruce Peninsula National Park: Singing Sands

On the Lake Huron side of the Bruce Peninsula National Park, **Singing Sands** is another world: a wide sandy beach, with a limestone and alvar shoreline, dunes, marshlands and forests. The unique meeting of ecosystems makes it a botanist's, or simply a flower-lover's, paradise. Here, you'll see a variety of orchids in bloom – 44 types exist in the park – as well as rare plants like the Scarlet Paintbrush and insect-eating Pitcher Plant. A 3km **forest trail** loops through the unique environs. There's also a 200m **boardwalk** overlooking the beach.

LOCAL KNOWLEDGE: ELVIS HAS LEFT THE BUILDING

Every July, the town of Collingswood gets all shook up for its annual four-day Elvis Festival. If you're at Blue Mountain – or anywhere in the vicinity – grab your blue suede shoes and join thousands of Elvis fans for a bout of Elvis-mania. 'Elvis Tribute Artists' or ETAs ('Elvis impersonator' is no longer the term of choice) take the stage in qualifying and semi-final rounds, to earn a spot in festival's grand finale. Judges are looking for authenticity, attention to detail, singing and physical technique and a bit of that special sauce Elvis was known for. Of course, the festival is more than a singing competition – there are street parades, open-mic events, guest performances, dinner concerts, Elvis-themed aerobics and oh-so-much more. Collingswood is a preliminary contest for the Ultimate Elvis Tribute Artist Contest, held every August in Graceland, the King of Rock 'n' Roll's home-turned-museum in Memphis, Tennessee. Winning at Collingswood, or any of the dozens of Elvis festivals and contests around the US, Canada and the globe, earns ETAs a ticket to compete in Memphis. Collingswood's first festival in 1996 drew 30 ETA hopefuls; today the number is more than double that. And the crowds have grown too – the peak year was 2014, with nearly 30,000 fans in attendance and a visit from Priscilla Presley, the King's daughter.

The Drive » Head back to Hwy 6 and turn left for Tobermory, 10km north along the wooded country highway.

4 Tobermory

The charming village of Tobermory is the jumping-off point for **Fathom Five National Marine Park** (☎519-596-2233; www.pc.gc.ca/fathomfive; adult/child $5/free; 👪), home to **Flowerpot Island**. A small island with two trails, it's surrounded by crystal-clear turquoise waters and has dramatic limestone formations (aka the Flowerpots), created from hundreds of years of waves hitting its shores. Book a glass-bottom-boat tour with **Bruce Anchor Cruises** (☎519-596-2555; http://bruceanchor.com; 7468 Hwy 6; adult/child from $34/25; ⏰May-Oct) to access the island; on the way, you'll float over two or three shipwrecks – there are **22 shipwrecks** in Fathom Five – before heading to the island and being dropped off for DIY exploring. After disembarking, head east along the **Loop Trail**, a 2.6km flat, leafy path that follows the shoreline, passing the Flowerpots, and ends at the lighthouse before turning back through the hilly, forested center. Back on the mainland, book a snorkeling or diving trip with **Diver's Den** (☎519-596-2363; www.diversden.ca; 3 Bay St; diving from $85, adult/child snorkeling from $65/45; ⏰May-Oct) to explore more shipwrecks, many in shallow waters. The oldest, a schooner called the *Cascaden*, dates to 1871.

PAUL MURPHY/500PX ©

Flowerpot Island A tugboat passes the eponymous limestone 'flowerpots'

The Drive » Take Hwy 6 south 64km to Red Bay Rd (look for the Top Valu gas station). Take a right, staying on Red Bay for 6km until it hits Hwy 13. Turn left, heading to Southampton, where it merges with Hwy 21. Stay on Hwy 21 for 150km, passing several lakeside villages and towns, the last of which is Grand Bend.

✕ 🛏 p226

5 Pinery Provincial Park

Opening onto gorgeous Lake Huron, **Pinery Provincial Park** (☎info 519-243-2220, reservations 888-668-7275; www.ontarioparks.com; 9526 Lakeshore Rd RR #2; per car $17; ⏰8am-10pm; P 👪) has one of the best **beaches** in Ontario – 10km of wide, sandy beach, emerald waters and picturesque dunes on either side. Perfect for a day of beachcombing or just chilling out on the sand. Inland, explore the Pinery's 6300 acres of protected forest – the largest in Southwestern Ontario. On the south side of the park, take the **Nippissing Trail**, a tough 2km loop that winds its way up and down spectacularly tall dunes covered in rare Oak Savanna, an ecosystem of oak trees, prairie grasses and wildflowers. Stairs are built into the steepest sections of the hike; a platform on the far end reveals a view of the forest's expanse and Lake Huron beyond. Afterwards, rent a kayak and paddle along the **Old Ausable Channel**, a lush wetlands area that cuts through the park's core, home to many of the 325 species of birds spotted here.

The Drive » Take Hwy 21 west for 100km as it cuts south through farmlands, becoming Country Rd 8. Continue south, along country roads until Hwy 401. Head west on Hwy 401 for 50km, exiting on Queen's Line Rd to County Rd 1 south. It eventually hits Country Rd 34 west and Country Rd 33 south to Point Pelee National Park, 37km later.

p227

6 Point Pelee National Park

Opening onto Lake Erie, **Point Pelee National Park** (☎519-322-2365; www.pc.gc.ca; 1118 Point Pelee Dr, Leamington; adult/child $8/free; ⏰park dawn-dusk, visitors center 10am-6pm Mon-Fri, to 7pm Sat-Sun Jun-Aug, reduced hrs rest of year; P) is one of the world's best birding sites. It is set on two migratory paths, and more than 390 bird species have been spotted here – May and September see the highest concentration of birds, especially songbirds and raptors. It also serves as a resting spot for thousands of migrating monarch butterflies – a fluttering vision in the fall. Grab your binoculars, and head out on the **West Beach Footpath**, a 2km narrow trail running through restored savannahs, views of Lake Erie shimmering

DETOUR: MANITOULIN ISLAND

Start: 4 Tobermory

A two-hour ferry ride from Tobermory takes you to another world: Manitoulin Island. A 2766-sq-km landmass, it's the world's largest fresh-water island. A landscape of farmlands and forests, Manitoulin is dotted with villages and small towns, many of them First Nations communities. Start at the **Ojibwe Cultural Foundation** (☎705-377-4902; www.ojibweculture.ca; 15 Hwy 551, M'Chigeeng; by donation; ⏰8:30am-4pm Mon-Fri; P) in M'Chigeeng, to learn about the culture and heritage of the Ojibwe, Odawa and Pottawatomi peoples, the original inhabitants of the island. Down the street, book a tour with **Great Spirit Circle Trail** (☎705-377-4404; www.circletrail.com; 5905 Hwy 540, M'Chigeeng; activities & tours from $40; ⏰May-Oct), a consortium of eight First Nations communities offering cultural tours and outdoors excursions such as paddling on ancient canoe routes. Afterwards, head east to the **Cup & Saucer Trail** (6301 Bidwell Rd, Sheguiandah) for a 9km hike along the Niagara Escarpment, with its 70m cliffs and granite outcrops leading to spectacular views of the North Channel. Try to catch a show at the **Debajehmujig Creation Centre** (☎705-859-1820; www.debaj.ca; 43 Queen St, Manitowaning; ⏰10am-5pm Mon-Fri) in Manitowaning, home of Canada's most prestigious indigenous theater company. And if you're on the island in early August, head to Wiikwemkoong, the proudly unceded First Nations reserve – its people never relinquished their land rights to the Canadian government. Here, Manitoulin celebrates its largest **powwow** (Wiikwemkoong Annual Cultural Festival; ☎705-859-2385; www.wikwemikongheritage.org; Thunderbird Park, Wiikwemkoong; adult/child $10/2; ⏰Aug) with lively dance competitions, drumming and traditional games. Everyone is welcome. The **Chi-Cheemaun ferry** (☎800-265-3163; www.ontarioferries.com; adult/child/car $17/9/38; ⏰May-late Oct) carries passengers and vehicles from Tobermory to South Baymouth two to four times daily. A swing bridge in Little Current on the north end of the island also connects it to the mainland.

through the trees. The path feeds into the beachfront **Tip Trail**, a 1km path to the very tip of the park, mainland Canada's southernmost point, like a pencil nib jutting out into the lake. Take a pic! Afterwards, head to the spectacular **Marsh**, with its boardwalk floating in a sea of cattails, beavers swimming by and painted turtles sunning themselves. Climb the observation tower for a bird's-eye view then rent a kayak to explore the waterways.

TOP TIP: PARKING AT THE GROTTO

Parking permits are required to visit The Grotto in the Bruce Peninsula National Park (p221). Good for four hours, permits have pre-scheduled start/end times. Don't overstay your visit – ticketing and towing are enforced! Permits can be purchased online or by phone; call well in advance for summer visits.

The Drive » Take the quiet lakefront road – Point Pelee Drive, which becomes Robson Rd after the docks – to the town of Leamington, 7km away. Turn left on its main drag, Erie St. It leads straight to the ferry docks of Pelee Island Transportation. A modern, multistoried ferry crosses Lake Erie's blue expanse to Pelee Island here from April to December.

p227

7 Pelee Island: Near the Ferry

Pelee Island feels a world apart from mainland Canada. With about 200 residents, everything moves just a little slower, with most folks getting around on bikes, small homes dotting the forested island and beachfront trails here and there. Across from the ferry dock, pop into the **Pelee Island Heritage Centre** (519-724-2291; www.peleeislandmuseum.ca; 1073 West Shore Rd, Pelee Island; adult/child $4/2; 10am-4pm May-Oct; P). Inside, you'll get a good lay of the land with an excellent natural history collection and well-curated displays explaining Pelee's history, from its early indigenous inhabitants to the present day. Don't miss the fascinating exhibit on the shipwrecks surrounding the island. Afterwards, walk 950m south along the lakefront to the **Pelee Island Winery** (800-597-3533; www.peleeisland.com; 20 East-West Rd, Pelee Island; tour with tasting adult/child $5/free; 11am-4pm Oct-May, to 8pm Jun-Sep; P), one of Canada's oldest vineyards.

The Drive » Head south on West Shore Rd, which turns into McCormick Rd after Pelee Island Winery. Continue for 3.6km, with Lake Erie to your right and the forest and farmlands to your left.

p227

8 Pelee Island: Fish Point Provincial Nature Reserve

The **Fish Point Provincial Nature Reserve** (519-825-4659; www.ontarioparks.com/park/fishpoint; 1750 McCormick Rd, Pelee Island; dawn-dusk; P) is a popular birding spot and home to one of the best swimming beaches on the island. A flat 3.2km trail leads through the dense forest, past Fox Lagoon and eventually near to the shoreline. Rare plants, such as the prickly pear cactus and hop tree, can be seen throughout, with black-crowned night herons and other migrating shorebirds showing their feathers. At the end, the beach finishes in a long, curving point forming a thin peninsula, the calm waters of Lake Erie on either side. This is the southernmost spot of inhabited Canada!

The Drive » Make your way to the ferry, looping around the small island. Back on the mainland, head north on Erie St through farmland until it becomes Hwy 77. After 27km, take Hwy 401 east. Cutting through the middle of southwestern Ontario, it will merge with Hwy 403 outside Woodstock, 185km away. Continue on Hwy 403 east for 135km to Toronto.

Eating & Sleeping

Blue Mountain ❶

Grandma Lambe's — Market $

(☎519-538-2757; http://grandmalambes.com; 206570 Hwy 26, Meaford; ⌚8am-6pm) You won't regret the trek to Grandma Lambe's (west on Hwy 26 just outside of Meaford). The store is a delicious jumble of maple syrup vintages, butter tarts, bushels of vegetables, and tables piled high with pies, buns and jellies.

Tremont Cafe — European $$$

(☎705-293-6000; www.thetremontcafe.com; 80 Simcoe St, Collingwood; mains $16-35; ⌚11am-3pm & 5:30-9:30pm Wed-Mon) Come for a mouthwatering weekend brunch or classic dinner at this delightful fine-dining cafe in the historic Tremont building. Will you have the duck confit or PEI mussels after your lamb lollipops? Dinner menus change regularly.

Blue Mountain Inn — Hotel $$

(☎705-445-0231; www.bluemountain.ca; 110 Jozo Weider Blvd, Blue Mountain; r/ste from $147/237; P ⊖ ❄ @ ≋) Accommodations range from standard guest rooms to roomier one-bedroom suites, all of which have seen a face-lift in recent years. Though far from luxurious, the rooms are comfortable enough and the location near the lifts is tough to beat. The outdoor hot tubs and indoor pool are pluses. Check the website for the best rates.

Westin Trillium House — Resort $$$

(☎705-443-8080; www.westinbluemountain.com; 220 Gord Canning Dr, Blue Mountain; d/ste from $369/409; P ❄ @ 📶 ≋ 👪 🐾) Couple-friendly, pet-friendly and family-friendly, this Westin upholds its brand's reputation for excellence in service. A wide range of guest rooms and suites are all luxuriously furnished and most overlook the Blue Mountain Village, pond or outdoor pools. Experiment with your dates for the best rates and packages.

Bruce Peninsula National Park ❷

The Fitz Hostel — Hostel $

(☎519-793-3267; https://thefitzhostel.com; 4 Mills St, Lions Head; dm $45, r with shared bath $120; P 📶) A friendly, well-run hostel in an updated 19th-century house, the Fitz offers two sunny four-bed dorms and a cozy private room. Guests share a a spick-and-span bathroom, a spacious living room, and a fully stocked kitchen. There's also a leafy backyard where occasional live-music performances take place. The affable owner, a fifth-generation local, possesses a wealth of information.

Cyprus Lake Campground — Campground $

(☎519-596-2263; www.pc.gc.ca; Cyprus Lake Rd; back-country/sites/yurts from $9.80/23.50/120, reservations $13.50; P) Sites at the most central and substantial campground within the Bruce Peninsula National Park (p221) must be reserved through Parks Canada in advance (recommended) or at one of the visitor centers (there's one near the campground entrance). You can even glam it up in a yurt! Back-country sites are available.

Tobermory ❹

Shipwreck Lee's Pirate Bistro — Fish & Chips $

(☎705-888-5946; https://shipwrecklees.com; 2 Bay St; mains $11-17; ⌚11am-8:30pm May-Oct; 👪) Tiki meets maritime at this colorful, quirky eatery filled with murals, pirate mannequins, and picnic tables (indoors and out). All-you-can-eat fish and chips is the way to go: baskets of melt-in-your-mouth whitefish with piles of fresh fries, all topped with a cocktail umbrella.

Innisfree — B&B $$

(☎519-596-8190; www.tobermoryaccommodations.com; 46 Bay St; r with shared bath incl breakfast $160, r incl breakfast $170; ⌚May-Oct; P ⊖ 📶) Whether it's due to the scent of fresh blueberry muffins, or the stunning harbor views from the sunroom and large deck, guests will adore this charming country home. Minimum two-night stay on weekends. Rates drop dramatically in the shoulder season.

Peacock Villa Motel $$

(☎519-596-2242; www.peacockvilla.com; 30 Legion St; d $109-165; ⏰Apr-Oct; P Wi-Fi) Six simple, pleasantly furnished motel rooms and four cozy cabins in a peaceful, woodsy setting, a hop-skip-and-jump from the harbor, offer excellent value. Friendly owner Karen is a wealth of information about the town and surrounds.

Pinery Provincial Park 5

Whispering Pines Motel Motel $$

(☎519-238-2383; www.whisperingpinesmotel.org; 10456 Lakeshore Rd; d $129-189; P ❄ Wi-Fi Pool) This friendly family-run motel is located in a wooded lot just south of Grand Bend. It has comfortable rooms with grannie decor (quilts and frilly curtains), old school air-con and gleaming bathrooms. Great value for families, the motel also has a nice pool and offers free passes to Pinery Provincial Park. An on-site restaurant is the frosting on the cake.

Point Pelee National Park 6

Point Pelee National Park Tented Camp $$

(☎519-322-2365; www.pc.gc.ca; 1118 Point Pelee Dr, Leamington; up to six people $120; P) Sleep in Point Pelee's (p224) tall forests in a comfortable oTENTik, a tented A-frame on a raised wood floor. Each sleeps six on comfy foam beds, has an eating/lounging area plus a grill (and a wildlife-proof food storage locker). Even tableware is included. And did we mention the porch with Adirondack chairs? In winter, a wood stove warms up the place by remote control.

Pelee Island 7

The Bakery Deli $

(☎519-724-2321; www.theislandbakery.ca; 5 Northshore Dr, Pelee Island; sandwiches from $7; ⏰8:30am-7pm Mon & Thu, to 4pm Tue, to 9pm Fri-Sun May-Oct) Tiny house turned bakery-deli-pizzeria. Stop here for hearty wraps and salads, pizza and all manner of baked goods (cinnamon buns, anyone?). Coffee drinks – even the fancy stuff – are sold too. Eat at one of the picnic tables on the leafy lakefront property or take your eats to go. A treat!

Wandering Dog Inn Inn $$

(☎519-724-2270; https://thewanderingdoginn.com; 1060 East West Rd; r with shared bath from $100, ste from $175; P ❄) A charming 125-year-old farmhouse with seven cozy rooms, all decorated in a simple country style. All share four full bathrooms – there's rarely a wait – plus a lounge with loads of board games and books. For a bit more privacy, opt for a suite. In a separate building, each room has a private bathroom plus screened-in porches with hammocks and grills. Just steps from the beach.

Thousand Island Parkway

On this drive, you'll experience a region full of artisanal food and locally produced drinks, dramatic vistas stretching across the river and a fascinating look at Canada's history.

TRIP HIGHLIGHTS

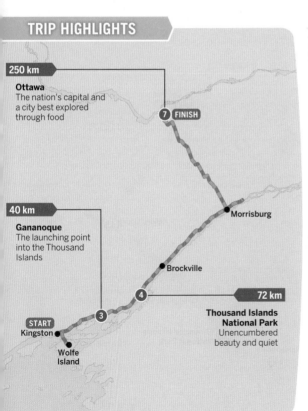

250 km
Ottawa
The nation's capital and a city best explored through food

7 FINISH

Morrisburg

40 km
Gananoque
The launching point into the Thousand Islands

Brockville

4

72 km
Thousand Islands National Park
Unencumbered beauty and quiet

3

START
Kingston

Wolfe Island

7 DAYS 250KM/155 MILES

GREAT FOR...

BEST TIME TO GO

May to June when the weather is not too hot and crowds are smaller.

ESSENTIAL PHOTO

A panoramic photo at the 1000 Islands Tower.

BEST FOR HISTORY

Being transported to the 1860s at Upper Canada Village in Morrisburg.

Thousand Islands National Park (p232) View of the park in autumn

21 Thousand Island Parkway

This is a trip for people who want to slow things down. Most jump on Hwy 401 to speed to Ottawa, but they miss one of the best parts of Ontario. The drive hugs the St Lawrence River and you'll be tempted to stop in every little hamlet to see what is on offer. The area is a haven for small craft producers – think beer and whisky rather than trinkets.

❶ Kingston

Kingston was Canada's first capital for three years due to its strategic location, and this still rings true today. Pretty much in between Toronto and Ottawa, it's a lovely small city to grab a bite to eat and stretch your legs at the waterfront. It's also a Canadian historian's dream to visit **Bellevue House** (☎613-545-8666, toll-free 888-773-8888; www.pc.gc.ca/en/lhn-nhs/on/bellevue; 35 Centre St; adult/child 6-16yr

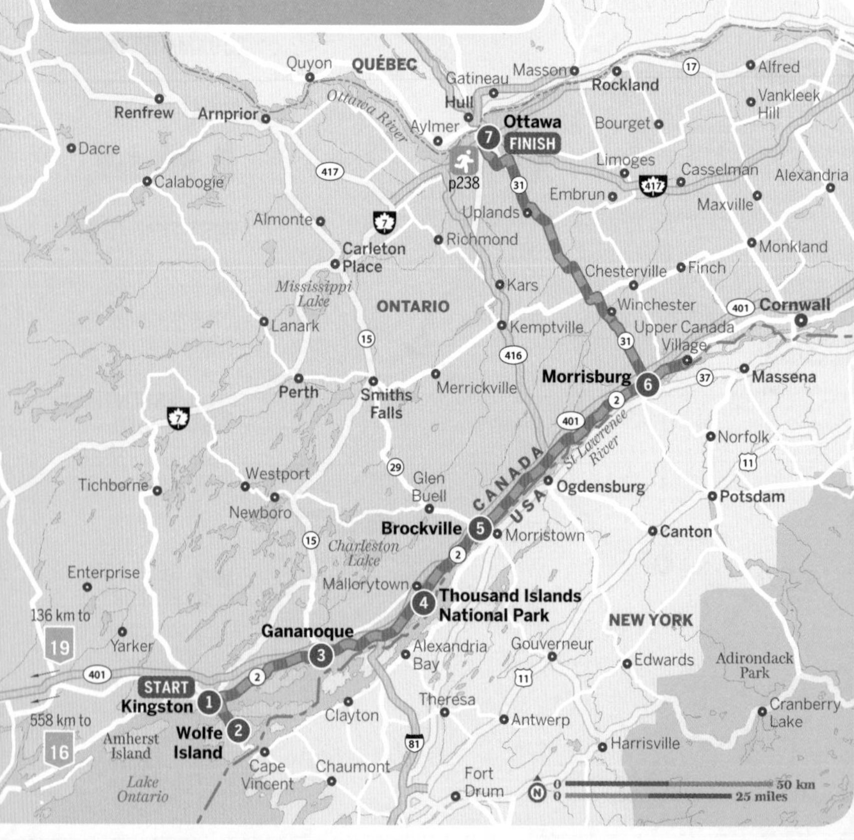

$4/free; ⏲10am-5pm Jul-Aug, Thu-Mon late May, Jun, Sep & early Oct), which was briefly home to the first prime minister, Sir John A Macdonald, or the **Fort Henry National Historic Site** (☎613-542-7388; www.forthenry.com; Fort Henry Dr; adult/child $20/13; ⏲9:30am-5pm late May-early Sep, to 10pm Wed Jul & Aug), a restored British fortification dating from 1832. If that bores you, then head downtown to Princess St and sample local beers at **Stone City Ales** (☎613-542-4222; www.stonecityales.com; 275 Princess St; mains $15; ⏲noon midnight Mon-Thu, from 11am Fri & Sat, 11am-10pm Sun) or book ahead for a fusion meal at **Chez Piggy** (☎613-549-7673; www.chezpiggy.com; 68 Princess St; lunch/dinner mains $17/35; ⏲11:30am-11pm Mon-Sat, from 10am Sun) – you won't be disappointed. End with a stroll by the waterfront, embracing the charm of a city that cherishes its role in Canada's history.

The Drive » Once in downtown Kingston, head north for several blocks until you see signs for the Wolfe Island Ferry – that's your next stop. The ferry is free for both pedestrians and vehicles. The 25-minute journey is best spent on the deck as the views of Kingston are spectacular. The ferry will drop you off on Centre St on the island.

✕ 🛏 p235

LINK YOUR TRIP

16 Lake Superior Coastline

Combine your drive north with a trip to the edge of Ontario. Sudbury is 250km from the northwest gate of Algonquin Provincial Park via Hwy11/17.

19 The Kawarthas

Continue your drive up to the north of the province by heading northwest from Kingston for around 200km to Peterborough.

2 Wolfe Island

Wolfe Island is the largest of the Thousand Island's 1800-plus islands. Much of the island is undeveloped and that is its draw. The main town, Marysville, has a few restaurants and accommodations, but the main draw is the general feeling of remoteness despite being so close to Kingston. The 2009 addition of hundreds of wind turbines adds to the surreal feeling, rather than detracting from the peaceful drive around the island or the calm walk around the coast. Bring a picnic from Kingston's artisanal shops and enjoy a few hours of thoughtful pondering before getting back on the road.

3 Gananoque

One of the largest towns in the Thousand Islands region, Gananoque is the perfect place from which to set out and explore. The more adventurous can choose a multiday kayak trip with **1000 Islands Kayaking** (☎613-329-6265; www.1000islandskayaking.com; 110 Kate St; half-day rentals/tours from $45/85), but we recommend travelling with the **Gananoque Boat Line** (☎888-717-4837; www.ganboatline.com; 280 Main St; 1hr cruise adult/child 6-12yr from $24/14; ⏲May–mid-Oct), which has several cruise options, including a trip to **Boldt Castle** (☎in season 315-482-9724, off season 315-482-2501; www.boldtcastle.com; Heart Island, Alexandria Bay, NY, USA; adult/child US$10/7; ⏲10am-6:30pm May-late Sep, 11am-5pm late Sep–mid-Oct), where the salad dressing was reportedly invented. If you do choose this trip, be sure to bring your passport as it is technically in the US.

Gananoque has several great places to sleep and even more places to eat and drink, but since you are here to see the Thousand Islands, you might as well stay as close as possible by renting a houseboat from **Houseboat Holidays** (☎613-382-2842; www.houseboatholidays.ca; 11 Clark Dr, RR3; weekend/midweek/weekly rates from $600/800/1100).

The Drive » Continue east up King St E/Hwy 2 until you are out of the city. The highway will fork – go right to take the scenic route via the Thousand Islands Parkway. It's a wonderful 32km drive to the next stop and be sure to get a panoramic snap up the 130m-high 1000 Islands Tower, which is roughly 20km from Gananoque.

p235

4 Thousand Islands National Park

Just south of Mallorytown is the **Thousand Islands National Park** (613-923-5261; www.pc.gc.ca/pn-np/on/lawren/index.aspx; 2 County Rd 5, Mallorytown; parking $7, tent sites without hookup $16, OTENTik camping $100-121; visitors center 10am-4pm Sat & Sun late May-Jun, daily Jul-Sep), a collection of 20 small islands and a lush archipelago. Splurge and stay in the park's luxurious oTENTik roofed safari tents as you explore the area for turtles and rare birds. There is very little light pollution here so the stargazing opportunities are fantastic, as is the kayaking and hiking trails. It's also amazingly child-friendly and the Mallorytown Landing Visitors Centre, just before the park entrance, has a playground, live animal shows and a bike path.

The Drive » Once you've recharged your batteries, hop back in the car and continue to meander east along the parkway. After around 11km you'll come to a large interchange. Hwy 401 is a slightly longer route but quicker and with more traffic, so we suggest taking Hwy 2, which continues along the St Lawrence River until you reach Brockville.

5 Brockville

Brockville, the 'City of the Thousand Islands' is an attractive place with historical gothic buildings and riverfront parks that will make you want to stay almost indefinitely. Head first for the riverfront for a short stroll and then take the children (or any young-at-hearts) to the **Aquatarium** (613-342-6789; www.aquatarium.ca; Tall Ships Landing, 6 Broad St, Brockville; adult/child $20/10; 10am-5pm mid-May–Aug, 10am-5pm Wed-Sun Sep–mid-May;), an interactive museum detailing the history and ecology of the St Lawrence seaway. From here, walk along Water St until you reach the **Brockville Railway Tunnel** (www.brockvillerailwaytunnel.com; cnr Water St E & Block House Island Pkwy; 9am-9pm), a 15-minute walk through a converted railway tunnel with a sound-and-light show. It's a great way to escape the heat in summer. You'll emerge at Pearl St, and we suggest turning left and walking 200m to Buell St, down which you'll find the highly rated **Buell Street Bistro** (613-345-2623; www.buellstreetbistro.com; 27 Buell St; mains $16-35; 11:30am-10pm Mon-Fri, from 4:30pm Sat & Sun) for dinner.

The Drive » When leaving Brockville, ignore the signs directing you to Hwy 401 – it's quicker but there is not much to see. Instead, stay on King St/Hwy 2 for 65km until you reach Morrisburg. The St Lawrence River will stay on your right the whole way, making you wonder why anyone would take a larger highway over this route.

p235

TOP TIP: TAKE THE SCENIC ROUTE

Don't follow your GPS for this route – it will always send you to Hwy 401 to shave off time. Take Hwy 2, which skirts along the coast, and enjoy the drive – there's less traffic and, while the speed limit is slower, you won't want to travel too fast anyway.

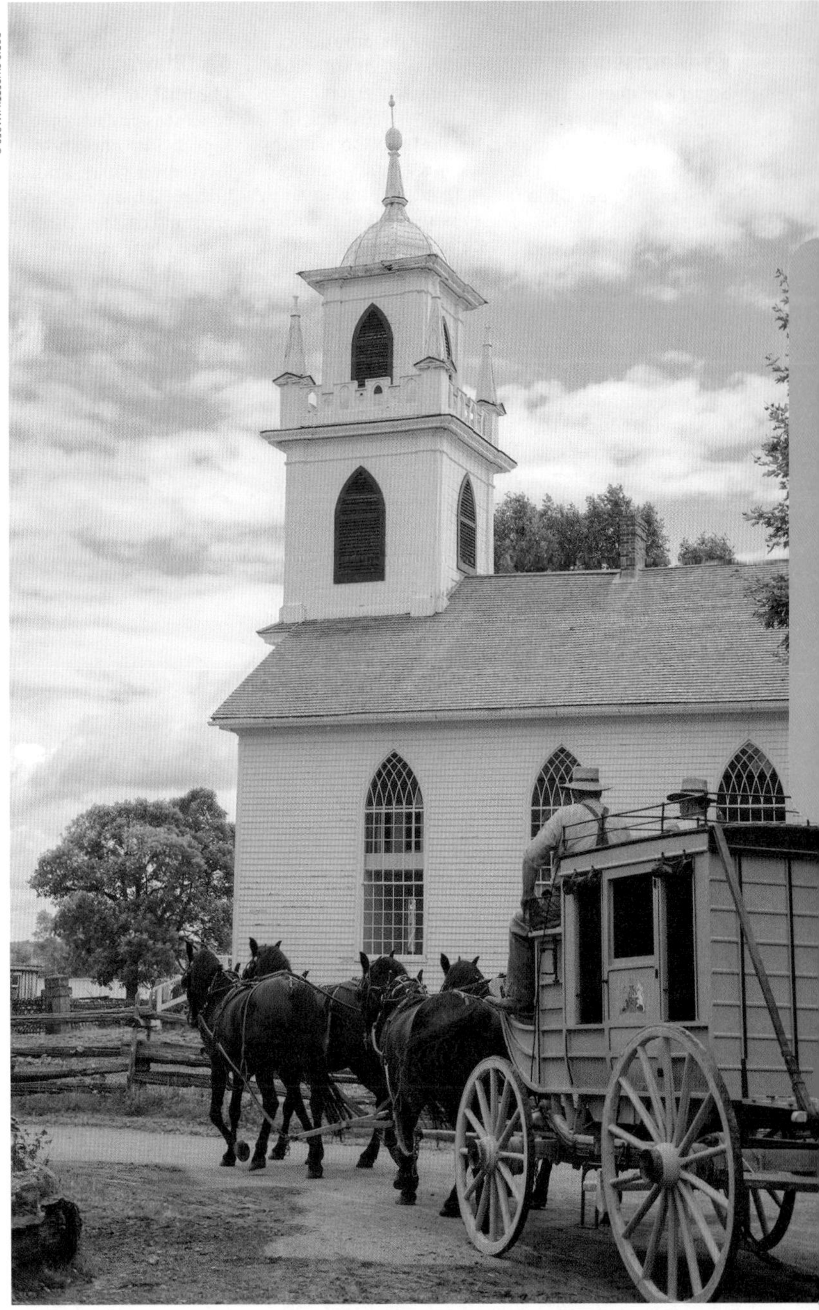

BORIS SV/GETTY IMAGES ©

Morrisburg Horses and stagecoach in Upper Canada Village (p234)

❻ Morrisburg

Small and quaint, the stop in Morrisburg is really just for one thing – the preeminent historic attraction, **Upper Canada Village** (☎613-543-4328; www.uppercanadavillage.com; 13740 County Rd 2, Morrisburg; adult/child $22/13; ⏰9:30am-5pm May-early Sep, tours 10:30am, 1pm & 3pm early Sep–mid Oct; 👪). Here costume-clad interpreters emulate life in the 1860s, never breaking character no matter what you try. There are around 40 historic buildings to discover, including a blacksmith, tavern, schoolhouse and a wool factory. We suggest staying over in Montgomery House, a historical log house, and trying each of the four restaurants for authentic (but still modern and tasty) food.

The village is one of the best ways to learn about Canada's history without reading about it, so is an ideal visit with children or adults with shorter attention spans. Try to come for a weekend in summer when they host special events, such as a haunted walk and musical celebrations.

The Drive » Trace your steps back west on Hwy 2 for 11km until you see the turnoff to the right on Hwy 31. Travel north for 66km heading for Ottawa. You'll have a very short drive on Hunt Club Rd before heading into town on the Airport Pkwy/Hwy 79. This 10km will take you right to downtown Ottawa.

❼ Ottawa

The final stop of our trip encompassing multiple aspects into one city – lovely river views, grand historical buildings and artisanal cuisine. Ottawa is a city best explored through food so head to the Rideau Centre, just south of the famous Byward Market. Once you park, get out and stretch your legs (p238) as you explore Canada's capital city.

✕ 🛏 p235

Eating & Sleeping

Kingston 1

Pan Chancho Fusion **$$**

(613-544-7790; www.panchancho.com; 44 Princess St; mains $17; 7am-3pm) This phenomenal bakery and cafe fuses unlikely ingredients into palate-pleasing dishes such as Vietnamese spring rolls and sesame tuna meatballs. The Moroccan-style, cumin-spiced lamb pita wrap with chickpeas is heartily recommended. The all-day breakfast menu features dishes such as curried eggs. Kingstonians crowd the rear courtyard on summer days.

Rosemount Inn B&B **$$**

(613-480-6624; www.rosemountinn.com; 46 Sydenham St; r incl breakfast from $225; P) Enjoy a decadent stay at this former dry-goods merchant's home in a historic district. Built in 1850, the massive stone, Tuscan-style villa has been magnificently preserved in its 19th-century finery from the arched entrance to the ceiling roses. A small spa offers wine-based facials and chocolate body wraps, and rates include full breakfast and afternoon tea loaded with homemade goodies.

Gananoque 3

Stonewater Pub Pub Food **$$**

(613-382-2542; www.stonewaterpub.com; 490 Stone St S; mains $18; 11am-9pm Sun-Wed, to 1am Thu-Sat) Below a B&B, this homely little waterfront Irish pub and restaurant serves up hearty and delicious fare: the 'Irish tenderloin' (grilled, bacon-wrapped ground lamb and beef) and 'porky pig' (pork loin burger) are both must-tries for self-respecting carnivores. There's a bunch of creative salads too. The vibe is straight out of *Moby Dick*, and especially delightful when there's live music.

Misty Isles Lodge Lodge **$$**

(613-382-4232; www.mistyisles.ca; 25 River Rd, Lansdowne; r from $115, campsites with hookup $40;) Located about 5km east of Gananoque on the Thousand Islands Pkwy, you'll find this laid-back beachfront property boasting comfortable units with wicker furnishings. A variety of adventure outfitting is offered as well, including kayak rentals (half day $40) and tours (half day $80), and camping packages on some of the river's shrubby islands.

Brockville 5

Dewar's Inn B&B **$$**

(877-433-9277, 613-925-3228; www.dewarsinn.com; 1649 County Rd 2; r $103-108, cottage $150-170;) These quaint riverside cottages, efficiency units and motel rooms are pleasantly furnished and spotlessly clean. The property is built on the site of an early-19th-century brewery, and scuba dives in the backyard have revealed sunken bottles of old brew. Decks along the river's edge have views of Ogdensburg, NY. Rates include breakfast. No pets or children under 12.

Ottawa 7

ByWard Market Square Market **$**

(613-244-4410; www.bywardmarketsquare.com; ByWard Market Sq; 10am-8pm) Anchoring the market district, this sturdy brick building is the perfect place to stop when hunger strikes. Aside from the fresh produce and cheese, an array of international takeaway joints offers falafel, spicy curries, flaky pastries, sushi… the list goes on. Look for the stand selling beavertails, Ottawa's signature sizzling flat-dough dish. Between William, Byward, George and York Sts.

Hostelling International (HI) Ottawa Jail Hostel **$**

(613-235-2595; www.hihostels.ca/ottawa; 75 Nicholas St; dm members $37-41, nonmembers $43-53, jail r $61-141; P@) This quirky hostel occupies nine floors of the 155-year-old former Ottawa Jail, considered to be one of the city's most haunted buildings. Guests can lock themselves away in a room or dorm in an actual cell, or opt for a more conventional four- to eight-bed dorm or en suite room. Rates include a continental breakfast.

STRETCH YOUR LEGS TORONTO

Start/Finish: Harbourfront Centre

Distance: 4.6 km

Duration: 3 hours

A feast for the eyes and belly, a walk through Toronto's bustling Financial and Old Town districts provides insight into the city's present and past, while the Waterfront is all about art and shimmering lake views.

Take this walk on Trips

Habourfront Centre

Set on Lake Ontario, the **Harbourfront Centre** (www.harbourfrontcentre.com; 235 Queens Quay W; 10am-11pm Mon-Sat, to 9pm Sun; P; 509, 510) is the place to start. A cultural hub, it's an easy place to wander and explore. It has galleries and open artist studios, an outdoor concert stage and even an ice rink. **Boxcar Social** (www.boxcarsocial.ca; mains $12-18; 9am-5pm Mon, to 11pm Tue-Thu, to late Fri, 10am-late Sat, to 8pm Sun; 509, 510), an industrial-chic cafe, is a good place to stop for a salad or cappuccino. For more art, head next door to the engaging **Power Plant Contemporary Art Gallery** (www.thepowerplant.org; 231 Queens Quay W; 10am-5pm Tue, Wed & Fri-Sun, to 8pm Thu; P; 509, 510) – if in doubt, look for its smoke stack.

The Walk » Head west on Queens Quay W and take a right on Rees St. At the top of the hill, dogleg east on Bremner Av to the towering CN Tower.

CN Tower

Toronto's iconic **CN Tower** (La Tour CN; www.cntower.ca; 301 Front St W; Tower Experience adult/child $38/28; 8:30am-11pm; ; S Union) is impossible to miss – it dominates the city skyline. Standing 553m tall, it was once the highest freestanding structure in the world. A ride to the top will reveal breathtaking 360-degree views of the city and a glass-bottom floor that will test your backbone. Afterwards, consider popping into **Ripley's Aquarium of Canada** (www.ripleysaquariumofcanada.com; 288 Bremner Blvd; adult/child $32/22; 9am-11pm; ; S Union) next door.

The Walk » Continue north on the pedestrian bridge adjacent to the CN Tower. Take a right on Front St, passing the historic Union Station, Toronto's longtime transportation hub. At Yonge St, take a left.

Hockey Hall of Fame

On the corner sits Canada's mecca to its beloved national sport: the **Hockey Hall of Fame** (www.hhof.com; Brookfield Place, 30 Yonge St; adult/child $20/14; 9:30am-6pm

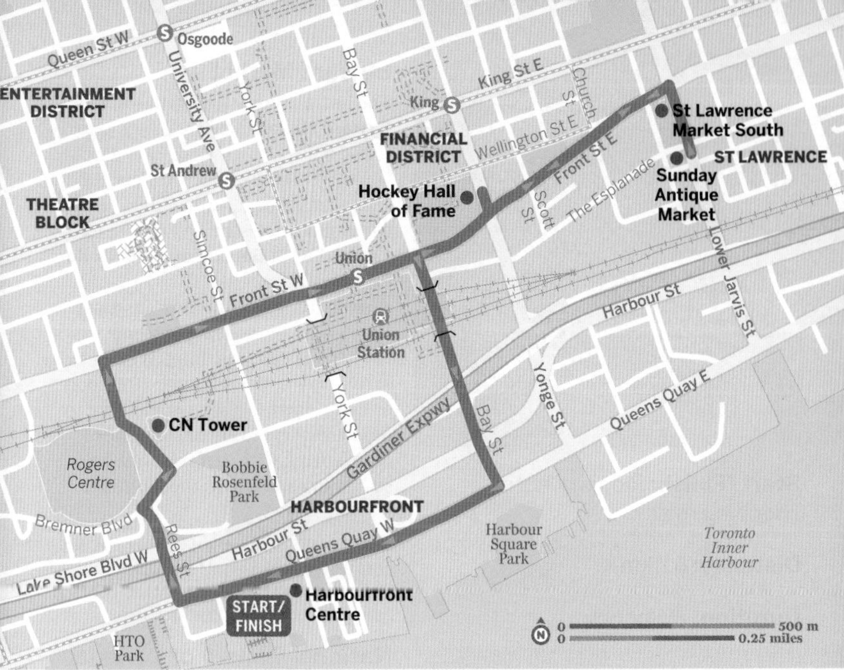

Mon-Sat, 10am-6pm Sun Jun-Sep, 10am-5pm Mon-Fri, 9:30am-6pm Sat, 10:30am-5pm Sun Oct-May; 👪; S Union). It's a spectacular tribute to the game, at which visitors learn all about hockey's greats with loads of memorabilia, documentaries and hands-on exhibits such as taking slap shots on simulated NHL goalies or calling a game in a newsroom, teleprompters and all.

The Walk » Return to Front St and head east, passing the striking Flatiron Building, a favorite of photographers.

St Lawrence Market South

St Lawrence Market (www.stlawrencemarket.com; 92-95 Front St E; ⏰8am-6pm Tue-Thu, to 7pm Fri, 5am-5pm Sat; P; 🚋503, 504) is the heart of Old Town, a public meeting place since the 1800s. Head inside the Market South building, a beautifully restored complex with more than 120 food stalls and shops selling everything from organic turnips to fresh lake perch. If you're looking for souvenirs, go downstairs to **GiftWorks** (⏰8am-6pm Tue-Thu, to 7pm Fri, 5am-5pm Sat; 🚋503, 504), a little shop packed with quality mementos.

The Walk » Head back to Front St and take a right on Lower Jarvis St to The Esplanade.

Sunday Antique Market

Directly behind St Lawrence Market South is a huge, semi-permanent tent. On Sundays, you'll find Toronto's **best antique market** (www.facebook.com/SundayAntiqueMarket; 125 The Esplanade; ⏰7am-4pm Sun; 🚋503, 504) here (the Market North building, its permanent home, is being reconstructed). Rows and rows of vendors sell treasures from the past: tea cups and old photos and leather-bound books. It's a perfect place to wander through, poke around and shop. On Saturdays, the tent transforms into a **Farmers Market**, overflowing with local produce and artisanal goods.

The Walk » Return to Jarvis St and turn left on Front St, retracing your steps. Take a left on Bay St, admiring the mural of notable indigenous Canadians under the train tracks, circling straight back to Queens Quay W.

STRETCH YOUR LEGS OTTAWA

Start/Finish: Rideau Centre shopping mall

Distance: 6.4km

Duration: 2½ hours

Ottawa is a walking town. The mix of leafy parks, historic buildings and large sidewalks create the perfect atmosphere for a stroll through Canada's capital. This walk takes you along Ottawa's main sites – don't forget your camera!

Take this walk on Trip

21

ByWard Market

The heart of downtown Ottawa, the **ByWard Market** (☎613-562-3325; www.byward-market.com; cnr York & ByWard Sts; ⏰6am-6pm) is Ottawa's top place for shopping, eating and drinking. Meander around at leisure and stop in for a quick bite at **Boulangerie Moulin de Provence** (☎613-241-9152; www.moulindeprovence.com; 55 ByWard Market Sq; items from $3, mains $14; ⏰7am-10pm) for some pastries and people-watching. Whether you arrive here in the morning, afternoon or night, there is always something to do, somewhere to eat or someone to have a drink with, but this walk assumes you are here in the morning.

The Walk » From Rideau Ave, enter the market via Williams St, passing the Highlander Pub, and on to the shops, restaurants and market stalls. Meander around until you reach St Patrick St and turn left towards the National Art Gallery.

National Gallery of Canada

The top **gallery** (☎613-990-1985, 800-319-2787; www.gallery.ca; 380 Sussex Dr; adult/child $16/free, 5-8pm Thu free; ⏰10am-6pm daily May-Sep, 10am-5pm Tue-Sun Oct-Apr, to 8pm Thu year-round) in Canada featuring indigenous and local artists. Trace Canada's history through its paintings and view special exhibitions from other famous international artists. Even if you're not an art lover, the gallery is worth visiting just for the iconic building, with several areas that have stunning panoramas across the city. If you are doing this walk with kids, the fun art classes offered at the gallery on weekends are the perfect distraction before continuing on your walk.

The Walk » Walk along St Patrick St until you see the Maman Statue, a 30ft-tall statue in front of the imposing gallery. From the gallery, walk down Mackenzie Ave until you reach the Chateau Laurier and turn right to the Ottawa Locks.

Ottawa Locks

While the **locks** are an engineering feat, the real star here is the view across the Ottawa River to Quebec. It's a gorgeous

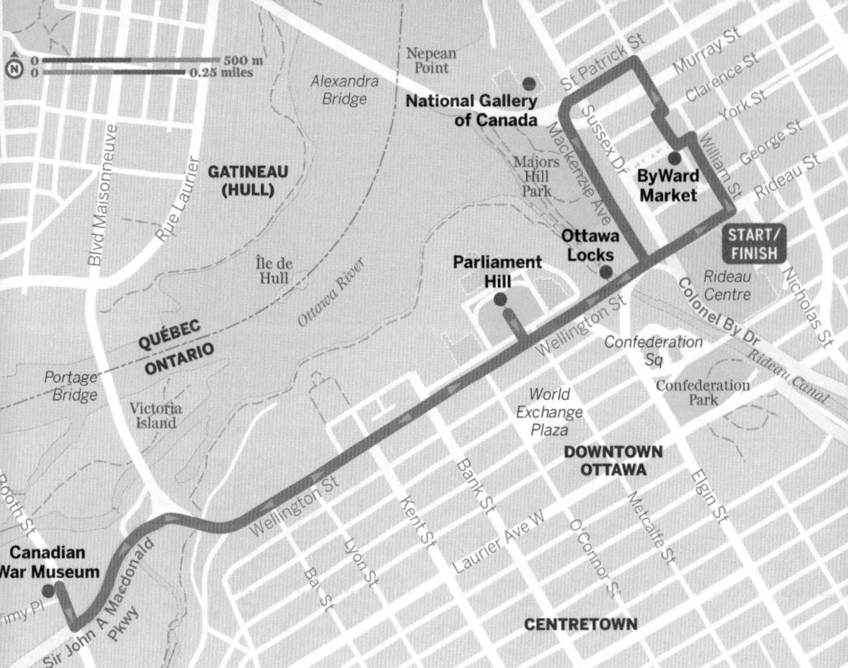

view during the day, but particularly lovely at sunset. In summer, you cannot miss the locks for all of the selfie-taking tourists – this makes it easy to find but harder to get that amazing photo. The best option is to put the camera away and enjoy the view.

The Walk » After the obligatory picture, keep walking on Wellington St towards Parliament Hill. Just a short walk from the locks, continue down Wellington St and turn left into the Parliament Hill grounds.

Parliament Hill

The home of Canada's legislature, **Parliament Hill** (613-996-0896; https://visit.parl.ca; 111 Wellington St; East Block tours 8:30am-4:30pm Jul-early Sep, West Block tours 8:30am-4:30pm) is a must-visit sight in Ottawa. The copper-topped turrets and Gothic revival gargoyles strike an imposing image, and the changing of the guard (10am daily in summer) is enjoyed by all ages. The centre-block is undergoing renovations until at least 2028, but the grounds are still magnificent and worth a walk around. There are more paths behind the buildings with views across the river that rival the Ottawa Locks.

The Walk » Exit at the Centennial Flame back on to Wellington St. Continue heading down Wellington St, passing the turnoff to Quebec. You'll see the war museum with textured concrete walls meant to resemble a bunker.

Canadian War Museum

The **war museum** (819-776-7000; www.warmuseum.ca; 1 Vimy Pl; adult/child 3-12yr $17/11; 9:30am-5pm Fri-Wed, to 8pm Thu Sep-Mar, from 9am May-Aug) turns Canada's pacifist reputation on its head, detailing the country's military history through thought-provoking exhibitions. Some of the exhibits can be a bit intense for younger children, but there is a wide variety of other activities that will keep them entertained, especially on weekends.

The Walk » Once finished with Canada's military history, head back up Wellington St, retracing your steps. Wellington St becomes Rideau Ave after Colonel By Dr, and you'll see the Rideau Centre on your left shortly after this crossing.

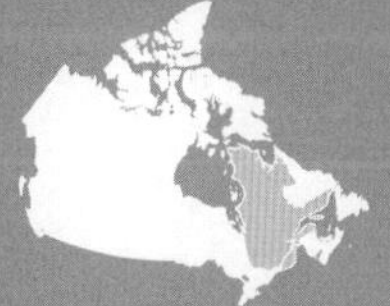

Québec

A ROAD TRIP INTO QUÉBEC FEELS LIKE A JOURNEY TO ANOTHER COUNTRY. Of course, this *is* Canada, with its interplay of vast wilderness and cosmopolitanism, but Québec's embrace of *terroir*, its language, its passion for everything from winter snow to wine to gastronomy, is something else, an 'else' that encompasses identities both distinctly North American and European.

Beyond the captivating cities of Montréal and Québec City, the francophone province unfolds in all its rare beauty: encompassing the chiseled peaks of the Laurentians, the breathtaking coasts of the unblemished Gaspé Peninsula and the pine-studded cliffs of the dramatic Saguenay Fjord. The St Lawrence also plays a starring role here, with expansive forests, lakeside villages and huge river islands setting the stage for memorable road trips near the famed waterway.

Saguenay Fjord (p283) Reflections on the waters of the fjord

Québec

22 **Up to the Laurentians 2 Days**
Wandering laid-back villages, hiking wooded trails and relaxing amid mountain scenery.

Classic Trip **23** **Eastern Townships 1 Day**
Forested lakes, rolling vineyards, and fine food and antique markets make for rewarding exploring.

24 **Montréal to Québec City 1 Day**
Delve into Québécois pop culture, lounge on a river beach and catch a show in a former hydroelectric plant.

Around, Over & In the St Lawrence River 3 Days
Eat local delicacies on the Île d'Orléans, feel the power of thundering Montmorency Falls and spot wildlife on Cap Tourmente.

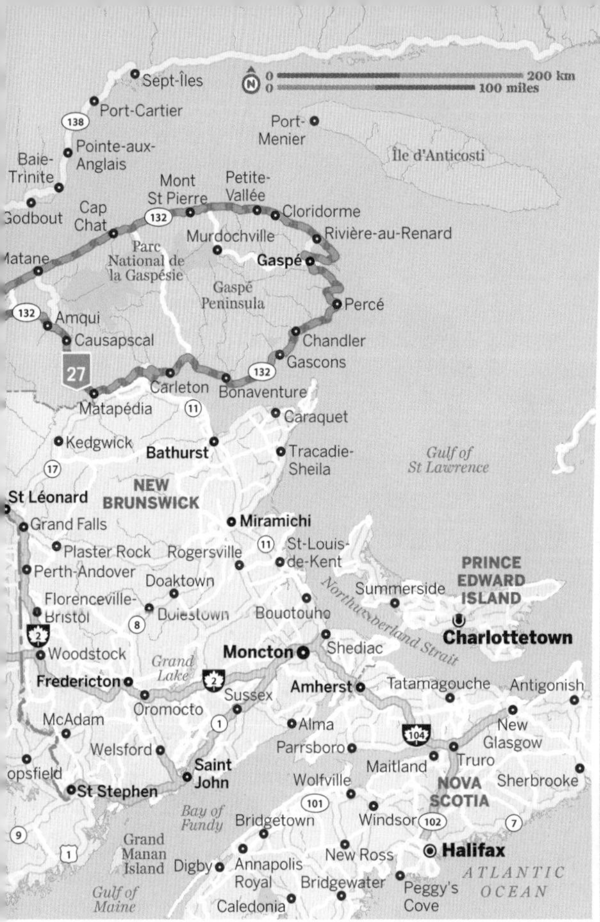

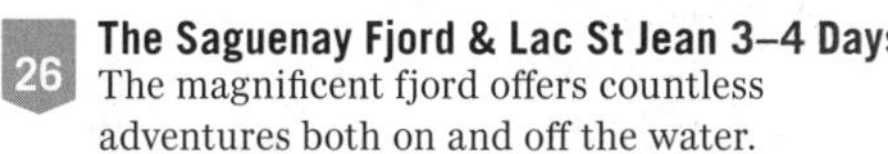

26 The Saguenay Fjord & Lac St Jean 3–4 Days
The magnificent fjord offers countless adventures both on and off the water.

27 Circling the Gaspé Peninsula 7–8 Days
Get your nature fix amid coast and mountains, then indulge in the peninsula's famed seafood.

DON'T MISS

Parc National du Mont-Tremblant

Admire the beauty of Québec's iconic national park amid pristine forests, lakes, rivers and mountains. Hit the trails on Trip 22

Abbaye St-Benoît-du-Lac

At this old-world abbey, you can listen to chanting monks, pick up locally made cider and enjoy the peaceful lakeside scenery. Go there on Trip 23

Montmorency Falls

Feel the power of nature at these thundering waterfalls, even higher than Niagara. Get there on Trip 25

Kayaking Saguenay Fjord

Enjoy dramatic views of the rocky cliffs and towering forests above the water's mirror-like surface. Grab a paddle on Trip 26

Parc National de Miguasha

Peel back the eons in this fossil-rich showcase from the Devonian period. Travel back in time on Trip 27

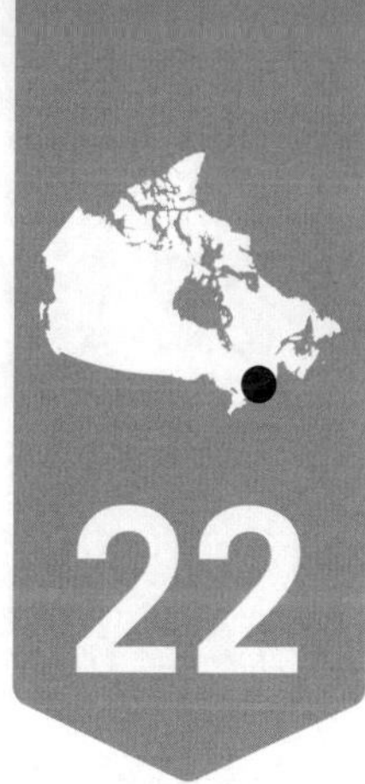

Up to the Laurentians

The Laurentians (Les Laurentides in French) are Montréal's playground. With gentle rolling mountains, crystal-blue lakes and meandering rivers bordered by towns and villages too cute for words, they're an irresistible draw.

TRIP HIGHLIGHTS

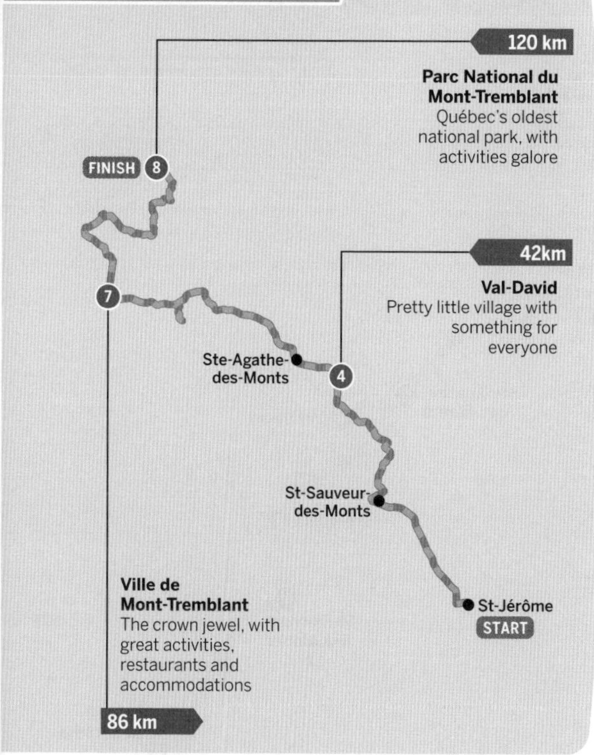

120 km

Parc National du Mont-Tremblant
Québec's oldest national park, with activities galore

FINISH 8

42km

Val-David
Pretty little village with something for everyone

7

Ste-Agathe-des-Monts

4

St-Sauveur-des-Monts

St-Jérôme
START

Ville de Mont-Tremblant
The crown jewel, with great activities, restaurants and accommodations

86 km

2 DAYS
120KM/75 MILES

GREAT FOR...

BEST TIME TO GO

Winter for the region's best skiing; May/June for spring flowers; September/October for a colorful fall display.

ESSENTIAL PHOTO

The base of Mont-Tremblant as the skiers descend.

BEST FOR OUTDOORS

Parc National du Mont-Tremblant for hiking, cycling, canoeing and wildlife.

Mont-Tremblant (p250) Ski season in full swing

22 Up to the Laurentians

This straightforward road trip will take you through more than a half-dozen delightful towns and villages, from St-Jérôme, the acknowledged gateway to the Laurentians and busy St-Sauveur-des-Monts to Val-David, perhaps the best place to put up your feet and chow down along the way, and Ville de Mont-Tremblant, *la crème* of your Laurentians gâteau. It will also introduce you to Québec province's oldest national park.

1 St-Jérôme

This sizable town, the largest in the region, may not overwhelm you, but it is officially recognized as the gateway to the Laurentians. It's also the southern terminus of the **Parc Linéaire du P'tit Train du Nord** (Little Train of the North Linear Park; ☎450-745-0185; www.laurentides.com/parclineaire; cross-country skiing/cycling $14/free; 👪), a trail built on top of old railway tracks for cyclists and cross-country skiers. Despite its administrative and industrial

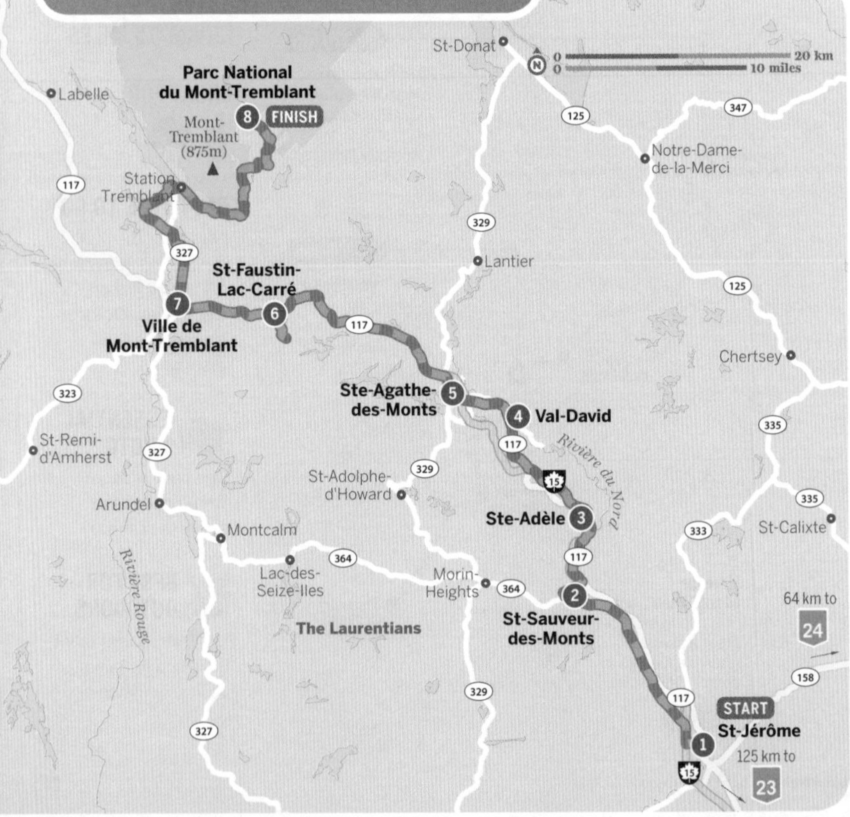

look and feel, St-Jérôme is worth a stop for its neo-Romanesque, Byzantine-style **cathedral** (450-432-9741; https://paroissestj.ca/paroisse-saint-jerome; 355 Pl du Curé-Labelle; 7:30am-3pm Mon-Fri, from 8am Sat, 8:30am-6pm Sun; P), a castle-like structure built in 1897 with stunning stained-glass windows and Venetian chandeliers. Nearby is the town's **Musée d'Art Contemporain des Laurentides** (450-432-7171; www.museelaurentides.ca; 101 Pl du Curé-Labelle; by donation; noon-5pm Tue-Fri & Sun, from 10am Sat), a contemporary-art museum with small but excellent exhibitions of work by regional artists. St-Jérôme is about 50km northwest of Montréal. Reach it via Rte 15 Nord and take exit 43E.

LINK YOUR TRIP

Eastern Townships

Drive an hour east of Montréal for charming villages and lakeside beauty.

Montréal to Québec City

From St-Jérôme, drive 85km northeast to the start of this memorable journey to Québec's oldest city.

The Drive » Rejoin Rte 15 Nord and follow it for just under 20km to exit 60, which will lead to Chemin Jean-Adam (Rte 364 Ouest) then Ave de la Gare and lastly Ave de l'Église in the center of St-Sauveur-des-Monts.

2 St-Sauveur-des-Monts

Usually just called St-Sauveur, this busy village is often deluged with day-trippers due to its proximity to central Montréal, 70km to the southeast. A pretty church anchors Rue Principale, the attractive main street, which is lined with restaurants, cafes and stylish boutiques. The main draw here is Les Sommets, five major ski hills with about 100 runs for all levels of expertise. The biggest hill, **Sommet St-Sauveur** (450-227-4671, 514-871-0101; www.montsaintsauveur.com; 350 Ave St-Denis; all-day lift ticket adult/youth/child $62/53/40, night skiing $47/36/31; 9am-10pm Mon-Fri, 8:30am-10pm Sat & Sun Nov-Mar;), is famous for its night skiing. Thrill-seekers might also enjoy other attractions here like Le Dragon, a double zip-line, the Viking, a scenic, dry 1.5km-long toboggan ride through rugged mountain terrain, and, in summer, **Parc Aquatique** (Water Park; 514-871-0101, 450-227-4671; ww.sommets.com/en/water-park-saint-sauveur; 350 Rue St-Denis; adult/youth/child per day $40/32/20; 10am-5pm Jun, to 7pm Jul-late Aug, to 6pm late Aug-early Sep;). Cross-country skiers flock to the more than 150km of interconnecting trails at Morin Heights, 8km to the west. The **Factoreries Tanger St-Sauveur** (St-Sauveur Tanger Outlets; 450-240-0880; www.tangeroutletcanada.com/saintsauveur/stores; 100 Ave Guindon; 10am-6pm Mon-Wed, to 9pm Thu & Fri, to 5pm Sat & Sun), factory outlets representing some 30 big-name brands – from Reebok and Puma to Guess and OshKosh B'gosh, are another draw in St-Sauveur.

The Drive » The easiest way to reach Ste-Adèle, some 10km to the north, is to follow Rue Principale east to Rte 117 Nord and take it to Blvd de Ste-Adèle and the center.

p252

3 Ste-Adèle

Ste-Adèle may not be as pretty as St-Sauveur, but there are plenty of things to keep families and outdoor enthusiasts happy, especially in and around picturesque Lac Rond (Round Lake).

If you're traveling to Mont-Tremblant – the town and/or the national park – this might be a good place to stop awhile as it has some excellent accommodations. Go for Au Clos Rolland (p252), a B&B in a sprawling 1904 mansion with gorgeous public spaces and vast grassy lawns surrounding it. Au Clos Rolland is only 300m from the Parc Linéaire du P'tit Train du Nord recreation path, making this a great option for cyclists and cross-country skiers. A favorite place for a meal is the Adèle Bistro (p252) right on Lac Rond with serious French dishes. Rue Morin, which runs from Lac Rond down to Rte 117, is lined with bars and other places to drink after dark.

The Drive » To reach Val-David, head southeast on Blvd de Ste-Adèle to Rte 15 Nord. Follow that for about 6km when it merges with Rte 117 Nord. You'll reach Rue de l'Église in Val-David after about 4km.

p252

4 Val-David

Arguably the most attractive village in the Laurentians, little Val-David offers great food, lovely wooded trails and views of the narrow Rivière du Nord running through the heart of town. Its charms have made it a magnet for artists, whose studios and galleries line the main street, Rue de l'Église, where you'll also find a number of agencies like **Roc & Ride** (819-322-7978; https://rocnride.com; 2444 Rue de l'Église; cross-country skiing equipment per half-/full-day $20/25; 9am-5pm Sat-Wed, to 6pm Thu & Fri) that will get you skiing, climbing, cycling or canoeing. The town's **tourist office** (ext 4235 888-322-7030, ext 4235 819-324-5678; www.valdavid.com; 2525 Rue de l'Église; 9am-5pm daily mid-Jun–mid-Oct, Fri-Sun mid-May–mid-Jun, Thu-Sun mid-Oct–mid-May), in a cute old train station, is conveniently located alongside the Parc Linéaire du P'tit Train du Nord recreation trail. Check out the nearby **Val-David Summer Market** (Marché d'Été de Val-David; http://marchesdici.org/nos-marches/val-david/#marche-d-ete; Rue de l'Académie; 9:30am-1:30pm Sat late May-early Oct) if you're in town on a Saturday morning. You'll also find artisanal bakeries, jazz music in cafes on summer weekends and more than a few arts-and-crafts people.

LOCAL KNOWLEDGE: PARC LINEAIRE DU P'TIT TRAIN DU NORD

Should you see roadside signs directing you to the Parc Linéaire du P'tit Train du Nord (Little Train of the North Linear Park), don't think it's showing you the way to something that goes 'choo-choo.' It's a trail system built on top of old railway tracks that wends its way for 232km north from Bois-de-Filion to Mont Laurier, passing streams, rivers, rapids, lakes and great mountain scenery. In summer it's open to bicycles and in-line skates, and you'll find rest stops, information booths, restaurants, B&Bs and bike rental and repair shops along the way. In winter the system lures cross-country skiers to the 42km-long section between St-Jérôme and Val-David, while snowmobile aficionados rule between Val-David and Mont Laurier (49km).

Val-David Village tourist office

The Drive » To reach Ste-Agathe-des-Monts, just less than 10km to the northwest, head southwest on Rue de l'Église toward the Parc Linéaire du P'tit Train du Nord then turn right onto Rte 117.

✕ 🛏 p252

5 Ste-Agathe-des-Monts

This mountain village, located about 9km northwest of Val-David, has a prime location on Lac des Sables. By the beginning of the 1900s, it was a well-known spa town. Later, famous guests included Queen Elizabeth, who came here during WWII, and Jackie Kennedy. Ste-Agathe is a stopover point on the Parc Linéaire du P'tit Train du Nord recreation path, making this a great option for cyclists and cross-country skiers. If you'd like to get out on the water, **Croisières Alouette** (☎0778-752-5098; www.croisierealouette.com; Quai Municipal; adult/youth/child $22/19/10.50; ⏰Jun-Oct) offers regular 50-minute cruises on Lac des Sables between two and five times a day in summer. The large **Hôtel Spa Watel** (☎800-363-6478, 819-326-7016; www.hotelspawater.com; 250 Rue St-Venant; r $120-220; P ❄ 📶 🏊), overlooking Lac des Sables, has spa facilities plus treatments and an indoor and outdoor pool. Three lakeside beaches are just opposite, including the large Plage Major. There is also quite a good restaurant in a lovely dining room here with views out to the lake.

The Drive » From Ste-Agathe-des-Monts join Rte 117 Nord and follow it for 20km to exit 107. Follow Chemin des Lacs for 3km into the center of St-Faustin-Lac-Carré.

MAPLE: AMBER NECTAR OF THE GODS

Québec is by far the largest producer of maple syrup in North America, with production exceeding 6.5 million gallons, and the Laurentians are a major contributor. That's more than three-quarters of the world's maple syrup, which is perhaps why it enjoys such pride of place here, appearing on everything from meat and desserts to foie gras, blended with smoothies and, of course, in maple beer. It's a very big business and worth a lot of money. It was thus not entirely a surprise when, over the course of several months in 2011 and 2012, nearly 3000 tons of syrup valued at $18.7 million was stolen from a storage facility in Québec. The Great Canadian Maple Syrup Heist was the most valuable in Canadian history. In late 2012, 17 men were arrested.

French settlers began producing it regularly in the 1800s after learning from indigenous people how to make it from maple-tree sap. Sap is usually extracted in March after enzymes convert starch into sugars over the winter. Once the weather warms and the sap starts flowing, the tree is tapped and the long process of boiling the raw sap down into syrup begins. It takes about 40L of sap to make 1L of syrup.

Quebecers head to *cabanes à sucre* (sugar shacks) out in the countryside during this time. There they sample the first amber riches of the season and do the *tire d'érable* (taffy pull), where steaming maple syrup is poured into the snow and then scooped up on a popsicle stick once it's cooled.

6 St-Faustin-Lac-Carré

The gateway to the region around Mont-Tremblant, St-Faustin has a couple of attractions in its own right, including a gorgeous slice of protected Laurentian wilderness at **Centre Touristique Éducatif des Laurentides** (CTEL; ☎819-326-9072; www.ctel.ca; 5000 Chemin du lac Caribou; adult/child $10/free; ⏲8am-5pm Sat-Thu, to 9pm Fri late Jun-early Sep, 8am-5pm Sat-Mon, to 9pm Fri mid-May–late Jun & early Sep–mid-Oct; P 👪), 20km by road to the south. This verdant park is a marvelous protected area and a great place to learn about local flora and fauna. The extensive trail network includes some wheelchair-accessible sections, and there are also kayak and canoe rentals to use in the dozens of lakes around here. Another reason to visit St-Faustin is **La Tablée des Pionniers** (☎855-688-2101, 819-688-2101; www.latableedespionniers.com; 1357 Rue St-Faustin; 4-/5-/6-course set menu $38/45/55; ⏲4:30-9:30pm Thu, 10am-10pm Fri-Sun late Feb-early May), a seasonal roadside eatery serving top-notch traditional Québécois cuisine in rustic country surroundings. Multicourse menus, served during maple-sugaring and apple-harvest seasons, feature such delights as split pea, cabbage and bacon soup; smoked-trout soufflés; pulled-pork and mushroom puff-pastry pies; and maple-walnut tarts – all accompanied by cider and maple from the family's orchards.

The Drive » From St-Faustin, follow Rte 117 Nord for 10km to exit 116 and Rte 327, which turns into Chemin du Village.

7 Ville de Mont-Tremblant

This village is the crown jewel of the Laurentians, lorded over by the 875m-high eponymous peak and surrounded by pristine lakes and rivers. It's a hugely popular winter playground, drawing ski bums from late October to mid-April. Founded in 1938, the **Mont-Tremblant Ski Resort** (☎514-764-7546; www.tremblant.ca;

1000 Chemin des Voyageurs, Station Tremblant; lift ticket adult/youth/child $99/88/66; ⌚8:30am-4pm late Nov–mid-Apr; 👪) is among the top-ranked international ones in eastern North America and includes more than 100 trails and 14 lifts. Its state-of-the-art summer facilities and activities include golf courses, water sports, cycling, tennis courts, hiking, yoga and zip-lines.

Ville de Mont-Tremblant is actually divided into three sections: Station Tremblant, the ski hill and pedestrianized tourist resort at the foot of the mountain; **Mont-Tremblant Village** (👪), a tiny cluster of homes and businesses about 4km to the southwest; and Mont-Tremblant Centre Ville, the main town and commercial center about 12km south of the mountain.

There's the full range of places to stay – from the basic-but-comfortable **Auberge Manitonga Hostel** (☎819-425-6008; www.manitongahostel.com; 2213 Chemin du Village, Mont-Tremblant Village; dm $30-42, r $74-120; P@📶) to the uber-luxurious **Hotel Quintessence** (☎866-425-3400; www.hotelquintessence.com; 3004 Chemin de la Chapelle, Station Tremblant; ste from $399; ❄@📶🏊). In-between is the favorite Auberge Le Lupin (p253), a log house with nine themed and spacious rooms just 1km away from the ski station and private beach access to sparkling Lac Tremblant. Among the best restaurants are **La Petite Cachée** (☎819-425-2654; www.petitecachee.com; 2681 Chemin du Village, Mont-Tremblant Village; mains $22-35; ⌚5-10pm) in a charming chalet halfway between the ski slopes and Mont-Tremblant Village, and sEb (p253), where seasonal, sustainable local ingredients are turned into culinary works of art.

The Drive ›› It's just under 30km from Ville de Mont-Tremblant to the Diable sector entrance of Parc National du Mont-Tremblant. Follow Chemin du Village (Rte 327) to Chemin Duplessis and Chemin du Lac Supérieur.

✕ 🛏 p253

8 Parc National du Mont-Tremblant

Québec province's oldest **park** (Mont Tremblant National Park; ☎819-688-2281, reservations 800-665-6527; www.sepaq.com/pq/mot; 4456 Chemin du Lac Supérieur, Lac-Supérieur; adult/child $8.60/free; 👪), which it opened in 1895, covers 1510 sq km of gorgeous Laurentian lakes, rivers, hills and woods. The park shelters rare vegetation (including silver maple and red oak) and is home to fox, deer, moose and wolves. It is also a habitat for almost 200 bird species, including a huge blue heron colony.

You'll find fantastic hiking and mountain-biking trails as well as camping and river routes for canoes. The half-day Méandres de la Diable route from Lac Chat to Mont de la Vache Noire is particularly popular. You won't be able to drive this far into the park. Reserve a canoe and a place on the shuttle bus by calling the park reservations line well in advance.

The Drive ›› From the Parc National du Mont-Tremblant you can return to Montréal via Rte 117 Sud and Rte 15 Sud (128km) and walk around Old Montréal.

Eating & Sleeping

St-Sauveur-des-Monts 2

Chez Bernard — Deli $

(450-240-0000; www.chezbernard.com; 407 Rue Principale; dishes $8-20; 10am-6pm Mon-Thu, to 8pm Fri, 9am-6pm Sat;) Superb deli with local specialties, some of which are homemade, plus full meals perfect for picnics.

Orange & Pamplemousse — Fusion $$

(450-227-4330; www.orangepamplemousse.com; 120 Rue Principale; 3-course set meals $28-40; 8am-2:30pm daily, 5-9pm Wed, Thu & Sun, to 9:30pm Fri & Sat) Billing itself as a *bistro actualisé* (up-to-date bistro), this restaurant is a great place to devour complex pasta dishes and extraordinary grilled fish to the relaxing gurgling of a Japanese bamboo water fountain. The breakfasts ($11 to $18) are also divine. Set meals are a snip at just $25 Wednesday and Thursday nights.

Le Petit Clocher — B&B $$

(450-227-7576; www.lepetitclocher.com; 216 Rue de l'Église; s $165-215, d $185-235; P) A gorgeous inn occupying a converted Dominican monastery on a little hillside above town, Le Petit Clocher has seven rooms decorated in French Country style, many of which have extraordinary views. Our favorite room was once a chapel and has beautiful old wood-paneled walls.

Auberge Sous L'Édredon — B&B $$

(450-227-3131; www.aubergesousledredon.com; 777 Rue Principale; r $169-249; P) This pretty inn with the cozy-sounding name (Under the Quilt) is overflowing with character. Some of the seven delightfully decorated rooms, named after gems and a lot more modern than the exterior suggests, have fireplaces and Jacuzzis. The inn is about 2km from the village center, close to a little lake and in full view of the ski slopes.

Ste-Adèle 3

Adèle Bistro — French $$

(450-229-4894; www.adelebistro.ca; 1241 Chemin du Chantecler; mains $21-32; 5-11pm Thu-Sun, 10am-3pm Sun) This stylish bistro opposite Lac Rond is the place to come to if you want serious French dishes: goose liver, bone marrow, blood pudding, *carbonnade* (selection of chargrilled meats). Host Jean-Marc Gandroz from Burgundy will walk you through the extensive wine list. Don't miss the killer bergamot-tea-flavoured crème brûlée. One of our favorite places for a meal in the Laurentians.

Au Clos Rolland — B&B $$

(450-229-1939; www.auclosrolland.com; 1200 Rue St-Jean; s $115-130, d $120-145;) Hidden in an otherwise-undistinguished neighborhood, this sprawling 1904 mansion surrounded by vast grassy lawns is an absolute gem. The public spaces downstairs – a library with piano, living room with fireplace and pretty glass-walled breakfast room – are instantly inviting, while the seven guest rooms, including a couple tucked under the eaves, have cozy beds, wood floors and 'old-house' charm.

The B&B is only 300m from the Parc Linéaire du P'tit Train du Nord (p252) recreation path, making this a great option for cyclists and cross-country skiers. Swiss nationals Carolyne and Pierre-André are the consummate hosts; the multicourse breakfasts are the repasts of gourmets.

Val-David 4

Le Mouton Noir — Fusion $

(819-322-1571; www.bistromoutonnoir.com; 2301 Rue de l'Église; mains $7.50-14.50; 8am-10.30pm Mon-Thu, to 1am Fri, 10am-10:30pm Sat & Sun, closed Mon & Tue winter) This artsy spot attracts a very Val-Davidian crowd of beards – some hippie-esque, some hipster-esque, some lumberjack-y. Everyone enjoys the funky Canadian fusion on old LP menus; you gotta love a place that serves bibimbap alongside poutine. Open mike on Friday and live music on Saturday keep the 'Black Sheep' baaing till late on weekends.

Au Petit Poucet — Québécois $$

(☎819-322-2246, 888-334-2246; https://aupetitpoucet.ca; 1030 Hwy 117; mains $9-21; ⏲6:30am-4pm) For the ultimate Québécois dining experience, head for this rustic cabin a couple of kilometers south of the village. In place since 1945, it's every local's go-to place for huge breakfasts and such specialties as *tourtière* (meat pie), ham-hock ragout and cassoulet with smoked ham.

Auberge Le Baril Roulant — Hostel $

(☎819-322-2280; www.barilroulant.com/auberge; 1430 Rue de l'Académie; dorm s $26-29, dorm $42-45, r $80-110, ste $110-130; P ❄ 📶 🐾) This wonderful inn and hostel on the river north of town is a welcome arrival in Val-David. There's a dorm with solid wooden bunk beds sleeping 14 people in 10 singles and two doubles, six rooms (with bathroom) named after winds (think Sirocco and Mistral) and a suite with a whirlpool tub.

There's a great kitchen and restaurant-pub (mains $9 to $20) open from noon to 10pm with dozens of craft beers on tap. Don't miss what they call 'the most zen terrace in the village' overlooking the Rivière du Nord.

La Maison de Bavière — B&B $$

(☎866-322-3528, 819-322-3528; www.maisondebaviere.com; 1470 Chemin de la Rivière; r $120-185; P @ 📶) Fall asleep to the sound of Rivière du Nord outside the window. This inn has hand-painted Bavarian stencils and wooden beams giving it the feel of a European ski chalet. Everything is geared toward a day of outdoors pursuits, from its location on the Parc Linéaire du P'tit Train du Nord (p248) trail to the energizing, full-gourmet breakfasts served each morning.

At the end of an activity-filled day, you can relax on the sprawling, pristine grounds overlooking the river. The restaurants and shops of Val-David are a short walk or bike ride away.

Ville de Mont-Tremblant ⑦

sEb — Canadian $$$

(☎819-429-6991; www.seblartisanculinaire.com; 444 Rue St-Georges, Mont-Tremblant Centre Ville; mains $32-55, 4-/7-course set menu $49/85; ⏲6-11pm Thu-Mon) Escape the mediocre and get a little taste of what culinary artisans can create with seasonal, sustainable local ingredients. A flexible, eager-to-please kitchen, an unforgettable menu and a never-ending wine list enhance the jovial atmosphere. sEb is best described as alpine chalet meets globetrotter (think African masks) meets Hollywood chic (Michael Douglas is a regular). Reservations essential.

Auberge Le Lupin — B&B $$

(☎819-425-5474; www.lelupin.com; 127 Rue Pinoteau, Mont-Tremblant Village; s $27-157, d $143-173; P @ 📶) Our favorite place to stay in Mont-Tremblant, this log house built in 1945 offers snug digs just 1km from the ski station, with private beach access to sparkling Lac Tremblant. The nine themed rooms are spacious and intelligently organised. The tasty breakfasts whipped up by hosts Pierre and Sylvie in the homey kitchen are a perfect start to the day.

Classic Trip

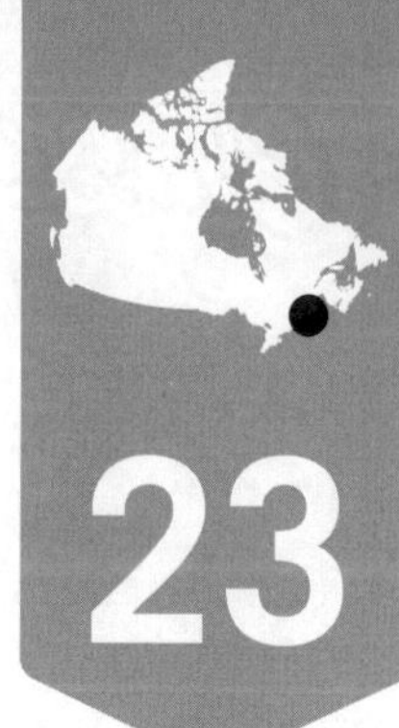

Eastern Townships

On this lake-villages drive you'll witness classic Québécois life in the region's Eastern Townships, with colorful wooden homes, sparkling lakes and ponds, maple-syrup–heavy cafes and interesting wineries.

TRIP HIGHLIGHTS

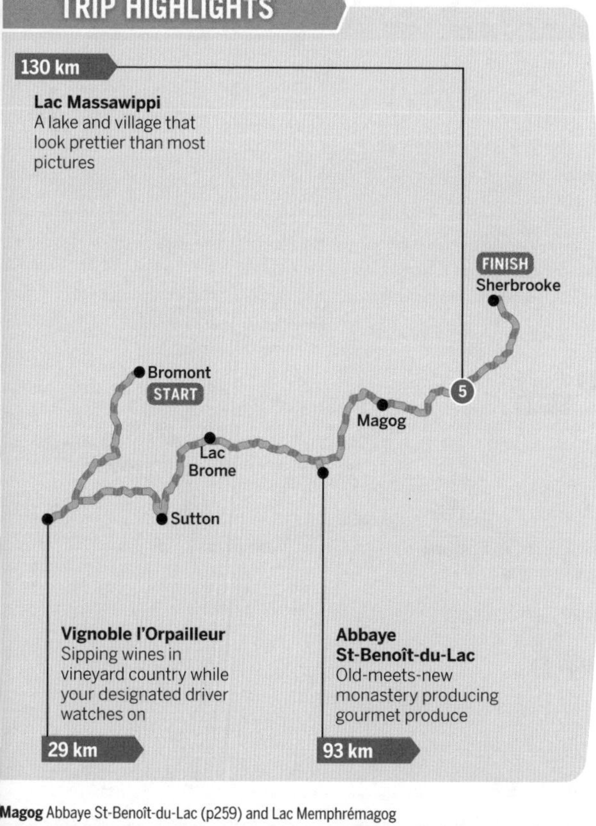

130 km

Lac Massawippi
A lake and village that look prettier than most pictures

FINISH
Sherbrooke

Bromont
START

5

Magog

Lac Brome

Sutton

Vignoble l'Orpailleur
Sipping wines in vineyard country while your designated driver watches on

29 km

Abbaye St-Benoît-du-Lac
Old-meets-new monastery producing gourmet produce

93 km

1 DAY
153KM/95 MILES

GREAT FOR...

BEST TIME TO GO

June and July has sunny weather with less traffic than in August.

ESSENTIAL PHOTO

At Abbaye St-Benoît-du-Lac with Lac Memphrémagog in the background.

BEST FOR CULTURE

Antique-store hopping for a glimpse of another era.

Magog Abbaye St-Benoît-du-Lac (p259) and Lac Memphrémagog

Classic Trip

23 Eastern Townships

This is a trip for people who like to take things at a leisurely pace, to experience local Québécois life with all its quirks – local produce, including cider and cheese made by monks, lakeside towns with duck festivals, and a treasure hunt of open-air murals. Between all the eccentricities, the ride is smooth and carefree.

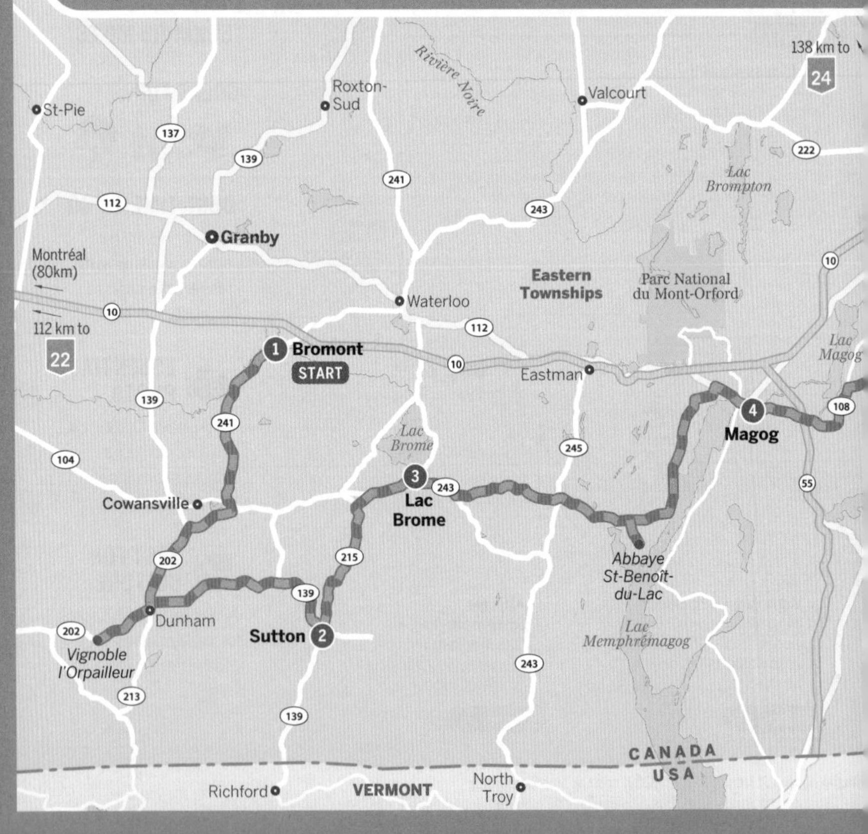

1 Bromont

From Montréal's Champlain Bridge take Hwy 10 for 75km and take Exit 78 to central Bromont. The ever-changing palette of Mt Brome is the highlight of stopping in this town. Its winter pines are laden with snow, luring skiers to **Ski Bromont** (☎450-534-2200; www.skibromont.com; 150 Rue Champlain; full/half day $42/34; 👪) with its roughly 140 trails, including almost 100 trails open for night skiing. In warmer weather the resort hosts a water park with fun slides, and its 100km of marked trails, including 15 thrilling downhill routes, have made it a mecca for mountain-bike aficionados (Bromont has hosted world championships). Even if you don't stop for long, a cruise by the edges of the 553m high mount is a fine start to the journey into the region and its hidden history – Mt Brome is what remains of an ancient series of volcanoes.

If that sounds too active, you might prefer to indulge with treats such as chocolate-covered cherries at the **Musée du Chocolat de la Confiserie Bromont** (☎450-534-3893; www.lemuseeduchocolatdelaconfiseriebromont.com; 679 Rue Shefford; meals from $13.25; ⏲8am-5pm). Its museum covers the history and process of chocolate making. And vegans can enjoy the taste sensations at Gaïa Resto Végan (p263).

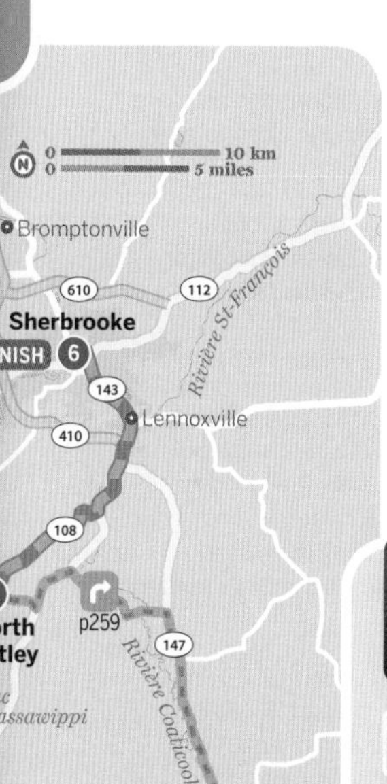

The Drive » Head south for 35km through Cowansville to Vignoble l'Orpailleur, a flat drive through the region's wineries and the long-flat houses with pruned lawns. As you head east from the wineries to Sutton, the 60km of road rise and there are three crossroads without any large signage. Instead, look for the small street signs to decide which street to follow.

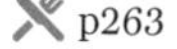
p263

2 Sutton

This is wine country and the most prestigious of them all, **Vignoble l'Orpailleur** (☎450-295-2763; http://orpailleur.ca; 1086 Rue Bruce, Dunham; ⏲10am-4:30pm), has a quirky display on the history of alcohol in Québec and offers wine tasting year round. The vineyard was established in 1982, but l'Orpailleur has pedigree – two of those in charge of the vines are sons of winemakers. The flat greenery is worth a peek, even if you are the designated driver. It has an attached restaurant, too.

LINK YOUR TRIP

22 Up to the Laurentians

After completing the trip, head two hours northwest to St-Jérôme for the start of a memorable ramble through the fabulous lake- and hillside scenery of the Laurentians.

24 Montréal to Québec City

From Sherbrooke, head northwest to Trois-Rivières, from where you can make a beeline for Québec City, or follow this itinerary in reverse to head back to Montréal.

Pause for a stroll through relaxed and beautiful Sutton and to linger at one of its cheery cafes. You might spot skiers getting warm after a trip on Mont Sutton during the winter, and hikers recovering from the climbs and rough camping on **Parc d'Environnement Naturel** (450-538-4085; www.parcsutton.com; adult/child $6/3; Jun-Oct;).

The Drive » The easy 18km drive northeast to Lac Brome is along Rte 215. In the south, the trees are sparser with grasslands and lawns stretching out into the distance. As you approach the town, you'll know it because of the mansion-like homes beaming as if recently painted, and pine trees on large lawns as if every day were Christmas.

 p263

3 Lac Brome

The traditional village-life essence of the Eastern Townships is encapsulated in downtown Lac Brome, the name given to a town made up of seven villages that converge on

NATIONAL PARKS

There are four national parks in the Eastern Townships, each with a slightly different flavour and all worth making extended stops.

Plan Your Trip
If you plan to camp or stay in a hut, check ahead; some accommodations are quite basic and not all parks are open year round. The trails leading to the national parks are gravel, so plan for your wheels to rough it a little.

Parc National du Mont Orford
This compact **park** (p261) is a delight in summer and a favorite with families for its gentle hiking trails, kayaking and canoeing in its lakes, and its small size, all conveniently reached 8km northwest from Magog.

Parc National du Mont-Mégantic
The standout feature in this **park** (819-888-2941; www.sepaq.com/pq/mme; 189 Rte du Parc; adult/child $8.75/free; P) at the eastern extremity of the townships 80km east of Sherbrooke is the **AstroLab** (819-888-2941; http://astrolab-parc-national-mont-megantic.org/en; 189 Rte du Parc, Notre-Dame-des-Bois; adult/child $19.25/free, Astronomy Evenings $25.25/free; 10am-4.30pm & 8pm-late Jun-Aug, check website for other times) observatory and educational center. If you have kids in tow, finish the day's road trip with an astronomy tour (reservations required).

Parc National de la Yamaska
At the heart of this 12-sq-km park near Bromont is an arrow-shaped lake ringed by towering forests. Come here in warm weather to rent sailboards, canoes and rowboats and then stay in a comfortable nature cabin. Visit in winter for snowshoeing and Nordic skiing.

Parc National de Frontenac
Wildlife lovers should make the trek 100km northeast of Sherbrooke to Frontenac to spot more than 200 species of bird and 30 of mammal. The park borders **Lac St-François**, with lakeside campsites and cabins, and has good family water activities as well as hiking and cycling.

DETOUR: COATICOOK

5 North Hatley

Cheese lovers will find the cheese map provided by the tourism office enough reason to detour to attractive Coaticook, a southern town of the Eastern Townships full of nature activities. The town's big magnet for outdoorsy types is the lush **Parc de la Gorge de Coaticook** (819-849-2331; www.gorgedecoaticook.qc.ca; 400 Rue St-Marc, Coaticook; adult/child $7.50/4.50; information desk 9am-5pm;) where you can explore the endless green space bordering the USA while riding horseback, mountain biking or hiking. If you have kids (or you are a big kid at heart), aim to visit on a summer evening for one of the highlights of Coaticook, **Foresta Lumina** (819-849-2331; www.forestalumina.com; 135 Rue Michaud, Coaticook; adult/child $19.50/11.50; 8:30-10:30pm Jul & Aug, Fri & Sat Jun, Sep & early Oct;), an outdoor light show where forest trails turn into colorful lit-up paths through the national park. At other times, there is an animal petting farm, and winter snow-tubing. Be sure to stop off for a maple syrup ice-cream at **Laiterie De Coaticook Ltée** at 1000 Rue Child.

From North Hatley head east on Rte 143 and then south along Rte 147 for 28km (30 minutes) to Parc de la Gorge de Coaticook. To rejoin the main part of the trip, head north on Rte 147, becoming Rte 143, for 33km (30 minutes) straight to Sherbrooke.

a lake of the same name. The town is home to the well-heeled, so the stores here cater to fine tastes with boutique clothing and gift stores, and more than a dozen well-curated antiques. Many stores are in converted Victorian houses, so there is a British flavor of yesteryear that is part of the highlight of stopping here. Stroll the lake and pop in for the area's famous duck products at **Brome Lake Duck Farm** (450-242-3825; www.canardsdulacbrome.com; 40 Chemin Centre; 8am-5pm Mon-Thu, to 6pm Fri, 9am-6pm Sat, 10am-5pm Sun). Lac Brome's prettiest village, **Knowlton**, is in the south and has the nickname the Knamptons (a play on the Hamptons) for the swanky **19th-century country houses**, owned by Montréalers who use the town as a summer getaway. It's worth driving off the main road for a peek at the architectural heritage.

The Drive » On the 43km drive from Knowlton, Lac Brome, to Magog, you'll first pass the Abbaye St-Benoît-du-Lac. Take Rte 243 east for five minutes and the left turnoff at Chemin de Glen, passing picturesque ponds and some unpaved roads to the abbey after 23km. Then follow the lakeside road north 20km to Magog.

4 Magog

Just 20km before you enter Magog from the south, the **Abbaye St-Benoît-du-Lac** (819-843-4080; www.abbaye.ca; 1 Rue Principale, St-Benoît-du-Lac; church 5am-8:30pm, shop 9-10:45am & 11:45am-6pm Mon-Sat) is an unmissable highlight of the townships. The complex mixes traditional architecture, such as a tall church tower, with modern features, such as colorful tiling. The abbey is framed by the wide dark expanse of Lac Memphrémagog and the mountains, resplendent in trees, which are particularly spectacular in the fall or dressed in winter snow. A visit is especially magical if you can coincide with the three-daily Gregorian chanting recitals. Drop by the abbey to buy products made by

Classic Trip

DO MI NIC/SHUTTERSTOCK ©

EZJAY/SHUTTERSTOCK ©

WHY THIS IS A CLASSIC TRIP

PHILLIP TANG, WRITER

This trip takes you into the heart of classic, slow Québécois life with wholesome, locally produced food. Many think that an abbey sounds like a dressed-up church, until they reach Abbaye St-Benoît-du-Lac and get to taste cheese and cider made by monks, who then break into Gregorian chanting. All this plus knock-out lakes and mountains once you continue on your merry way.

Above: Parc National du Mont Orford (p261)
Left: Historic inn, North Hatley (p261)
Right: Abbaye St-Benoît-du-Lac (p259)

WALTER BIBIKOW/GETTY IMAGES ©

monks, such as blueberries dipped in chocolate, cider and cheese. Continue on with a drive through pretty downtown Magog and around Lac Memphrémagog to ogle the waterfront properties. You can even take a narrated boat cruise on the lake, if you have extra time up your sleeve and book a month in advance. The **Parc National du Mont Orford** (☎819-843-9855; www.sepaq.com/pq/mor; 3321 Chemin du Parc, Orford; adult/child $8.75/free, parking $8.50; P 👪) is also nearby for winter skiing and summer hiking.

The Drive » The short but hilly 18km drive east from Magog to North Hatley passes by drool-worthy red-brick and colorful stately houses in the loftiest section and then the road narrows and becomes surrounded by thick trees just before North Hatley. If you can make it to North Hatley's Farmers Markets, enter by car along Capelton and park for free.

✕ 🛏 p263

5 North Hatley

North Hatley is what first-timers to the region picture as the Eastern Townships and it is this beauty, easily one of the top stunners in Québec, that makes the town worthy of a stop. Admire the postcard-perfect aspects of the village – hugging the north of sparkling **Lac**

Classic Trip

Massawippi, populated with visitors in colorful bathers and kayaks in summer, and polished-up centuries-old houses flanking the streets. A cruise along the main street is the best way to spot the restored historic houses and antique stores, which are filled with local treasures. Catch the local buzz by planning a visit to coincide with the North Hatley Farmers Market on Saturdays in warm weather, held at River Park. Tasting the locally produced honey, apples and pastries are part of the charm, but it's the buskers and the chance to chat with locals that makes it special. By night you can taste the local ingredients that go into four-course menus at Auberge Le Coeur d'Or.

The Drive » The 20km drive northeast from North Hatley to Circuit des Murales de Sherbrooke is a mostly straight, flat trip whether you take Rte 108 or the more southerly Rte 143, though the former does pass an asphalt plant, which might amuse those looking for a passing quirky sight. Traffic will get thicker as you enter Sherbrooke.

p263

6 Sherbrooke

More of a small city than a township, there are unusual but worthy attractions to make Sherbrooke, the last of the main Eastern Townships, your final destination for this trip. Hunt for the 11 **street murals** dotted downtown at the **Circuit des Murales de Sherbrooke** starting from the corner of Rue Frontenac and Wellington. Each piece tells a local story of the people and region, including painted life-size re-creations of shop facades that once stood in the area. From a distance, the facades are camouflaged by the adjacent real stores, adding to the hunt-and-discovery fun, especially for tired kids at the end of a road trip. At **Bishop's University** (www.ubishops.ca/st-marks-chapel; Rue du Collège, Lennoxville) original architecture abounds, with most of the two-dozen buildings dating from the 1840s. The most conventionally attractive architectural sight is St Mark's Chapel, which woos visitors with stained-glass windows and decorative pews.

Eating & Sleeping

Bromont 1

Gaïa Resto Végan Vegan $

(☎450-534-2074; www.legaia.ca; 840 Rue Shefford; mains $9-15; ⏰8am-3pm Thu-Mon, also 5-8pm Fri & Sat; 🌱) For vegans, Gaïa is easily the culinary drawcard for the Eastern Townships. Middle Eastern, South Asian and Québécois flavors go into knockout crepes, burgers, bowls and smoothies pretty enough to elicit oohs and ahs when served up. Details like cashew ricotta elevate fresh ingredients to gourmet dishes great enough to convince an omnivore, and staff have a local warmth. Reservations recommended.

Sutton 2

Le Pleasant Hôtel & Café Historic Hotel $$

(☎450-538-6188; www.lepleasant.com; 1 Rue Pleasant; r $125-259; ❄ @ 📶) This luxurious inn is a great place for a weekend escape or romantic interlude. Some of the sleek and modern rooms – well balanced by a classically historical facade – have views of **Mont Sutton**, and the breakfasts are memorable.

Magog 4

Fondissimo Swiss $$$

(☎819-843-8999; 276 Rue Principale Est; mains $26-34; ⏰5-10pm Jul & Aug, Thu-Sun only rest of year) With a name like Fondissimo, it's not hard to guess the specialty of this hip restaurant in an old renovated factory – there are eight varieties of Swiss fondue alone. Chinese fondue – meat, veggies and seafood, and a piping-hot vat of oil in which to cook it yourself – is also a popular choice.

À L'Ancestrale B&B B&B $$

(☎819-847-5555; www.ancestrale.com; 200 Rue Abbott; r incl breakfast $109-139; @ 📶) Wake up to a five-course gourmet breakfast at this intimate retreat. The five rooms are dressed in a romantic, countrified way and outfitted with refrigerators and coffeemakers. It's central but on a quiet street.

North Hatley 5

Auberge Le Coeur d'Or Québécois $$$

(☎819-842-4363; www.aubergelecoeurdor.com; 85 Rue School; 4-course meal $47; ⏰6-9pm, closed Mon & Tue Nov-Apr) For a delightful night out, head to this charming farmhouse inn. The restaurant's four- to five-course dinners make abundant use of local ingredients, including cheeses from Sherbrooke, rabbit from Stanstead, duck from Orford and smoked trout from East Hereford. Save room for profiteroles, chocolate mousse cake, or the Coeur d'Or's trademark trio of crème brûlées.

Manoir Hovey Resort $$$

(☎819-842-2421; www.manoirhovey.com; 575 Rue Hovey; d from $300, dinner & breakfast incl from $505; P ❄ @ 📶 🏊) This lovely resort offers handsomely set rooms in a picturesque lakeside setting. You'll find expansive gardens, a heated pool and an ice rink (in winter), and you can arrange numerous outdoor activities – windsurfing, lake cruises and golfing. The award-winning restaurant **Le Hatley** is among the best in the Eastern Townships, with four-course meals highlighting refined Québécois fare ($80 for nonguests).

Montréal to Québec City

The sparkle off the St Lawrence River will guide you to eclectic Trois-Rivières with stops for quirky pop-culture and race-car driving museums, zip-lining, potato donuts and circus performances.

TRIP HIGHLIGHTS

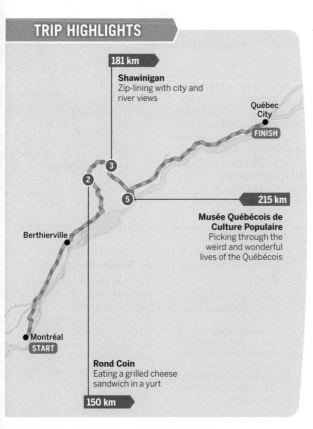

181 km
Shawinigan
Zip-lining with city and river views

Québec City
FINISH

215 km
Musée Québécois de Culture Populaire
Picking through the weird and wonderful lives of the Québécois

Berthierville

Montréal
START

Rond Coin
Eating a grilled cheese sandwich in a yurt
150 km

1 DAY
383KM/238 MILES

GREAT FOR...

BEST TIME TO GO

June and July has sunny weather, and less traffic than August.

ESSENTIAL PHOTO

Gliding on a zip line at Parc de L'Île Melville.

BEST FOR CULTURE

Delving into the minutiae of Québécois lives at quirky museums.

Montréal City skyline with Biosphere by architect Buckminster Fuller

24 Montréal to Québec City

This trip is for people who want to explore Québec's lesser-known Mauricie region, reachable in a couple hours from Montréal along the northern shore of the St Lawrence River, with stops at wonderfully weird museums. The backdrop is the ever-reassuring guiding line of the mighty waterway as well as a constant flow of quaint towns to pass through and compare.

1 Berthierville

From Montréal take scenic Hwy 40 east on the northern side of the St Lawrence River for 80km (one hour), to pause at pretty Berthierville. Fans of race-car driving should make a pit stop at **Musée Gilles-Villeneuve**, which commemorates the eponymous Québécois motorsport legend, who grew up in Berthierville. The small museum housed in an old post has a surprisingly large collection of race cars (including the one with which his son, Jacques Villeneuve, won the Indy 500), a mini race track and memorabilia galore such as helmets, race suits, competition snowmobiles.

For something more tranquil, the free **Park Scirbi** has three nature trails from 2km to 4.5km where you can spot more than 222 species of birds, grazing farm animals and wetlands. You can also participate in nature workshops. Parking is available.

Then drop by **Délices D'antan** (on Rang de la Rivière-Bayonne) for the local specialty, potato donuts.

The Drive » On the 70km drive northeast from Berthierville to St-Élie-de-Caxton, river-hugging Hwy 40 is quite flat until after Louiseville, where the road starts to climb away from the St Lawrence River and up through neighborhoods of white flat houses sporting spacious green lawns.

2 St-Élie-de-Caxton

A town circled by mountains and decorated with lakes might be whimsical enough to make you break into song. Indeed Québécois folk musician and storyteller Fred Pellerin was born here and has famously sung its praise. It's worth a stop to see the charming houses

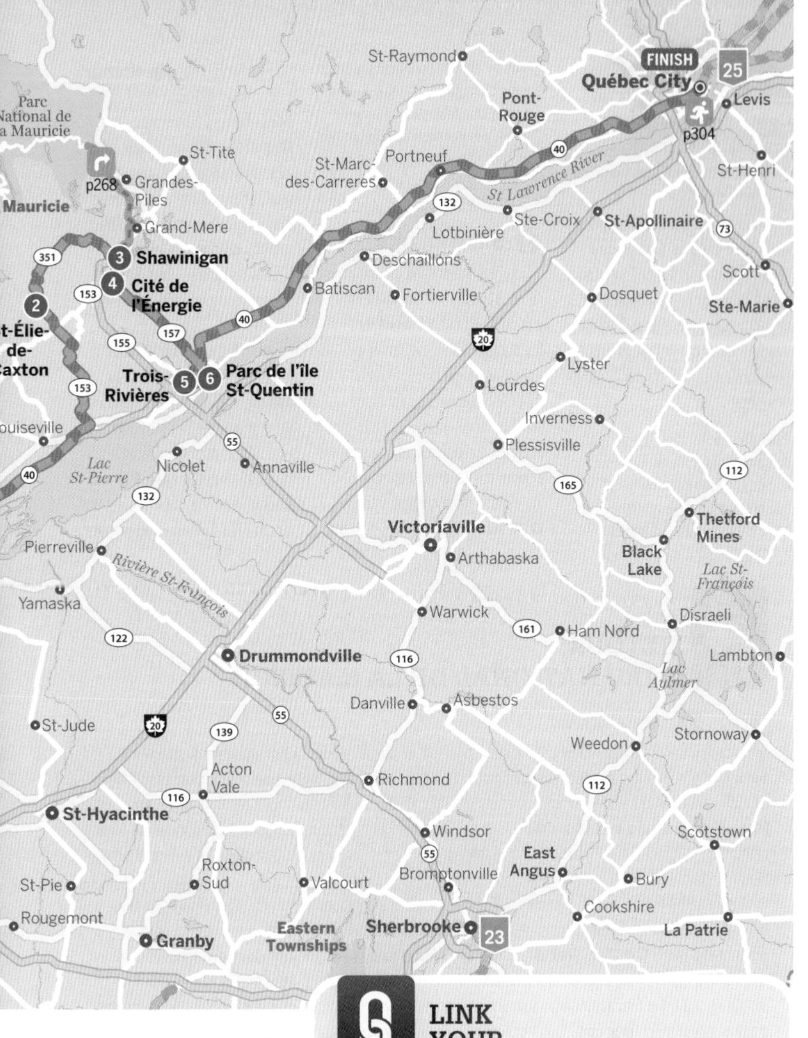

and shops that inspired him. Head to the Bureau d'Accueil Touristique at 52 Chemin des Loisirs for the free two-hour (on foot; 30 minutes if driving) self-guided **audio tour** (from June to October) 'Le Caxton Légendaire' narrated by Pellerin himself, which really brings it all to life, even if you have

LINK YOUR TRIP

23 Eastern Townships

From Trois-Rivières, head south to join this classic trip at Sherbrooke, then follow the itinerary in reverse for a picturesque route back to Montréal.

25 Around, Over & In the St Lawrence River

At this trip's end, continue to Île d'Orléans', just north of Québec City, for island roaming, waterfall gazing and abundant outdoor adventures.

never heard anything by him. Pop into the **Rond Coin** for an iconic eat the village, a boutique 'gridchize' (grilled cheese sandwich). While it's wholesome and delicious, half the fun is the location. The convivial restaurant and general store is inside a large round yurt, and it has novel accommodations set in old milk wagons.

The Drive » The 28km drive from St-Élie-de-Caxton to Shawinigan is extremely flat and easygoing on the northeasterly Rte 351, and a bit bumpier though slightly greener east on Rte 153 with narrower roads. Both take you by large Québécois homes that will make you envious of the space they have.

3 Shawinigan

Shawinigan's orderly downtown is modeled on Manhattan and set in a convenient grid of streets. Unlike central NYC, Shawinigan still maintains cute small stores and has river views from its cafes. Factor in some playtime with **D'Arbre en Arbre** on four very thrilling **zip-lining** courses in Parc de L'Île Melville. There are varying difficulties, which can get pretty challenging. It's set around the river with commanding views across downtown Shawinigan. Head to the river for a stroll, and if you have a spare couple of hours, you can rent a boat there for a cruise along the river. Then, if you plan to be here in the evening, book tickets to watch the **Cirque Éloize** show *Nezha,* about an orphan girl stranded on

DETOUR: PARC NATIONAL DE LA MAURICIE

Start: 3 Shawinigan

Moose foraging by an idyllic lake, the plaintive cry of a loon gliding across the water, bear cubs romping beneath a potpourri of trees waiting to put on a spectacular show of color in the fall – these are scenes you might possibly stumble across while visiting **Parc National de la Mauricie** (Mauricie National Park; ☎888-773-8888, 819-538-3232; www.pc.gc.ca/mauricie; adult/child $7.80/free; P). What may well be Québec's best-run and best-organized park is also among its most frequented.

The numerous walking trails, which can take anywhere from half an hour to five days to complete, offer glimpses of the indigenous flora and fauna, brooks and waterfalls (the **Chutes Waber** in the park's western sector are particularly worth the hike), as well as panoramic views onto delicate valleys, lakes and streams. The longest trail, Le Sentier Laurentien, stretches over 75km of rugged wilderness in the park's northern reaches. Backcountry campsites are spaced out every 7km to 10km. No more than 40 people are allowed on the trail at any time, making reservations essential. Topographic maps are for sale at the park.

The park is excellent for canoeing. Five canoe routes, ranging in length from 14km to 84km, can accommodate everyone from beginners to experts. Canoe and kayak rentals ($18/50 per hour/day; www.locationcanot.com) are available at three sites, the most popular being Lac Wapizagonke, which has sandy beaches, steep rocky cliffs and waterfalls. One popular day trip has you canoeing from the Wapizagonke campground to the west end of the lake, followed by a 7.5km loop hike to the Chutes Waber and back by canoe.

The park entrance is located about 25km north of Shawinigan. Reach it from Shawinigan by driving along Hwy 55 north and taking exit 226.

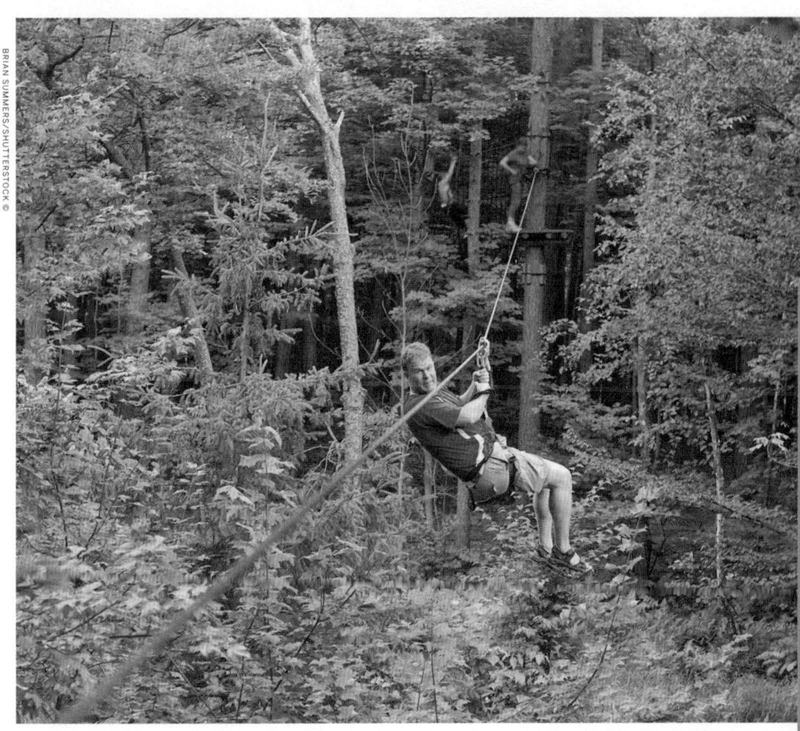

Shawinigan D'Arbre en Arbre

a pirate island, at the covered insulated amphitheater.

The Drive » It's a swift 4km drive south from downtown Shawinigan to Cité de l'énergie on Île Melville, where there is also Parc de L'Île Melville. There is free outdoor parking on the island.

4 Cité de l'Énergie

The **City of Energy** is a kind of science museum built around a 1901 hydroelectric power station, telling the story of how machinery is powered. It might sound dry, but the multimedia exhibits help to make it amusing and educational. Tours of the historic area, with a river crossing and a visit to the power plant itself are worth doing to make even more sense of the whole mini-city's past. Be sure to climb to the top of the observation tower for some fine views of the area. If you can visit on a summer evening, be sure to catch a show by **Cirque de Soleil**, reason enough to stop in the region. The musicians, dancers and acrobats put on a performance with the broad theme of energy.

Stop for a bite to eat at the **Roulotte Beauparlant**. The biggest claim to fame of this 1940s trailer-turned-diner is that former Prime Minister Jean Chrétien often ate here.

The Drive » The 35km drive southeast along Rte 157 from Cité de l'Énergie to Trois-Rivières runs downhill towards the St Lawrence River on an uneventful, easy trip. You'll pass by tightly packed houses that give way to low-level farmlands and then back to quiet suburban streets with detached houses.

5 Trois-Rivières

It's no surprise that this is the most common rest stop on the way to Québec, when you realize how much there is to see and do in the town of Trois-Rivières. The area

LOCAL KNOWLEDGE: QUEBECOIS CULTURE

Québécois are a true hybrid of Europe and North America. In the cities, folks Instagram their dinners; in rural areas, they may drive a Ford F-350 with camo plates. But across the board, people take life a little slower, and take time to enjoy a coffee, beer or wine with their meals. In general, people here are friendly but not overbearing; there is a reserve to locals that feels both Continental European and rooted in the cold climate. The French language and its preservation is an issue near and dear to many Québécois, including those raised in more anglophone-friendly Montréal.

The Québécois drink more alcohol than the average Canadian, and predominantly liberal views contribute to a laid-back atmosphere that feeds an effervescent nightlife in Montréal and Québec City and a passion for festivals across the province. On weekend evenings, city streets are often packed with pedestrians well into the early hours of the morning.

has a small selection of museums, but the quirky **Musée Québécois de Culture Populaire** (Musée POP; ☎819-372-0406; http://museepop.ca; 200 Rue Laviolette; adult/child $13/8; ⌚10am-6pm Jul & Aug, to 4pm Wed-Fri, to 5pm Sat & Sun Sep-Jun) is by far the most unique. Visit for the temporary exhibitions, which pick out lesser-known aspects of the social and cultural life of the Québécois. Known as Musée POP, themes are indeed pop, rather than highbrow, and in the past have included a quirky show on the social significance of garage sales, and one exhibiting woodcarvings of birds commonly spotted in the area.

Then visit the **Centre d'Histoire de l'Industrie Papetière Boréalis**, which focuses on the process and history of paper making. Kids particularly love the workshops, which take them through the process of making their own sheet of paper. They can then continue to the underground vaults for a **treasure hunt** using UV flashlights.

Finish off with a stroll along the attractive **riverfront promenade**, which leads to the oldest section of town along Rue des Ursulines.

The Drive » This brisk 4km drive north and then east across two bridges from central Trois-Rivières to Parc de l'île St-Quentin is easy. You can see the forested island for much of the ride. There is a $5 charge per person (including vehicle entry).

✕ 🛏 p271

❻ Parc de l'île St-Quentin

The island just across from the central Trois-Rivières waterside promenade has a riverside **beach** with yellow sand and a **pool** that are both worth visiting in warm weather for a splash about. City views form the backdrop. The park also has easy boardwalk trails dotted with black squirrels, picnic tables and a playground, making it a great stop if you have kids who have energy to use up.

The Drive » After spending the day at Trois-Rivières, you can head directly to Québec City, 130km east on Hwy 40, or head back to Montréal 142km on Hwy 40 west. A more scenic route to return to Montréal is via the charming Eastern Townships, taking Rte 55 southeast either 155km to bustling Sherbrooke, or 175km to picturesque North Hatley.

Eating & Sleeping

Trois-Rivières 5

Café Morgane — Cafe $

(819-694-1118; http://cafemorgane.com; 100 Rue des Forges; dishes $5-9; 6am-11:30pm Mon-Thu, to 12:30am Fri & Sat, 7am-11:30pm Sun;) On most afternoons, this branch of a local chain is the busiest spot in Trois-Rivières. Espresso, herbal teas and decadent sweets infuse the airy space with delightful smells. There's a free wi-fi connection here.

Le Poivre Noir — Fusion $$$

(819-378-5772; www.poivrenoir.com; 1300 Rue du Fleuve; mains $25-34, 3-course menu $46; 11:30am-2pm Wed-Fri, also 5:30-8:30pm Tue-Sat;) At this upmarket place by the riverfront, chef José Pierre Durand's inspired, often daring, blend of French, Québécois and international influences creates a memorable dining experience. Appetizers such as asparagus and blood-orange salad, or warm goat's-cheese 'snowballs' with tomatoes and pistachios are followed by main dishes such as Québécois deer with pine-nut and squash risotto and cranberry chutney. Reservations suggested.

Gambrinus — Brewery $

(819-691-3371; www.gambrinus.qc.ca; 3160 Blvd des Forges; dishes $5-16; 11am-1am Mon-Fri, 3pm-1am Sat) About 3km northwest of the riverfront, this decade-old brewery serves more than a dozen varieties of beer, including seasonal cranberry, raspberry and apple ales, an excellent IPA, and an unconventional hemp-and-honey blend called Miel d'Ange.

Auberge Internationale de Trois-Rivières — Hostel $

(819-378-8010; www.hihostels.ca; 497 Rue Radisson; dm/d $32/70; @) This wonderfully clean and friendly youth hostel is set in a two-story brick Georgian home, within easy walking distance of the riverfront and all the city's attractions. Dorms have four to eight beds each, and there are also reasonably priced private rooms. Bicycle rentals are available.

Le Fleurvil — B&B $$

(819-372-5195; www.fleurvil.qc.ca; 635 Rue des Ursulines; d $119-159;) Operated by a gregarious Harley aficionado with a knack for decorating, this homey inn within a stone's throw of the St Lawrence River and the walking promenade fronts a lush garden with a maple-shaded pool.

Classic Trip

Around, Over & In the St Lawrence River

With an island that's a locavore's paradise, waterfalls in spades, Québec's most sacred church, artsy towns and the St Lawrence River forever in view... What's not to love?

TRIP HIGHLIGHTS

290 km

Baie St Paul
Art town boasting lovely galleries and restaurants

La Malbaie

110 km

Ste-Anne de Beaupré
More than a basilica – a state of mind

9

137 km

Cap Tourmente National Wildlife Area
Bird sanctuary counting hundreds of species

6

4

1

Parc de la Chute-Montmorency

START/FINISH Québec City

Île d'Orléans
Paradise for locavores in the St Lawrence

13 km

3 DAYS
383KM/238 MILES

GREAT FOR...

BEST TIME TO GO

Visit May/June for springtime flowers and produce, September/October for magical fall colors.

ESSENTIAL PHOTO

La mer (the sea) that is the St Lawrence River from La Malbaie.

BEST FOR CULTURE

Baie St Paul is a food and arts hub.

Québec City View with the Fairmont Le Château Frontenac (p280)

Classic Trip

25 Around, Over & In the St Lawrence River

This drive, with the St Lawrence River at its heart, will circle you around idyllic Île d'Orléans, an island dotted with strawberry fields, apple orchards, windmills, workshops and galleries, across to the Côte de Beaupré, with a waterfall taller than Niagara Falls and Québec's largest basilica, and on to Charlevoix, a stunning outdoors playground with some lovely local towns crammed with artists' studios, galleries and boutiques.

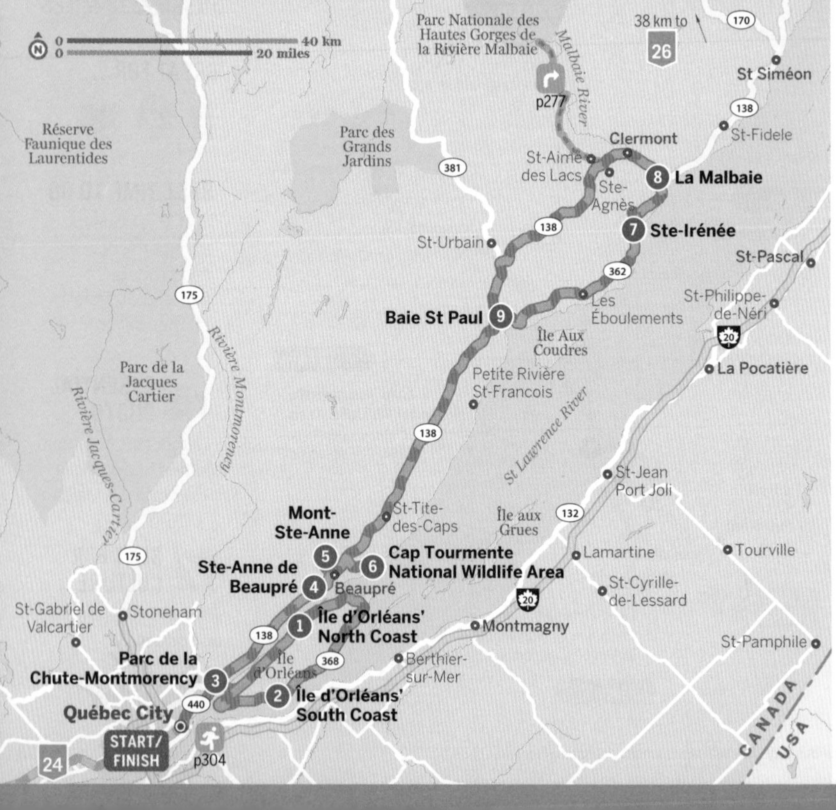

❶ Île d'Orléans' North Coast

'Orléans Island,' 15km northeast of Québec City, with a population of just 6825, is still primarily a farming region and has emerged as the epicenter of Québec's agritourism movement. Foodies from all around flock to the local *économusées* (workshops) to watch culinary artisans at work.

To reach the island from Québec City, take Rte 440 Est to the Pont de l'Île d'Orléans, the huge suspension bridge leading to the island, then join Rte 368. This 60km-long road encircles the island, with two more cutting across it north–south.

LINK YOUR TRIP

Montréal to Québec City

It's less than a two-hour drive from the Île d'Orléans to Trois-Rivières, where you can complete this road trip along the St-Lawrence in reverse.

The Saguenay Fjord & Lac St Jean

From Baie St-Paul, continue another 138km northeast to a spectacular journey along the Saguenay Fjord.

There are a half-dozen villages on the island. On the north side you'll find St-Pierre, Ste-Famille and St-François, each with its own attractions. Before setting out, though, stop in at the **Île d'Orléans tourist office** (☎866-941-9411, 418-828-9411; http://tourisme.iledorleans.com/en; 490 Côte du Pont, St-Pierre; ⏲8:30am-6pm early Jun-early Sep, to 4:30pm rest of year), which you'll come to after crossing the bridge. Its very complete *Autour de l'Île d'Orléans* (Around the Île d'Orléans) brochure is well worth the $1 charged for it.

Then make a beeline to any of the many workshops and boutiques lining the road in St-Pierre, including **Cassis Monna & Filles** (www.cassismonna.com/en; 1225 Chemin Royal, St-Pierre; ⏲10am-8pm Jun-Sep, 11:30am-5pm Oct-May), where everything from mustard to liqueur is made from blackcurrants, and **La Nougaterie Québec** (www.nougateriequebec.com; 1367 Chemin Royal, St-Pierre; ⏲10am-5pm Mon-Fri, from 11am Sat & Sun), where egg whites and honey are miraculously turned into nougat.

In Ste-Famille, the main draw is **Maison Drouin** (www.maisondrouin.com; 2958 Chemin Royal, Ste-Famille; adult/child $6/free; ⏲10am-6pm mid-Jun–early Sep, noon-4pm Sat & Sun early Sep–mid-Oct), a house dating back to 1730 that has never been modernized, while in St-François you have to climb the wooden **Observation Tower** (325 Chemin Royal, St-François; ⏲sunrise-sunset) for views over the St Lawrence River and the brooding mountains beyond.

The Drive ›› Nothing could be easier. Just continue on the only highway on the island – Rte 368 – which loops around the island and back to the bridge (33km).

p281

❷ Île d'Orléans' South Coast

The next three villages ahead of you on the island's southern coast are St-Jean, St-Laurent and Ste-Pétronille. Their edges are dotted with strawberry fields, orchards, cider producers, windmills, workshops and galleries. Some of the villages contain wooden and stone houses that are up to 300 years old.

If you're feeling peckish, stop off at **La Boulange** (www.laboulange.ca; 4624 Chemin Royal, St-Jean; light meals $5-12; ⏲7:30am-5:30pm Mon-Sat, to 5pm Sun late Jun–early Sep, see website for rest of the year), a memorable bakery and a grocery store in St-Jean. Devour to-die-for croissants while taking in views of the St Lawrence and the 18th-century **Église St-Jean** (Church of St John; ☎418-828-2551; 4623 Chemin Royal, St-Jean) next door.

Classic Trip

Further along in St-Laurent, the little **Parc Maritime de St-Laurent** (http://parcmaritime.ca/en; 120 Chemin de la Chalouperie, St-Laurent; adult/youth/child $5/3/free; ⌚10am-5pm mid-Jun–mid-Oct; 👪) is worth a look to understand the maritime heritage of the region. At the nearby **La Forge à Pique-Assaut** (www.forge-pique-assaut.com; 2200 Chemin Royal, St-Laurent; ⌚9am-5pm late Jun-early Sep, 9am-noon & 1:30-5pm Mon-Fri mid-Sep–mid-Jun), artisanal blacksmith Guy Bel makes and sells decorative objects at his *économusée*. Our last stop, in Ste-Pétronille, is the incomparable **Chocolaterie de l'Île d'Orléans** (www.chocolaterieorleans.com; 8330 Chemin Royal, Ste-Pétronille; ⌚9.30am-5pm Mon-Fri, to 6pm Sat & Sun), where *chocolatiers* above a delightful shop in a 200-year-old house churn out tasty concoctions.

The Drive » From Ste-Pétronille's center, continue along Rte 368 and back to the Pont de l'Île d'Orléans. Cross the bridge and join Rte 138 Ouest to the Blvd des Chutes exit and the Parc de la Chute-Montmorency (10km).

🛏 p281

3 Parc de la Chute-Montmorency

The waterfall in this national park just over the bridge from the Île d'Orléans is 83m high, topping Niagara Falls by about 30m (though it's not nearly as wide). What's cool is walking over the falls on the **suspension bridge** (La Chute-Montmorency) to see (and hear) them thunder down below.

Once you reach the park's entrance you have one of three choices: park the car and take the **cable car** (www.sepaq.com/destinations/parc-chute-montmorency; adult/child one way $12.25/6.30, return $14.35/7.20; ⌚8:30am-7:30pm late Jun–mid-Aug, shorter hours rest of year; P 👪) up to the falls; follow the Promenade de la Chute from the cable car's lower station and climb the 487-step Escalier Panoramique (Panoramic Staircase); or stay in the car and drive to the upper station and the **Manoir Montmorency** (www.sepaq.com/destinations/parc-chute-montmorency; 2490 Ave Royale; ⌚10am-6pm Apr-Oct, to 4pm Nov-Mar), a replica of an 18th-century manor house with an information counter, interpretation center about the falls and park, a shop and a terrace restaurant. To really get the adrenaline going, there's a zip-line that shoots across the canyon in front of the falls and three levels of via ferrata (cable-aided protected climbing trails).

The Drive » From Parc de la Chute-Montmorency, rejoin Rte 138 and this time travel east. The town and basilica of Ste-Anne de Beaupré are 25km to the northeast.

4 Ste-Anne de Beaupré

The drive along the Côte de Beaupré to the **pilgrimage church** (www.sanctuairesainteanne.org; 10018 Ave Royale; ⌚7am-9:30pm Jun-Aug, 8am-5pm Mon-Sat, to 6pm Sun Sep-May) at Ste-Anne de Beaupré is a delight in any season, including winter, when the ice floes in the St Lawrence shimmer in the sun under the bright blue sky. Approaching along Rte 138, the basilica tower's twin steeples dwarf everything else in town. Since the mid-1600s, the village has been an important Christian site; the annual pilgrimage around the feast day of St Anne (July 26) draws thousands of visitors. The awe-inspiring basilica you see today was constructed after a devastating blaze in 1922 and has been open since 1934. Inside, don't miss the lovely modern stained-glass windows (there are 214 of them), the impressive tilework and glittering ceiling mosaics depicting the life of St Anne.

DETOUR: PARC NATIONALE DES HAUTES GORGES DE LA RIVI RE MALBAIE

Start: 8 La Malbaie

This 225-sq-km **provincial park** (800-665-6527, 418-439-1227; www.sepaq.com/pq/hgo; 25 Blvd Notre-Dame, Clermont; adult/child $8.75/free; visitor center 9am-8pm mid-Jun–early Sep;) has several unique features, including the highest rock faces east of the Rockies. Sheer rock plummets (by as much as 800m) to the calm Malbaie River, creating one of Québec's loveliest river valleys. The park is located about 40km northwest of La Malbaie. To reach it, head northwest on Rte 138 toward Baie St Paul, then take the turn for St-Aimé des Lacs and keep going for another 30km.

There are trails of all levels, from ambles around the 2.5km loop of the L'Érablière (Maple Grove) to vigorous hikes of up to 11km ascending to permafrost. A highlight is the boat cruise up the river, squeezed between mountains. The river can also be seen from a canoe or kayak, which are available for hire, as are mountain bikes. Boat tickets and rentals are available at the Le Draveur Visitor Center at the park entrance.

A delightful spot to stop for lunch en route to the church is **Auberge Baker** (www.aubergebaker.com; 8790 Ave Royale, Château-Richer; mains $22-36; noon-2pm & 5-8:30pm). It's 5km to the southwest in Château-Richer on Rte 360, which runs parallel inland to Rte 138.

The Drive » Follow Rte 138 Est (also known as Blvd Ste-Anne in these parts) to the fork in the village of Beaupré and join the 360 Est (Ave Royale) to Mont-Ste-Anne.

p281

5 Mont-Ste-Anne

This immensely popular **ski resort** (www.mont-sainte-anne.com; 2000 Blvd du Beau-Pré, Beau-Pré; lift ticket adult/youth/child full day $83/57/40, half-day $58/46/30; 8:30am-4pm mid-Dec–Apr;) is just 50km northeast of Québec City so it gets a lot of weekend skiers, especially between mid-December and well into April. It counts nine lifts and 71 ski trails, nine of which are set aside for night skiing (from 4pm to 9pm). You'll find all sorts of other winter activities here, including cross-country skiing, snowshoeing, skating, ice canyoning and dog-sledding. You can rent skis and snowboards too.

During the summer, the resort features mountain biking, hiking and golfing opportunities. This is also the time to hike to **Jean Larose Waterfalls** (Chutes Jean Larose; 2000 Blvd du Beau-Pré; adult/child $7.80/5.50; 9am-4pm May-Oct) in a deep chasm to the south across Rte 360. With a drop height of 68m, it is one of the most beautiful (and least developed) waterfalls in Québec. You can walk around and across the falls via a series of steps (all 400 of them), ledges and bridges.

The Drive » From Mont-Ste-Anne, follow Rte 360 Ouest (Blvd Beaupré) back to Rte 138 Est and exit at the signposted Chemin du Cap Tourmente (15km).

6 Cap Tourmente National Wildlife Area

Lying at the confluence of the upper and lower estuaries of the St Lawrence River, this **wildlife sanctuary** (Réserve Nationale de Faune du Cap-Tourmente; 418-827-4591; www.canada.ca/en/environment-climate-change/services/national-wildlife-areas/locations/cap-tourmente.html; 570 Chemin du Cap Tourmente, St-Joachim; adult/youth/child under 12yr $6/5/free; 8:30am-5pm mid-Apr–Oct,

Classic Trip

ANDRIY BLOKHIN/SHUTTERSTOCK ©

DBVIRAGO/GETTY IMAGES ©

WHY THIS IS A CLASSIC TRIP STEVE FALLON, WRITER

This drive will introduce you to the best Québec has to offer: the agricultural delights and *économusées* (workshops) of the Île d'Orléans where artisans make everything from cider to nougat; the grandeur of Montmorency Falls; the awesomeness and spirituality of Ste-Anne de Beaupré; and the unspoiled beauty of Charlevoix with its pretty and very arty towns boasting a wide assortment of boutiques, galleries, cafes and restaurants.

Above: Basilica of Ste-Anne de Beaupré (p276)
Left: Montmorency Falls (p276)
Right: Rue St-Jean-Baptiste, Baie St Paul (p285)

to 4pm early Jan–mid-Apr;) offers contrasting landscapes shaped by the meeting of the river, large coastal marshes, plains and mountains. It shelters a multitude of habitats that are home to a very wide diversity of animal and plant species. The wildlife area is home to more than 180 bird species, including flocks of snow geese that migrate to wetlands in spring and autumn. Many of these species are at risk, including the peregrine falcon, the bobolink and the butternut. In addition, there are 30 mammal species, 22 types of forest stands and 700 plant species. The sanctuary is beyond the villages of St-Joachim and Cap-Tourmente; there's a visitor center here and a network of marked trails.

The Drive » Follow the Chemin du Cap Tourmente back up to Rte 138 Est. At Baie St Paul you have a choice, but we recommend following the Uoute du Fleuve along Rte 362 Est to Ste-Irénée (88km) and La Malbaie (108km). On the way back you can drive the ear-popping hills of the Route des Montagnes along Rte 138 Ouest.

---

7 Ste-Irénée

This stretch of the drive is particularly beautiful, with breathtaking views of the St Lawrence as you ride up and down the hills. The first major village is **Les Éboulements**, 'one of the prettiest villages in Québec,' the road signs tell us, with wonderful old wooden houses, an old mill and grazing sheep. Next up is Ste-Irénée, with full-frontal views of the river and its hilltop **Domaine Forget** (888-336-7438, 418-452-8111; www.domaineforget.com; 5 Rang St-Antoine), a music and dance academy with a 600-seat hall that attracts classical and jazz musicians and dancers from around the world, particularly during its annual festival in summer. Just down the hill from the village as you approach La Malbaie is the **Observatoire de l'Astroblème de Charlevoix** (www.astroblemecharlevoix.org; 595 Côte Bellevue, Pointe-au-Pic; 1/2/3 activities adult $14/26/36, child $7/13/18; 10am-5pm late Jun-early Sep, to 9pm when cloudy;), an observatory that examines how meteors created the valleys on which Charlevoix sits through multimedia exhibits.

The Drive » It's just 20km along Rte 362 Est to La Malbaie from Ste-Irénée.

8 La Malbaie

La Malbaie is a town on the St Lawrence River at the mouth of the Malbaie River. The river's so wide here that locals call it *la mer* (the sea). Formerly Murray Bay, it actually encompasses five once-distinct villages. The first you'll encounter along Rte 362 Est from Ste-Irénée is Pointe-au-Pic, a holiday destination for the wealthy at the beginning of the 20th century and Canada's first seaside resort. To learn more about the town's history, visit the **Musée de Charlevoix** (www.museedecharlevoix.qc.ca; 10 Chemin du Havre, Pointe-au-Pic; adult/child $8/6; 9am-5pm Jun–mid-Oct, 10am-5pm Mon-Fri, 1-5pm Sat & Sun mid-Oct–May;). It's right on the water so you'll get some lovely views of 'the sea.' For more dramatic ones, head up to the **Auberge des 3 Canards** (www.auberge3canards.com; 115 Côte Bellevue, Pointe-au-Pic) for lunch or tea and take a seat on the sprawling verandah. It's not far from the **Fairmont Le Manoir Richelieu** (www.fairmont.com/richelieu-charlevoix; 181 Rue Richelieu, Pointe-au-Pic), sister hotel to Québec City's **Fairmont Le Château Frontenac** (www.fairmont.com/frontenac; 1 Rue des Carrières, Old Upper Town), with almost as much history and prestige: it dates to 1899.

The Drive » For a little variety, take the Route des Montagnes (Mountain Route) along Rte 138 Ouest to Baie St Paul (49km).

p281

9 Baie St Paul

Arguably the most interesting of all the little towns along the St Lawrence, this unique blend of the outdoors and the bohemian – Cirque du Soleil originated here – may be the most attractive. Plan to kick off your shoes and stay awhile and if you do overnight, book the delightful Auberge à l'Ancrage and have a meal at either the Alsatian Le Diapason or the very French **Le Mouton Noir** (www.moutonnoirresto.com; 43 Rue Ste-Anne; set meals $37-43; 11am-3pm & 5-11pm, evenings only Wed-Sun winter). The architecturally arresting **Musée d'Art Contemporain de Baie St Paul** (www.macbsp.com; 23 Rue Ambroise-Fafard; adult/student/child $10/7/free; 10am-5pm mid-Jun–Aug, 11am-5pm Tue-Sun Sep–mid-Jun), with contemporary art by local artists and some photographic exhibits from its own collection of 3000 pieces, makes a valiant effort to present the town as an artistic hub but not entirely successfully. Instead, visit one of the local galleries such as the **Galerie d'Art Beauchamp** (www.galeriebeauchamp.com; 16 Rue St-Jean-Baptiste; 9:30am-5:30pm) just up from the helpful **Baie St Paul Tourist Office** (www.tourisme-charlevoix.com; 6 Rue St-Jean-Baptiste; 9am-6pm May-Sep, to 4pm Oct-Apr).

The Drive » From Baie St Paul you can return to Québec City via Rte 138 Ouest (95km) and walk around the Old Town's historical buildings and museums.

p281

Eating & Sleeping

Île d'Orléans' North Coast 1

Au Poste de Traite Québécois $

(418-829-9898; www.aupostedetraite.com; Chemin Royal, Ste-Famille; mains $8-17; 11am-8pm Tue-Sun, to 3pm most days winter) This roadside restaurant in Ste-Famille is a good place to stop for lunch when pootling around the island. Along with the usual poutine, rillettes and onion soup, it serves burgers and pasta dishes in all their guises and sandwiches too.

Île d'Orléans' South Coast 2

Auberge La Goéliche Boutique Hotel $$

(888-511-2248, 418-828-2248; www.goeliche.ca; 22 Rue du Quai, Ste-Pétronille; r $198-228; P) Probably the nicest place to stay on the island, the Victorian-style Auberge La Goéliche has 19 rooms individually decorated with antiques and wood furniture; all of them have balconies and stunning views of the river. Guests relax on the large porch, in the gardens or by the outdoor pool. The in-house **restaurant** is first class.

Ste-Anne de Beaupré 4

Auberge Baker Inn $$

(866-824-4478, 418-824-4478; www.aubergebaker.com; 8790 Ave Royale, Château-Richer; d $105-155) This lovely inn 5km to the southwest of Ste-Anne de Beaupré in Château-Richer has seven rooms of varying sizes but all with the same cozy comfort. The house dates from 1840, the surrounding gardens just up from the river are a delight, the restaurant is worth a detour and the owners are as welcoming as a spring day. A delight.

La Malbaie 8

Auberge des Eaux Vives B&B $$

(418-665-4808; www.aubergedeseauxvives.com; 39 Rue de la Grève, Cap à l'Aigle; r $145-175) Sylvain and Johanne are the perfect hosts at this three-room B&B with breakfasts to write home about – think smoothies and a four-course extravaganza on a sunny terrace overlooking the St Lawrence. The decor is modern and chic, and there's a guest-only nook with a Nespresso machine, a full kitchen, two fireplaces and killer views.

Baie St Paul 9

Le Diapason Alsatian $$

(418-435-2929; www.restolediapason.com; 1 Rue Ste-Anne; mains $19-32; 11:30am-2pm & 5-9pm) This pleasant surprise (Alsatian in Charlevoix?) serves all our favorites from eastern France: *flammekueche* (Alsatian 'pizza'), *tartiflette* (potatoes roasted with cheese) and, of course, *choucroute garnie* (sauerkraut simmered with assorted smoked meats and sausages). All the produce is locally sourced, the atmosphere more than convivial and the terrace a delight in summer.

Auberge à l'Ancrage Inn $$

(666-344-3264, 418-240-3264; www.aubergeancrage.com; 29 Rue Ste-Anne; r from $169) Arguably the most charming place to stay in Baie St Paul, this little inn on the Rivière du Gouffre counts but four rooms – two facing the river and two the street. There's a kind of maritime theme going on at the 'Anchorage,' with lots of antiques in public areas and a wonderful porch. The garden runs down to the river.

The Saguenay Fjord & Lac St Jean

Cruising deep-blue waters, exploring rocky cliffs and scouting for whales are all part of the maritime experience on the world's southernmost fjord.

TRIP HIGHLIGHTS

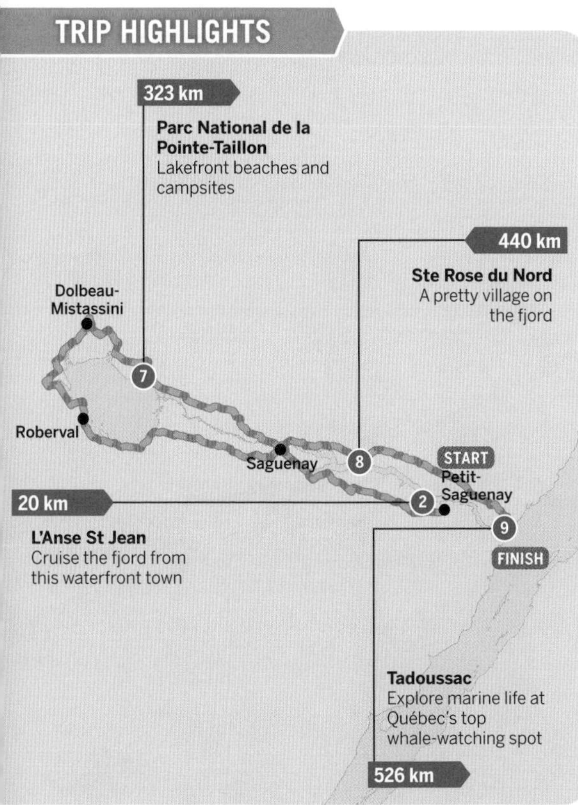

3–4 DAYS
526KM/327 MILES

GREAT FOR...

BEST TIME TO GO

Late August through mid-October for whale-watching, blueberry season and fall colors.

ESSENTIAL PHOTO

The rocky cliffs along the fjord from Ste Rose du Nord (or from a boat).

BEST FOR WILDLIFE

Whale-watching from Tadoussac.

Tadoussac (p289) One of the best spots for whale-watching

26 The Saguenay Fjord & Lac St Jean

The Saguenay region's glories start outdoors with the dramatic scenery along the fjord. Hop on a boat to check out its cliffs and forests, or venture out on a whale-watching tour. Nearby, Lac St Jean has sandy beaches, lakeside cafes and shoreside trails to hike or cycle. Naturally, there's food, too, from blueberries that blanket the fields in summer, to locally made cheeses, chocolates and craft beers ready to sample.

❶ Petit-Saguenay

Coming from Charlevoix or points south on Rte 138, leave the coast at St Siméon and turn northwest onto Rte 170, where the road, lined with evergreens, begins to climb into the hills, winding around and beneath steep rocky cliffs.

At the town of Petit-Saguenay, detour for your first glimpse of the fjord. Following the signs to the 'Quai de Petit Saguenay,' the municipal docks, bear right from Rte 170 onto Rue Tremblay, which

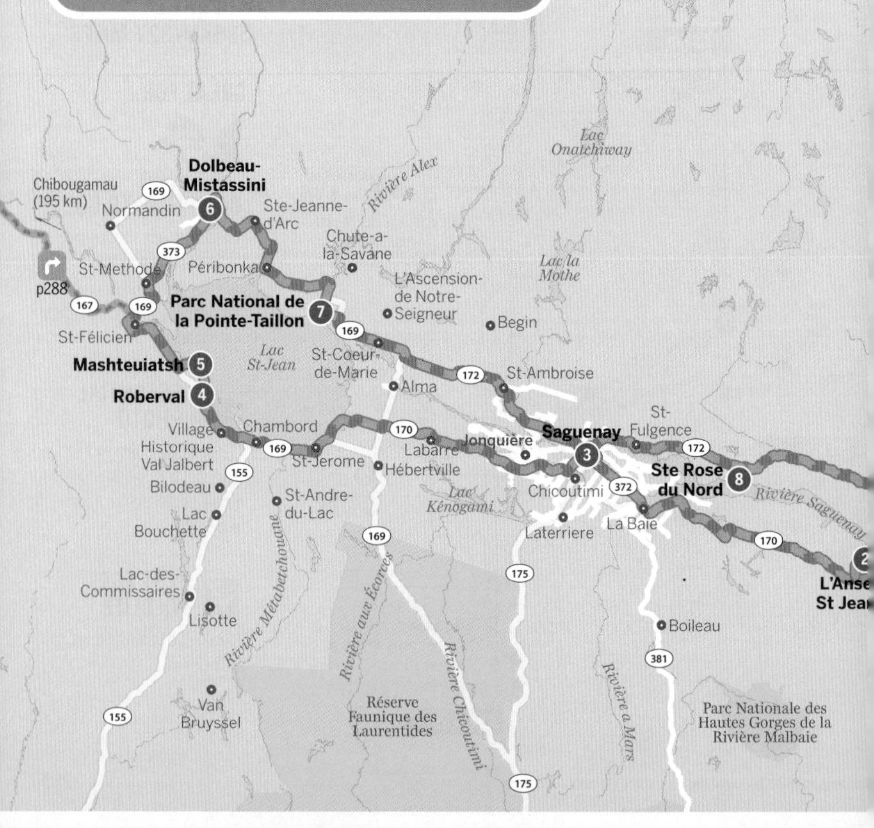

becomes Rue du Quai. Keep following this road as it narrows (it's closed to cars in winter) and continues for 4km where there's a small parking area at the edge of the rock-lined fjord. There's a lookout point and a small picnic area here, too, if you want to take a waterside break.

The Drive » Retrace your route back to Rte 170 and turn right to continue heading west on this highway. In about 13km, at the sign for L'Anse St Jean, turn right onto Rue du Coin, then make an immediate right onto Rue St-Jean-Baptiste, which will take you into the village.

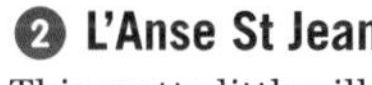

2 L'Anse St Jean

This pretty little village along the fjord is a great spot to get out on the water. Book a paddling excursion with **Fjord en Kayak** (☎866-725-2925, 418-272-3024; www.fjord-en-kayak.ca; 359 Rue St-Jean-Baptiste; 3hr/1-day tours $63/139; ⊙mid-May–mid-Oct; 👪), or a cruise on the fjord with **Navettes Maritimes du Fjord** (☎800-363-7248, 418-543-7630; www.navettesdufjord.com; 355 Rue St-Jean-Baptiste; fjord cruise adult/child from $59/30; ⊙Jun–mid-Oct; 👪); both companies offer a number of different options to suit your time and experience level. Back on land, if you're ready for a bite, dig into a plate of poutine or a burger at Bistro de L'Anse (p290), then stroll through the village and along the waterfront.

Drive west along the fjord to take in more scenic views at L'Anse de Tabatière. To get here, cross the covered bridge off Rue du Faubourg. Pause for a photo at the bridge, then follow Chemin St-Thomas to Chemin de l'Anse; it's about 5km to the beach.

Retrace your route to return to the highway, but stop along the way for a pastry and coffee at **Nuances de Grains** (☎418-608-8416; www.nuancesdegrains.com; 261 Rue St-Jean Baptiste; pastries $1.50-5; ⊙8am-6pm daily late Jun-Aug, to 5pm Fri-Sun Sep-Oct, hours vary Nov-late Jun), a *boulangerie* on Rue St-Jean-Baptiste next to the church.

The Drive » Follow Rue St-Jean-Baptiste back to Rte 170, and head west toward Saguenay. Leave Rte 170 at La Baie (stop at Musée du Fjord to learn more about the fjord's ecosystem) and continue west on Rte 372. This increasingly urban road isn't the most picturesque, but it leads into Chicoutimi, Saguenay's largest borough. The drive is 1¼ hours in total.

✕ 🛏 p290

LINK YOUR TRIP

25 Around, Over & In the St Lawrence River

Continue your road trip in Charlevoix. From Tadoussac, take the free ferry to Baie Ste Catherine, then continue south.

Circling the Gaspé Peninsula

Catch the ferry (Les Escoumins/Trois Pistoles, or Forestville/Rimouski) to the Gaspé Peninsula for more maritime scenery and excellent seafood.

3 Saguenay

Take a break from the fjord's scenic beauty with an urban interlude in Chicoutimi, Saguenay's largest borough. Hang out over coffee, a sandwich or a slice of cake at the cool Cafe Cambio (p290), and take a stroll along Rue Racine, Chicoutimi's main street, to browse the boutiques. You can walk to the riverfront here, too, where you'll often find summertime outdoor concerts, along with the lovely water views.

It's less than a 10-minute drive to **La Pulperie** (www.pulperie.com; 300 Rue Dubuc, Chicoutimi; adult/child $14.50/7; 9am-6pm daily mid-Jun–Aug, 10am-4pm Wed-Sun Sep–mid-Jun; P), an interesting history and culture museum in the buildings that once housed Canada's biggest pulp mill. Inside the museum, look for the House of Arthur Villeneuve, too; it's the vividly painted former home of a former barber who became a prolific folk artist. His house was moved in its entirety to La Pulperie. From downtown Chicoutimi, go west on Rte 372/Blvd du Saguenay, turn left onto Rue Price W, then right onto Rue Dréan, which leads to the museum.

Head back to Rue Racine when you're ready to eat again for pizza jazzed up with local ingredients at La Parizza (p290) or a build-your-own burger at **Rouge Burger Bar** (http://rougeburgerbar.ca; 460 Rue Racine E, Chicoutimi; mains $16-25; 5-9pm Sun, Tue & Wed, to 10pm Thu-Sat).

The Drive » Leave Saguenay's more urban precincts and head for Québec's third-largest lake – Lac St Jean. Follow Rte 170 west until it intersects with Rte 169, which will lead south and then west along the lakeshore. Exit Rte 169 onto Rue Brassard toward Roberval, then turn left when it comes to a 'T' intersection onto Ave St-Joseph, which leads toward the marina.

p290

4 Roberval

As you head west from Saguenay, you'll get your first glimpses of the lake after Rte 169 splits off from Rte 170, but when

BLUEBERRY LOVE

This is a place that loves its blueberries. More than 20 million kilos of the little blue fruits are harvested each summer in Saguenay-Lac St Jean, earning the region's inhabitants the nickname 'les Bleuets.' Its cycling route – a 256km network of bike trails through the area – is dubbed the **Véloroute des Bleuets** (Blueberry Bike Trail; https://veloroutedesbleuets.com/en) and an annual summertime fruit fest, **Festival du Bleuet de Dolbeau-Mistassini** (www.festivaldubleuet.com), includes concerts, activities for the kids and a giant blueberry pie.

You'll see farm stands selling fresh berries on local roads throughout the summer, and many local farms let you pick your own fruit. Late July or early August until early September is typically peak blueberry season. Strawberries, haskap berries (which resemble elongated blueberries but taste more tart) and raspberries also grow through the area. Strawberry season usually runs from late June through mid-July, haskaps ripen from mid-June until late July and raspberries peak from mid-July through August. Berries turn up in pies, jams and more at local markets, too.

A group of Trappist monks makes a particularly local berry treat: chocolate-covered blueberries, which are available only between mid-July and the middle of September. Get them at the shop on the grounds of their monastery, **La Chocolaterie des Pères Trappistes de Mistassini** (418-276-1122; www.chocolateriedesperes.com; 100 Rte des Trappistes, Dolbeau-Mistassini; 9am-4:30pm Mon-Fri, to 4pm Sat & Sun late Jun-early Sep). They make great road-trip snacks.

Chicoutimi Saguenay's largest borough

you pull into Roberval, you can really take in the watery expanse.

Stop at the marina where you can climb the lookout tower for views across the lake. An office of **Maison du Vélo** (Bicycle Tourism Information Center; ☎418-668-4541; https://veloroutedesbleuets.com/en; 1692 Ave du Pont N, Alma; ⏲8am-5:30pm mid-Jun–Aug) has information about cycling in the area, as well as a snack bar and restrooms.

Roberval is a good place to stop for lunch on your round-the-lake tour. Try the home-style Québec fare at La Bonne Cuisine de Roberval (p290) along the highway or the good-value set menus at Emporte-moi (p290) in town; the latter also serves a large assortment of teas.

The Drive » Continue along the lakeshore on Ave St-Joseph, then turn right onto Blvd Horace-J-Beemer, which becomes Rue Ouiatchouan as it enters the First Nations community of Mashteuiatsh.

✕ p290

5 Mashteuiatsh

Stop to visit **Musée Amérindien de Mashteuiatsh** (☎418-275-4842; www.cultureilnu.ca; 1787 Rue Amishk, Mashteuiatsh; adult/child $13/9; ⏲9am-5pm daily mid-May–mid-Oct, closed Mon & Sun mid-Oct–mid-May; P), a small museum in a contemporary building above the lakeshore, where you can learn more about this indigenous community's culture and heritage. The exhibits highlight the cultures of the local Pekuakamiulnuatsh people and of other First Nations in Québec. There are excellent vistas across Lac St Jean from this town as well.

The Drive » To continue your tour around the lake, leave Mashteuiatsh heading north and then west on Rue Ouiatchouan,

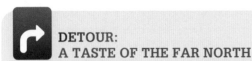

DETOUR: A TASTE OF THE FAR NORTH

Start: 5 Mashteuiatsh

Get a taste of Québec's Far North with a detour to Chibougamau, gateway to the Eeyou Istchee Baie-James region, and to the nearby Cree community of Oujé-Bougoumou, where you can learn about this indigenous culture.

You'll need at least an extra two to three days for this excursion. Chibougamau is 250km, or just less than a three-hour drive, northwest of Mashteuiatsh, toward the west end of Lac St Jean. And as you follow Rte 167 away from the lake, the terrain feels increasingly remote.

The Chibougamau region offers a variety of outdoor activities that introduce you to Québec's north, from fishing to hiking to canoeing on undeveloped lakes. The lovely waterside **Gîte de La Rivière** (418-748-7063; www.gitedelarivierechibougamau.com; 18 Chemin du Lac-Dulieux; s/d/ste incl breakfast from $78/88/124; P) would make an excellent base for outdoor explorations.

From Chibougamau, drive 45 minutes west (take Rte 167 south to Rte 113 west) to the Cree community of Oujé-Bougoumou. This young community, which was constructed in the 1990s, has an excellent cultural center, **Aanischaaukamikw Cree Cultural Institute** (418-745-2444; http://creeculturalinstitute.ca; 205 Opemiska Meskino; adult $10; 9am-noon & 1-4pm Mon-Fri; P), where you can learn more about this First Nation, its history and its culture. Local outfitters like **Nuuhchimi Wiinuu Cree Culture Tours** (418-770-4144; creeculturaltours@hotmail.com) offer other experiences that can introduce you to this indigenous culture, while you have fun outdoors.

To return to the Saguenay-Lac St Jean region, take Rte 167 south and continue 230km to Saint-Félicien. Turn east onto Rte 169 to continue your tour around the lake. Alternatively, from Chibougamau, you can take Rte 113 west toward Val d'Or and the Abitibi-Témiscamingue region for more northern experiences.

which becomes Chemin de la Pointe Bleue. Turn right onto Rte 169, which will meander through the town of Saint-Félicien before heading northwest to Saint-Methode. From there, follow Rte 373 north along the lake and into Dolbeau-Mistassini.

6 Dolbeau-Mistassini

The main reason to stop in this town near the west end of Lac St Jean is chocolate. Trappist monks run a chocolate shop, La Chocolaterie des Pères Trappistes de Mistassini (p286), on the forested grounds of their rural monastery outside Dolbeau-Mistassini.

The don't-miss confection? Chocolate-covered blueberries, which are available only in late summer and early autumn when the local blueberry season in the Saguenay-Lac St Jean region is at its peak. Even if you're not here at the right time for the blueberries, though, the shop sells a variety of other chocolate treats.

The Drive » Return to Rte 169, which is now on the north side of Lac St Jean, and follow it as it snakes back toward the water near Péribonka. Stay on 169 to the entrance for Parc National de la Pointe-Taillon.

7 Parc National de la Pointe-Taillon

On a peninsula jutting into Lac St Jean, this **provincial park** (www.sepaq.com/pq/pta; 835 Rang 3 W, Saint-Henri-de-Taillon; adult/child $8.75/free; Jun–mid-Oct; P) has sandy beaches and more than 40km of cycling paths. Stop to cool off with a swim, or go for a paddle along the lake; the park rents canoes, kayaks and stand-up paddleboards.

For a longer stay, you can settle into a campsite here for a night or more. The park has 'ready-to-camp' tents, too.

The Drive » Return to Rte 169 going east. When the road intersects Rte 172, follow Rte 172 to stay along the lake's north shore. It's 120km or about 90 minutes from the park to the turnoff for Ste Rose du Nord onto Rue du Quai, which leads into the village.

p291

8 Ste Rose du Nord

One of Québec's prettiest towns, the village of Ste Rose du Nord sits directly on the fjord. Explore the forests along the shore – there are walking paths in the woods near the quay – or drive up winding Rue de la Montaigne to a lookout point with expansive views. Have lunch at one of the cafes by the quay or pick up picnic essentials from the town's market to enjoy outdoors.

Above the fjord, off Rte 172 west of town, you can stay the night at Pourvoirie du Cap au Leste (p291), which has a collection of cute cabins and a well-regarded restaurant serving regional cuisine. There are more opportunities to go hiking or canoeing from the property as well.

The Drive » As you leave the village, turn right (east) onto Rte 172. At the intersection of Rte 138, turn right (south) to Tadoussac. It's 85km, or about an hour's drive.

p291

9 Tadoussac

Tadoussac sits at the mouth of the Saguenay Fjord, where the North Shore region of the St Lawrence River officially starts, and Rte 138 continues north to ever-more-remote coastal communities. But stay in Tadoussac for at least a day or two; it's one of the best spots in the region for whale-watching.

Learn more about the local marine life at the **Centre d'Interprétation des Mammifères Marins** (CIMM; 418-235-4701; http://gremm.org; 108 Rue de la Cale Sèche; adult/child $14/free; noon-5pm mid-May–mid-Jun, 9am-8pm mid-Jun–mid-Sep, 11am-6pm mid-Sep–mid-Oct;), then head out on the water yourself. **Croisières AML** (www.croisieresaml.com; 177 Rue des Pionniers; trips adult/child from $70/40; May-Oct;) runs a variety of different whale-watching excursions from Tadoussac, while **Mer et Monde** (418-232-6779; www.meretmonde.ca; 148 Rue du Bord de l'Eau; 3hr kayak trips from $58, whale-watching from $68) leads guided sea-kayaking excursions.

Tadoussac has plenty of places to eat, so wrap up your road trip with a special dinner. Both Chez Mathilde (p291) and La Galouïne (p291) serve first-rate local seafood with plenty of produce from around the region.

If you want to stay in town, Hôtel Tadoussac (p291) is a good choice, looking out over the bay; you can't miss the white clapboard exterior and red roof of this historic property. Or you can camp nearby between the trees at **Domaine des Dunes** (www.domainedesdunes.com; 585 Chemin du Moulin à Baude; tent & RV sites $31-36, trailer or motorhome sites $45, chalets $149-177, tipi $149; May-Oct; P). Reserve in advance for any accommodations if you're visiting in the busy summer months of July and August.

Before you leave the fjord region and its many maritime pleasures, head for **Microbrasserie Tadoussac** (www.microtadoussac.com; 145 Rue du Bord de l'Eau; 11am-11pm daily) to raise a glass to your Québec adventures.

p291

Eating & Sleeping

L'Anse St Jean 2

Bistro de L'Anse Pub Food $$

(☎418-272-4222; www.bistrodelanse.com; 319 Rue St-Jean-Baptiste; mains $15-20; ⏰noon-midnight late Jun-Aug, from 5pm mid-May–late Jun & Sep–mid-Oct) Popular local hub where you can tuck into poutines, salads and burgers on the verandah and catch live music on the weekends. Try a beer from the owners' nearby nano-brewery, **Microbrasserie La Chasse-Pinte**.

Auberge des Cévennes Inn $$

(☎418-272-3180, 877-272-3180; www.auberge-des-cevennes.qc.ca; 294 Rue St-Jean-Baptiste; r from $85-110; P 📶) You can hear the river gurgling across the street at this lovely inn, overlooking the covered bridge. The interior is old-school, even a little grandma's cottage-y, but the decor fits the location, and the owners are as friendly as anything. A buffet breakfast is available (adult/child $7/5); rooms have microwaves and refrigerators if you prefer to make your own.

Chalets du Fjord Inn $$

(☎800-561-8060, 418-272-3430; www.chalets-sur-le-fjord.com; 354 Rue St-Jean-Baptiste; studios/condos/chalets from $119/170/194; P 📶 🏊) Accommodations ranging from studios to condos to hillside cabins of varying sizes and amenities. It overlooks the marina and has its own quality restaurant, **Chez Montagner**, serving salads, pizzas and seafood (mains $18 to $27). Book well in advance.

Saguenay 3

Cafe Cambio Cafe $

(☎418 549-7830; https://cafecambio.ca; 414 Rue Racine E, Chicoutimi; mains $6-10; ⏰7am-11pm Mon-Fri, from 8am Sat & Sun; 📶 👪) This spacious and airy coffeehouse draws locals from morning till night, to get work done, hang out with friends or linger over an espresso and slice of cake. Food-wise, there are eggs, toasts and waffles to start the day, then salads, sandwiches and sweets from lunchtime on.

La Parizza Pizza $$

(☎418-973-9732; https://lp.pizza; 337 Rue Racine E, Chicoutimi; pizzas $17-27; ⏰4pm-midnight Tue & Wed, to 3am Thu-Sat; 🌶) Pizza, objectively, is awesome. The Québec obsession with *terroir* ingredients is also awesome. When these two culinary concepts collide, you get La Parizza, which features such brilliant creations as Margherita pizza served with a veritable charcuterie of local meats; pizza topped with wild shrimp, scallops and smoked salmon; and a pie containing spinach, goat's cheese, pancetta and walnuts.

Roberval 4

La Bonne Cuisine de Roberval Diner $

(☎418-275-6605; https://labonnecuisine.ca; 562 Blvd Marcotte (Rte 169), Roberval; mains $5-15; ⏰4am-midnight; P) This traditional roadside diner in a little house on the highway serves local Québec classics, from breakfasts of eggs, meat and beans, to smoked meat, poutine and *tourtière* (meat pie). In the summer, there's blueberry pie. And in case you're circling the lake and need a coffee before dawn, it opens at 4am.

Emporte-moi Bistro $$$

(☎418-765-0171; 815 Ave Saint-Joseph, Roberval; dinner mains $27-40; ⏰7:30am-8pm Mon-Fri, from 8am Sat & Sun) A short walk from the marina in the center of Roberval, this restaurant and tea shop serves home-style fare with a bit of flair. The midday set menus, which offer a soup, a choice of fish, pasta or meat, plus dessert and coffee or tea, are a good value at $14 to $16.

Parc National de la Pointe-Taillon 7

Auberge Île du Repos Campground, Hostel $

(☎418-347-5649; www.iledurepos.com; 105 Chemin de Île du Repos, Péribonka; campsites/dm/r from $27/38/80; P) Taking up an entire little island off Péribonka, near Parc National de la Pointe Taillon, this lodging features dorms, kitchen facilities, private chalet rooms, camping, a cafe-bar, a beach with all kinds of water sports, croquet and volleyball.

Ste Rose du Nord 8

Pourvoirie du Cap au Leste — Cabin $$

(418-675-2000; www.capauleste.com; 551 Chemin du Cap à l'Est; r $120-160, ste $180-220;) The frugal but charming cabins here have balconies, and the restaurant (set evening meals from $36) serves superb regional cuisine; nonguests should reserve. Hiking, canoeing and climbing can be organized. Signposted off Rte 172 between Ste-Fulgence and Ste Rose du Nord, this spot is worth the bumpy 7km ride for its dramatic views over a large stretch of the fjord.

Tadoussac 9

Café Bohème — Cafe $$

(418-235-1180; www.lecafeboheme.com; 239 Rue des Pionniers; mains lunch $15-22, dinner $21-31; 7am-11pm Jul & Aug, 8am-10pm May-Jun & Sep-Oct;) This village hangout is a prime place to sip an espresso or nitro cold brew and breakfast on fruit and yogurt or crepes filled with duck confit. Later, choose between dishes such as a baguette stuffed with local lobster and shrimp or a smoked-salmon pancake at lunch, or venison braised with haskap berries or fresh pasta in the evening.

Chez Mathilde — Canadian $$$

(418-235-4443; www.chezmathildebistro.com; 227 Rue des Pionniers; mains $15-30, set meals $50-75; noon-3pm & 6-11pm Jun-Oct;) The stellar chef at this colorful little house utilizes plenty of local products, from seafood to greens to cheeses, in the short but creative menu. The innovative dishes are served up alongside a view of the port from the airy patio.

La Galouïne — Québécois $$$

(418-235-4380; www.lagalouine.com; 251 Rue des Pionniers; mains $22-34; 7:30am-10pm May-Oct) Local ingredients dominate the table here, from fresh scallops, salmon and shrimp from the nearby waters to venison caught from the woods. An extensive wine list makes it that much easier to enjoy your evening.

Hôtel Tadoussac — Hotel $$

(418-235-4421, 800-561-0718; www.hoteltadoussac.com; 165 Rue du Bord de l'Eau; r from $179; May-Oct;) Commanding the sweep of Tadoussac's bay, this hotel is winning the location contest, hands down. There's a sense of historic heritage as well; it's been hosting guests since 1870. Functional rooms have plush carpets, ceiling fans and river views. Rates vary outside of the July-August high season.

If the hotel's white clapboards and red roof look familiar, it may be because the lodging's exterior was used as the Hotel New Hampshire, in the 1984 film of the same name based on John Irving's novel about a quirky New England hotel.

Circling the Gaspé Peninsula

Hiking maritime mountains, exploring offshore islands and devouring fresh-caught seafood are all on the itinerary as you circle La Gaspésie, the seaside peninsula on Québec's eastern shores, on Rte 132.

TRIP HIGHLIGHTS

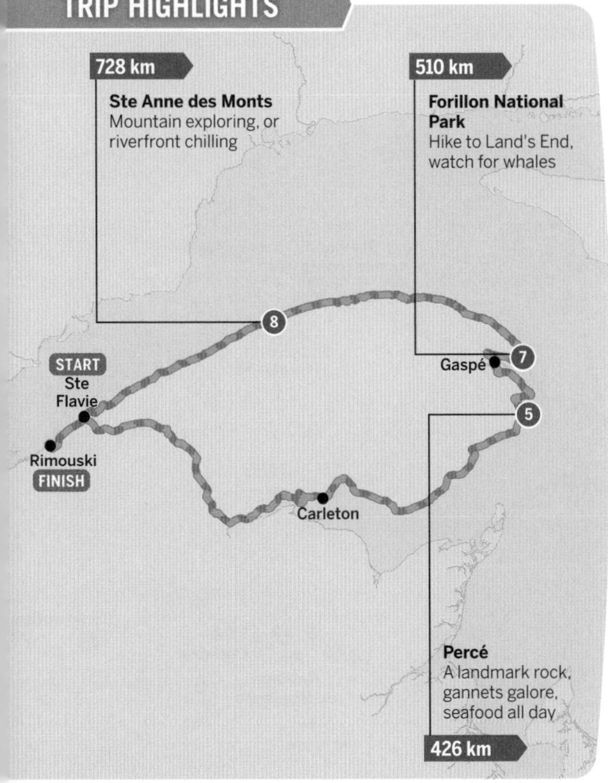

728 km
Ste Anne des Monts
Mountain exploring, or riverfront chilling

510 km
Forillon National Park
Hike to Land's End, watch for whales

8

7

Gaspé

START
Ste Flavie

5

Rimouski
FINISH

Carleton

Percé
A landmark rock, gannets galore, seafood all day

426 km

7–8 DAYS
900KM/560 MILES

GREAT FOR...

BEST TIME TO GO

Late June or early September draw fewer crowds than busy July and August.

ESSENTIAL PHOTO

Percé Rock from a boat or kayak.

BEST FOR OUTDOORS

Hiking to Land's End in Forillon National Park.

Percé Rocher Percé (p296)

27 Circling the Gaspé Peninsula

Cue up the Québécois sea shanties and hit the road in this Francophone region, where each waterfront village is cuter than the next, and the landscape along the Gulf of St Lawrence varies from forested peaks to sea as far as you can see. Québec's first national park, plus several provincially protected beauties, offer excellent hiking. You can spot wildlife, too, from seabirds to whales (and lobster – on your plate).

1 Ste Flavie

Kick off your trip with an unusual art installation – a line of stone figures marching out of the St Lawrence. *Le Grand Rassemblement* (The Great Gathering) was created by local artist Marcel Gagnon in this riverside village, on Rte 132, 350km northeast of Québec City.

Gagnon bought a cottage here in 1984, with the idea of opening a small art gallery. Two years later, he crafted the grand series of sculptures

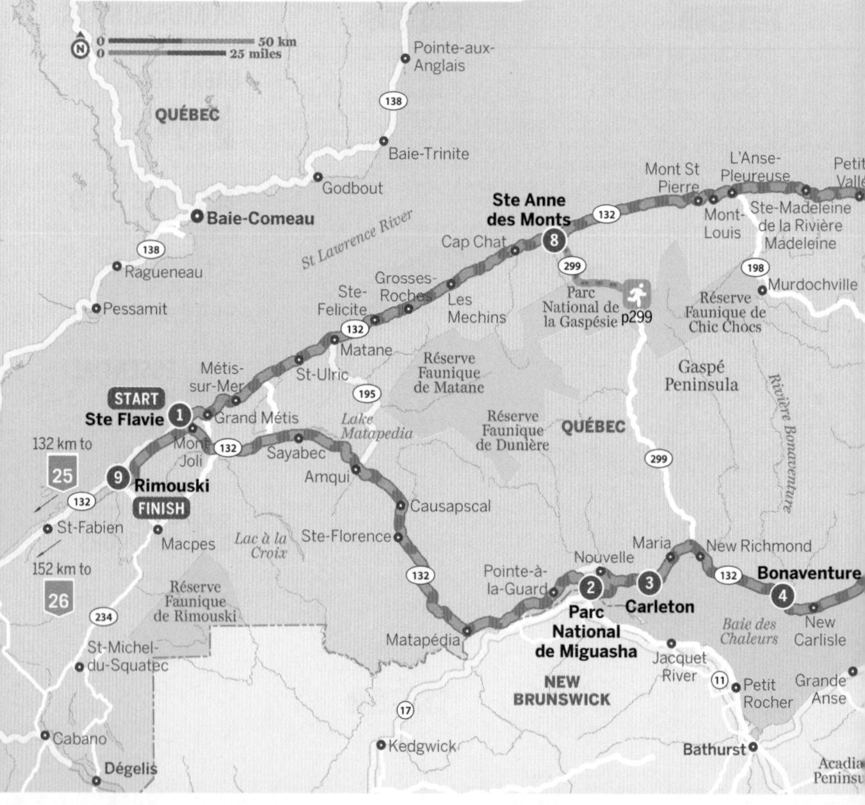

– installing them in the river behind his gallery – that would become his best-known work. That gallery, expanded into the **Centre d'Art Marcel Gagnon** (☎866-775-2829, 418-775-2829; www.centredart.net; 564 Rte de la Mer; ⌚7:30am-9pm May-Sep; P), showcases work by Gagnon and several family members; his son Guillaume now manages the business, which includes a restaurant and an upstairs *auberge* with several guest rooms.

Down the road, score your first lobster of the trip at **Capitaine Homard** (☎418-775-8046; http://capitainehomard.com; 180 Rte de la Mer; mains $18-40; ⌚4-10pm May, from 11am Jun-Aug; P 👪), a casual nautical-themed eatery, where you can choose whether you have your crustaceans boiled, grilled, in a tartare with local shrimp, or in a *guédille au homard* (lobster-salad sandwich).

The Drive » From Ste Flavie, turn inland onto Rte 132 and drive through urban Mont Joli, following signs for Amqui, Causaspcal and Matapédia. The scenery gradually becomes more dramatic as you wind past inland lakes and forested hills. This 200km route takes you to an unusual national park; turn right at Escuminac, following signs for Parc National de Miguasha.

2 Parc National de Miguasha

As you follow the road along the Baie-des-Chaleurs, you get your first glimpse of Le Gaspésie's red cliffs, which give this park its name. Miguasha is a Mi'kmaq word meaning 'red earth.'

The region around what is now **Parc National de Miguasha** (☎418-794-2475; www.sepaq.com/pq/mig; 231 Rte Miguasha W, Nouvelle; adult/child $8.75/free; ⌚9am-5pm Jun-Oct, reduced hours Nov-May; P) is a geologic highlight. It's the world's top fossil site for illustrating the 'age of fish,' the Devonian period more than 350 million years ago, when sea creatures began evolving into tetrapods, which could walk on land. The park's collection includes more than 11,000 specimens, some of which are on exhibit in the informative **Information Center & Museum** (☎418-794-2475; www.sepaq.com/pq/mig; 231 Rte Miguasha W, Nouvelle; museum adult/child $10.85/free, plus park $8.75/free; ⌚9am-5pm Jun-Oct, reduced hours Nov-May; P 👪). Watch a short film to learn more about this heritage, and allow time for a guided walk with a park naturalist along

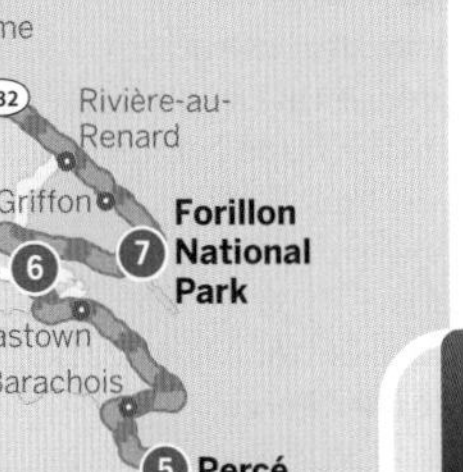

LINK YOUR TRIP

25 Around, Over & In the St Lawrence River

For more riverside adventures and excellent eating, road trip through Charlevoix. Take the ferry to St Siméon, then turn south.

26 The Saguenay Fjord & Lac St Jean

Want more whales and maritime scenery? Ferry to St Siméon and loop the Saguenay Fjord.

the bay and cliffs where many of the fossils were unearthed.

The Drive » Turn right from the Information Center to make a scenic loop around the peninsula on Route de Miguasha, which rejoins Rte 132 near the town of Nouvelle. Turn right onto Rte 132 and continue another 16km east to Carleton.

3 Carleton

This waterfront town overlooking Baie-des-Chaleurs is a relaxing spot to stay for a night (or more) – Manoir Belle Plage (p301) is a comfortable updated motel – with good restaurants, **a craft brewery** (☎418-364-5440; www.lenaufrageur.com; 586 Blvd Perron; ⏲3-10pm), a contemporary arts and performance center, and a bayside quay to stroll. You can drive – or hike if you're really energetic (it's 555m above town) – up to **Mont St-Joseph** (☎418-364-3723; www.montsaintjoseph.com; 837 Rue de la Montagne; chapel tours adult/child $8.50/free; ⏲chapel 8am-6pm late Jun-Aug, 9am-5pm Sep–mid-Oct), a chapel with expansive views across the bay.

Before getting back on the road, stop for coffee at the local roastery, **Brûlerie du Quai** (☎418-364-6788; www.bruleriedu quai.com; 200 Rte du Quai; coffees from $2; ⏲7:30am-6pm, to 9pm Jul & Aug), and pick up pastries or a picnic lunch at **La Mie Véritable** (☎418-364-6662; 578 Blvd Perron; baked goods $2-6; ⏲7am-5:30pm Tue-Sat; P 📶 ✎), a first-rate bakery-cafe.

The Drive » Leave town heading east on Rte 132. The highway briefly climbs up from the coast, then, as you descend toward the town of Maria, the whole bay suddenly spreads out before you. Continue on Rte 132 into Bonaventure.

✕ 🛏 p301

4 Bonaventure

Acadians founded this town back in the 1700s, and you can learn something about this heritage at the interesting **Musée Acadien du Québec** (☎418-534-4000; www.museeacadien.com; 95 Ave de Port-Royal; adult/child $13/9; ⏲9am-5pm Jul-Oct, reduced hours Nov-Jun; P). Across the street, take a peek inside the stone **Église de Bonaventure** (99 Ave Grand-Pré; ⏲8am-6pm), an 1860 church with a grand gilded ceiling.

To break up your drive with a more active adventure, go for a guided paddle – by canoe, kayak or stand-up paddleboard – along Rivière Bonaventure with **Cime Aventure** (☎800-790-2463, 418-534-2333; www.cimeaventure.com; 200 Chemin Athanase-Arsenault; campsites/yurts/ecolodges/chalets from $33/100/159/239; ⏲Jun-Sep; 👪).

The Drive » Continue following Rte 132 east along the coast. It's 135km – about a two-hour drive – to Percé.

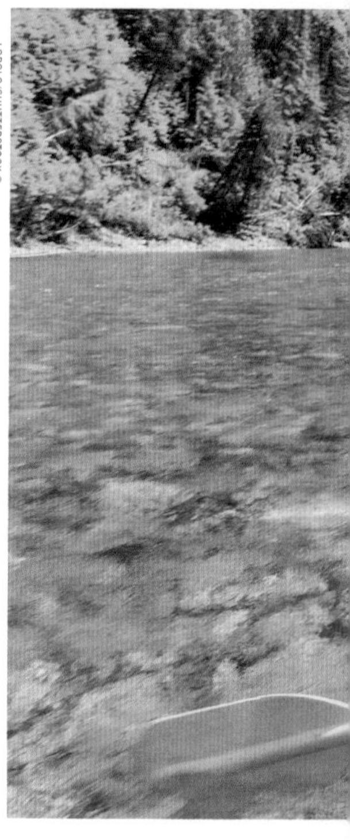

LOPOLO/SHUTTERSTOCK ©

5 Percé

Stay alert as you approach this small town at the Gaspé Peninsula's east end. You'll come down a hill where – surprise! – you'll glimpse its famous stone landmark: **Rocher Percé** (Pierced Rock). Perhaps it's fitting that this stretch of coastline has been called 'La Côte-Surprise.'

Take a boat tour to **Parc National de l'Île-Bonaventure-et-du-Rocher-Percé** (☎418-782-2240; www.sepaq.com/pq/bon; 4 Rue du Quai; adult/child $8.75/free; ⏲8:30am-5pm mid-May–mid-Oct; P),

Bonaventure Kayaking

the protected area that encompasses both the arched rock and the nearby **Île Bonaventure** and together houses North America's largest migratory bird refuge. On the island, the highlight is a hike to see the colony of more than 100,000 gannets, a strikingly beautiful seabird. The boat operators all offer whale-watching trips, too.

Back on land, head for **Géopark de Percé** (Percé Unesco Global Geopark; ☎418-782-5112; www.geoparcdeperce.com; 180 Rte 132 W; trail access free, glass platform adult/child $9/5.50, zip-line $21/12.25; ⏰8am-9pm Jun-Sep, reduced hours Nov-May) to hike in the hills above town or take in the views of the rock and island from a glass-floored lookout platform cantilevered over the cliffs.

The more you adventure, the more you'll appreciate your seafood dinner at one of the village restaurants overlooking the water. Both **La Maison du Pêcheur** (www.maisondupecheur.ca; 157 Rte 132 W; pizzas $15-28, mains $22-49; ⏰11:30am-3pm & 5:30-9:30pm Jun-Oct; P 📶) and **Restaurant La Maison Mathilde** (www.aubergelestroissoeurs.com; 85 Rte 132 W; set meals $24-49; ⏰7-11:30am & 5:30-10pm Jun-Sep; P) are good options for dishes from the sea.

The Drive » Leave Percé heading north on Rte 132, which twists between the cliffs and the sea. Pull off at the rest stop just outside town for great views of the gulf and back toward Rocher Percé. Then continue on Rte 132 until it meets Rte 198, which will take you north into the town of Gaspé.

🛏 p301

6 Gaspé

Get some culture at the **Musée de la Gaspésie** (☎418-368-1534; http://museedelagaspesie.ca; 80 Blvd Gaspé; adult/child $15.25/9.25;

⌚9am-5pm Jun-Oct, from 10am Tue-Fri, from 12:30pm Sat & Sun Nov-May; P 👪), which highlights the region's maritime heritage. Check out the museum's cool virtual-reality exhibit where you head out to sea with a couple of fisherfolk. Just beware if you get seasick – it's surprisingly realistic! Or visit **Site d'Interpretation Micmac de Gespeg** (☎418-368-7449; www.micmacgespeg.ca; 783 Blvd Pointe-Navarre; adult/child $11.25/8.75; ⌚9am-5pm early Jun-early Oct; P 👪) to learn something about the area's indigenous culture.

Gaspé has a fun local eatery, **Bistro Bar Brise-Bise** (☎418-368-1456; www.brisebise.ca; 135 Rue de la Reine; mains $13-34; ⌚11am-10pm, to late on show nights), which serves excellent seafood and often hosts live music, while its craft brewery, **Microbrasserie Cap Gaspé** (☎418-360-9000; 286 Blvd de York S; ⌚noon-9pm Jul-Sep, Thu-Sat only Oct-Jun; 📶), is a popular spot for a beer. The town also has several hotels and inns, including the lovely Auberge sous les Arbres (p301), that could serve as your base for exploring Forillon National Park (your next stop), if you don't want to camp or stay in one of the hostels just outside the park.

The Drive » Follow Rte 132 north out of town toward Forillon National Park. From Gaspé, it's 20km to the park's Penouille Visitor Centre and about 30km to the south entrance gate.

✕ 🛏 p301

7 Forillon National Park

Plan at least a couple of days to explore this majestic national park, though there's plenty to do to fill a week or more.

There's a sandy beach near the **Penouille Visitor Centre** (1238 Blvd de Forillon, Gaspé; ⌚9am-5pm late Jun–mid-Oct), where you can rent kayaks or paddleboards. After you've had fun on the water, continue east on Rte 132 to the park's south gate, where you can explore the heritage buildings at Grande-Grave, then gear up for the park's don't-miss hike: the 8km round-trip Les Graves trail from L'Anse-aux-Amérindiens to **Land's End**.

If you didn't go whale-watching in Percé, or you want another look at these massive mammals, book an excursion departing from Grande-Grave Wharf with **Croisières Baie de Gaspé** (Baleines Forillon; ☎418-892-5500; www.baleines-forillon.com; 2448 A Blvd de Grande-Grève, Quai de Grande-Grave; adult/child $80/50; ⌚Jun-early Oct; 👪). Also at Grande-Grave is a heritage site where you can poke around a group of historic homes and a restored general store.

Up for another hike? Consider the Mont-Saint-Alban trail, which climbs to a lookout with a panoramic vista. Then continue driving north on Rte 132, where Canada's tallest lighthouse stands guard at Cap des Rosiers, and you have more views across the water and cliffs. The short Du Banc trail serves up more cliff vistas nearby.

The Drive » The 200km drive on Rte 132 from Forillon to Ste Anne des Monts takes you through some of La Gaspésie's most striking scenery, as the highway hugs the coast between steep cliffs and the sea. For a coffee break or local-produce menu lunch, stop at Auberge l'Amarrée, a colorful cafe along the main road in Mont Louis.

TOP TIP: WHICH WAY TO LOOP

You can do this loop trip in either direction, but if you travel counter-clockwise around the peninsula, as we've suggested here, you'll always have the water on your right – where it's easier to pull over for photos or gawk at the views.

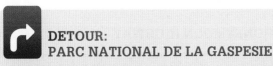

DETOUR: PARC NATIONAL DE LA GASPESIE

Start: 8 Ste Anne des Monts

As you leave the coast and wind your way into this 800-sq-km park, the trees get denser and the mountains higher, with spiky peaks that almost begin to resemble those of the Canadian Rockies. If you'd like to break up your road trip with some hiking in the mountains, head inland to Parc National de la Gaspésie.

The park has more than two-dozen summits that top 1000m, including Mont Jacques Cartier, which at 1268m, is Québec's second-highest mountain. Several of the park's peaks are accessible to day hikers, and a section of the International Appalachian Trail runs through the park as well. All in, there are 140km of hiking paths to explore.

You can easily day-trip to the park from Ste Anne des Monts. From Rte 132, turn south on Rte 299, which leads to the park's **Interpretation Center** (8am-8pm daily Jul & Aug, reduced hours Sep-Jun;). While it's only a 35-minute drive from town, if you want to stay longer, consider overnighting at **Gîte du Mont Albert** (418-763-2288, 866-727-2427; www.sepaq.com/pq/gma; 2001 Rte du Parc; r from $169; Jun-Oct & Jan-Mar; P), the comfortable park lodge.

8 Ste Anne des Monts

This pretty town on the river is a good spot to spend the night. The town has several lovely inns; you can watch the sunset over a bowl of seafood chowder at Auberge Château Lamontagne (p301). Grab a beer at the local microbrewery (p301) or party till the wee hours at the riverside hostel, **Auberge Festive Sea Shack** (418-763-2999, 866-963-2999; www.aubergefestive.com; 292 Blvd Perron E; campsites $20, yurts from $30, dm from $38; P).

In the morning, you can learn more about the marine life of the St Lawrence at **Exploramer** (418-763-2500; www.exploramer.qc.ca; 1 Rue du Quai; adult/child $18/12; 9am-5pm Jun–early Oct; P), the town's aquarium. If you have time, detour off the coast for some hiking in one of the peninsula's most spectacular mountain regions, **Parc National de la Gaspésie** (418-763-7494; www.sepaq.com/pq/gas; adult/child $8.75/free; year-round; P), where you can explore the trails for a day or more.

The Drive » Continue west on Rte 132; it's 185km from Ste Anne des Monts to Rimouski. After Ste Anne des Monts, the landscape starts feeling more urban. But just when you think you're done with the scenic part of your road trip, another expanse of river opens up beside the highway or you find one more cute beach town along the shore.

p301

9 Rimouski

Whether you're heading back toward Québec City or going on to another adventure, wrap up your Gaspé Peninsula road trip in Rimouski. As you're following Rte 132 into the city, stop at **Pointe-au-Père National Historic Site** (418-724-6214; www.shmp.qc.ca; 1000 Rue du Phare; 3-attraction ticket adult/child $25/14.50; 9am-6pm Jun–mid-Oct, museum only 9am-5pm Thu-Sun Mar-May; P), where you can check out a historic lighthouse and visit the well-designed **Empress of Ireland Museum** (418-724-6214; www.shmp.qc.ca; 1000 Rue du Phare; museum only adult/child $10/6.50; 9am-6pm Jun–mid-Oct, to 5pm Thu-Sun Mar-May; P) to learn

QUEBEC'S HONEYMOON HIGHWAY

Rte 132, which circles the Gaspé Peninsula, celebrated its 90th anniversary in 2019, and many Québécois will tell you that the highway played a role in anniversary celebrations in their own families. By the mid-1900s, the road, which was completed in 1929 (it was originally called Rte 6), became one of the most popular destinations in Québec – for honeymooners.

The Québec government wanted to bring tourists to this newly completed roadway, which – with unfortunate timing – opened just at the start of the Great Depression. The province began producing a series of visitor guides, starting with an illustrated 32-page brochure, *Romantic Gaspé*, published in 1929, to introduce visitors to the peninsula's charms.

Apparently, this promotion – and many subsequent marketing campaigns – worked. The local tourism bureau estimated that in 1925, before the road was constructed, only about 100 tourists visited La Gaspésie. By the 1950s, the region was drawing nearly 100,000 road trippers, including many newlywed couples, in an average summer, lured by the sea, the mountains and the Francophone joie de vivre. Today, that number is more than 700,000.

Of course, the Gaspé Peninsula has yet to approach the romantic popularity of Canada's 'Honeymoon Capital,' Niagara Falls, a region that draws more than 14 million annual visitors. But head for the La Gaspésie, instead, young lovers. Because, really, if you're on your honeymoon, you don't need 14 million other people hanging around.

about the worst maritime disaster since the *Titanic*.

Cheer yourself up with a pastry from **Pâtisseries & Gourmandises d'Olivier** (☎418-727-6564; 102 Rue St-Germain E; pastries $3-5; 7am-6pm Wed, Sat & Sun, to 7pm Thu & Fri) or with an excellent sweet or savory pancake at **Le Crêpe Chignon** (☎418-724-0400; www.crepechignonrimouski.com; 140 Ave de la Cathédrale; mains $9-15; 7am-9pm Mon & Tue, to 10pm Wed & Thu, to 11pm Fri, 8am-10pm Sat, to 9pm Sun;). If you haven't had enough seafood, you can fill your crepe with local shrimp or cold-smoked salmon before you leave this maritime region.

Have time for one more stop? Continue south to **Parc National du Bic** (☎418-736-5035; www.sepaq.com/pq/bic; 3382 Rte 132; adult/child $8.75/free; year-round), off Rte 132, 20km south of Rimouski, for more hiking, kayaking or just exploring the shore. In the summer, you might even spot seals swimming or sunning on the rocks.

Eating & Sleeping

Carleton 3

Le Marin d'Eau Douce Seafood $$$

(☎418-364-7602; www.marindeaudouce.com; 215 Rte du Quai; mains $25-30; ⏰5-10pm) An inviting dockside eatery right on the water that serves fresh seafood and other specialties using local ingredients. It has an upscale feel and friendly staff.

Manoir Belle Plage Hotel $$

(☎800-463-0780, 418-364-3388; www.manoirbelleplage.com; 474 Blvd Perron; r incl breakfast from $89; P ❄ @ 📶) Modern rooms with luxurious linens await in this cheery hotel on the highway. There's an upscale restaurant on-site serving local produce and a tasteful, whimsical nautical theme throughout the hotel – think strategically placed driftwood and marine poetry.

Percé 5

Hôtel La Normandie Hotel $$

(☎418-782-2112, 800-463-0820; www.normandieperce.com; 221 Rte 132 W; r $119-349; ⏰mid-May–mid-Oct; P @ 📶) The classiest spot in town, the retreat-like Normandie has serious amenities: the beach, room balconies, a dining room for seafood and expansive lawns with panoramic views of the rock.

Gaspé 6

Marché des Saveurs Gaspésiennes Deli $

(☎418-368-7705; https://marche-de-saveurs-gaspesiennes.business.site; 119 Rue de la Reine; sandwiches $7-12; ⏰8am-7pm Mon-Wed, to 7:30pm Thu-Fri, to 6pm Sat, 10am-6pm Sun) This small gourmet market makes sandwiches, from duck rillettes with pickles, to smoked salmon or smoked meat, and sells pastries, cheeses, jams and other products from around the region. You can eat at one of the few tables or take a picnic down to the river.

Auberge sous les Arbres Inn $$

(☎418-360-0060; www.aubergesouslesarbres.com; 146 Rue de la Reine; r $125-160; P ❄ 📶) Book in advance to score a gilded room at this lovely old home, which has been converted into a stately country cottage/inn. The interior decor has an early-20th-century summer-retreat vibe, while the central location gives guests easy access to town.

Ste Anne des Monts 8

Microbrasserie Le Malbord Pub Food $$

(☎418-764-0022; www.lemalbord.com; 178 1e Ave W; mains $8-17; ⏰11am-midnight Jul-Aug, from 3pm Tue-Sat Sep-May; P) Nothing will warm you up after a long day of hiking in Parc National de la Gaspésie (p299) like a tall glass of red beer and some bacon and cheese melted over potatoes, or pizza with smoked salmon, or a hearty smoked-meat sandwich. All this – local beer, good grub – plus a busy live music schedule.

Auberge Château Lamontagne Inn $$

(☎418-763-7666; www.chateaulamontagne.com; 170 1e Ave E; r $99-140, ste & chalets from $175; P 📶) This colorful inn has an expansive river-view terrace and seven refined rooms with polished oak floors in a brick manor overlooking the St Lawrence. Also on the property are three two-room chalets facing the waterfront. The inn's upscale, romantic restaurant highlights local products from land and sea; try the seafood chowder topped with gooey melted cheese.

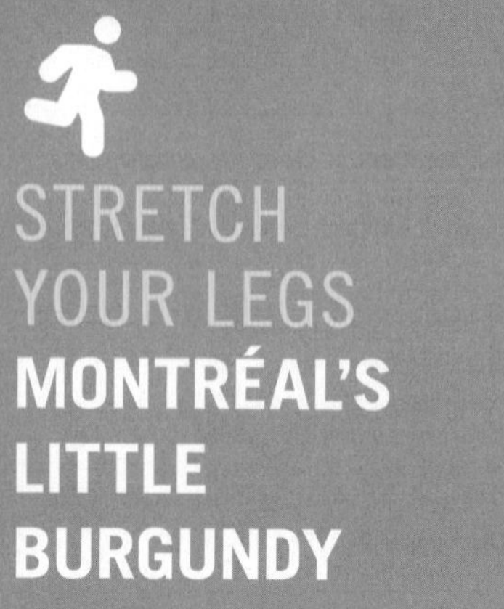

STRETCH YOUR LEGS MONTRÉAL'S LITTLE BURGUNDY

Start/Finish: Marché Atwater

Distance: 1.5 miles

Duration: 1½ to 2 hours

Delightful Little Burgundy is made for relaxed strolling. As you walk around this town by a canal, you'll see locals buying fresh produce, cycling for pleasure and eating in casually cool restaurants. You'll also spot enviable converted warehouse homes.

Take this walk on Trips

Marché Atwater

The fantastic **Atwater Market** (☎514-937-7754; www.marchespublics-mtl.com; 138 Ave Atwater; ⏰7am-6pm Mon-Wed, to 7pm Thu, to 8pm Fri, to 5pm Sat & Sun; Ⓜ Atwater) has a mouthwatering assortment of fresh produce from local farms, excellent wines, crusty breads, fine cheeses and other delectable fare. The market's specialty shops operate year-round, while outdoor eatery stalls open from March to October. It's housed in a 1933 brick hall, topped with a clock tower, and little bouts of live music pop off with pleasing regularity. The grassy banks overlooking the Canal de Lachine are great for a picnic with produce from the market.

The Walk » From the southern exit of the market, walk south 100m to the canal. You'll pass the faux-grass square rest area with picnic tables and a mini-stage for occasional performances. Head west, east or across the bridge to the leafy park – whichever takes your fancy.

Canal de Lachine

A perfect marriage of urban infrastructure and green civic planning, Canal de Lachine incorporates a 14km cycle-and-pedestrian pathway with picnic areas and outdoor spaces. Flotillas of pleasure boats glide along its waters. Old warehouses converted into luxury condos cluster near Atwater Market. If time allows, it's well worth heading out along the canal path on a hired bike or in-line skates from **My Bicyclette** (☎514-317-6306; www.mybicyclette.com; 2985 Rue St-Patrick; bicycle per 2hr/day from $22/45; ⏰10am-6pm; Ⓜ Charlevoix), or on the water in a kayak or boat, available at nearby **H2O Adventures** (☎514-842-1306; www.h2oadventures.com; 2727b Rue St-Patrick; pedal boat/tandem kayak/electric boat/voyageur canoe per hour $25/35/50/50; ⏰9am-9pm Jun-Aug, noon-7:30pm Mon-Fri, 10am-7:30pm Sat & Sun Sep-May; Ⓜ Charlevoix).

The Walk » Cross back by the westside of Marché Atwater along Ave Atwater, passing by a small playground before hitting Rue Notre-Dame

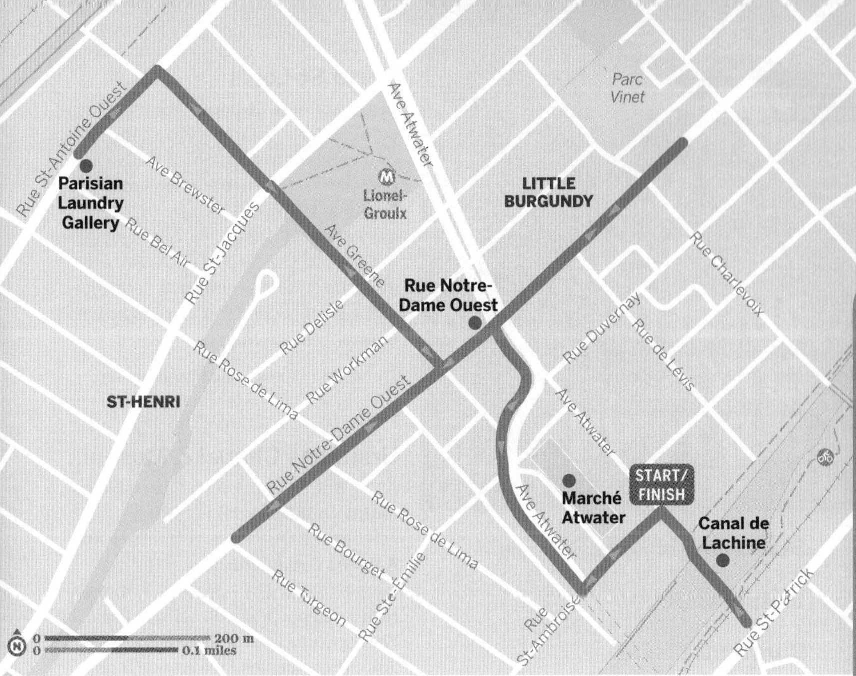

Ouest after 450m. Look out for street art on the main drag. You'll also spot thrift and antique stores, another local attraction.

Rue Notre-Dame Ouest

Soak up Little Burgundy's alternative/ gentrifying vibe with a stroll by its many cafes, restaurants and stores. The pick of the top spots to eat on the street's west side is Asian-retro chic **Satay Brothers** (514-933-3507; www.sataybrothers.com; 3721 Rue Notre-Dame Ouest; mains $9-15; 11am-11pm Wed-Sun; M Lionel-Groulx) for Malaysian laksa; to the east, the famous **Joe Beef** (514-935-6504; www.joebeef.ca; 2491 Rue Notre-Dame Ouest; mains $30-55; 6pm-late Tue-Sat; M Lionel-Groulx) restaurants serve a changing selection of hearty Québécois dishes (reservations required), or head to **Le Bon Vivant** (514-316-4585; https://lebv.ca; 2705 Rue Notre-Dame Ouest; mains $15-30; 5-11pm Mon-Fri, from 11am Sat & Sun; M Lionel Groulx) for a select menu from grilled octopus to freshly made beef or salmon tartare and weekend bagel brunches.

The Walk » This 600m walk north from Rue Notre Dame Ouest along Ave Greene to Parisian Laundry Gallery, takes you to the fringes of St Henri, giving you a peek at the local neighborhood along the way with its up-down houses, red-brick apartments and converted warehouses.

Parisian Laundry Gallery

A former industrial laundry turned monster gallery (1400 sq meters), this space is worth a trip for the old red-brick building itself, even if you're not a fan of contemporary art. The two (visible) stories of the converted warehouse are seemingly comprised of only windows, some arched, letting in plenty of natural light. Previous exhibitions have included works by New York conceptual artist Adam Pendleton and Québec sculptor Valérie Blass. Be sure to check out exhibits upstairs and in the basement.

STRETCH YOUR LEGS
QUÉBEC CITY'S OLD TOWN

Start/Finish: Porte St-Louis

Distance: 3km

Duration: 2 hours

This historical walking tour encompasses a mix of well-known and lesser-known attractions and sights in Vieux-Québec, the city's attractive Old Town. Set off early, before the tour buses arrive.

Take this walk on Trip

Porte St-Louis

Begin at **Porte St-Louis** (Rue St-Louis, Old Upper Town), an impressive gate first erected in 1693, which is also an entrance to the **Fortifications of Québec National Historic Site** (www.pc.gc.ca/eng/lhn-nhs/qc/fortifications/index.aspx; 2 Rue d'Auteuil). At the corner of Rue St-Louis and Rue du Corps-de-Garde, a cannonball sits embedded in a tree at the base (allegedly since 1759).

The Walk » The walk is a straightforward 320m-long stroll from the Porte St-Louis to where Rue St-Louis meets Rue du Corps-de-Garde.

Ursulines Chapel & Museum

At 34 Rue St-Louis, a traditional house dating to 1676 contains the long-established Québécois restaurant **Aux Anciens Canadiens** (www.auxanciens canadiens.qc.ca; 34 Rue St-Louis). The restaurant's steeply pitched roof was typical of 17th-century French architecture. Along adjoining Rue des Jardins you'll pass the **Ursulines Chapel** (www.museedes ursulines.com; 12 Rue Donnacona; ⏲10:30am-noon & 1-4:30pm Tue-Sun May-Oct, 1-4:30pm Sat & Sun Nov-Apr) with the finest woodcarving in Québec where French General Louis-Joseph Montcalm lay from the time of his death in 1759 until 2001. Across from the chapel is the **Ursulines Museum** (www.poleculturel desursulines.ca; 10 Rue Donnacona; adult/youth/child $10/5/free; ⏲10am-5pm Tue-Sun May-Sep, 1-5pm Tue-Sun Oct-Apr) in the convent where generations of nuns educated both French and Indigenous girls starting in 1641.

The Walk » From the Ursulines Museum, walk north along Rue des Jardins then turn left (west) onto Rue Ste-Anne (210m).

Édifice Price

On Rue Ste-Anne is the elegant 1870 **Hôtel Clarendon** (www.hotelclarendon.com; 57 Rue Ste-Anne), Québec City's oldest hotel. Just next door is **Édifice Price** (Price Building; www.ivanhoecambridge.com/en/office-buildings/properties/edifice-price; 65 Rue Ste-Anne), one of Canada's first skyscrapers, built in 1929 for $1 million. Enter

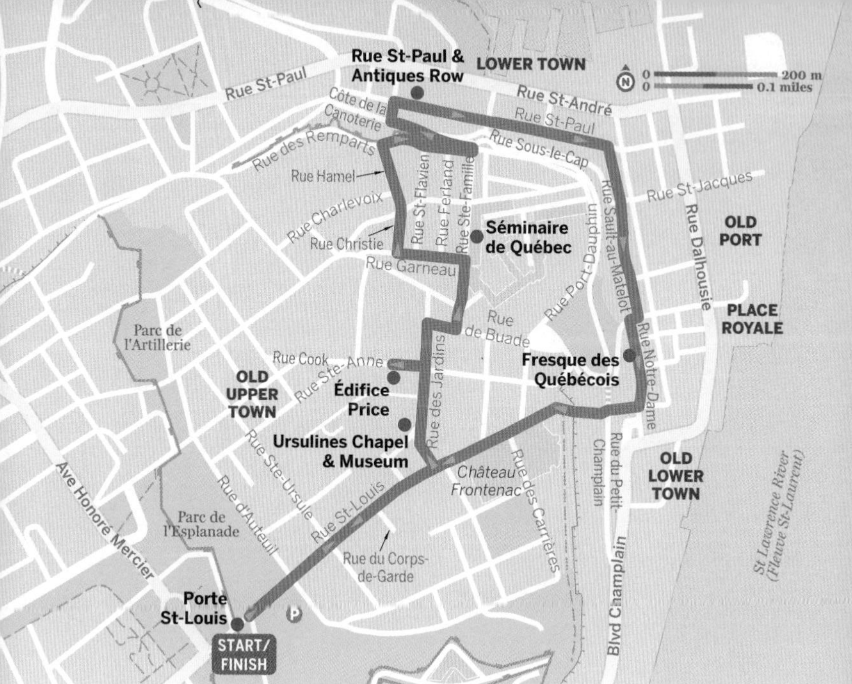

for a look at the art-deco lobby with its fine bronze friezes of loggers at work as well as the stunning coffered ceiling and its brass chandeliers.

The Walk » A short stroll along Rue des Jardins and then Rue de Buade brings you face-to-face with the heavily restored Basilique-Cathédrale Notre-Dame-de-Québec, which dates in its present form from 1925.

Séminaire de Québec

Just to the left (north) of the cathedral is the entrance to the **Séminaire de Québec** (Côte de la Fabrique,) founded in 1663 and its fabulous **Musée de l'Amérique Francophone** (Museum of French-Speaking America; www.mcq.org/en/informations/maf; 2 Côte de la Fabrique). American officers were imprisoned here after their unsuccessful siege of Québec in 1775–76. Detour down pretty Rue Garneau, then descend to Rue des Remparts for fine views over Québec City's waterfront factory district.

The Walk » Descend Côte de la Canoterie, a historical link between the Lower and Upper Towns. Turn right at Rue St-Thomas and then right again onto Rue St-Paul.

Rue St-Paul & Antiques Row

Rue St-Paul is lined with galleries, antiquarian shops and bric-a-brac stores and is always a delightful place to stroll and browse.

The Walk » Turn right and follow pretty Rue Sault-au-Matelot to the impressive trompe l'oeil Québec fresco.

Fresque des Québécois

The impressive 420-sq-meter trompe l'oeil **Fresque des Québécois** (Québec City Mural; 29 Rue Notre-Dame, Parc de la Cetière) is where you can pose for the requisite tourist pic alongside historical figures like Jacques Cartier and Samuel de Champlain. The whimsical multistory mural was painted in 1998 by a group of artists from Québec and Lyon in France.

The Walk » The easiest way to return to Porte St-Louis is to take the funicular up to the Old Upper Town, walk across Place d'Armes to the Château Frontenac and then walk southwest along Rue St-Louis.

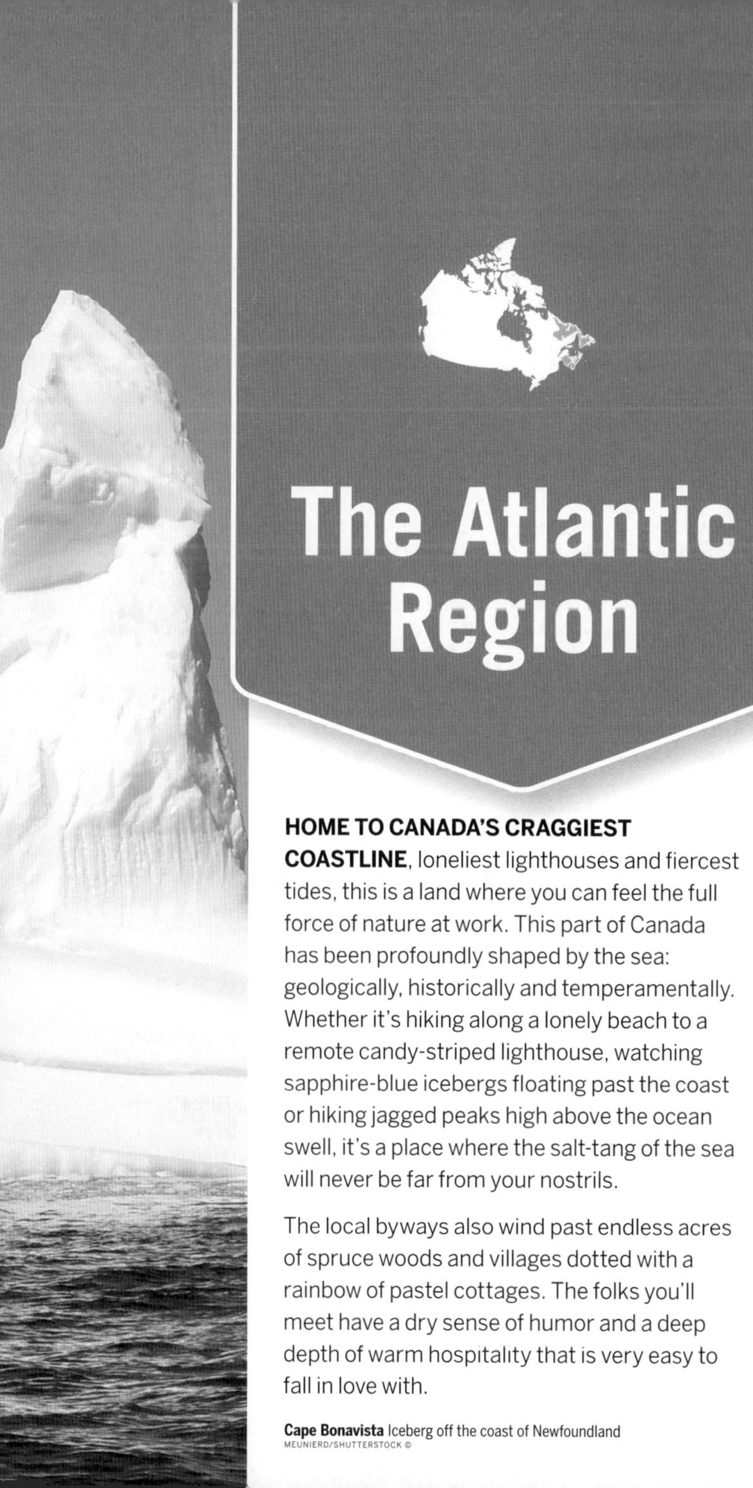

The Atlantic Region

HOME TO CANADA'S CRAGGIEST COASTLINE, loneliest lighthouses and fiercest tides, this is a land where you can feel the full force of nature at work. This part of Canada has been profoundly shaped by the sea: geologically, historically and temperamentally. Whether it's hiking along a lonely beach to a remote candy-striped lighthouse, watching sapphire-blue icebergs floating past the coast or hiking jagged peaks high above the ocean swell, it's a place where the salt-tang of the sea will never be far from your nostrils.

The local byways also wind past endless acres of spruce woods and villages dotted with a rainbow of pastel cottages. The folks you'll meet have a dry sense of humor and a deep depth of warm hospitality that is very easy to fall in love with.

Cape Bonavista Iceberg off the coast of Newfoundland

The Atlantic Region

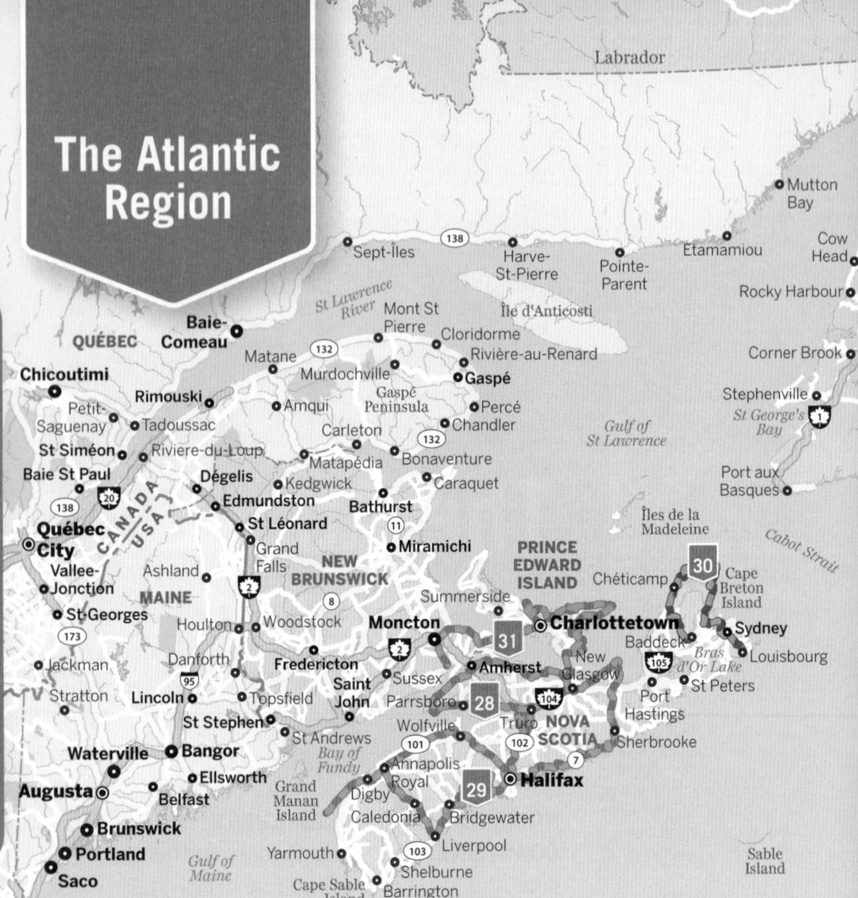

28 Central Nova Scotia 10 Days
A fascinating medley of easy-going towns, secluded beaches and dramatic coastal parks.

29 South Shore Circular 10 Days
Iconic coastal scenery, plus plenty of surprises – including vineyards and age-old petroglyphs.

Classic Trip
30 The Cabot Trail 2–3 Days
Legendary road trip traversing verdant forests, soaring clifftops and sparkling fog-kissed bays.

31 Two Islands, Three Provinces 8 Days
Admire the grandeur of the Maritime provinces, amid captivating island allure and superb seafood.

Icebergs, Vikings & Whales 5 Days
Fall in love with Newfoundland, while spotting whales, hiking past sea cliffs and exploring island culture.

DON'T MISS

Highland Games

Follow the wail of bagpipes at this wondrous Celtic competition held in Antigonish each July. Get there on Trip 28

Kejimkujik National Park

Travel back in time while studying ancient rock art on a guided canoe trip into Nova Scotian wilderness. Reconnect with nature on Trip 29

Skyline Trail

Spot birds of prey and breaching whales while walking through forest and up to sea cliffs high above the shoreline. Find your way there on Trip 30

Greenwich Dunes

Enjoying the end-of-the-world peacefulness on a stroll amid a long, dune-covered stretch of coastline. Go there on Trip 31

Twilingate

Head out on a whale-watching and iceberg-spotting cruise from this island town on the Central Coast. Get there on Trip 32

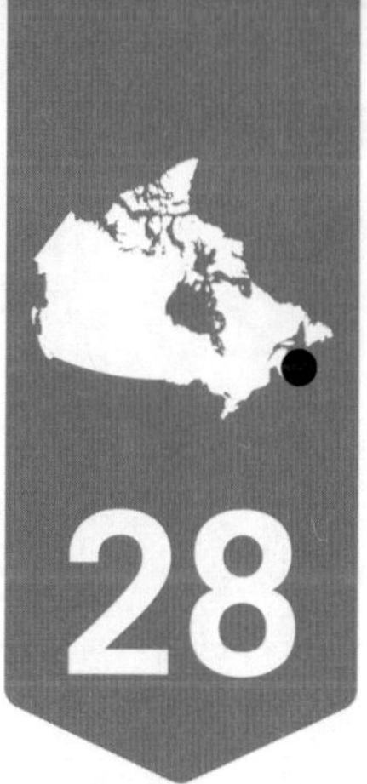

Central Nova Scotia

Follow the road less travelled and loop around Nova Scotia's middle, from the Bay of Fundy all the way to the little-known Eastern Shore.

TRIP HIGHLIGHTS

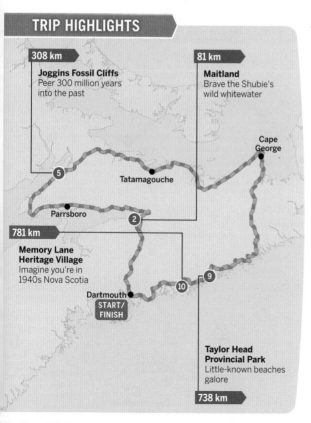

308 km
Joggins Fossil Cliffs
Peer 300 million years into the past

81 km
Maitland
Brave the Shubie's wild whitewater

781 km
Memory Lane Heritage Village
Imagine you're in 1940s Nova Scotia

738 km
Taylor Head Provincial Park
Little-known beaches galore

Cape George
Tatamagouche
Parrsboro
Dartmouth
START/ FINISH
5
2
9
10

10 DAYS
861KM/535 MILES

GREAT FOR...

BEST TIME TO GO
June to September

The view from Cape George Lighthouse.

Kayaking the islands and inlets around Tangier.

Cape George The lighthouse (p315) overlooks St Georges Bay

28 Central Nova Scotia

Sandwiched between the lighthouse-strewn South Shore and the wild roads of Cape Breton – it's easy to see why central Nova Scotia gets overlooked by many visitors. But that's such a shame, as the middle part of the province has so much to recommend it: wild whitewater, remote peninsulas, fantastic sea-kayaking, fossil-studded cliffs and no shortage of off-the-radar beaches.

1 Dartmouth

Eclipsed by its big city neighbor across the harbor, working-class Dartmouth is fast becoming a hipster hotbed for young folk, creatives and commuters. Founded in 1750, it has plenty of history and an excellent foodie scene: try the **Battery Park Beerbar** (☎902-446-2337; www.batterypark.ca; 62 Ochterloney St; ⏰11:30am-midnight Sun-Thu, to 1am Fri & Sat) for craft brews, **Portland Street Creperie** (☎902-466-7686; www.portlandstreetcreperie.com;

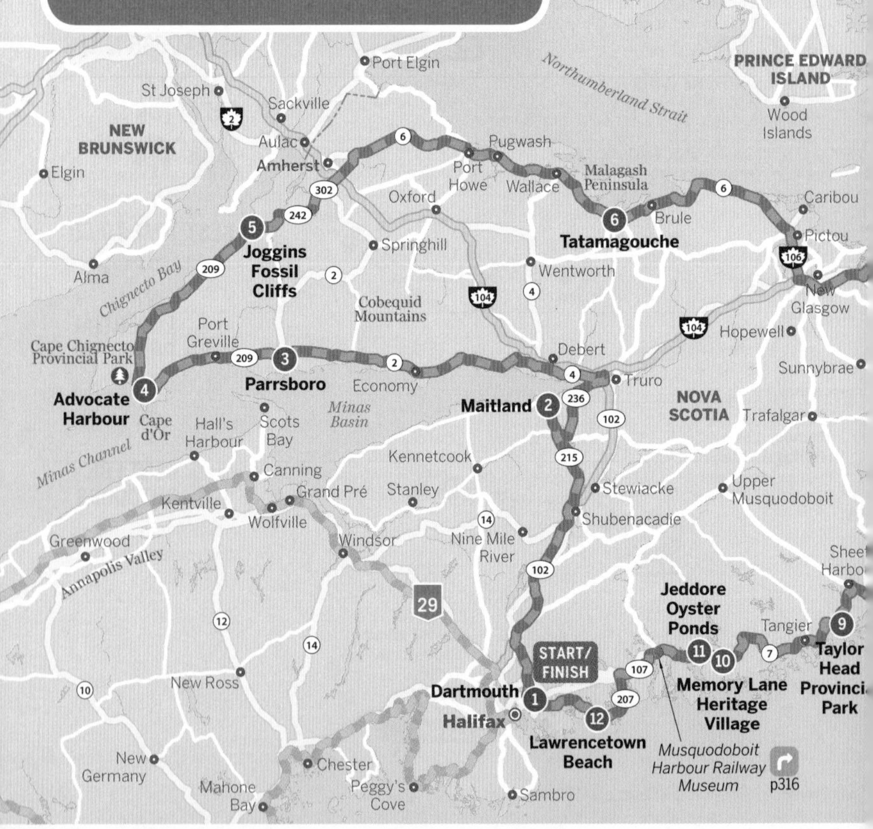

p316

55 Portland St; crepes $6-9; 8:30am-5pm Mon-Thu & Sat, to 7pm Fri, 10am-2:30pm Sun) for pancakes, or the smart Canteen (p317) for bistro food. The best way across is aboard the Halifax–Dartmouth ferry, which runs several times an hour; Dartmouth's accommodation choice isn't great, but there are plenty of options in Halifax.

The Drive » It's a fast drive from Dartmouth on Hwys 122 and 102 straight to Maitland, 80km north.

p317

2 Maitland

Tiny Maitland is the place to brave the Shubenacadie River's legendary tidal bore, a mass of churning whitewater caused by the river's outflow meeting the blasting force of the incoming Fundy tides. Depending on the phase of the moon, the tidal bore can create wave heights of up to 10ft, a wild, washing machine of whitewater that has to be experienced to be believed. **Shubenacadie River Runners** (902-261-2770, 800-856-5061; http://riverrunnersns.com; 8681 Hwy 215; 2/3hr tour $65/85; Jun-Sep) and **Shubenacadie River Adventures** (902-261-2222; www.shubie.com; 10061 Hwy 215; tours from $85; Jun-Sep) run trips on outboard-powered Zodiacs that plunge through the maelstrom for the two to three hours that the rapids exist.

LINK YOUR TRIP

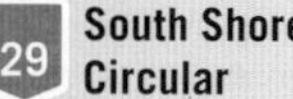

South Shore Circular

You've done Nova Scotia's middle; now it's time to go west.

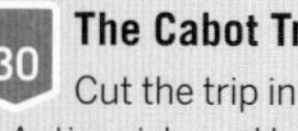

The Cabot Trail

Cut the trip in half at Antigonish, and head east onto Cape Breton.

The Drive » The drive to Parrsboro around the Minas Basin is long: 122km. Take Hwy 236 to Truro, then turn onto Hwy 4, then Hwy 2 (the Glooscap Trail). Count on 2½ to three hours.

p317

3 Parrsboro

On the opposite side of the Minas Basin, Parrsboro is renowned among rock hounds for its geological deposits. The best place to get a grounding is the **Fundy Geological Museum** (902-254-3814; http://fundygeological.novascotia.ca; 162 Two Islands Rd; adult/child $6/4; 10am-5pm mid-May–mid-Oct), where you can view fossils and dinosaur skeletons dug out around the Fundy coastline, and peer into a working lab where new specimens are being processed.

The Drive » Parrsboro makes an obvious overnight stop, with several B&Bs and hotels around town. The next stretch follows the coastal 209 from Parrsboro to Advocate Harbour, 46km west. Along the way, stop offs include the Age of Sail Museum in Port Greville and a little lighthouse at Spencer Island.

p317

4 Advocate Harbour

Advocate Harbour is a breathtaking cove with a 5km-long beach piled high with driftwood that changes dramatically with the tides. Behind the beach, salt marshes – reclaimed with dikes by the Acadians – are replete with birds. Its best-known sight is the **Cape d'Or Lighthouse** (☎902-670-0534; www.capedor.ca; 1 Cape d'Or Rd, Diligent River), where the old keeper's residence has now been converted into a seasonal guesthouse and restaurant. Even if you're not staying, it's worth the rough dirt road drive just for the Fundy views.

The Drive » Continue on Hwy 209 to Joggins, 58km north. En route you'll pass turnoffs to Cape Chignecto Provincial Park, a renowned hiking area.

✕ p317

5 Joggins Fossil Cliffs

Hidden in the cliffs around **Joggins** (www.jogginsfossilcliffs.net; 100 Main St, Joggins; tours from $10.50; ⏲9:30am-5:30pm Jun-Aug, 10am-4pm late Apr-May, Sep & Oct), is archeological treasure: 300-million-year-old fossils dating from the Coal Age, aka the Carboniferous Period, long before the first dinosaurs. Guided tours from the visitor center view fossils buried in the rock, including lycopsid trees, root systems known as stigmaria and shrimp-like creatures called pygocephalus. Tour times are tide-dependent; consult the website for schedules.

The Drive » The next stage of the drive cuts across to Tatamagouche via the busy town of Amherst, 188km west via Hwys 242, 302 and 6. The coastal section from Port Howe to Tatamagouche is the most interesting; if you like, you can stop off at a wildlife reserve at Wallace Bay.

6 Tatamagouche

The **Malagash Peninsula**, which juts out into protected Tatamagouche Bay, is a low-key, bucolic loop for a drive or bike ride. Tatamagouche makes a great base for exploring. There's loads to see and do round here: top stops include a tasting session at **Jost Winery** (☎902-257-2636; www.jostwine.ca; 48 Vintage Lane, Malagash; tours $5; ⏲wine store 10am-5pm Mar-Dec, tours noon & 3pm Mon-Fri, 11am Sat Jun-Sep), wildlife watching at **Blue Sea Beach** (https://parks.novascotia.ca/content/blue-sea-beach; 651 Blue Sea Rd, Malagash Point) or **Rushton's Beach** (http://parks.novascotia.ca/content/rushtons-beach; 723 Hwy 6, Brule), and a visit to the excellent **Tatamagouche Brewing Co** (☎902-657-4000; www.tatabrew.com; 235 Main St; ⏲10am-6pm Sun-Thu, to 9pm Fri, to 8pm Sat). There are a few hotels and B&Bs around town if you want to overnight.

The Drive » Take Hwy 6 for 55km to Pictou, then Hwys 106 and 104 to Sutherlands River for 32km. Here you'll turn off onto Hwy 245, then Hwy 337, around the edge of Cape George; this stretch is about 61km.

DETOUR: CANSO

Start: 8 Antigonish

One of North America's oldest seaports, Canso today stands as a lonely cluster of boxy fishers' homes on a treeless bank of Chedabucto Bay. Just offshore, **Grassy Island Fort** (☎902-366-3136; www.pc.gc.ca/en/lhn-nhs/ns/canso/culture/grassyislandfort; 1465 Union St; ⏲10am-6pm Jun-Sep) was built in 1720 by the British to counter the French, who had their headquarters in Louisbourg. The fort was destroyed in 1744, but you can wander freely among the ruins. Boats run across until 4pm.

The most direct route is 115km southeast of Antigonish along Hwy 16. A slightly more circuitous route is to take the junction off Hwy 7 between Lochaber and Aspen onto Hwy 276 E, then follow signs to Hwys 316 and 16.

7 Cape George

The jaunt to Cape George is a mustn't miss: with its remote beaches, cliffs and sea scenery, it's been compared in beauty to parts of the Cabot Trail. There are numerous beaches to stop off at – **Arisaig Provincial Park** and **Malignant Cove** are highlights – but the real pleasure here is the drive itself, all breezy bluffs and open ocean vistas.

The 360ft **Cape George Point Lighthouse** (www.parl.ns.ca/lighthouse) overlooks the calm waters of St Georges Bay. The present light (the third) was built in 1961, but there's been a beacon here since 1861. If it's nearing lunch time, head just around the cape to the fish-and-chip truck near the **Ballantyne's Cove Tuna Interpretive Centre** (902-863-8162; 57 Ballantyne's Cove Wharf Rd; 10am-5:30pm Jul-Sep), then work off the fried goodness with a dip or a stroll at **Crystal Cliffs Beach** (Crystal Cliffs Farm Rd).

The Drive » From Cape George, the coastal 337 meanders south to Antigonish, about 30km away.

MOLLIEGPHOTO/SHUTTERSTOCK ©

Joggins Fossil Cliffs Fossilized stone

8 Antigonish

Antigonish is best-known for its well-regarded seat of learning, St Francis Xavier University, and for its Celtic roots: since 1861, the town has hosted an annual **Highland Games** (www.antigonishhighlandgames.ca) every July and it still attracts thousands of visitors. A 4km hiking and cycling trail to the nature reserve at **Antigonish Landing** begins just across the train tracks from the Antigonish Heritage Museum: you might see eagles, ducks and ospreys. If you don't stay in Tatamagouche, Antigonish is the next obvious place to take a break.

The Drive » The cross-country journey to the Eastern Shore is via Hwy 7, which travels to Liscomb, then turns westwards and tracks the coast. Point-to-point, it's 155km from Antigonish to Taylor Head.

✕ p317

9 Taylor Head Provincial Park

A little-known highlight of Nova Scotia, this spectacular **park** (902-772-2218; http://parks.novascotia.ca/content/taylor-head; 20140 Hwy 7, Spry Bay) encompasses a peninsula jutting 6.5km into the Atlantic. On one side is a long, very fine, sandy beach fronting a protected bay. Some 17km of hiking trails cut through the spruce and fir forests. The Headland Trail, an 8km round-trip, is the longest and follows the rugged coastline to scenic views at Taylor Head. The shorter Bob Bluff Trail is a 3km round-trip hike to a bluff with good views.

About 14km southwest of Taylor Head Provincial Park, Tangier is one of the best settings for kayaking in the Maritimes. Based at Mason's Cove, **Coastal Adventures Sea Kayaking** (www.coastaladventures.com; half-/full-day tour $85/125; Jun-Sep) explores the isolated '100 Wild Islands' nearby.

DETOUR: MUSQUODOBOIT HARBOUR RAILWAY MUSEUM

Start: ⓫ Jeddore Oyster Ponds

This wonderful little **railway museum** (902-889-2689; www.mhrailwaymuseum.com; 7895 Hwy 7, Musquodoboit Harbour; by donation; 9am-5pm Jun-Sep), loved by train buffs and kids alike, looks a little incongruous in its surroundings: it's hard to believe there was once a passenger service through here. Housed in the 1918 railway station on its original site, the museum has train memorabilia inside and original rolling stock outside. It's near the small village of Musquodoboit Harbour, about 14km west of Jeddore Oyster Ponds on Hwy 7.

The Liscombe Lodge Resort is the barea's best place to stay, or you can pitch at one of a number of wild campgrounds dotted along the shoreline.

The Drive » From Tangier, stick to Hwy 7; the twisting road carries you on towards Lake Charlotte, 43km west, with flashes of forest and coastline en route.

p317

⓾ Memory Lane Heritage Village

A 20-minute drive from Tangier, **Memory Lane Heritage Village** (877-287-0697; https://heritagevillage.ca; 5435 Clam Harbour Rd, Lake Charlotte; adult/child $8/3; 9:30am-4pm Jun-Sep) re-creates a 1940s Eastern Shore village in a series of lovingly relocated and restored buildings, chock-full of hands-on antiques, as if frozen in time. You'll find vintage cars, a farmstead with animals (great for kids), a schoolhouse, a church, a miner's hut, a blacksmith, shipbuilding shops and much more.

Just to the south, in **Clam Harbour Provincial Park**, there's a fine beach for sunbathing.

The Drive » From Memory Lane Heritage Village, the Jeddore Ponds and Fisherman's Life Museum are 7km further west along Hwy 7.

⓫ Jeddore Oyster Ponds

The tiny **Fisherman's Life Museum** (902-889-2053; http://fishermanslife.novascotia.ca; 58 Navy Pool Loop, Jeddore Oyster Pond; adult/child $4/3; 9am-4pm Wed-Sun Jun, Tue-Sun Jul-Sep), located 35km west of Tangier near a series of pools known as the Jeddore Oyster Ponds, paints a convincing picture of the tough lives of the people – particularly the women – who lived along the Eastern Shore at the turn of the century. The simple wooden house here belonged to Ervine Myers, his wife Ethelda and their 13 daughters; in summer, Ervine spent weeks away at his fish shack on Roger Barren Island, and worked away at local lumber camps in winter, leaving his wife and daughters to look after the family home. The museum is dotted with family memorabilia, and costumed guides offer tea, tales and hospitality. It's surprisingly moving in its own homespun way.

The Drive » Hwys 107 and 207 traverse the deep inlets of the Eastern Shore. You'll reach Lawrencetown Beach after 42km.

⓬ Lawrencetown Beach

Learning to surf might not be foremost in your mind when you plan a trip to Nova Scotia, but there are some surprisingly good swells (this is the Atlantic, after all). Surf central is Lawrencetown Beach, where Nova Scotia's only pro surfer offers lessons through his **East Coast Surf School** (902-449-9488; www.ecsurfschool.com; 4348 Lawrencetown Rd, East Lawrencetown; lessons from $75).

The Drive » Hwy 207 will carry you directly back to Dartmouth, 23km to the west.

Eating & Sleeping

Dartmouth 1

Canteen — Bistro $$

(902-425-9272; www.thecanteen.ca; mains lunch $10-18, dinner $18-24; 11am-2:30am & 5-11pm Tue-Fri, 10am-2pm & 5-11pm Sat) This pared-back bistro has become Dartmouth's dining hot spot for its fresh, flavoursome dishes: big bowls of mussels, panzanella salad, lobster tagliatelle and scallop risotto, all driven by the seasons and served in a light, minimal space. It's very popular, so bookings are advised. If you miss out, its sandwich takeout, **Little C**, is next door.

Maitland 2

Cresthaven by the Sea — B&B $$

(902-261-2001; www.cresthavenbythesea.com; 19 Ferry Lane; r $159; May-Oct; Wi-Fi) There are three sweet rooms on offer in this immaculate white Victorian house on a bluff right over the point where the Shubenacadie River meets the bay. All rooms have river views; the lower ones are wheelchair accessible.

Parrsboro 3

Black Rock Bistro — Bistro $$

(902-728-3006; www.blackrockbistro.ca; 151 Main St; mains $14-20; 7am-8pm; P) This downtown bistro is pretty much the pick of Parrsboro's eating places. Steak-frites, handmade burgers, slow-roasted ribs, and the odd pasta and risotto dish will make sure you don't leave hungry.

Gillespie House Inn — B&B $$

(902-254-3196; www.gillespiehouseinn.com; 358 Main St; d $129-149; P Wi-Fi) The pick of Parrsboro's B&Bs, this lovingly restored sea captain's mansion has heritage-themed rooms stocked with burnished sleigh beds, clawfoot tubs, antique settees and wingback chairs. There's a fabulous staircase and verandah, a yoga studio and a blueberry field where you can pick your own berries in summer. A real stunner.

Advocate Harbour 4

Wild Caraway Restaurant & Cafe — Canadian $$

(902-392-2889; www.wildcaraway.com; 3721 Hwy 209; mains lunch $8-16, dinner $22-38; 11am-3:30pm & 5-7:30pm Thu-Mon mid-May–Oct; Wi-Fi) Local products and seasonal cooking underpin the menu at this superb coastal cafe, in a little house with a view of the driftwood-strewn beach of Advocate Harbour. The food is as good as you'll find in this part of Nova Scotia: crumbed fishcakes, mackerel bento bowls, pan-seared scallops, and cheeses from That Dutchman's Cheese Farm.

Antigonish 8

Brownstone Restaurant — Cafe $$

(902-735-3225; www.brownstonecafe.ca; 244 Main St; mains $8-20; 11am-9pm Mon-Sat) This attractive little cafe on Main St has some surprises inside, including Italianate murals, brick-effect wallpaper and a bizarre copper-effect stucco ceiling. It's the town's any-time-of-day choice for something to eat, with generous breakfasts; big salads and flatbread pizzas for lunch; and stir-fries, steaks and pasta for dinner.

Taylor Head Provincial Park 9

Liscombe Lodge Resort — Resort $$

(902-779-2307; www.liscombelodge.ca; 2884 Hwy 7, Liscomb; r/chalets from $155/189; May-Oct; P pool) A nature-lover's dream, this rambling country lodge comprises 30 spacious, nicely decorated riverside rooms in the main lodge, five rustic four-room cottages, and 17 sweeter-than-sweet chalets with fireplaces as well as decks overlooking the woodsy grounds and river. There's loads to keep kids occupied, including an indoor pool, a tennis court, free bikes and kayaking.

South Shore Circular

The Nova Scotia of your imagination – lonely lighthouses, wild beaches, pretty fishing coves and sprawling forests, with the briny scent of the sea never far from your nostrils.

TRIP HIGHLIGHTS

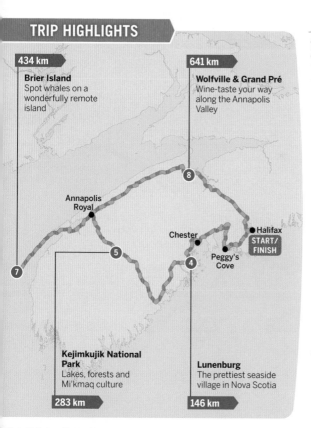

434 km
Brier Island
Spot whales on a wonderfully remote island

641 km
Wolfville & Grand Pré
Wine-taste your way along the Annapolis Valley

Annapolis Royal
Chester
Halifax
START/ FINISH
Peggy's Cove

Kejimkujik National Park
Lakes, forests and Mi'kmaq culture
283 km

Lunenburg
The prettiest seaside village in Nova Scotia
146 km

10 DAYS 734KM/456 MILES

GREAT FOR...

BEST TIME TO GO

June to September

ESSENTIAL PHOTO

Standing next to the world-famous lighthouse at Peggy's Cove.

BEST FOR OUTDOORS

Paddling a canoe around the peaceful shores of Kejimkujik Lake.

Kejimkujik National Park (p322) Canoeing on Kejimkujik Lake

29 South Shore Circular

This trip makes a scenic circuit round the western half of Nova Scotia, meandering along the South Shore from Halifax (locally dubbed 'The Lighthouse Route'), before cutting inland to explore the forests and lakes of Kejimkujik National Park, circling back via the vineyards and orchards of the Annapolis Valley. It captures the essence of Nova Scotia in all its salty, sea-facing, good-natured glory: by the end, you'll feel like a true Maritimer.

1 Halifax

Big in Nova Scotian terms, titchy in Canadian terms, the port city of Halifax makes a fine place to begin. The city has some great museums, and the waterfront boardwalk (p358) has super views across the harbor to Dartmouth and Georges Island, plus pop-up food shacks and summer events aplenty. You'll need at least a couple of days in the city to explore.

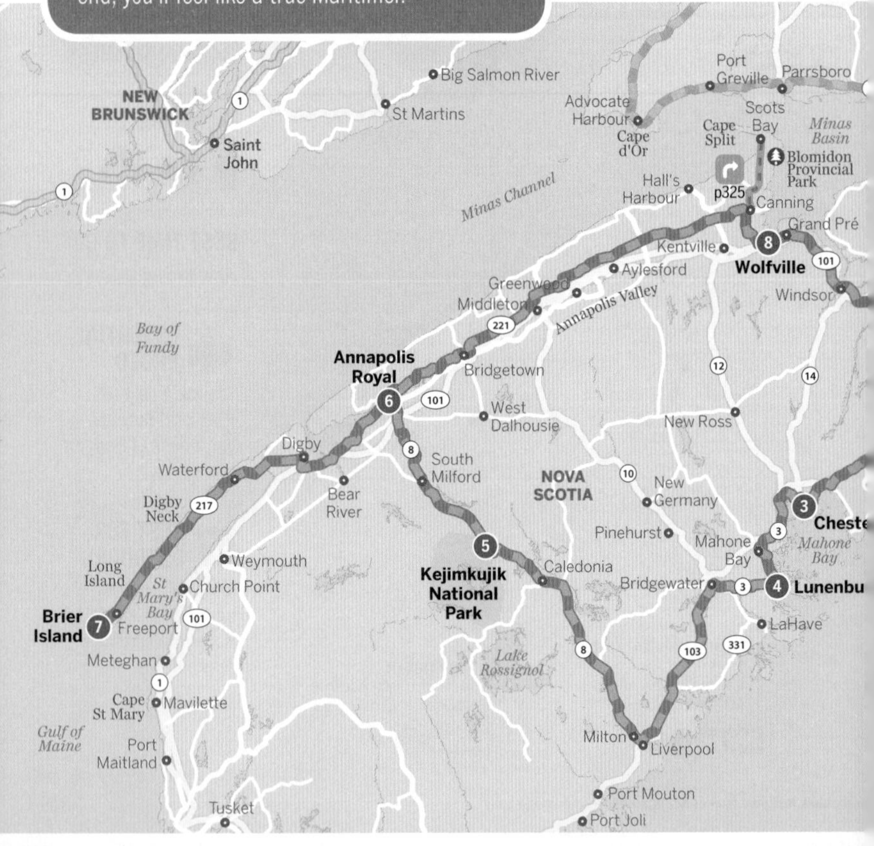

The Drive » The drive out of Halifax on Hwy 33 makes a pleasant start to the trip (so long as you manage to avoid any rush-hour traffic). This is the official beginning of the Lighthouse Route, for which you'll see plenty of signs. It's 42km to Peggy's Cove, a journey of 45 minutes to an hour depending on traffic.

 p326

2 Peggy's Cove

With its red-and-white striped lighthouse, colorful clapboard cottages and boulder-strewn shoreline, this tiny little fishing cove presents the classic picture that literally every visitor to Nova Scotia wants to snap. In summer you'll be doing battle with hordes of coach trippers for the prime spot, so it's much better to hit the cove very early or late in the day when it's still relatively tranquil. Built in 1914, the **lighthouse** (185 Peggys Point Rd; 9:30am-5:30pm May-Oct) is apparently the most photographed in Canada, and rather bizarrely served as a post office for many years.

If the crush gets too much, you'll find the same kind of vibe at the cute-as-a-button cove of **Lower Prospect**, 30km to the east via Terence Bay. Admittedly, there's no lighthouse, but the tranquility more than makes up for its absence.

The Drive » Head north from Peggy's Cove, following the coast through Glen Margaret and Tantallon; at Upper Tantallon, turn onto Hwy 3, which will take you on a scenic route along the coast via Boutiliers Point, Queensland and East River (the alternative is the fast but dull main Hwy 103). It's a winding route of about 70km.

 p326

3 Chester

The seaside village of Chester is one of the prettiest stop-offs along the south shore. Established in 1759, it's had a colorful history as the haunt of pirates and Prohibition-era bathtub-gin smugglers, and it keeps its color today via the many artists' studios about town. It's also a popular place for well-to-do Haligonians to buy a summer home. Many visitors to Chester also take a day trip out to **Big Tancook Island** (www.tancookcommunitynews.com; adult/child round-trip $7/free), the largest of the islets in Mahone Bay, which offers some great walking and interesting settlement history. The one-way trip takes about 50 minutes.

Just along the coast is Mahone Bay, where you can wander along Main St, which is scattered with shops selling antiques, quilts, pottery

LINK YOUR TRIP

28 Central Nova Scotia

From Halifax, hop across the harbor to Dartmouth for the start of this journey to dramatic coastal scenery.

31 Two Islands, Three Provinces

Extend the adventure from Halifax with a jaunt north on the Nova Scotia–Prince Edward Island combo.

and works by local painters. The town's seafront skyline is punctuated by three magnificent old churches that provide useful landmarks for sailors.

The Drive » Skip the dull Hwy 103 in favor of Hwy 3 along the coast. It runs for 25km from Chester to Mahone Bay. Another 11km will bring you to Lunenburg. It's a pretty stretch of road, with plenty of sea views to enjoy en route.

❹ Lunenburg

With its brightly painted weatherboard houses, lawned squares and slate-topped churches, lovely Lunenburg almost looks like a model. And in some ways, that's exactly what it is: it was designed according to the standard British blueprint for colonial settlements in the 18th century, and seems barely to have changed since it was built. The old town's beautifully preserved architecture has earned it Unesco World Heritage site status, and deservedly so. The town's sea-going past is exhaustively covered at the **Fisheries Museum of the Atlantic** (☎902-634-4794; http://fisheriesmuseum.novascotia.ca; 68 Bluenose Dr; adult/child $13/3.50; ⏲9:30am-5pm or 5:30pm mid-May–Oct), and if you're lucky, you might be able to take a cruise aboard the **Bluenose II** (☎902-634-1963; https://bluenose.novascotia.ca; 2hr cruises adult/child $65/36) – successor to the original *Bluenose*, the fabled racing yacht that still graces the Canadian dime.

With plenty of B&Bs around town, it's also an obvious place to overnight.

The Drive » From Lunenburg, Hwy 3 west joins Hwy 103 for a quick route to Liverpool, where you turn off onto Hwy 8, the only road into Kejimkujik National Park. It's about 134km, a good two- to 2½-hour drive. A much slower alternative are the coastal Hwys 332 and 331 via Crescent Beach and Broad Cove, offering views of the LeHave Islands. This route adds 25km to 30km and another 45 minutes to an hour.

NANCY ROSE/GETTY IMAGES ©

✕ 🛏 p326

❺ Kejimkujik National Park

Known as 'Keji' by locals, the vast 381-sq-km national park of Kejimkujik is home to the last tracts of true wilderness in Nova Scotia. Generations of Mi'kmaq people paddled, camped and hunted here, and the area is dotted with ancient camping sites, many marked by

THE RUM RUNNERS TRAIL

Had enough of driving? Then take a break on this excellent **bike route** (www.rumrunnerstrail.ca), which runs from Halifax to Lunenburg via most of the main south shore towns, including St Margaret's Bay, Chester and Mahone Bay. It's 119km if you do the whole thing, but the website and route maps handily split the route into seven subsections that can each easily be done in a day. The 10km Mahone Bay to Lunenburg section is an ideal starter; you can hire bikes at **Sweet Ride Cycling** (☎902-531-3026; www.sweetridecycling.com; 523 Main St; half-/full-day rentals $25/35; ⏲10am-5pm Mon-Sat, noon-5pm Sun).

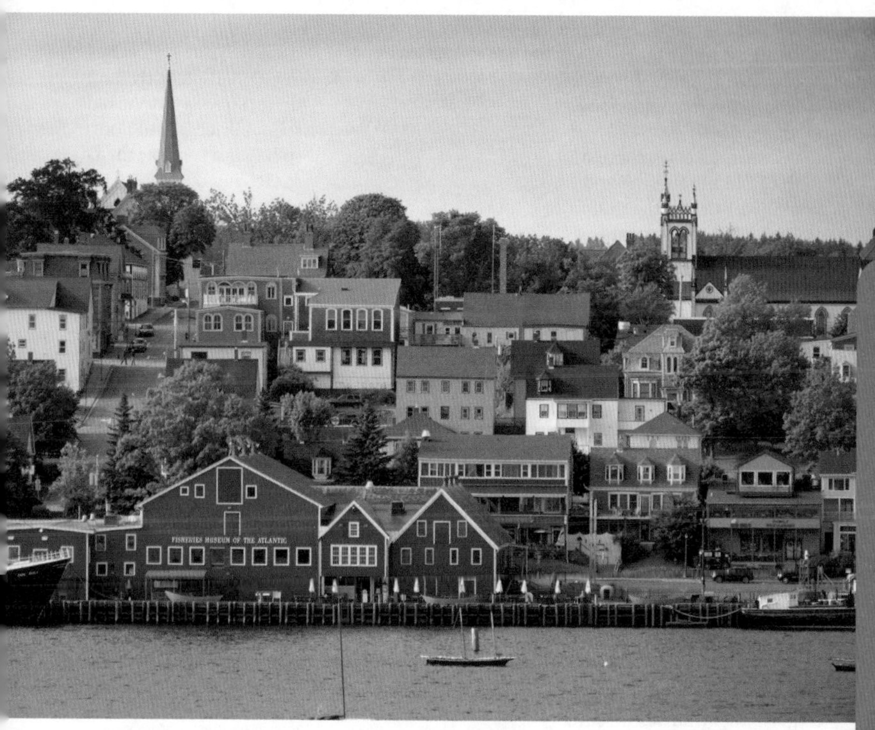

Lunenburg Views of the town's well-preserved architecture

rock engravings known as petroglyphs: in summer you can take a fascinating guided hike in the company of native guides. Incredibly, even today, less than 20% of Keji's wilderness is accessible by car; the rest can only be reached on foot or by canoe.

Whynot Adventure (Keji Outfitters; ☎902-682-2282; www.whynotadventure.ca; 1507 Main Pkwy; canoe rental per hour/day/week from $15/40/165; ⏰8am-8pm Jun-Sep) runs guided kayaking and canoeing trips from its base near Jakes Landing, on the shores of the enormous Kejimkujik Lake. The **national park visitor center** (☎902-682-2772; www.parkscanada.gc.ca/keji; 3005 Main Pkwy, Maitland Bridge; park entry adult/child $6/3; ⏰8:30am-7pm or 8pm mid-Jun–Aug, to 4:30pm mid-May–mid-Jun & Oct) has details on local campgrounds where you can overnight in pre-pitched oTENTiks or cozy cabins.

The Drive » The main national park visitor center is near Maitland Bridge, roughly halfway between the south and north coast. From the visitor center, it's 48km to Annapolis Royal on Hwy 8.

🛏 p326

6 Annapolis Royal

There are many reasons to stop off in the well-to-do town of Annapolis Royal – great restaurants, lovely gardens, a fine brewery and a wondrous riverside location not least among them – but it's the dramatic 17th-century stronghold of **Fort Anne** (☎902-532-2397; www.parkscanada.gc.ca/fortanne; Upper St George St; adult/child $3.90/free; ⏰9am-5:30pm daily mid-Jun–Aug, Tue-Sat only mid-May–mid-Jun & Sep–mid-Oct) that most visitors come to see. The town's strategic importance on the Annapolis River meant the fort witnessed many bloody battles between its construction in the 1630s and the end of hostilities in the mid-1700s; the battlements and bulwarks are now largely grassed over, but you can still get a sense of the imposing presence the fort must have presented to prospective attackers. There's an interesting museum in the old Officers' Quarters, with exhibits including a four-panel tapestry depicting 400 years of the fort's history.

Another couple of facts that might be worth retaining for a pub quiz: Annapolis Royal was the location of Canada's first permanent European settlement, and also served as the capital of Nova Scotia until the founding of Halifax in 1749.

The Drive » Take the coastal Hwy 1 to Digby, then head towards Long Island and Brier Islands via Hwy 217. It's a super drive, with little traffic and brilliant views of the Bay of Fundy. The two car ferries run hourly (after midnight they're 'on call'). Each costs $7, payable only on travel towards Brier Island (the return fare is free); ferry times can be found at www.brierisland.org. From Annapolis Royal to Westport on Brier Island it's 101km: two hours if you time the crossings right.

p327

7 Brier Island

Some people might see it as a detour, but the there-and-back trip to Brier Island is an integral part of this trip. This huge basin is famous for its tides (which are the most extreme in the world), and also for its whales: plankton stirred up by the strong Fundy tides attracts finback, minke and humpback whales, as well as the endangered and hard-to-see North Atlantic right whale. Several operators offer whale-watching trips from **Westport**, at the far end of Brier Island, including the excellent **Brier Island Whale & Seabird Cruises** (902-839-2995; www.brierislandwhalewatch.com; 223 Water St, Westport; adult/child from $50/28; mid-May–Oct). It's a fairly long drive, so a stay at the old-school Brier Island Lodge (p327) is a sensible idea.

Getting out to the island is almost as much fun: you'll traverse two chugging ferries en route, and be treated to plenty of gloriously untouched island scenery. The workaday town of Digby makes a handy base before or after the trip: it's renowned for its scallops, which you can sample at restaurants all over town.

The Drive » Backtrack to Annapolis Royal, then continue along the valley to Wolfville: Hwy 221 offers a more scenic route than main Hwy 101, passing through several small towns along the way. It's a pretty long drive of 208km and probably 3½ to four hours thanks to the ferry crossings; overnighting in Annapolis Royal makes it a more leisurely prospect.

p327

8 Wolfville

If you mention the Annapolis Valley to Nova Scotians, one image is likely to spring to mind: a glass of ice-cold white wine, preferably served alongside a big pile of seafood. The area's nutrient-rich soils and temperate climate on the Bay of Fundy makes it perfect for viticulture: in fact, the first vines in Nova Scotia were planted here way back in the early 1600s. The area's wineries are scattered around

KEJI SEASIDE ADJUNCT

The main part of Kejimkujik National Park is supplemented by a smaller Keji Seaside Adjunct, 107km to the south, protecting an important coastal habitat of dunes, beaches and creeks between Port Joli and Port Mouton Bay. It's a popular place for backcountry hiking and kayaking. Most people camp, but if you prefer not, the nearby towns of Liverpool and Shelburne make the most obvious bases.

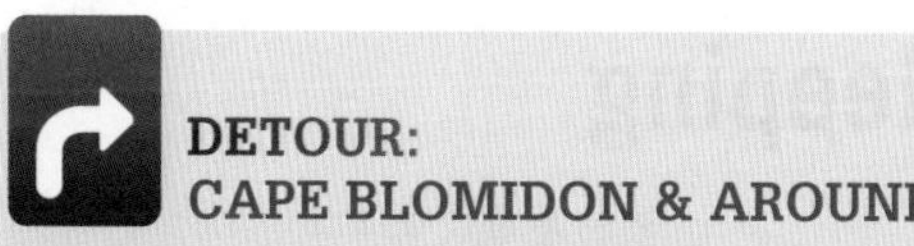

DETOUR: CAPE BLOMIDON & AROUND

Start: 8 Wolfville & Grand Pré

The area to the north of the Annapolis Valley is dominated by the high ridge of the North Mountain, which comes to an end at windswept **Cape Blomidon**. It's an under-explored area that's perfect for a detour. Key stops include the rustic **Halls Harbour Lobster Pound** (902-679-5299; www.hallsharbourlobster.com; 1157 W Halls Harbour Rd, Centreville; mains $15-24; noon-7pm mid-May–Jun, Sep & Oct, 11:30am-9pm Jul & Aug), where you can gorge yourself on ocean delicacies straight from the source; the quaint town of **Canning**; and the renowned **Blomidon Estate Winery** (902-582-7565; www.blomidonwine.ca; 10318 Hwy 221, Canning; 10am-6pm Mon-Fri, to 7pm Sat, 11am-6pm Sun Jun-Sep). Another must-see is the **Look-Off**, a well-signposted viewpoint that has a panoramic perspective of the the Annapolis Valley and, if you're lucky, bald eagles soaring overhead.

Hwy 358 ends in Scots Bay, where the dramatic 13km **Cape Split** hiking trail offers some of the finest views of the Minas Basin and the Bay of Fundy. If you're not up for the hike, nearby **Blomidon Provincial Park** (902-582-7319; https://parks.novascotia.ca/content/blomidon; 3138 Pereau Rd, Canning; campsites $26.70-35.60; mid-May–mid-Oct) has a picnic area and plenty of easier walks.

the university town of Wolfville and nearby **Grand Pré**, a national historic site steeped in Acadian history.

The valley is littered with world-class wineries, all of which offer guided tours and tastings, including the best-known local appellation, Tidal Bay. Among the oldest and most prestigious is Domaine de Grand Pré (p327), whose vintages include a delicious spicy muscat and a nice sparkling Champlain Brut. The winery also has a renowned fine-dining restaurant, Le Caveau (p327).

There's a slightly more contemporary vibe at **Lightfoot & Wolfville** (902-542-7774; www.lightfootandwolfville.com; 11143 Evangeline Trail; 10am-6pm Mon-Wed, to 9pm Thu-Sun mid-Jun–mid-Oct, shorter hours rest of year), an organic, biodynamic vineyard producing a range of wines, from a bubbly rosé and blanc de blancs to a crisp chardonnay and an ice wine. The tours ($15) are informative and last about 45 minutes, exploring the estate's ecofriendly approach and ethos, and including a taste of three wines. Afterwards you can lunch at their excellent bistro.

For a different taste, it's also worth stopping off in Wolfville for a visit to the **Annapolis Cider Company** (902-697-2707; www.drinkannapolis.ca; 388 Main St, Wolfville; 10am-7pm), which uses heirloom and heritage apples to makes all its brews.

The Drive » Hwy 101 cuts directly across the island from Wolfville to Halifax: a distance of 93km, but you'll do it in less than 1½ hours if the traffic's okay.

p327

Eating & Sleeping

Halifax 1

Edna — Canadian $$

(902-431-5683; www.ednarestaurant.com; 2053 Gottingen St; brunch $12-20, mains $24-36; 5-11pm Fri & Sat, 5-10pm Tue-Thu & Sun) At the edge of the North End, this hipster diner has strong competition but is still many people's first choice. It's bare bones as far as decor goes: a long wooden table for communal dining, a tiled bar, metal stools and tables for two. Food is modern bistro: risotto, seared scallops, classic steaks, all lovingly prepared. Edna equals excellence.

Bar Kismet — Bistro $$

(902-487-4319; www.barkismet.com; 2733 Agricola St; small plates $12-15, large plates $25-27; 5pm-midnight Tue-Sun) Impeccable small plates of seafood have made this tiny bar-bistro a favorite among foodie North Enders, and deservedly so: dishes zing with surprising combinations and flavors, such as bass with morel mushrooms and artichokes, or raw scallop with lemongrass and turnip. The decor's stripped right back – bare wood, mirrors, pendant lights – putting the focus firmly on the food.

Halliburton — Inn $$

(902-420-0658; www.thehalliburton.com; 5184 Morris St; d $169-229, ste $299-350; P ❄ @ 📶) Smart, refined and with a dash of Haligonian history that's getting increasingly hard to find, the Halliburton occupies a classic red-brick Victorian edifice in the middle of downtown. It offers 29 traditionally decorated rooms with varying layouts, and a very pleasant hidden garden out the back.

Peggy's Cove 2

Oceanstone Seaside Resort — Resort $$

(902-823-2160; www.oceanstoneresort.com; 8650 Peggy's Cove Rd, Indian Harbour; r $170-235, ste $270-315, cottages $410-570; P ⊖ ❄ @ 📶 🐾) Smart rooms and lovely sea-view cottages are on offer at this large complex just a short drive from Peggy's Cove. The decor is very stylish, with lots of distressed wood, maritime detailing and big windows that make the most of the briny scenery. **Rhubarb** (mains $15 to $17), the inn's dining room, is considered one of the region's best seafood restaurants.

Lunenburg 4

South Shore Fish Shack — Seafood $$

(902-634-3232; www.southshorefishshack.com; 108 Montague St; mains $12-20; 11am-8pm Sun-Wed, to 9pm Thu-Sat) There are two main reasons to swing by this place: to eat the best fish-and-chips in Lunenburg and to enjoy the view from the deck. Chuck in great lobster buns, panko-crusted scallops and a fun sea-shack vibe, and you really can't go wrong.

Sail Inn B&B — B&B $$

(902-634-3537; www.sailinn.ca; 99 Montague St; r $120-180; P ⊖ 📶) If you want to be down by the harbor, this smart B&B is a really lovely choice. It's housed in a heritage building, but the rooms are bright, airy and modern, and all have harbor views. On the ground floor look out for the old well that's been turned into a fishpond!

Kejimkujik National Park 5

Jeremy's Bay Campground — Campground $

(877-737-3783; www.pc.gc.cax; campsites $25.50-29.40, cabins & yurts $70, oTENTiks $100; May-Oct) This excellent campground is one of the best places in the park to sleep under the stars. There's a wide choice of campsites (both serviced and unserviced), plus rustic wooden cabins, yurts and pre-pitched tents (called oTENTiks) that come with mattresses, furniture, a private deck, a firebox and a picnic area. It's in a great lakeside location near Jake's Landing.

Mersey River Chalets Cabin **$$**

(☎902-682-2447; www.merseyriverchalets.ns.ca; 315 Mersey River Chalets Rd E, Caledonia; tipis $90-120, cabins $185-208;) Get back to nature at this cabin complex, deep in the woods beside Harry's Lake. There's a choice of pine chalets, a spacious log house, a four-room lodge and (best of all) tipis. Cabins have wood-burning stoves and private porches with barbecues; rooms in the lodge have private decks with lake views; and the cozy tipis have fully equipped kitchens. Canoes and kayaks are available for guests.

Annapolis Royal 6

Queen Anne Inn Inn **$$**

(☎902-532-7850; www.queenanneinn.ns.ca; 494 Upper St George St; r $129-209; May-Oct; P) The most elegant property in Annapolis Royal, this eye-popping B&B looks as though it's blown straight off the *Gone with the Wind* set. Built in 1865 as a private home for local notables William Ritchie and Fanny Foster, it's a real museum piece: sweeping staircases, carriage clocks, four-poster beds, Tiffany-lamp replicas and a glorious central turret.

Brier Island 7

Shoreline Restaurant Seafood **$$**

(☎902-245-6667; 88 Water St; mains $12-30; 11am-9pm) This is *the* spot in Digby for top-notch scallops – and clams, crab, lobster, haddock and pretty much every other fish you care to mention – along with salads and steaks. Grab a booth or head out to the waterfront deck and dig in. It's easy to miss, located at the back of a gift shop.

Hillside Landing B&B **$$**

(☎902-247-5781; www.hillsidelanding.com; 152 Queen St; d $150-180) Originally from Ontario, owners Henry and Linda have renovated this wonderful mansion with real love and care. The three rooms are spankingly stylish: one looks over the street, while Vye and Rutherford both have panoramic aspects over the harbor. Throw in posh jet showers, a magnificent verandah and a copious breakfast, and you have Digby's top B&B.

Brier Island Lodge Lodge **$$**

(☎902-839-2300; www.brierisland.com; 557 Water St, Westport; r $109-169; May-Oct;) Atop cliffs 1km east of Westport, Brier Island Lodge has 37 rooms, many with ocean views. Its pine-paneled **restaurant** (mains $10 to $30) has views on two sides, friendly service and fabulously fresh seafood. Boxed lunches are available.

Wolfville 8

Le Caveau European **$$$**

(☎902-542-1753; https://grandprewines.com/pages/le-caveau; 11611 Hwy 1, Grand Pré; mains lunch $14-21, dinner $28-38; 11:30am-2pm & 5-9pm May-Oct) Overseen by head chef Jason Lynch, this upscale bistro at the **Domaine de Grand Pré winery** has become a destination in its own right. The ethos is rich, indulgent dining with a taste for game and seafood; as much produce as possible comes from surrounding farms. The beautiful patio is paved with fieldstones and shaded with grapevines.

Olde Lantern Inn & Vineyard Inn **$$**

(☎902-542-1389; www.oldlanterninn.com; 11575 Hwy 1, Grand Pré; r $137-157;) Among the world-famous Grand Pré vines, this little vineyard has a pleasant guesthouse with four attractive, clutter-free rooms, all with whirlpool bath. Two are in the timber-framed main house, while another two are in a modern wing. There are wonderful views over the Bay of Fundy and the Grand Pré landscape.

Classic Trip

30

The Cabot Trail

Wild coast, cloud-capped mountains, back-of-beyond beaches – there's a reason that the Cabot Trail is the drive every visitor to Nova Scotia wants to do.

TRIP HIGHLIGHTS

244 km
Bay St Lawrence
Spot whales at this far northern harbor

313 km
Skyline Trail
The classic hike to take on the Cabot Trail

210 km
Neil's Harbour to White Point
A coastal detour with incredible Atlantic views

START
Sydney

Baddeck
FINISH

35 km
Louisbourg
A fortress packed with colonial history

2–3 DAYS
420KM/261 MILES

GREAT FOR...

BEST TIME TO GO

September and October for fall colors and fewer jams.

ESSENTIAL PHOTO

Standing at the end of the Skyline Trail.

BEST FOR WILDLIFE

Taking a whale-watching tour to spot minke whales, pilot whales and fin whales.

Nova Scotia The Cabot Trail (p330) snakes along the sea in Cape Breton

Classic Trip

30 The Cabot Trail

This is the big one: the looping, diving, dipping roller coaster of a road that snakes its way around the northern tip of Cape Breton, with epic views of rolling seas, mountain passes, thick forests and – if you're lucky – the chance to spot a moose, eagle or even a whale en route. Take your time: this is a Maritime classic to relish.

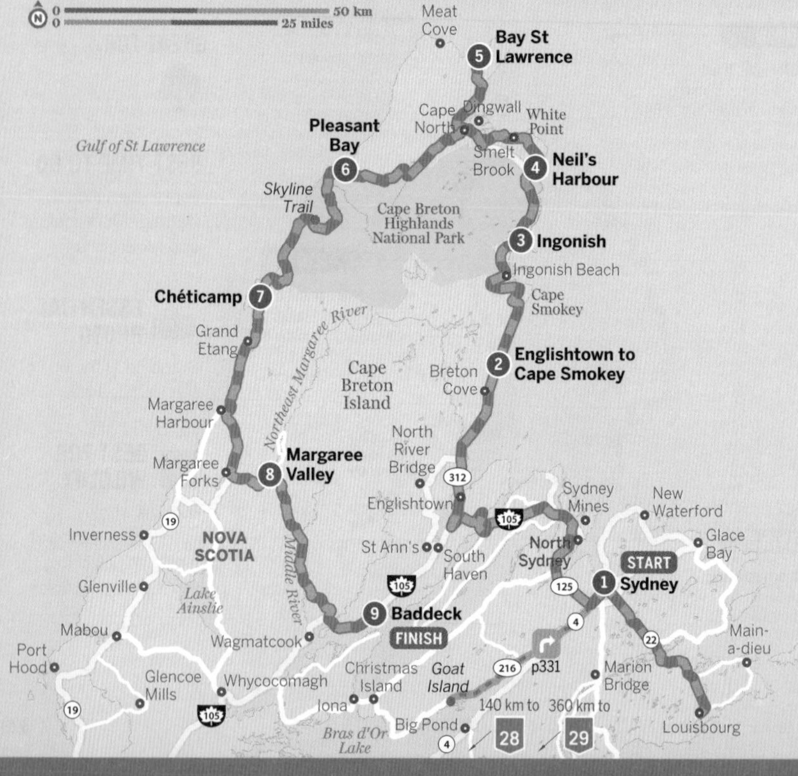

1 Sydney

The trip begins in Sydney, Cape Breton's largest city, which built its fortune on coal mining and steelmaking, but suffered hard when those industries began to decline. It's a handy base for exploring one of Cape Breton's premier sites: the famous **Fortress of Louisbourg** (902-733-3552; www.fortressoflouisbourg.ca; 58 Wolfe St; adult/child $17.60/free; 9:30am-5pm mid-May–mid-Oct, to 4pm Mon-Fri mid-Oct–mid-May), which sits on a peninsula 35km southwest of the city via Hwy 22. Built in the early 18th century, it was the site of numerous sieges and battles between the English and French armies, but finally fell for good following the conquest of Québec in 1760, when it was razed to the ground. It's since been painstakingly rebuilt as it would have appeared c 1744, with more than 50 buildings to explore, and costumed soldiers, cooks, orderlies, musicians, gardeners and artisans on hand to bring the place to life. Though the scale of the reconstruction is massive, three-quarters of the fort remains in ruins: a 2.5km trail winds through on its way to the Atlantic coast.

DETOUR: ESKASONI CULTURAL JOURNEYS

Start: 1 Sydney

Forty kilometers southwest of Sydney, Goat Island is home to one of Nova Scotia's largest **Mi'kmaq communities** (902-322-2279; www.eskasoniculturaljourneys.ca; 1 Goat Island Trail; adult/child $40/20; 9am-5pm Mon-Fri May-Oct). Here local guides offer enthralling tours along a 2.4km trail that provide an introduction into Mi'kmaq culture, including the chance to weave baskets, learn traditional dances, hunting and cooking techniques, hear tribal stories and participate in a smudging ceremony (a cleansing smoke bath used for purification). You'll also get to try some bush tea and luskinigan, a bannock-style bread cooked over an open fire (sometimes known as 'four-cent bread' because it's so cheap to make).

LINK YOUR TRIP

Central Nova Scotia

You'll have to cut into the route halfway, but it's easy to join up Cape Breton with an exploration of central Nova Scotia.

South Shore Circular

It's a bit of a drive back to Halifax, but the spin along the South Shore is another mustn't miss.

The Drive » From Sydney, follow Hwy 125 and Hwy 105 for about 55km till you reach the junction with Hwy 312 towards Englishtown. A small 24-hour passenger ferry ($7) crosses the inlet to Jersey Cove, then leads north straight onto the main Cabot Trail.

p337

2 Englishtown to Cape Smokey

The stretch of road north from **Englishtown** gives you your first taste of the main Cabot Trail in all its forested, coastal glory. It's an easy drive, framed by thick woodland and rolling hills, with occasional flashes of ocean between the trees. There aren't too many reasons to stop, but if you're peckish, there are a couple of pleasant cafes en route: try the **Clucking Hen** (902-929-2501; 45073 Cabot Trail; mains $7-18; 7am-7pm May-Oct) for sandwiches, salads and fresh-baked cakes, or the **Dancing Moose** (902-929-2523; www.thedancingmoosecafe.com; 42691 Cabot Trail, Birch Plain; pancakes $5-10; 7:30am-4pm Jun-Oct) for Dutch-style pancakes.

Eventually, you'll reach the dramatic point of **Cape Smokey**, where the road climbs sharply up the mountainside; in bad weather it's wreathed in fog, but with luck it'll be clear and you'll be treated to sweeping views over Ingonish Bay.

The Drive » It's a straight-up drive of about 55km from Englishtown to Ingonish.

3 Ingonish

Up and over Cape Smokey, the trail leads you down into the broad bay of Ingonish, a collection of small seaside villages set around the shores of a sheltered lagoon. It's a scenic setting, and while there's not a huge amount to do in town (save for the big, sandy beach), it makes a useful staging spot to overnight, with plenty of B&Bs and motels around town, not to mention a famous golf course and one of Nova Scotia's plushest hotels, the Keltic Lodge at the Highlands (p337). Even if you're not staying, it's well worth stopping in at the hotel for the chance to walk the **Middle Trail** out to the coast.

The Drive » After overnighting in Ingonish, aim for an early start on the trail. You'll pass the National Park Information Centre as you drive north out of Ingonish: stop here to buy your park permit, review your route and get trail advice from park staff. It's a drive of about 27km from the park entrance north to Neil's Harbour.

p337

4 Neil's Harbour

From Ingonish, you enter into the boundaries of the Cape Breton Highlands National Park. The road hugs the coast, dipping and diving around several scenic inlets where you can stop off for photo ops. After 27km, you'll spy the turnoff to Neil's Harbour; here, you actually exit out of the park again, following a stunningly scenic stretch of road that hugs the coast, offering views of the restless Atlantic, clapboard houses and bobbing boats. It's well worth stopping at **White Point**, where a short 2km hiking trail leads out to a dramatic rocky headland, which has claimed many shipwrecks over the centuries; unfortunate sailors are said to have been buried around the point in unmarked graves.

The Drive » From Neil's Harbour to White Point is about 7km; from here, the road loops back round to rejoin the main Cabot Trail after about 15km.

5 Bay St Lawrence

Not long after rejoining the main route, you need to keep your eyes peeled for another turnoff at North Cape, this time signposted for the remote Bay St Lawrence. The road dips down into a lovely green valley, passing **Cabots Landing Provincial Park** (902-662-3030; https://parks.novascotia.ca/content/cabots-landing), where the globetrotting explorer is said to have landed in 1497 (becoming the first recorded European to set foot in North America)

TOP TIP: ROUTE DIRECTION

The vast majority of drivers do the Cabot Trail from west to east, starting in Chéticamp and ending in Ingonish, but there's a good case for doing it in the opposite direction: there's less traffic this way, and you get to drive coast-side for the whole route, making for better views and easier stop-offs. It also means that, if you do the trail in a day, you'll hit the west coast for sunset: cue photo ops aplenty. Note that there are very few petrol stations along the trail: be sure to fill up in Chéticamp or Ingonish before you set out.

BENEDEK/GETTY IMAGES ©

Fortress of Louisbourg (p331) Imposing entrance gate

and where you'll also find picturesque beaches around Aspy Bay.

Another 7km brings you to the eponymous bay, still a working fishing harbor. Here you can take one of the best whale-watching trips in Nova Scotia in the company of the uber-experienced **Captain Cox** (☎902-383-2981; www.whalewatching-novascotia.com; 578 Meat Cove Rd, St Margaret Village; adult/child $45/25; ⏰mid-Jun–Oct), who's been running expeditions since the 1970s. Sightings aren't guaranteed, but if anyone knows how to find you a whale or two, it's this man. With luck, you'll see pilot whales, minke whales and dolphins without too much trouble; fin whales are much rarer.

The Drive » From the turnoff at North Cape, it's about 18km to Bay St Lawrence and another 18km back. An optional detour is to take a rough, slippery gravel track for 14km to the unedifyingly named Meat Cove: it's about as far north as you can get in Nova Scotia by road, but unless you've got a sturdy SUV or 4x4, it's probably not worth the hassle.

6 Pleasant Bay

Once you've rejoined the trail again at North Cape, you'll begin climbing into one of the most dramatic areas of the national park, tracking along a deep 40km-long ravine known as the **Aspy Fault**, caused by the movement of tectonic plates. There are several places to stop en route to marvel at the scenery: look out for bald eagles soaring overhead. Eventually you'll crest over the pass and drop down the other side into the aptly named Pleasant Bay. If you haven't already done a whale-watching tour, there are several operators around town; alternatively, you can make the rather more surprising pilgrimage out to **Gampo Abbey** (☎902-224-2752; www.gampoabbey.org; 1533 Pleasant Bay Rd; ⏰tours 1:30-3:30pm Mon-Fri Jun-Sep), a Tibetan Buddhist monastery just along the coast. You're free to wander the grounds, or you can take a guided tour.

The Drive » From Pleasant Bay, the road climbs again over Mackenzie Mountain and French Mountain, dropping down along the coast to reach Chéticamp after 43km.

✕ p337

7 Chéticamp

The stretch of the trail leading south towards Chéticamp is a real eye-popper, looping and veering along the cliffs, with wonderful sea views

Classic Trip

ADWO/SHUTTERSTOCK ©

ROB CRANDALL/SHUTTERSTOCK ©

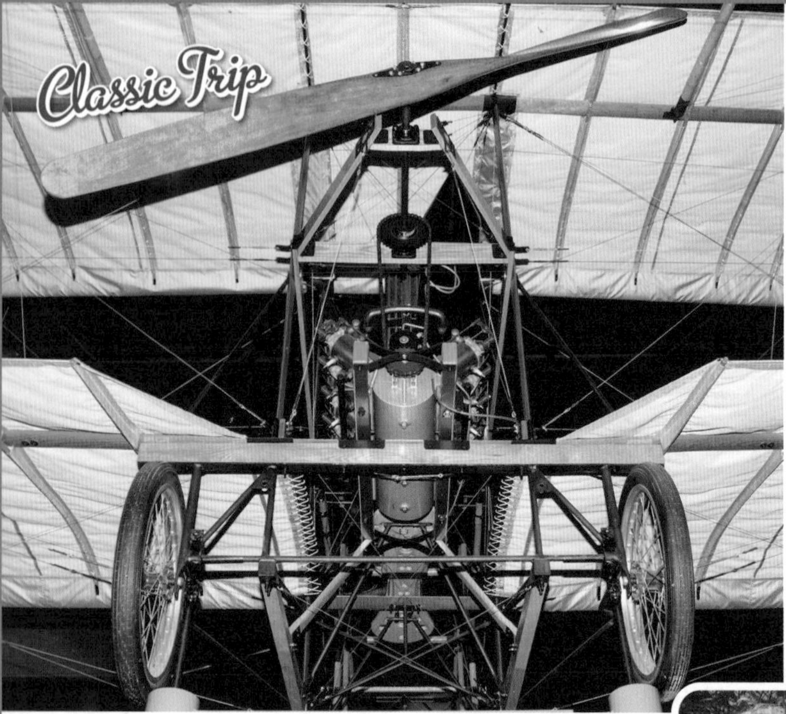

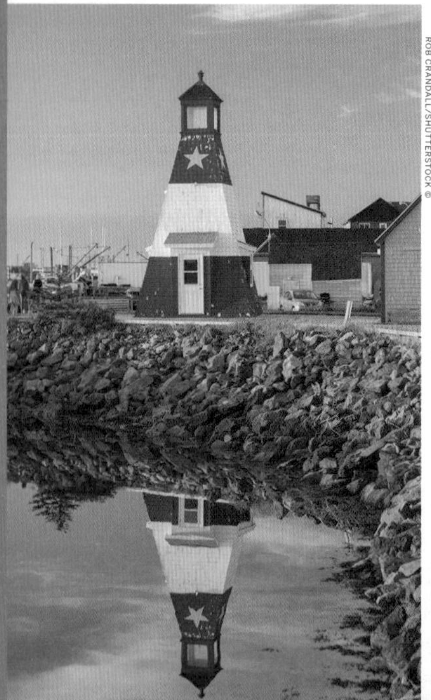

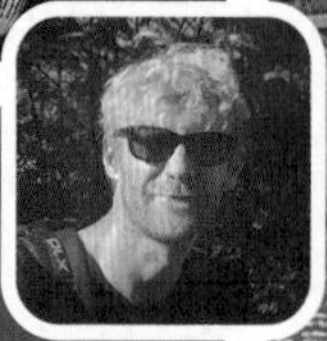

WHY THIS IS A CLASSIC TRIP

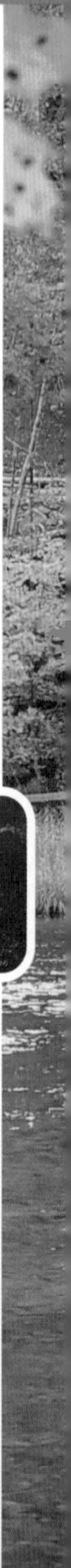

OLIVER BERRY, WRITER

Completed in 1932 to link Cape Breton's isolated coastal communities, this is the original Maritime road trip: people have been looping the loop for the last nine decades, and the trail remains as popular as ever. Traversing the edge of the Cape Breton Highlands National Park, it's home to some of the province's grandest scenery, richest wildlife and best hiking trails: basically, it's a Nova Scotian rite of passage.

Above: Scale model of *Silver Dart* airplane, Alexander Graham Bell National Historic Site (p336)
Left: Lighthouse, Chéticamp (p333)
Right: Fly fishing for salmon, Margaree River

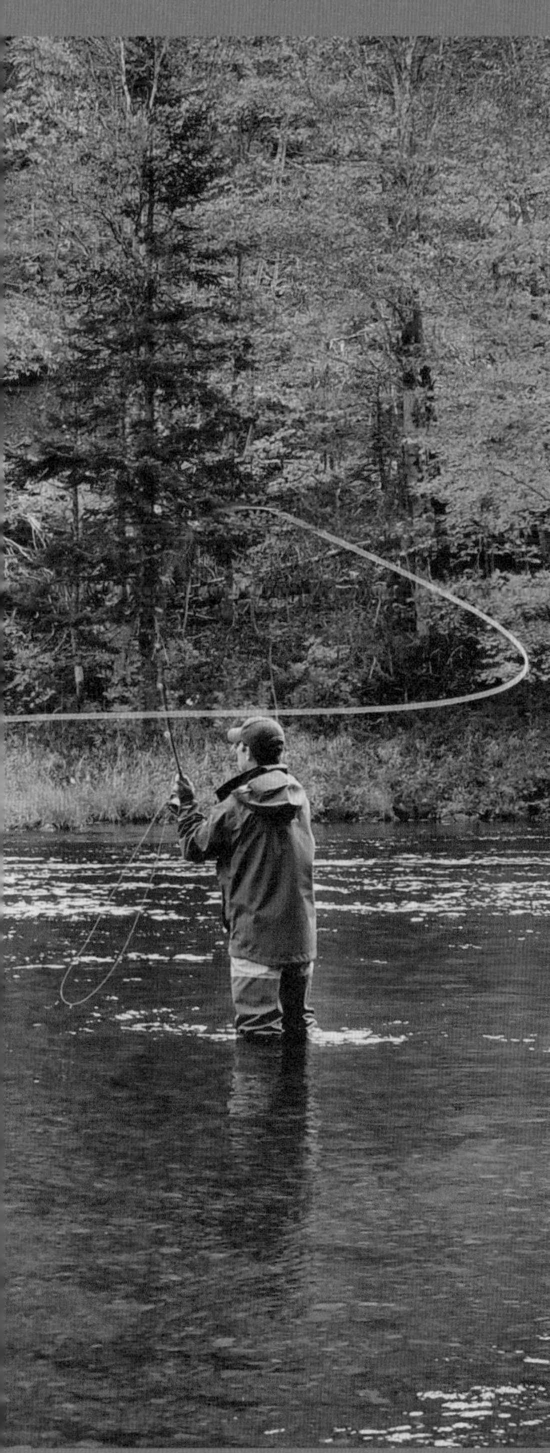

around every bend: ideally you want to hit this bit of the road for sunset, when the photo opportunities will have you stopping at every pull-out. You'll pass through the national park gate on the edge of town, then head on towards the distinctive profile of **Chéticamp Island**. The town itself is home to Nova Scotia's most vibrant and thriving Acadian community, owing much of its cultural preservation to its geographical isolation (the road didn't make it this far until 1949). It's a busy little fishing town, famous for rug-hooking; the **Trois Pignons** (☎902-224-2642; www.lestroispignons.com; 15584 Cabot Trail; adult/child $5/4; ⊙8:30am-6pm Jul & Aug, to 5pm mid-May–Jun & Sep–mid-Oct) museum has a fine collection. With luck you should be able to catch some live music over dinner at one of the town's lively restaurants and bars. There's plenty of accommodation too, making this the ideal place to stop overnight.

The Drive » After a night in Chéticamp, spin 25km south along the trail to Margararee Harbour, then continue inland along the Margaree Valley.

🛏 p337

8 Margaree Valley

The route veers inland along the course of the lovely **Margaree River**, renowned for its trout and salmon fishing. The **Margaree Salmon Museum** (902-248-2848; 60 E Big Intervale Rd; $2; 9am-5pm mid-Jun–mid-Sep) explores the history of fishing in the valley, with a collection of rods, reels, flies and vintage photos; you can also visit the **Margaree Fish Hatchery** (902-248-2845; 115 Hatchery Rd; 9am-4pm Jun-Aug) to see how the river is kept stocked, and stop off at various points along the valley to explore riverside trails. It's well worth popping in for lunch at the cafe-bakery **Dancing Goat** (902-248-2727; www.facebook.com/DancingGoatCafe; 6289 Cabot Trail, Margaree Valley; items $5-13; 8am-5pm Sat-Thu, to 8pm Fri;), or if you're here in the evening, the quaint **Normaway Inn** (902-248-2987; www.thenormawayinn.com; Egypt Rd; mains $12-28, 3-course dinner menu from $40) for some traditional fiddle music.

The Drive » It's an easy drive along the valley of about 88km back to Baddeck.

THE SKYLINE TRAIL

The Cape Breton Highlands has some wonderful hikes, but none is better-known than the Skyline Trail, an 8.2km loop via boreal forest and windswept clifftops onto a spectacular ridge, ending at a stunning lookout: you might well spy bald eagles, moose and possibly whales swimming along the Gulf of St Lawrence from the viewing platforms. Several areas of the trail are boarded to allow for habitat regrowth: stick to the trail to avoid unnecessary erosion. The loop walk is fairly flat; allow two to three hours to complete it. If you don't follow the loop, it's about 6.5km return from the parking lot.

The trailhead starts near the top of French Mountain, about 22km north of Chéticamp, and 20km south of Pleasant Bay.

9 Baddeck

Our last stop is Baddeck, a small town hunkered on the shores of the majestic **Bras d'Or Lake** – which, at 1099 sq km, is the largest lake in Nova Scotia, more like an inland sea. The town's main claim to fame is its association with the pioneering inventor Alexander Graham Bell, who fell in love with the hilly scenery in the 1870s (apparently it reminded him of his Highland home). He built himself a grand summer residence on a peninsula nearby, and the town is now home to the **Alexander Graham Bell National Historic Site** (902-295-2069; www.pc.gc.ca/en/lhn-nhs/ns/grahambell; 559 Chebucto St; adult/child $7.80/free; 9am-5pm May-Oct) – a fascinating museum that explores the great man's experiments in telecommunications, electricity, aviation, ship design, kite-flying and plenty more besides. Don't miss the scale model of his groundbreaking *Silver Dart* airplane, which made its first flight from the frozen ice of Baddeck Bay on February 23, 1909 (just over five years after the Wright Brothers).

The Drive » From Baddeck, you can head back to Sydney, 78km east (perhaps to catch a ferry from nearby North Sydney to Newfoundland) or head west towards Port Hawkesbury and mainland Nova Scotia beyond.

p337

Eating & Sleeping

Sydney 1

Kiju's — Native American $$$

(902-562-6220; www.kijus.com; 50 Maillard St, Membertou; mains $22-46, 3-course menu $40; 11am-9pm Sun-Thu, to 10pm Fri & Sat) Based at **Membertou Heritage Park** (www.membertouheritagepark.com), this restaurant provides the rare opportunity to try Mi'kmaw-inspired dishes, such as four-cent bread, cedar-plank salmon, barbecued duck and a foraged-fruit-and-berry salad.

Colby House — B&B $$

(902-539-4095; www.colbyhousebb.com; 10 Park St; r $100-130;) This 1904 house makes a grand spot to stay in Sydney, with three handsome rooms tricked out in turn-of-the-century style. It's been beautifully maintained, from the central staircase to the elegant verandah, and the tree-lined location is surprisingly peaceful. A real delight.

Ingonish 3

Main Street Restaurant & Bakery — Canadian $$

(902-285-2225; 37764 Cabot Trail, Ingonish Beach; mains $10-24; 8am-8pm) Come breakfast, brunch, lunch or dinner, Ingonish's friendly diner is the place most people head for when they're feeling hungry. Chunky BLT sandwiches, homemade waffles, big plates of chicken, pasta and seafood, and yummy cakes – what's not to like?

Keltic Lodge at the Highlands — Lodge $$$

(902-285-2880; www.kelticlodge.ca; Ingonish Beach; r $189-279, ste $510-600; May-Oct; P) Especially favored by golfers, this upmarket Tudor-style resort on its own peninsula has been a luxurious retreat since the 1950s. It's been attractively renovated, with plush loft-style rooms divided between the gabled Main Lodge, two separate houses and a complex of cottages dotted around the lawned grounds. There's also a lovely spa and a refined restaurant (mains $15 to $35).

Pleasant Bay 6

Rusty Anchor — Diner $$

(902-224-1313; 23197 Cabot Trail; mains $10-28; 11am-9pm) Pit stops are few and far between on the Cabot Trail, which makes this waterfront diner a boon if you've run out of picnic snacks. The food's mostly good; pan-fried fish, scallops and lobster rolls are all on offer.

Chéticamp 7

Chéticamp Outback Inn — Motel $$

(902-224-8025; cheticampoutbackinn@bellaliant.com; 909 Chéticamp Back Rd; r $155-225; P) Inland from Chéticamp, this back-road country motel looks standard, but the rooms are a bit of a surprise: they have wood-effect walls, enormous TVs, comfy beds with scatter cushions, and a work desk with coffee machine. Each room has a small deck area for mountain contemplation.

Baddeck 9

Highwheeler Cafe — Cafe $

(902-295-3006; www.visitbaddeck.com/highwheeler-cafe; 486 Chebucto St; sandwiches $9; 7am-6pm Tue-Sun May-Oct;) Everyone's choice for lunch, this Baddeck cafe ticks all the boxes: grilled sandwiches, delicious quesadillas, homemade soups, and delicious muffins and blueberry-raspberry scones, plus a pleasant deck. You can phone ahead and ask for a packed lunch if you're hiking or hitting the Cabot Trail.

Silver Dart Lodge — Lodge $$

(902-295-2340; www.silverdartlodge.com; 257 Shore Rd; r/chalets from $165/195; P) Cracking views over Bras d'Or Lake are the main selling point here. There's a wide choice of accommodations, with rooms divided between the original main house, three motel-style lodges and several cute clapboard chalets, and you can eat with a lake view in McCurdy's Dining Room.

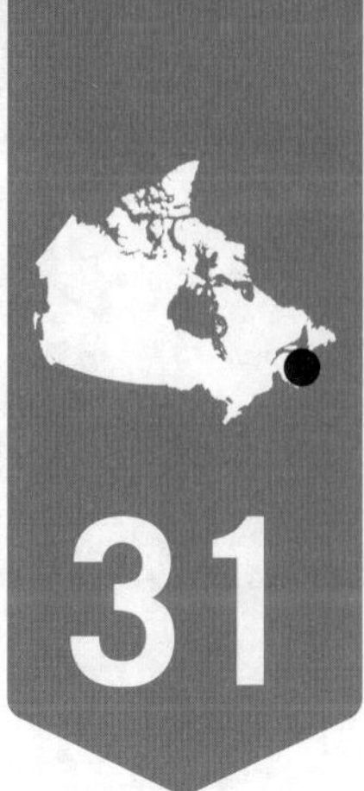

Two Islands, Three Provinces

Get a taste of three different sides of the Maritimes: historic Nova Scotia, pretty Prince Edward Island and coastal New Brunswick.

TRIP HIGHLIGHTS

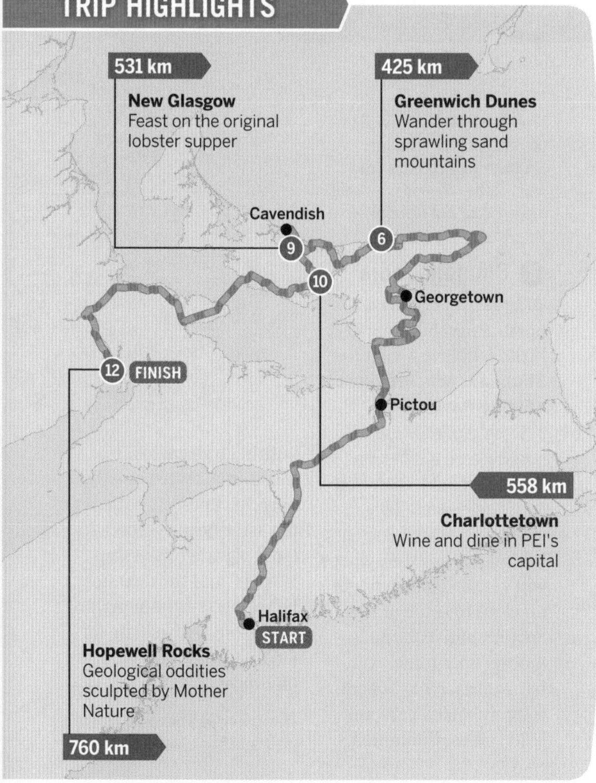

531 km
New Glasgow
Feast on the original lobster supper

425 km
Greenwich Dunes
Wander through sprawling sand mountains

Cavendish
9
6
10
Georgetown
12 FINISH
Pictou

558 km
Charlottetown
Wine and dine in PEI's capital

Halifax
START

Hopewell Rocks
Geological oddities sculpted by Mother Nature
760 km

8 DAYS
760KM/472 MILES

GREAT FOR...

BEST TIME TO GO

June to September

ESSENTIAL PHOTO

Sunbathing on the beach at Brackley or North Rustico.

BEST FOR FOODIES

Tucking into a crustacean-themed feast in New Glasgow.

Prince Edward Island National Park (p343) North Rustico beach

31 Two Islands, Three Provinces

This three-province loop is a great way of experiencing the diversity of the Maritime provinces, especially if you have limited time. On Nova Scotia, you'll visit the capital city and a superb wildlife park before catching a boat over to potato-crazy PEI, home of some of the finest beaches in Atlantic Canada, as well as everyone's favourite flame-haired heroine, Anne of Green Gables. You'll finish in New Brunswick, with a walk among weird rock formations overlooking the incredible Bay of Fundy.

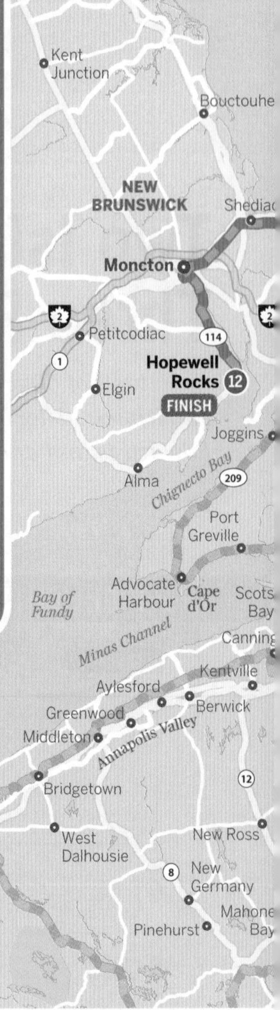

❶ Halifax

Maritime Halifax marks the start of this tripartite road trip. If you've only got limited time in the city, a great way to make the most of it is with a guided tour courtesy of **Halifax Free Tours** (www.halifaxfreetours.wixsite.com/halifaxfreetours; ⏲10am & 3pm Jun-Sep), or hire a bike from **I Heart Bikes** (www.iheartbikeshfx.com; 1507 Lower Water St; rentals per hour from $12; ⏲10am-6pm May, 9am-8pm Jun-Aug) to take a scenic spin along the waterfront. Later on, you could take an evening cruise on the **Tall Ship Silva** (☎1-800-565-9662; www.tallshipsilva.com; 1½hr cruises adult/child $33/21.50).

The Drive » It's a fast 61km up Hwy 101 from Halifax to Shubie; Hwy 2 runs parallel most of the way, and is arguably more scenic, but much slower.

❷ Shubenacadie

To break up the drive north, kids (both big and little) will love a visit to **Shubenacadie Provincial Wildlife Park** (☎902-758-2040; https://wildlifepark.novascotia.ca; 149 Creighton Rd, Shubenacadie; adult/child $4.75/2; ⏲9am-6:30pm mid-May–mid-Oct, to 3pm Sat & Sun mid-Oct–mid-May), where you get the chance to get up close to some of Nova Scotia's native fauna: moose, porcupines, timber wolves, lynx, bobcat, cougar, black bears and bald eagles. Contained within large enclosures, the animals were mostly born in captivity, but a few have been rescued from private ownership as 'pets' and thus cannot be released into the wild. Check out the website for feeding times and hands-on events.

The Drive » The easiest route to Pictou is on main Hwys 102 and 104. It's 105km but with luck you should be there in a little over an hour, traffic willing.

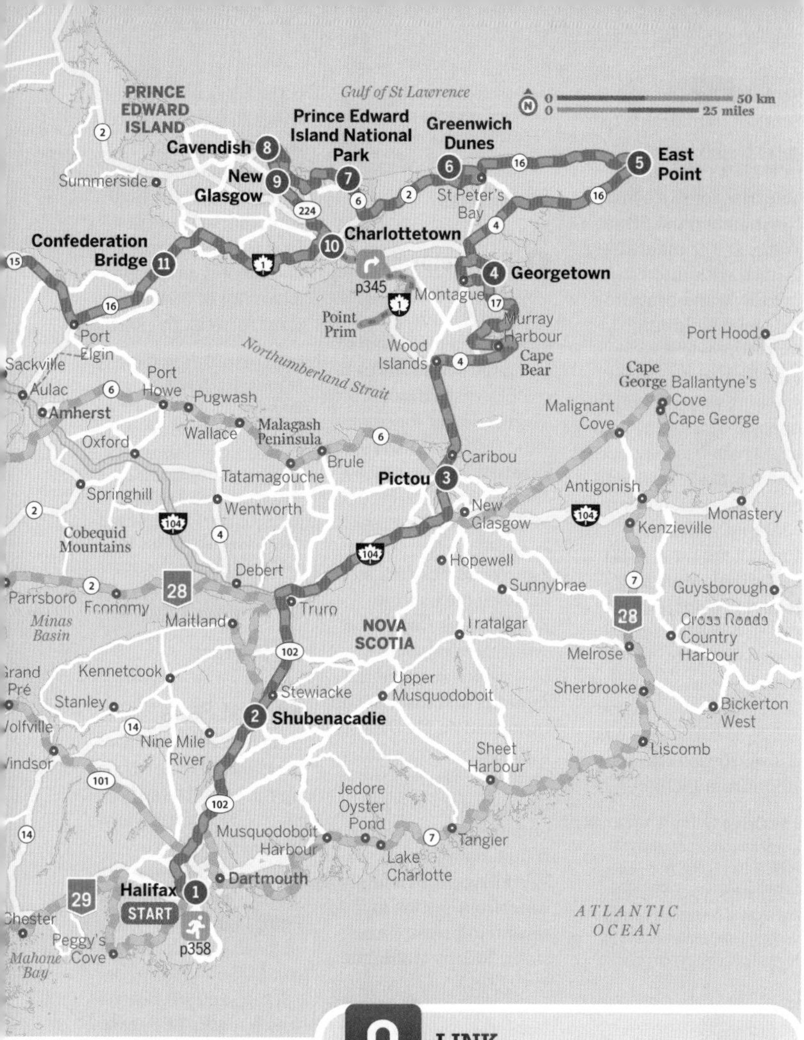

3 Pictou

The small seaside town of Pictou is mainly familiar to most Nova Scotians as the terminus for ferries to Prince Edward Island; it's also sometimes known as the 'Birthplace of New

LINK YOUR TRIP

28 Central Nova Scotia

After crossing the Confederation Bridge, continue 115km southeast to Tatamagouche for the second half of this great ramble around Nova Scotia.

29 South Shore Circular

Since it begins and ends in Halifax, this Nova Scotian loop can be tacked on before this route.

Scotland' because the first Scottish immigrants to Nova Scotia landed here in 1773. It's also an enjoyable base for exploring Northumberland Strait. Water St, the main street, is lined with interesting shops and beautiful old stone buildings; unfortunately the views are blighted by a giant smoking pulp mill on the opposite side of the estuary, which has long been slated for closure due to environmental concerns.

While you're in town, head for a swim at **Caribou-Munroes Island Provincial Park** (902-485-6134; https://parks.novascotia.ca/content/caribou-munroes-island; 2119 Three Brooks Rd; campsites $26.70-35.60), which has a lovely beach less than 10km from Pictou.

The Drive » The ferry terminal is a few kilometers north of Pictou. Bay Ferries runs over to Wood Islands on PEI; there are around five sailings a day in spring and autumn, and up to nine per day in summer, so there should be no reason to have to overnight – but if you do, Pictou has several decent places to stay.

p346

4 Georgetown

The ferry will deposit you at Wood Islands, a strung-out settlement extending along the southern coast of PEI's eastern side. Make a detour for some wine-tasting at **Rossignol Estate Winery** (902-962-4193; www.rossignolwinery.com; 11147 Shore Rd, Murray River; 10am-5pm Mon-Sat, from noon Sun May-Oct), stop in to see the historic lighthouse at **Cape Bear** (www.capebearlighthouse.com), which received the Titanic's first distress call, then head on via the artsy little fishing community of Murray Harbour to Georgetown, once an important shipbuilding center, now a sleepy seaside village with a lovely waterfront setting and several impressive mansions. Nearby **Montague** is the service center for Kings County; its streets lead from the breezy, heritage marina area to modern shopping malls, supermarkets and fast-food outlets. Georgetown and Montague both have a handful of B&Bs if you want to break the journey.

The Drive » From the ferry, head east on Hwy 4 along the coast for 18km to Murray Harbour, then take the scenic Hwy 17 through Gaspereaux and past the lighthouse on Panmure Island. This will bring you into Montague and Georgetown across the bay. To East Point, it's an easy-going 70km spin along Hwys 4 and 16 all the way.

p346

5 East Point

From Georgetown, it's a pleasant drive northwest up the coast towards Souris, with great views of the coast practically the whole way. The objective here is **East Point Lighthouse** (www.eastpointlighthouse.ca; adult/child $6/3.50; 10am-6pm Jun-Aug), an 1867 beacon which marks PEI's easternmost point – but there are a couple of interesting diversions along the way.

Elmira Railway Museum (Rte 16A; adult/student/family $5/4/10; 9:30am-4pm daily Jul & Aug, Mon-Fri Jun & Sep) stands at the end of the island's short-lived railway (now the popular Confederation Bike Trail); the old station has been turned into a museum ex-

TOP TIP: BY BRIDGE OR FERRY

You've got two options for getting to and from PEI: the Wood Islands ferry or the Confederation Bridge. The ferry is useful for heading onwards to Cape Breton and eastern Nova Scotia, while the bridge is handier for New Brunswick or central Nova Scotia, but there's another consideration: cost. Since you only pay the toll when you *leave* the island, it's actually about $30 cheaper to take the ferry to PEI, and leave via the bridge ($79 versus $47.75).

ploring the history of the line. Train nerds will love the miniature choo-choo, which winds its way through nearby forest.

Also worth a stop is **Basin Head Provincial Park** (www.tourismpei.com/provincial-park/basin-head; Basin Head), which many PEIers think has some of the island's finest beaches – including the famed Singing Sands Beach, where the sand audibly squeaks underfoot when it's dry.

The Drive » You can't get lost on the next section: just follow Hwy 16 west, tracking the north coast to Greenwich, which you'll reach after 58km.

p346

6 Greenwich Dunes

The next stage of the trip takes you eastwards towards the small coastal community of **Saint Peter's Bay**.

The highlight of this section of the trip is the amazing Greenwich Dunes, a 6km stretch of rolling, shifting wall of sand overlooking an awesome, often empty beach. The avant-garde **Greenwich Interpretation Centre** (902-961-2514; Rte 13; 9:30am-7pm Jul & Aug, to 4:30pm May, Jun, Sep & Oct) details the ecology of the dune system and the archaeological history of the site; from the centre, you can follow the Greenwich Dunes Trail (4.5km return, 1½ hours)

MMACKILLOP/GETTY IMAGES ©; DESIGNER: JEAN M. MULLER

Confederation Bridge (p345) Views of the bridge on a summer morning

out into the sandbanks themselves.

The Drive » Round Saint Peter's Bay, join Hwy 2 and then follow it for 45km to the junction with Hwy 6; here you'll see signs to Prince Edward Island National Park.

p346

7 Prince Edward Island National Park

As you round the inlet of Tracadie Bay, and head north to Grand Tracadie, you're entering into the borders of **Prince Edward Island National Park** (902-672-6350; www.pc.gc.ca/eng/pn-np/pe/pei-ipe/visit.aspx; day pass adult/child $7.80/free; admission fees apply mid-Jun–Sep). For most Canadians, this is quintessential PEI – a sprawling expanse of dune-backed beaches and red sandstone bluffs, a landscape synonymous with summer. Established in 1937, the park runs in a narrow strip for 42km along the island's north coast, ranging in width from a few kilometers to just a few hundred metres. Backed by areas of wetland and woodland the park provides an important habitat for plants, animals and birdlife, including the red fox and endangered piping plover.

In summer, this is sunbathing central – from east to west, the main beaches are **Dalvay, Stanhope, Brackley, North Rustico, MacNeills Brook** and **Cavendish**. If crowds aren't your thing, the beaches further east tend to be quieter – parking can be a real headache in July and August.

The Drive » To get the most out of the views, follow the Gulf Shore parkway wherever possible; it dips in and out along the coastline, rejoining Hwy 6 at various points. Note that park entry fees are payable in summer. From Tracadie to Cavendish, it's about 45km via the coast road.

8 Cavendish

Cavendish is famous across Canada as the home town of Lucy Maud Montgomery (1874–1942), author of the beloved *Anne of Green Gables* stories (round here she's known simply as Lucy Maud or LM). But far from a quaint country village filled with clapboard houses and clip-clopping horses, modern Cavendish is a busy tourist mecca. The **Green Gables Heritage Place** (www.pc.gc.ca/en/lhn-nhs/pe/greengables; 8619 Hwy 6; adult/child $7.80/free; ⏲10am-5pm May-Oct) is the main point of interest; owned by her grandfather's cousins, it's been painstakingly restored to reflect how it would have appeared in Anne's day, including furniture, furnishings and decor.

A 1.1km trail leads through the 'Haunted Wood' to **Lucy Maud Montgomery's Cavendish Homestead** (www.lmmontgomerycavendishhome.com; 8523 Cavendish Rd; adult/child $6/free; ⏲9:30am-5:30pm Jul & Aug, 10am-5pm May, Jun & Oct), which arguably offers a more authentic picture of LM's life and times: she lived here from 1876 to 1911 with her maternal grandparents Alexander and Lucy Macneill, after her mother Clara died of tuberculosis. It's here that she wrote books including *Anne of Green Gables* and *Anne of Avonlea*. There's a small museum and an Anne-themed bookshop.

The Drive » From Cavendish, take Hwy 13 to New Glasgow for 10km.

p347

9 New Glasgow

Lobster suppers are a PEI tradition, and the old-fashioned **restaurant** (www.peilobstersuppers.com; 604 Rte 258; lobster dinners from $37.95; ⏲4-8pm Jun–mid-Oct) in New Glasgow claims to be their spiritual home – it's been serving these indulgent shellfish feasts since 1958. Getting messy while you crack your crustacean is part of the fun – but leave room for chowder, mussels, salads, breads and a mile-high lemon pie.

The Drive » Take Hwy 224 and Hwy 2 to Charlottetown, traveling through classic PEI countryside of fields, farmsteads and small towns. It's 28km and should take only 30 minutes when the traffic's good, likely longer in summer.

p347

THE CONFEDERATION TRAIL

Following the route of the railway that once cut across PEI, the Confederation Trail (www.tourismpei.com/pei-confederation-trail) is one of the best cycling routes in Canada. Winding through a varied landscape of fields, forests, rivers, valleys and coastline, it's a pleasure to cycle – not least because it's almost entirely flat. Some sections of the trail are completely canopied; in late June and the early weeks of July the trail is lined with bright, flowering lupines, and in fall, the changing colors of the foliage are a wonder.

The tip-to-tip distance from Tignish in the northwest to Elmira in the northeast is 273km, but it's easily done in sections, since the main trail passes through major towns including Summerside, Kensington and Mt Stewart, with branches to other towns, including Charlottetown, Souris and Montague. Since prevailing winds on PEI blow from the west and southwest, cycling in this direction is easier.

You can download a trail map and route guide from the Tourism PEI website, and information centers can help with route guidance, accommodations and bike hire.

⑩ Charlottetown

PEI's handsome capital, Charlottetown has stayed true to its small-town roots, with a lovely, low-rise downtown that still retains many of the red-brick facades and Victorian buildings of its late-19th-century heyday. Covering just a few blocks inland from the harbor, the old part of town was deliberately designed to be walkable, and it pays to wander around and soak up the sights – including the impressive mock-Gothic **St Dunstan's Basilica** (902-894-3486; www.stdunstanspei.com; 45 Great George St; 9am-5pm) and a surfeit of heritage homes, shops and colorful clapboard buildings. There aren't that many must-see sights – the real pleasure of Charlottetown is just having a good wander – but the town does have a wealth of excellent places to eat and drink. Sink some craft beer at **Craft Beer Corner** (Upstreet Craft Brewing; www.upstreetcraftbrewing.com; 156 Great George St; noon-midnight), have a taco or two at **Sugar Skull Cantina** (www.sugarskullcantina.ca; 83 Water St; mains $9-13; noon-8pm), and treat yourself to a slap-up dinner at the Brickhouse (p347).

The Drive » Hwy 1 runs directly from Charlottetown to the Confederation Bridge, passing through the pleasant towns of Victoria and Crapaud en route. It's 56km, usually an hour's drive.

 p347

⑪ Confederation Bridge

Opened in 1997, and a marvel of Canadian engineering, the **Confederation Bridge** (www.confederationbridge.com; car/motorcycle $47.75/19; 24hr) spans 12.9km linking Prince Edward Island and New Brunswick. It's the longest bridge that crosses ice-covered water in the world. Unfortunately the 1.1m guardrails do a fairly good job of obscuring the view, but still, driving over the bridge is a PEI rite of passage.

The Drive » The standard bridge toll covers travel to and from the island, and includes one car and all passengers (the toll is only charged on departure from PEI). Once you're over the bridge, it's a fairly long drive to Hopewell Rocks: 95km via Hwy 15 to Moncton, and another 40km to Hopewell Rocks Park on Hwy 114.

⑫ Hopewell Rocks

On the far side of the bridge, you'll touch down in New Brunswick, your third Maritime province of the trip. A fine finish is provided by the Hopewell Rocks, a fantastical landscape of sandstone formations etched out by the awesome Fundy tides. They've been sculpted into a bewildering array of forms – arches, towers, ice-cream cones – and at low tide, you can get right in among them. From here, many more Fundy area adventures await, or you can loop back into mainland Nova Scotia; Halifax is around a three-hour drive away.

DETOUR: POINT PRIM

Start: ⑩ Charlottetown

Reaching out into the Northumberland Strait, this skinny spit of land makes a rewarding detour from Charlottetown. It's covered in wild rose, Queen Anne's lace and wheat fields through summer and has views of red-sand shores on either side. At the tip is the **Point Prim Lighthouse** (www.pointprimlighthouse.com; 2147 Point Prim Rd, Belfast; adult/child $5/3.50; 10am-6pm mid-Jun–mid-Sep): the province's oldest and, we think, the prettiest. If you're lucky, you'll be able to climb to the top to pump the foghorn.

Eating & Sleeping

Pictou 3

Harbour House Pub $

(☎902-485-1047; 41 Coleraine St; mains $10-20; ⏰11:30am-9pm Sun-Thu, to 11pm Fri & Sat) A pleasant portside watering hole that has lots of Nova Scotian ales to try, plus basic pub dishes. Opening hours can be a little erratic.

Pictou Lodge Resort $$

(☎902-485-4322; www.pictoulodge.com; 172 Lodge Rd; r $199-239, cottages $215-445;) In business since the 1920s, this complex feels rather quaint, with cedar-log cabins, paddleboats and family-friendly 60-hectare grounds (including a private beach). Cabins range in size from one to three bedrooms, or you can book lodge-style rooms; most have been attractively renovated. The restaurant (mains $25 to $30) is the best place for dinner in town.

Georgetown 4

Clam Diggers Seafood $$

(☎902-583-3111; www.clamdiggerspei.com; 6864 Water St, Georgetown; mains $12-35; ⏰11:30am-9pm) Quite recently relocated to a creekside spot, this popular seafood diner is a brilliant place for brunch, lunch or dinner, with local specialties such as breaded clams, old-fashioned shanty bake (basically fish pie) and hot scallop Caesar. The cooks also do a mean lobster roll and seafood chowder, and the big glass windows offer fine water views.

Georgetown Inn & Dining Room Inn $$

(☎902-652-2511; www.peigeorgetownhistoricinn.com; 62 Richmond St, Georgetown; d from $120;) Eight island-themed rooms are on offer at this fine old Georgetown house, including a spacious captain's room with jet tub and a shared outside deck, a bay-windowed harbor room and (of course) a Green Gables suite. The restaurant is good too (mains from $15).

East Point 5

FireWorks Canadian $$$

(☎902-687-3745; https://innatbayfortune.com/fireworks; 758 Rte 310, Bay Fortune; per person $155; ⏰from 5pm) Since taking over the Inn at Bay Fortune in 2015, Food Network star Michael Smith has created one of PEI's most unique dining experiences: the 'FireWorks feast,' based around a monstrous 7.5m brick-lined, wood-burning oven. It features a smorgasbord of oysters, hot-smoked fish, flame-grilled steaks, seafood chowder and fire-oven bread, served at long butcher-block tables: a truly epic barbecue banquet.

Guests staying at the Inn automatically receive a reservation at the feast. The event also includes a tour of the kitchen garden and farm.

Johnson Shore Inn Inn $$

(☎902-687-1340; www.jsipei.com; 9984 Northside Rd, Hermanville; r from $120; ⏰May-Jan;) Coastal luxury and stunning views of St Lawrence Bay are the calling cards at this lovely seaside inn, clad in white clapboard and full of Atlantic Canadian character. Rooms are priced according to the quality of the sea view, but they're all extremely elegant.

Greenwich Dunes 6

Trailside Cafe & Inn Cafe $$

(☎902-628-7833; www.trailside.ca; 109 Main St, Mt Stewart; mains $12-17) This stomping venue is one of the best places in eastern PEI to catch some live music – owners Pat and Meghann are passionate music lovers, and they attract top artists to their nighttime performances. The shingled building, dating from 1897, makes an intimate space, and you can dine on pizzas, cheese and charcuterie platters while you enjoy the show.

There are also four rooms upstairs. If you can't make a dinner show, try and catch the Hillsborough River Gospel Brunch ($22), held on summer Sundays in July and August.

Cavendish 8

Carr's Oyster Bar — Seafood $$

(902-886-3355; www.carrspei.ca; 32 Campbellton Rd, Stanley Bridge; mains $16-40; 11am-8pm) Dine on oysters straight from Malpeque Bay, or lobster, mussels and seafood you've never even heard of, like quahogs from Carr's own saltwater tanks (the menu helpfully divides dishes up into raw, steamed, fried or baked). There is also plenty of fish on offer.

Kindred Spirits Inn & Cottages — Inn $$

(902-963-2434; www.kindredspirits.ca; 46 Memory Lane; r from $165; P) This prim, spread-out complex goes big on the storybook style. Rooms are every *Anne of Green Gables* fan's dream, with dotty floral prints, glossy wood floors and fluffy, comfy beds: they're split between the main inn and a separate gatehouse. It's worth bumping up the price bracket for more space and comfort.

New Glasgow 9

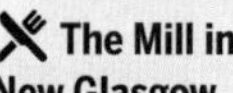

The Mill in New Glasgow — Canadian $$

(902-964-3313; www.themillinnewglasgow.com; 5592 Rte 13; mains $18-35; noon-3pm & 5-9pm Wed-Sun) Chef Emily Wells has turned this lakeside restaurant into a destination address since winning the 'Taste Our Island' competition in 2015. The ethos is comfort food with an upscale twist, often with an Asian-inspired or Provençal flair (fish cakes with sriracha lime mayo, or chicken stuffed with arborio rice, feta, parmesan, almonds and dried cranberries).

Charlottetown 10

Brickhouse Kitchen & Bar — Canadian $$

(902-566-4620; http://brickhousepei.com; 125 Sydney St; mains $16-30; 11am-10pm) An upscale-grub pub that's crammed with rough-bricked, industrial chic, from the trendy booth seats and open-view kitchen to the pop-art prints on the walls. Dishes take their cue from PEI ingredients – chef Seth's seafood chowder is a favorite, as is the tandoori-spiced roasted hen.

Great George — Boutique Hotel $$

(902-892-0606; www.thegreatgeorge.com; 58 Great George St; d/ste from $199/259) This colorful collage of celebrated buildings along Charlottetown's most famous street has rooms ranging from plush and historic to bold and contemporary. Its room designs cover all bases – from multiroom layouts (ideal for families) to self-contained suites. All feel indulgent and elegant.

Classic Trip

Icebergs, Vikings & Whales

Slate-gray ocean, wind-carved cliffs, endless forests and floating ice: on this trip, you'll experience the best of the relentless playground of elemental beauty that is Newfoundland.

TRIP HIGHLIGHTS

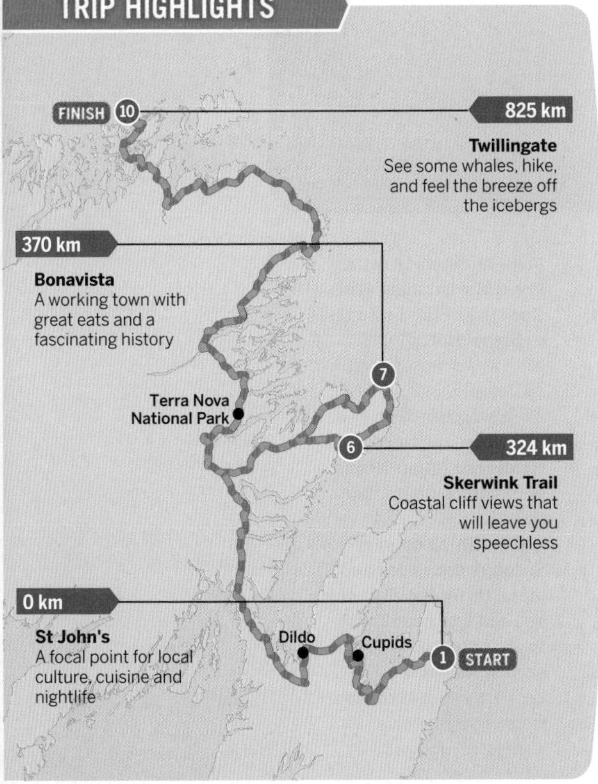

FINISH 10 — 825 km

Twillingate
See some whales, hike, and feel the breeze off the icebergs

370 km

Bonavista
A working town with great eats and a fascinating history

7

Terra Nova National Park

6 — 324 km

Skerwink Trail
Coastal cliff views that will leave you speechless

0 km

St John's
A focal point for local culture, cuisine and nightlife

Dildo

Cupids

1 START

5 DAYS
825KM/513 MILES

GREAT FOR...

BEST TIME TO GO

July and August are busy, but the weather is great. May and June are colder, but have less crowds.

ESSENTIAL PHOTO

From a clifftop on the Skerwink Trail.

BEST FOR FOODIES

A refined meal at Bonavista's Boreal Cafe.

Newfoundland The Skerwink Trail (p353) winds past massive cliff faces along the coast

Classic Trip

32 Icebergs, Vikings & Whales

There are no straight roads in Newfoundland. Rather, this is a land that is off the beaten track seemingly by design. The province is cut through by winding loops of asphalt that connect the villages of remote peninsulas, several of which you'll explore on this journey, which gives travelers a taste of this province's warm hospitality and raw, severe beauty.

❶ St John's

Newfoundland's capital is also its largest city, yet for many visitors St John's feels like a pleasant small town. Like all of the province, this is a neighborly, warm place, but it is a capital, meaning there's lots to do here. Failing that, you can visit the **Rooms** (☎709-757-8000; www.therooms.ca; 9 Bonaventure Ave; adult/child $10/5, 6-9pm Wed free; ⏲10am-5pm Mon, Tue, Thu & Sat, to 9pm Wed, to 10pm Fri, noon-5pm Sun, closed Mon Oct-Apr; 👪), the province's main museum, to get a sense of what makes this Rock tick. Take a spin up to **Signal Hill** (☎709-772-5367; www.pc.gc.ca/signalhill; 230 Signal Hill Road; ⏲grounds 24hr, visitor center 10am-6pm; P), where the **North Head Trail** stands as one of Canada's great urban treks.

The dining options in St John's are varied and fantastic for the city's size. You can't go wrong with fresh oysters on the half shell at **Adelaide** (☎709-722-7222; www.facebook.com/theadelaideoysterhouse; 334 Water St; small plates $8-17;

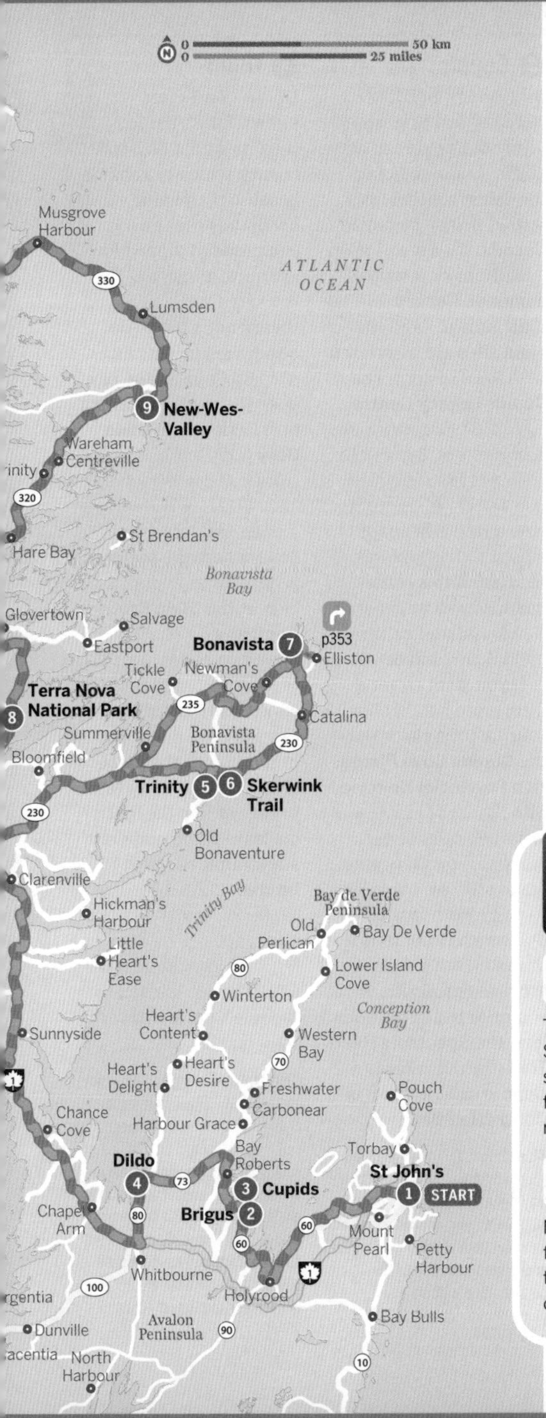

⌚5-11pm Mon-Wed, to midnight Thu, to 1am Fri, 11am-3pm & 5pm-1am Sat, 11am-3pm & 5pm-midnight Sun), or a premium handcrafted pizza at **Piatto** (www.piattopizzeria.com; 377 Duckworth St; mains $12-19; ⌚11:30am-10pm Mon-Thu, to 11pm Fri & Sat, to 9pm Sun; 👪). Consider making a stop at the **Outfitters** (www.theoutfitters.nf.ca; 220 Water St; ⌚10am-6pm Mon-Wed & Sat, to 9pm Thu & Fri, noon-5pm Sun), a one-stop shop for all your outdoor needs. This town's famous for its nightlife, and while it's no fun driving with a hangover, consider at least catching some live music on George St, or a beer at the **Duke of Duckworth** (www.dukeofduckworth.com; McMurdo's Lane, 325 Duckworth St; ⌚noon-2am; 📶).

The Drive » You can drive to Brigus by heading westbound on the Trans-Canada Hwy, and there is something to be

LINK YOUR TRIP

28 Central Nova Scotia

Take the ferry to North Sydney, and drive 185km southwest to Antigonish for the second half of this road trip.

30 The Cabot Trail

After exploring Newfoundland, catch the ferry from Port aux Basques to North Sydney for this classic Nova Scotia ramble.

said for starting that iconic road at its easternmost point. Still, we recommend taking NL 60 W, which hugs the coast and meanders through some attractive small towns.

❷ Brigus

Brigus is so bucolic, in such a quintessentially English-cottage-y way, you halfway expect to see a cast member from *Downton Abbey* ride by on an old-time bicycle. This was once a prosperous port and a home for seafaring captains; now it's (more or less) a prosperous retirement community that attracts tourists who love tea, jams and a slow pace of life. You can kill a few hours here just walking around and appreciating how pretty everything is; make sure you get a scone at the Country Corner (p357), and don't forget to walk through the **Brigus Tunnel** (The Walk) – an artificially dug stone passageway that once connected the main part of town to a deep water berth.

The Drive » It's an easy, short drive (about 4.5km) on NL 60 from Brigus to Cupids.

p357

❸ Cupids

Brigus may look like a stereotypical English village, but Cupids can actually lay claim to being the oldest continuously settled British colony in Canada. It's a small town – really, more a strip of homes on Conception Bay than a town – and the main sites are associated with local history. The **Cupids Legacy Centre** (709-528-1610; www.cupidslegacycentre.ca; Seaforest Dr; adult/child $8/4; 9:30am-5pm Jun-Oct; P) is, for its size, a rather brilliant museum that explores the past of this settlement, as well as general Newfoundland culture, in great depth and detail.

If you want to get a little more hands-on with your history, check out the **Cupids Cove Plantation Provincial Historic Site** (709-528-3500; www.seethesites.ca/the-sites/cupids-cove-plantation.aspx; Seaforest Dr; adult/child $6/free; 9:30am-5pm May-Oct; P), which is not only a museum, but a working archaeological site. If you need to stretch your legs, the **Spectacle Head Trail** (Quay Rd) affords some excellent views of Conception Bay.

The Drive » To get to Dildo, you can either cut across the Bay de Verde peninsula on NL 73W, or you can take the loooong (but pretty) way around and drive to the top of the peninsula, and then down.

p357

❹ Dildo

Dildo is far better known for its name then its actual physical beauty, which is a shame, because the phallic headlands the town is (supposedly) named for are quite gorgeous. This is a small settlement and there's not a ton to do besides snap some nice sunset photos of the bay, pose with a statue of Captain Dildo at the **Dildo Dory** (709-582-3799; www.dildodorygrill.ca; 9 Front Rd; mains $11-22; 11:30am-8pm Jun-Sep, weekends only spring & fall), where the seafood is quite nice, or sink a beer at the **Dildo Brewing Company** (709-582-3335; www.dildobrewingco.com; 1 Front Rd; 11am-10pm), which has figured out you can sell anything if you brand it with the name 'Dildo.' If you really want to eat out like the locals do, leave Dildo and drive a few minutes north to **Pitchers** (709-582-2097; 89 Main Rd, New Harbour; mains $6-10; 7am-11pm; P), a grocery store with a full service kitchen to the side that serves very solid meals.

The Drive » Time to hop on the highway. The Trans-Canada cuts through Newfoundland, but as you'll see, much of the province lives on the peninsulas that stick like amoeba arms off the TCH. Take NL 80 south from Dildo to the Trans-Canada, then take the highway north about 120km and exit onto NL 230; drive this road about 70km to Trinity.

5 Trinity

Trinity is another village with a preserved-in-amber vibe, largely because the main driver of the economy here is no longer fishing, but rather, tourism (and to a degree, the kind of tourism that indulges the idea that this is still a fishing village). This is an exceptionally pretty town, all heritage homes and narrow lanes. One of the foodiest food experiences in the province can be found at the **Twine Loft** (www.trinityvacations.com/our-restaurant; 57 High St; prix-fixe $55).

The main thing to do here is tour historical properties via a multiuse ticket purchased at the **Trinity Museum** (www.trinityhistoricalsociety.com; Church Rd; 7-site admission adult/child $20/free; 9:30am-5pm mid-May–mid-Oct). If it's summer, make sure you pop by the **Rising Tide Theatre** (www.risingtidetheatre.com; 40 West St; Jun-Sep), which has a busy performance schedule of shows that engage the area's history and culture. Most of these shows are of the dramedy hybrid school of theatre, so expect laughs and lumps in your throat.

The Drive » Take NL 230 east/north out of Trinity, then turn onto Rocky Hill Rd and drive about 2km to find the trailhead to the Skerwink Trail.

p357

DETOUR: ELLISTON

Start: 7 Bonavista

About 7km east of Bonavista, the little town of Elliston is famous for its sealing history and contemporary puffin-watching opportunities. Learn about the former at the **Sealers Interpretation Centre** (John C. Crosbie Sealers Interpretation Centre; 709-476-3003; www.homefromthesea.ca; Elliston; $7; 9am-5:30pm May-Oct; P), a modern museum dedicated to educating the public about this traditional hunting practice. Fair warning, this spot makes no apologies for the seal hunt. From here you can drive to a small parking area and walk a kilometer out to a small cliff. Across the water is a series of rocks and sea stacks where you can see hundreds if not thousands of puffins poking their heads out of their dens, seemingly prepping themselves for the cutest marine avian life photoshoot ever. Grab a meal at **Nanny's Root Cellar** (709-468-5050; 177 Main St, Elliston; mains $8-16; 8am-8pm; P), an excellent provider of hearty Newfoundland meals cooked in a fresh, innovative way.

6 Skerwink Trail

The 5km **Skerwink Trail** (www.theskerwinktrail.com) is simply one of the best hikes in the province, if not Canada. If you're reasonably fit, it takes around two hours to complete this loop, although you'll want to factor in time to enjoy the views.

And oh, the views. The Skerwink winds past massive cliff faces and foggy coves and affords great views of Trinity and other small settlements clinging to the coast. It's just drop dead gorgeous, and the highlight of many a trip to Newfoundland.

If you're pressed for time, consider hiking the trail 'backwards' (it's a loop, so there is no front or back, but most people start by hiking toward **Dog Cove**). The other end of the trail terminates at **Sam White's Cove**, a rocky beach with some lovely sea stacks, so while you're cheating a little, you are getting a taste of some nice coastal scenery while putting in half the work.

The Drive » Get back on NL 230 and head north; you'll want to follow it around 45km to the town of Bonavista.

Classic Trip

ELENA ELISSEEVA/SHUTTERSTOCK ©

EMKAPLIN/GETTY IMAGES ©

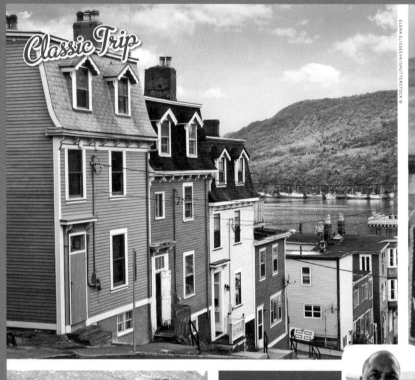

WHY THIS IS A CLASSIC TRIP
ADAM KARLIN, WRITER

Newfoundland's physical beauty cannot be overstated, but neither can its size. While this island may look small on a map, it's a bear of a landmass to tackle. This trip is a best-of itinerary that helps you grapple with its logistics – if you time it right, you'll experience a ridiculous amount of stunning vistas; even more so, you'll gain an authentic sense of Newfoundland's unique allure.

Above: Colorful houses, St John's (p350)
Left: Brigus Tunnel (p352)
Right: Dildo Brewing Company (p352)

SCOTT HEANEY/SHUTTERSTOCK ©

❼ Bonavista

Bonavista is nowhere as immediately beautiful as Brigus or Trinity. It's a working fishing village, or at least a fishing village that supports itself via a hybrid economy of fishing and, increasingly, tourism. You'll be hard pressed to find a friendlier place in Newfoundland. The big physical attraction is **Dungeon Park** (Cape Shore Rd, off Rte 230; P), a dramatic sea arch that was carved out of the coast when Poseidon was apparently having a very bad day. You'll also want to spend a few hours poking around **Ryan Premises** (www.pc.gc.ca/en/lhn-nhs/nl/ryan; Ryans Hill Rd; adult/child $3.90/free; ⏲10am-6pm Jun-Sep) and **Ye Matthew Legacy** (www.matthewlegacy.com; Roper St; adult/child $7.25/3; ⏲9:30am-5pm Jun-Sep); the former is a reconstructed merchant warehouse complex that's now a museum of fisheries history, while the latter is a rebuilt version of the boat John Cabot sailed here in 1497.

The Boreal Diner (p357) is one of the best restaurants in the province; come for local ingredients artfully massaged into Canadian contemporary cuisine that's delicious without being pretentious. If you want to tap your toes, the **Garrick Theatre** (www.garricktheatre.ca; 18 Church St) is great for a show.

The Drive » Take NL 235 back to the Trans-Canada, then take the highway westbound for 160km to reach Terra Nova.

p357

8 Terra Nova National Park

Fantastic strands of spruce forest blanket this **national park** (709-533-2801; www.pc.gc.ca/terranova; adult/child/family per day $5.80/free/11.75) in a taiga-esque quilt year round. There are many trails to explore, but if you need a little break after the rigours of the Skerwink, **Sandy Pond** (P) is an easy stroll over boardwalks and crushed gravel. Sandy Pond is a local body of water (way bigger than what you may think when you hear 'pond') where lots of folks enjoy waterfront views and a slow pace of walking. If you're up for it, there are plenty more challenging trails in the park.

The Drive » Continue on the Trans-Canada for about 35km, then hop on the exit for NL 320 north. Follow this narrow road past bays and forest for about 75km.

9 New-Wes-Valley

This small town is a very Newfoundland kind of village – a friendly spot where there's not much to do but appreciate the stony shore, which is best done from **Pool's Island** (Quay Rd), where you'll find walking trails that wind over boulders and moorland. Just north of here, **Norton's Cove Studio** (709-536-2533; www.nortonscove.com; 113 Main St, Brookfield; 10am-6pm daily Jul & Aug) is managed by a local artist; it's a cool spot for unique prints and embroidery, and the nearby **cafe** (www.nortonscove.com/pages/cafe; 114 Main St, Brookfield; mains $8-22; 10am-8pm Thu-Tue; P) is a great spot for a waterfront meal of locally sourced goodness. At the very least, get yourself a cup of strong coffee, because you've got a long drive ahead of you.

The Drive » Jump on NL 330, and drive north about 170km to Twillingate. On the way, you'll pass some stunning coastal views and a range of tiny villages, each as scenic as the last.

10 Twillingate

The town is composed of a series of islands, considered by many to be the tourism jewel of the Central Coast. Many visitors come here to go on a whale-watching and/or iceberg tour by boat, an activity we highly recommend. Less known is the **Lower Little Harbour Trail** (Lower Little Harbour Rd), which wends its way past ghostly abandoned fishing villages and rugged coastline. Be sure to grab some baked goods and excellent coffee (or a hot chocolate – or even better a mocha for the best of both worlds!) at the **Crow's Nest Cafe** (709-893-2029; www.facebook.com/CrowsNestCafe; Main St, Crow Head; 10am-5pm Tue-Sat & 8-10pm Wed, Fri & Sat, 11am-4pm Sun). If you need something stronger, the **Stage Head Pub** (709-893-2228; www.splitrockbrewing.ca; 119 Main St; noon-midnight) is a very highly regarded local microbrewery. Pop into the **Artisan Market** (709-884-8477; www.twillingateandbeyond.com/artisan-market.html; 96 Main St; 9am-9pm) for some locally produced art, a perfect and unique souvenir to mark the end of this epic road trip across the island.

p357

Eating & Sleeping

Brigus 2

Country Corner — Canadian $$

(709-528-1099; www.thecountrycorner.ca; 14 Water St; mains $11-18; 11am-7pm Sun-Thu, to 9pm Fri & Sat;) A combination restaurant and gift shop, the Country Corner is especially notable for its warm bowls of cod chowder and a slew of baked goods cooked with tart partridgeberries. Has a kids' menu.

Cupids 3

Cupid's Haven B&B and Tea Room — B&B $$

(709-528-1555; www.cupidshaven.ca; Burnt Head Loop; r $119-169;) An old Anglican church was converted into this divine B&B. Each of the four rooms has a private bathroom, vaulted ceilings and Gothic arched windows that let light stream in.

Trinity 5

Two Whales Cafe — Coffee

(709-464-3928; http://twowhales.com; 99 Main Rd, Port Rexton; 10am-6pm) An adorable coffee shop serving the full-octane variety and lemon blueberry cake that's off the charts. It also does good vegetarian fare and organic salads.

Artisan Inn & Campbell House — Inn $$

(709-464-3377; www.trinityvacations.com; 57 High St; r incl breakfast $159-235; mid-May–Oct;) A fantasy coastal getaway, these gorgeous properties are adjacent to each other and managed by the same group. Both have ocean vistas. The three-room inn hovers over the sea on stilts; set further back, Campbell House has lush gardens.

Bonavista 7

Boreal Diner — Canadian $$

(709-476-2330; www.theborealdiner.com; 61 Church St; mains $13-19; noon-9pm Mon-Thu, to 10pm Fri & Sat, 5-9pm Sun;) In a bright-red colonial house, this innovative restaurant manages what many others aspire to: creative, international takes on local Newfoundland ingredients. Thus: Crab pot stickers, cod in tarragon sauce, and polenta with wild mushroom stew are all potential options on the ever-shifting menu. It also does vegan and gluten free.

Russelltown Inn & Vacation Homes — Inn $$

(www.russelltowninn.com; 134 Coster St; r $140-193, pods $80, cottages $275-350) This property manages several accommodations throughout town: a main inn with clean, understated but attractive rooms, several guest cottages (minimum two-night stay) and 'glamping' in eco pods – effectively, nicely renovated studio shacks – with solar lighting.

Twillingate 10

Doyle Sansome & Sons — Seafood $$

(709-628-7421; www.sansomeslobsterpool.com; 25 Sansome's Place, Hillgrade; mains $8-24; 11am-9pm; P) Head out of your way for this classic cash-only seafood spot, serving crisp cod, fish cakes with rhubarb relish, and fresh lobster. If it's a nice day, the dock seating provides a fine view. Don't be fooled by the name – a slew of friendly women cook here. The village of Hillgrade is about 17km from Twillingate.

Anchor Inn Hotel — Hotel $$

(709-884-2777; www.anchorinntwillingate.com; 3 Path End; r $150-190; Mar-Dec; P) The waterfront Anchor has attractive rooms with deliciously soft beds and heart-melting scenic vistas. Amenities include the hotel's view-worthy deck and the barbecue grill for do-it-yourself types.

STRETCH YOUR LEGS HALIFAX

Start/Finish Canadian Museum of Immigration at Pier 21

Distance 5.4km

Duration 3 hours

This walking tour makes a circuit around Halifax's historic downtown, taking in the harbor, the waterfront, the art museum and the city's hilltop citadel en route. It can be done any time of day, but afternoon means sunset views from the citadel.

Take this walk on Trips

Canadian Museum of Immigration at Pier 21

From the parking lot outside the Cunard Centre, you'll see **Pier 21** (www.pier21.ca; 1055 Marginal Rd; adult/child $12/8; 9:30am-5:30pm May-Nov, reduced hours Dec-Apr) dead ahead on the harborside. Between 1928 and 1971, this was the Canadian version of Ellis Island, where all prospective immigrants to the country arrived.

The Walk » From the museum, head out onto the harborfront and follow the boardwalk north.

Halifax Boardwalk

In centuries past, Halifax's harborfront wharves would have bristled with maritime traffic – tugboats, clippers, frigates and fishing schooners. Even though the days of sail are long gone, the city's epic 2.5-mile seafront boardwalk still makes a fine stroll. If you're feeling parched, stop in at the **Garrison Brewing Company** (www.garrisonbrewing.com).

The Walk » The Maritime Museum is on the boardwalk; you'll reach it after 1.6km.

Maritime Museum of the Atlantic

This briny **museum** (http://maritimemuseum.novascotia.ca; 1675 Lower Water St; adult/child May-Oct $9.55/5.15, Nov-Apr $5.15/3.10; 9:30am-5pm May-Oct, closed to 1pm Sun & all day Mon Nov-Apr) covers Atlantic Canada's nautical activities, from merchant shipping and small boat building to the World War convoys.

Outside you can visit the WWII corvette **HMCS Sackville**, the last surviving veteran of the Battle of the Atlantic.

The Walk » Follow Lower Water St, then turn left away from the harbour onto Prince St and right onto Hollis St.

Art Gallery of Nova Scotia

At the province's premier **art institution** (www.artgalleryofnovascotia.ca; 1723 Hollis St; adult/child $12/5, 5-9pm Thu free; 10am-5pm Sat-Wed, to 9pm Thu & Fri), you can see a replica of the house that belonged to folk artist Maud Lewis, who turned the

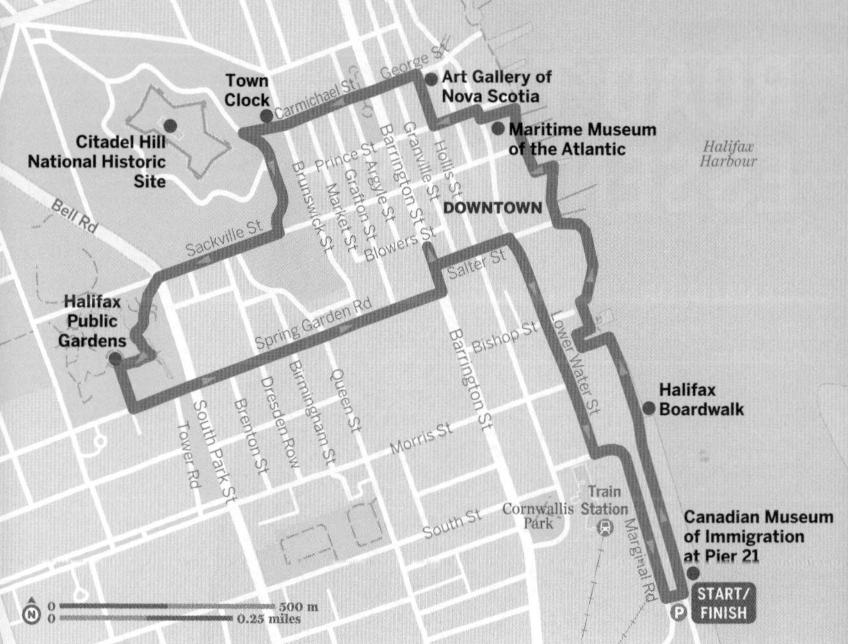

house, measuring 3m by 4m, into her very own living canvas. Look out for two portraits of Halifax notables by the master Joshua Reynolds: Edward Cornwallis, the first governor and founder of Halifax, and George Montagu-Dunk, 2nd Earl of Halifax.

The Walk » From the museum, head uphill along George St and Carmichael St; you'll see the clock dead ahead.

Town Clock

This Palladian-styled town clock looks like it would be more at home in a Venetian lane, but it has been faithfully keeping time here for more than 200 years. The inner workings arrived in Halifax from London in 1803, after being ordered by Prince Edward, the Duke of Kent.

The Walk » A path leads up the grassy slope from the town clock to the citadel.

Citadel Hill National Historic Site

Looming over town, Halifax's star-shaped **Citadel** (www.pc.gc.ca/en/lhn-nhs/ns/halifax; 5425 Sackville St) is the fourth fortress to stand on this spot, built from 1818 to 1861. The grounds and battlements are open year-round; between May and October, you can visit rooms including the soldiers' barracks, guards' room, signal post, engineer's store and gunpowder magazines.

The Walk » Follow the winding road down to Sackville St, and hike along to the corner of South Park St. Enter through the park gates.

Halifax Public Gardens

Opened to the public in 1875, Halifax's delightful 16-acre **public gardens** (www.halifaxpublicgardens.ca) are a fine example of Victorian horticultural planning. Stocked with lakes, statues, fountains, bridges, ponds and a huge variety of trees and formal flower beds.

The Walk » Exit on Spring Garden Rd. Follow it downhill, passing the central library on your right. As you near Barrington St, admire North America's largest freestanding granite spire at St Mary's Cathedral Basilica, before returning to Pier 21 via Lower Water St.

ROAD TRIP ESSENTIALS

Canada Driving Guide

Canada is a fabulous place for road trips, with an extensive network of highways, breathtaking scenery and friendly locals to help out if you should lose your way.

DRIVER'S LICENSE & DOCUMENTS

In most provinces, visitors can legally drive for up to three months with their home driver's license. In some, such as British Columbia, this is extended to six months.

If you're spending considerable time in Canada, think about getting an International Driving Permit (IDP), which is valid for one year. Your automobile association at home can issue one for a small fee. Always carry your home license together with the IDP.

INSURANCE

Canadian law requires liability insurance for all vehicles, to cover you for damage caused to property and people.

- The minimum requirement is $200,000 in all provinces except Québec, where it is $50,000.
- Americans traveling to Canada in their own car should ask their insurance company for a Nonresident Interprovince Motor Vehicle Liability Insurance Card (commonly known as a 'yellow card'), which is accepted as evidence of financial responsibility anywhere in Canada. Although not mandatory, it may come in handy in an accident.
- Car-rental agencies offer liability insurance. Collision Damage Waivers (CDW) reduce or eliminate the amount you'll have to reimburse the rental company if there's damage to the car itself. Some credit cards cover CDW for a certain rental period if you use the card to pay for the rental and decline the policy offered by the rental company. Always check with your card issuer to see what coverage it offers in Canada.
- Personal accident insurance (PAI) covers you and any passengers for medical costs incurred as a result of an accident. If your travel insurance or your health-insurance policy at home does this as well (and most do, but check), then this is one expense you can do without.

RENTAL

Car

To rent a car in Canada you generally need to be at least 25 years old (some companies will rent to drivers between the ages of 21 and 24 for an additional charge); hold a valid driver's license (an international one may be required if you're not from an English- or French-speaking country); and have a major credit card.

Driving Fast Facts

Right or left? Drive on the right

Legal driving age 16

Top speed limit Varies by province; 90km/h in Prince Edward Island, 100km/h in Ontario and 120km/h in British Columbia

Best radio station The commercial-free Canadian Broadcasting Corporation (CBC)

Canada Playlist

Feist Mushaboom

Tragically Hip Wheat Kings

Keep the Car Running Arcade Fire

Prémonition Coeur de Pirate

Electric Pow Wow Drum A Tribe Called Red

Bridge to Nowhere Sam Roberts

Tôt ou Tard Eli Rose

I Don't Know The Sheepdogs

Colossus of Rhodes The New Pornographers

Crabbuckit K-OS

Fous n'Importe Où Charlotte Cardin

Heart of Gold Neil Young

When the Night Feels My Song Bedouin Soundclash

Renta-car rates generally include unlimited mileage, but expect surcharges for additional drivers and one-way rentals. Major international car-rental companies usually have branches at airports, train stations and in city centers. In Canada, on-the-spot rentals often are more expensive than pre-booked packages (ie cars booked with a flight or in advance).

Child and infant safety seats are legally required; reserve them (around $15 per day, or $50 per trip) when booking your car.

International car-rental companies with hundreds of branches nationwide include:

Avis (☎800-230-4898; www.avis.com)

Budget (☎800-268-8900, French 800-268-8970; www.budget.com)

Dollar (☎800-800-5252; www.dollarcanada.ca)

Enterprise (☎844-307-8008; www.enterprise.ca)

Hertz (☎800-654-3131; www.hertz.com)

National (☎toll free 844-307-8014; www.nationalcar.ca)

Practicar (☎toll free 800-327-0116; www.practicar.ca) Often has lower rates. It's also affiliated with Backpackers Hostels Canada and Hostelling International.

Thrifty (☎800-334-1705; www.thriftycanada.ca)

Motorcycle

Several companies offer motorcycle rentals and tours. A Harley Heritage Softail Classic costs about $210 per day, including liability insurance and 200km mileage. Some companies have minimum rental periods, which can be as much as seven days. Riding a hog is especially popular in British Columbia.

Cycle BC (☎604-709-5663; http://cyclebc.ca) Tours and rentals out of Victoria and Vancouver in British Columbia.

McScoots Motorcycle & Scooter Rentals (☎250-763-4668; www.mcscoots.com) Big selection of Harleys; also operates motorcycle tours. It's based in Kelowna, British Columbia.

RVs & Campervans

The RV market is biggest in the west, with specialized agencies in Calgary, Edmonton,

Driving Tips

➡ Never let the gas tank go below a third of a tank, even if you think there's cheaper fuel up the road. When traveling out west, always fill up before heading to your next destination. Sometimes, the next station is a long way off!

➡ In some areas you can drive for hours without cell service, so plan carefully for emergencies.

➡ Moose, deer and elk are common on rural roadways, especially at night. There's no contest between a 534kg bull moose and a Subaru, so keep your eyes peeled.

➡ A word for Canada's southern neighbors: don't forget that speed limits are in kilometers - not miles - per hour!

Road Distances (km)

	Banff	Calgary	Edmonton	Halifax	Inuvik	Jasper	Montréal	Ottawa	Québec City	St John's	Toronto	Vancouver	Whitehorse	Winnipeg
Calgary	130													
Edmonton	410	290												
Halifax	4900	4810	4850											
Inuvik	3440	3515	3220	8110										
Jasper	280	415	370	5250	3150									
Montréal	3700	3550	3605	1240	6820	3950								
Ottawa	3450	3340	3410	1440	6620	3770	200							
Québec City	3900	3800	3880	1020	7060	4210	250							
St John's	6200	6100	6150	1480	9350	6480	2530	2730	2310					
Toronto	3400	3400	3470	1790	6680	3820	550	450	800	3090				
Vancouver	850	970	1160	5880	3630	790	4580	4350	4830	7130	4360			
Whitehorse	2210	2290	2010	6830	1220	1930	5620	5390	5840	8150	5450	2400		
Winnipeg	1450	1325	1330	3520	4550	1670	2280	2140	2520	4820	2220	2290	3340	
Yellowknife	1800	1790	1510	6340	3770	1590	5050	4900	5350	7620	4950	2370	2540	2800

These distances are approximate only.

Whitehorse and Vancouver. For summer travel, book as early as possible. The base cost is roughly $250 per day in high season for smaller vehicles, although insurance, fees and taxes add a hefty chunk to that. Diesel-fueled RVs have considerably lower running costs.

Canadream Campers (☎925-255-8383; www.canadream.com) Based in Calgary, with rentals (including one-way rentals) in eight cities, including Vancouver, Whitehorse, Toronto and Halifax.

Cruise Canada (☎403-291-4963; www.cruisecanada.com) Offers three sizes of RVs. Locations in Halifax, and in central and western Canada; offers one-way rentals.

BRINGING YOUR OWN VEHICLE

There's minimal hassle driving into Canada from the USA, as long as you have your vehicle's registration papers, proof of liability insurance and your home driver's license.

MAPS & APPS

- **National Geographic Road Atlas** is one of the best ink-and-paper maps, with special attention paid to national parks and forests.
- **Google Maps** (http://maps.google.com) Turn-by-turn driving directions with estimated traffic delays. Be sure to download offline maps so you have mapping details when you lack cell phone service.
- **Waze** (www.waze.com) Popular, free crowd-sourced traffic and navigation app.
- **GasBuddy** (www.gasbuddy.com) Website and app that finds the cheapest places to gas up nearby.
- Most tourist offices distribute free provincial road maps.
- You can also download and print maps from GeoBase (http://geogratis.gc.ca).

ROAD CONDITIONS

Road conditions are generally good, but there are a few things to keep in mind.

Fierce winters can leave potholes the size of landmine craters. Be prepared to swerve. Winter travel in general can be hazardous due to heavy snow and ice, which may cause roads and bridges to close periodically. **Transport Canada** (☎613-990-2309; www.tc.gc.ca/en/transport-canada.html) provides links to road conditions and construction zones for each province.

If you're driving in winter or in remote areas, make sure your vehicle is equipped with four-season radial or snow tires, and emergency supplies in case you're stranded.

ROAD RULES

➡ Canadians drive on the right-hand side of the road.

➡ Seat belt use is compulsory. Children who weigh less than 18kg must be strapped into child-booster seats, except infants, who must be in a rear-facing safety seat.

➡ Motorcyclists must wear helmets and drive with their headlights on.

➡ Distances and speed limits are posted in kilometers. The speed limit is generally 40km/h to 50km/h in cities and 90km/h to 110km/h outside town.

➡ Slow down to 60km/h when passing emergency vehicles (such as police cars and ambulances) stopped on the roadside with their lights flashing.

➡ Turning right at red lights after coming to a full stop is permitted in all provinces (except where road signs prohibit it, and on the island of Montréal, where it's always a no-no). There's a national propensity for running red lights, however, so don't assume 'right of way' at intersections.

➡ Driving while using a hand-held cell phone is illegal in Canada. Fines are hefty.

➡ Radar detectors are not allowed in most of Canada (Alberta, British Columbia and Saskatchewan are the exceptions). If you're caught

Driving Problem-Buster

What should I do if my car breaks down? Put on your hazard lights (flashers) and carefully pull over to the side of the road. Call the roadside emergency assistance number of your car-rental company or, if you're driving your own car, your automobile association.

What if I have an accident? If it's safe to do so, pull over to the side of the road. For minor collisions with no major property damage or bodily injuries, be sure to exchange driver's license and auto-insurance information with the other driver, then file a report with your insurance provider or notify your car-rental company as soon as possible. If you distrust the other party, call the police, who will fill out an objective report. For major accidents, call ☎911 and wait for the police and emergency services to arrive.

What should I do if I am stopped by the police? Be courteous. Don't get out of the car unless asked. Keep your hands where the officer can see them (eg on the steering wheel). For traffic violations, there is usually a 30-day period to pay a fine; most matters can be handled by mail. Police can legally give roadside sobriety checks to assess if you've been drinking or using drugs.

What should I do if my car gets towed? Immediately call the local police in the town or city that you're in and ask where to pick up your car. Towing and hourly or daily storage fees can quickly total hundreds of dollars.

What if I can't find anywhere to stay? If you're stuck and it's getting late, it's best not to keep driving on aimlessly – just pull into the next roadside chain motel or hotel with the 'Vacancy' light lit up.

Road Trip Websites

Canadian Automobile Association (www.caa.ca) Offers services, including 24-hour emergency roadside assistance, to members of international affiliates, such as AAA in the USA, AA in the UK and ADAC in Germany. The club also offers trip-planning advice, free maps, travel-agency services and a range of discounts on hotels, car rentals etc. Autoclub membership is a handy thing to have in Canada.

Canada Road Conditions (https://www.th.gov.bc.ca/drivebc_supp/canada_map.htm) Check the status of road conditions in all 13 provinces and territories.

driving with a radar detector, even one that isn't being operated, you could receive a fine of $1000 and your device may be confiscated.

➡ The blood-alcohol limit for drivers is 0.08%, but provincial limits can be lower. Driving while drunk or high is a criminal offense.

PARKING

Free parking is plentiful in small towns and rural areas, but scarce and often expensive in cities. Municipal parking meters and centralized pay stations usually accept coins and credit or debit cards.

When parking on the street, carefully read all posted regulations and restrictions (eg 30-minute maximum, no parking during scheduled street-cleaning hours) and pay attention to colored curbs, or you may be ticketed and towed. In some towns and cities, overnight street parking is prohibited downtown and in designated areas reserved for local residents with permits.

At city parking garages and lots, expect to pay at least $2 per hour and $12 to $40 for all-day or overnight parking.

FUEL

Most gas stations in Canada are self-service. You'll find them on highways outside of most towns, though the options are few and far between in sparsely populated areas.

Gas is sold in liters (3.78L equals one US gallon). The current cost for regular fuel in Canada ranges from $1.10 to $1.55. Prices are higher in remote areas, with Yellowknife usually setting the national record; drivers in Calgary typically pay the least for gas.

Fuel prices are usually lower in the USA, so fill up south of the border if that's an option.

SAFETY

Vehicle theft, break-ins and vandalism are a problem mostly in urban areas. Be sure to lock your vehicle's doors, leave the windows rolled up and use any anti-theft devices that have been installed (eg car alarm, steering-wheel lock). Do not leave any valuables visible inside your vehicle; instead, stow them in the trunk before arriving at your destination, or else take them with you once you've parked.

Canada Travel Guide

GETTING THERE & AWAY

AIR

Airports & Airlines

Toronto is far and away Canada's busiest airport, followed by Vancouver. The international gateways you're most likely to use:

Calgary (Calgary International Airport; www.yyc.com)

Edmonton (Edmonton International Airport; http://flyeia.com)

Halifax (Halifax Stanfield International Airport; http://halifaxstanfield.ca)

Montréal (Montréal Trudeau International Airport; www.admtl.com)

Ottawa (Ottawa International Airport; http://yow.ca)

St John's (St John's International Airport; http://stjohnsairport.com)

Toronto (Toronto Pearson International Airport; www.torontopearson.com)

Vancouver (Vancouver International Airport; www.yvr.ca)

Winnipeg (Winnipeg International Airport; www.waa.ca)

Air Canada (www.aircanada.com), the national flagship carrier, is considered one of the world's safest airlines. All major global airlines fly to Canada. Other companies based in the country and serving international destinations:

WestJet (www.westjet.com) Calgary-based low-cost carrier serving destinations throughout Canada as well as across the US and Caribbean.

Porter Airlines (www.flyporter.com) Flies around eastern Canada and to US cities, including Boston, Chicago, Washington, DC, and New York.

Air Transat (www.airtransat.com) Charter airline from major Canadian cities to holiday destinations (ie southern USA and Caribbean in winter, Europe in summer).

CAR & MOTORCYCLE

The highway system of the continental USA connects directly with the Canadian highway system at numerous points along the border. These Canadian highways then meet up with the east–west Trans-Canada Hwy further north. Between the Yukon Territory and Alaska, the main routes are the Alaska, Klondike and Haines Hwys.

If you're driving into Canada, you'll need the vehicle's registration papers, proof of liability insurance and your home driver's license. Cars rented in the USA can usually be driven into Canada and back, but make sure your rental agreement says so. If you're driving a car registered in someone else's name, bring a letter from the owner authorizing use of the vehicle in Canada.

SEA

Ferry

Various ferry services on the coasts connect the USA and Canada:

➡ Bar Harbor, Maine, to Yarmouth, NS: **Bay Ferries Limited** (www.ferries.ca/thecat)

➡ Eastport, Maine, to Deer Island, NB: **East Coast Ferries** (www.eastcoastferriesltd.com)

➡ Seattle, WA, to Victoria, BC: **Victoria Clipper** (www.clippervacations.com)

➡ Ketchikan, Alaska, to Prince Rupert, BC: **Alaska Marine Highway System** (www.ferryalaska.com)

➡ Bella Bella, BC, to Prince Rupert, BC: **BC Ferries** (www.bcferries.com)

➡ Sandusky, Ohio, to Pelee Island, ON: **Pelee Island Transportation Service** (www.ontarioferries.com)

➡ Port Angeles, WA, to Victoria, BC; **Black Ball Ferry** (www.cohoferry.com)

➡ Anacortes, WA, to Sidney, BC; **Washington State Ferries** (www.wsdot.wa.gov/ferries)

Freighters

An adventurous, though not necessarily inexpensive, way to travel to or from Canada is aboard a cargo ship. Freighters carry between three and 12 passengers and, though considerably less luxurious than cruise ships, they give a salty taste of life at sea. **Maris Freighter Cruises** (www.freightercruises.com) has more information on the ever-changing routes.

TRAIN

Amtrak (www.amtrak.com) and **VIA Rail Canada** (www.viarail.ca) run three routes between the USA and Canada: two in the east and one in the west. Customs inspections happen at the border, not upon boarding.

Train Routes & Fares

Route	Duration (hr)	Frequency (daily)	Fare (US$)
New York–Toronto (Maple Leaf)	13¾	1	131
New York–Montréal (Adirondack)	12	1	70
Seattle–Vancouver (Cascades)	4	2	41

DIRECTORY A–Z

ACCESSIBLE TRAVEL

Canada is making progress when it comes to easing the everyday challenges facing people with disabilities, especially those who have mobility requirements.

➡ Many public buildings, including museums, tourist offices, train stations, shopping malls and cinemas, have access ramps and/or lifts. Most public restrooms feature extra-wide stalls equipped with hand rails. Many pedestrian crossings have sloping curbs.

➡ Newer and recently remodeled hotels, especially chain hotels, have rooms with extra-wide doors and spacious bathrooms.

➡ Interpretive centers at national and provincial parks are usually accessible, and many parks have trails that can be navigated in wheelchairs.

➡ Car rental agencies offer hand-controlled vehicles and vans with wheelchair lifts at no additional charge, but you must reserve them well in advance.

➡ Download Lonely Planet's free Accessible Travel guides from http://lptravel.to/AccessibleTravel.

➡ For accessible air, bus, rail and ferry transportation, check **Access to Travel** (www.accesstotravel.gc.ca), the federal government's website. In general, most transportation agencies can accommodate people with disabilities if you make your needs known when booking.

Other organizations specializing in the needs of travelers with disabilities:

Mobility International (www.miusa.org) Advises travelers with disabilities on mobility issues and runs an educational exchange program.

Society for Accessible Travel & Hospitality (www.sath.org) Travelers with disabilities share tips and blogs.

ACCOMMODATIONS

In popular destinations, such as Ottawa, Banff and Jasper, it pays to book ahead in the height of the summer, especially during major festivals, and in the ski season.

Plan Your Stay Online

For more accommodations reviews by Lonely Planet authors, check out www.lonelyplanet.com. You'll find independent reviews, as well as recommendations on the best places to stay.

B&Bs From purpose-built villas to heritage homes or someone's spare room, they are often the most atmospheric lodgings.

Motels Dotting the highways into town, these are often family-run affairs that offer the most bang for your buck.

Hotels From standard to luxurious with a burgeoning number of boutique options.

Hostels Young backpacker hangouts, but favored by outdoor adventurers in remoter regions.

Camping Campgrounds are plentiful; private grounds often have fancier facilities.

Seasons

- Peak season is summer, basically June through August, when prices are highest.
- It's best to book ahead during summer, as well as during ski season at winter resorts, and during holidays and major events, as rooms can be scarce.
- Some properties close down altogether in the off-season.

B&Bs

- **Bed & Breakfast Online** (http://m.bbcanada.com) is the main booking agency for properties nationwide.
- In Canada, B&Bs (*gîtes* in French) are essentially converted or purpose-built private homes whose owners live on-site. People who like privacy may find B&Bs too intimate, as walls are rarely soundproof and it's usual to mingle with your hosts and other guests.
- Standards vary widely, sometimes even within a single B&B. The cheapest rooms tend to be small, with few amenities and a shared bathroom. Nicer ones have added features such as a balcony, a fireplace and an en suite bathroom.
- Breakfast is always included in the rates (though it might be continental instead of a full cooked affair).
- Not all B&Bs accept children.
- Minimum stays (usually two nights) are common, and many B&Bs are only open seasonally.

Hotels & Motels

Most hotels are part of international chains, and the newer ones are designed for either the luxury market or businesspeople, with in-room cable TV and wi-fi. Many also have swimming pools and fitness and business centers. Rooms with two double or queen-sized beds sleep up to four people, although there is usually a small surcharge for the third and fourth people. Many places advertise 'kids stay free,' but sometimes you have to pay extra for a crib or a rollaway (portable bed).

In Canada, like the USA (both lands of the automobile), motels are ubiquitous. They dot the highways and cluster in groups on the outskirts of towns and cities. Although most motel rooms won't win any style awards, they're usually clean and comfortable and offer good value for travelers. Many regional motels remain typical mom-and-pop operations, but plenty of North American chains have also opened up across the country.

Camping

- Canada is filled with campgrounds – some federal or provincial, others privately owned.
- The official season runs from May to September, but exact dates vary by location.
- Facilities vary widely. Backcountry sites offer little more than pit toilets and fire rings, and have no potable water. Unserviced (tent) campgrounds come with access to drinking water and a washroom with toilets and sometimes

Sleeping Price Ranges

The following price ranges refer to a double room with private bathroom in high season, excluding tax (which can be up to 17%).

$ less than $100

$$ $100–$250

$$$ more than $250

Practicalities

Newspapers The most widely available newspaper is the Toronto-based *Globe and Mail*. Other principal dailies are the *Montréal Gazette, Ottawa Citizen, Toronto Star* and *Vancouver Sun*. *Maclean's* is Canada's weekly news magazine.

Radio & TV The Canadian Broadcasting Corporation (CBC) is the dominant nationwide network for both radio and TV. The CTV Television Network is its major competition.

Smoking Banned in all restaurants, bars and other public venues nationwide. This includes tobacco, vaping and cannabis.

Weights & Measures Canada officially uses the metric system, but imperial measurements are used for many day-to-day purposes.

showers. The best-equipped sites feature flush toilets and hot showers, and water, electrical and sewer hookups for recreational vehicles (RVs).

➡ Private campgrounds sometimes cater only to trailers (caravans) and RVs, and may feature convenience stores, playgrounds and swimming pools. It is a good idea to phone ahead to make sure the size of sites and the services provided at a particular campground are suitable for your vehicle.

➡ Most government-run sites are available on a first-come, first-served basis and fill up quickly, especially in July and August. Several national parks participate in Parks Canada's **camping reservation program** (☎519-826-5391; http://reservation.pc.gc.ca; reservation fee online/call center $11/13.50), which is a convenient way to make sure you get a spot.

➡ Nightly camping fees in national and provincial parks range from $25 to $35 (a bit more for full-hookup sites); fire permits often cost a few dollars extra. Backcountry camping costs about $10 per night. Private campgrounds tend to be a bit pricier. British Columbia's parks, in particular, have seen a hefty rate increase in recent years.

➡ Some campgrounds remain open for maintenance year-round and may let you camp at a reduced rate in the off-season. This can be great in late autumn or early spring, when there's hardly a soul about. Winter camping, though, is only for the hardy.

DISCOUNT CARDS

Discounts are commonly offered for seniors, children, families and people with disabilities, though no special cards are issued (you get the savings on-site when you pay). AAA and other automobile association members can also receive various travel-related discounts.

International Student Identity Card (www.isic.org) Provides students with discounts on travel insurance and admission to museums and other sights. There are also cards for those who are under 26 years but not students, and for full-time teachers.

Parks Canada Discovery Pass (adult/family $68/137; www.pc.gc.ca) Provides access to more than 100 national parks and historic sites for a year. Can pay for itself in as few as seven visits; also provides quicker entry into sites. Note that there's no charge for kids under 18 years, and a 'family' can include up to seven people in a vehicle, even if they're unrelated.

Many cities have discount cards for local attractions, such as the following:

Montréal Museum Pass (www.museesmontreal.org; $75)

Ottawa Museums Passport (www.museumspassport.ca; $35)

Toronto CityPASS (www.citypass.com/toronto; adult/child $73/50)

Vanier Park ExplorePass (Vancouver; www.spacecentre.ca/explore-pass; adult/child $42.50/36.50)

ELECTRICITY

Type A
120V/60Hz

Type B
120V/60Hz

FOOD

Canadian cuisine is nothing if not eclectic, a casserole of food cultures blended together from centuries of immigration. Poutine (French fries topped with gravy and cheese curds), Montréal-style bagels, salmon jerky and pierogi jostle for comfort-food attention. For something more refined, Montréal, Toronto and Vancouver have well-seasoned fine-dining scenes, while regions across the country have rediscovered the unique ingredients grown, foraged and produced on their doorsteps – bringing distinctive seafood, artisan cheeses and lip-smacking produce to menus.

It's worth booking ahead for popular places, especially on the weekend – which, in the Canadian restaurant world, includes Thursdays. Most cafes and budget restaurants don't accept reservations.

Local Flavors

If you're starting from the east, the main dish of the Maritime provinces is lobster – boiled in the pot and served with a little butter – and the best place to sample it is a community hall 'kitchen party' on Prince Edward Island. Dip into some chunky potato salad and hearty seafood chowder while waiting for your crustacean to arrive, but don't eat too much; you'll need room for the mountainous fruit pie coming your way afterwards.

Next door, Nova Scotia visitors should save their appetites for butter-soft Digby scallops and rustic Lunenburg sausage, while the favored meals of nearby Newfoundland and Labrador often combine rib-sticking dishes of cod cheeks and sweet snow crab. If you're feeling really ravenous, gnaw on a slice of seal flipper pie – a dish you're unlikely to forget in a hurry.

Québec is the world's largest maple syrup producer, processing an annual 6.5 million gallons of the syrup used on pancakes and as an ingredient in myriad other dishes. In this French-influenced province, fine food is a lifeblood for the locals, who happily sit down to lengthy dinners where the accompanying wine and conversation flow in equal measures.

The province's cosmopolitan Montréal has long claimed to be the nation's fine-dining capital, but there's an appreciation of food here at all levels that also includes hearty pea soups, exquisite cheeses and tasty pâtés sold at bustling markets. In addition, there's also that national dish, poutine, waiting to clog your arteries, plus smoked-meat deli sandwiches.

Ontario – especially Toronto – is a microcosm of Canada's melting pot of cuisines. Like Québec, maple syrup is a super-sweet flavoring of choice here, and it's found in decadent desserts such as beavertails (fried, sugared dough) and on breakfast pancakes the size of Frisbees. Head south to the Niagara Peninsula wine region and you'll also discover restaurants

Eating Price Ranges

The following price ranges are for main dishes:

$ less than $15

$$ $15–25

$$$ more than $25

fusing contemporary approaches and traditional local ingredients, such as fish from the Great Lakes.

Nunavut in the Arctic Circle is Canada's newest territory, but it has a long history of Inuit food, offering a real culinary adventure for extreme-cuisine travelers. Served in some restaurants (but more often in family homes – make friends with locals and they may invite you in for a feast), regional specialties include boiled seal, raw frozen char and *maktaaq* – whale skin cut into small pieces and swallowed whole.

In contrast, the central provinces of Manitoba, Saskatchewan and Alberta have their own deep-seated culinary ways. The latter, Canada's cowboy country, is the nation's beef capital – you'll find top-notch Alberta steak on menus at leading restaurants across the country. If you're offered 'prairie oysters' here, though, you might want to know (or maybe you'd prefer not to!) that they're bull's testicles, prepared in a variety of ways designed to take your mind off their origin. In the Rockies things get wilder – try elk, bison and even moose.

There's an old Eastern European influence over the border in Manitoba, where immigrant Ukrainians have added comfort food staples such as pierogi and thick, spicy sausages. Head next door to prairie-land Saskatchewan for dessert. The province's heaping fruit pies are its most striking culinary contribution, especially when prepared with tart Saskatoon berries.

In the far west, British Columbians have traditionally fed themselves from the sea and the fertile farmlands of the interior. Okanagan Valley peaches, cherries and blueberries – best purchased from seasonal roadside stands throughout the region – are the staple of many summer diets. But it's the seafood that attracts the lion's share of culinary fans. Tuck into succulent wild salmon, juicy Fanny Bay oysters and velvet-soft scallops and you may decide you've stumbled on foodie nirvana. There's also a large and ever-growing influence of Asian food in BC's Lower Mainland.

INTERNET ACCESS

➡ It's easy to find internet access. Libraries and community agencies in practically every town provide free wi-fi and computers for public use. The only downsides are that usage time is limited (usually 30 minutes), and some facilities have erratic hours.

➡ Internet cafes are scarce, limited to the main tourist areas in only certain towns; access generally starts around $2 per hour.

➡ Wi-fi is widely available. Most lodgings have it (in-room, with good speed), as do many restaurants, bars and Tim Hortons coffee shops.

LGBTIQ+ TRAVELERS

Canada is tolerant when it comes to LGBTIQ+ people, though this outlook is more common in the big cities than in rural areas. Same-sex marriage is legal throughout the country (Canada was the fourth country in the world to legalize same-sex marriage, in 2005).

Montréal, Toronto and Vancouver are by far Canada's gayest cities, each with a humming nightlife scene, publications and lots of associations and support groups. All have sizable Pride celebrations, too, which attract big crowds.

Attitudes remain more conservative in the northern regions. Throughout Nunavut, and to a lesser extent the Northwest Territories, there are some retrogressive attitudes toward homosexuality. The Yukon, in contrast, is more like British Columbia, with a live-and-let-live West Coast attitude.

The following are good resources for LGBTIQ+ travel; they include Canadian information, though not all are exclusive to the region:

Damron (www.damron.com) Publishes several travel guides; gay-friendly tour operators are listed on the website, too.

Out Traveler (www.outtraveler.com) Gay travel magazine.

Purple Roofs (www.purpleroofs.com) Website listing queer accommodations, travel agencies and tours worldwide.

Queer Events (www.queerevents.ca) A general resource for finding events that are aimed at the gay community.

Xtra (www.xtra.ca) Source for gay and lesbian news nationwide.

MONEY

➡ All prices quoted are in Canadian dollars ($), unless stated otherwise.

➡ Canadian coins come in 5¢ (nickel), 10¢ (dime), 25¢ (quarter), $1 (loonie) and $2 (toonie or twoonie) denominations. The gold-colored loonie features the loon, a common Canadian waterbird, while the two-toned toonie is decorated with a polar bear. Canada phased out its 1¢ (penny) coin in 2012.

➡ Paper currency comes in $5 (blue), $10 (purple), $20 (green) and $50 (red) denominations. The $100 (brown) and larger bills are less common. The newest bills in circulation – which have enhanced security features – are actually a polymer-based material; they feel more like plastic than paper.

➡ For changing money in the larger cities, currency exchange offices may offer better conditions than banks.

ATMs

➡ Many grocery and convenience stores, airports and bus, train and ferry stations have ATMs. Most are linked to international networks, the most common being Cirrus, Plus, Star and Maestro.

➡ Most ATMs also spit out cash if you use a major credit card. This method tends to be more expensive because, in addition to a service fee, you'll be charged interest immediately (in other words, there's no interest-free period as with purchases). For exact fees, check with your own bank or credit card company.

➡ Visitors heading to Canada's truly remote regions won't find an abundance of ATMs, so it is wise to cash up beforehand.

➡ Scotiabank, common throughout Canada, is part of the Global ATM Alliance. If your home bank is a member, fees may be less if you withdraw from Scotiabank ATMs.

Cash

Most Canadians don't carry large amounts of cash for everyday use, relying instead on credit and debit cards. Still, carrying some cash, say $100 or less, comes in handy when making small purchases. In some cases, cash is necessary to pay for rural B&Bs and shuttle vans; inquire in advance to avoid surprises. Shops and businesses rarely accept personal checks.

Credit Cards

Major credit cards such as MasterCard, Visa and American Express are widely accepted in Canada, except in remote, rural communities, where cash is king. You'll find it difficult or impossible to rent a car, book a room or order tickets over the phone without having a piece of plastic. Note that some credit card companies charge a 'transaction fee' (around 3% of whatever you purchased); check with your provider to avoid surprises. If you are given an option to pay in your home currency, it is usually better to not accept, as they charge a higher interest rate for the point-of-sale transaction.

For lost or stolen cards, these numbers operate 24 hours:

American Express (☎800-869-3016; www.americanexpress.com)

MasterCard (☎800-307-7309; www.mastercard.com)

Visa (☎416-367-8472; www.visa.com)

Tipping

Tipping is a standard practice. Generally you can expect to tip for the following:

Restaurant waitstaff 15% to 20%

Bar staff $1 per drink

Hotel bellhop $1 to $2 per bag

Hotel room cleaners From $2 per day (depending on room size and messiness)

Taxis 10% to 15%

OPENING HOURS

Opening hours vary throughout the year. We've provided high-season opening hours; hours will generally decrease in the shoulder and low seasons.

Banks 10am–5pm Monday to Friday; some open 9am–noon Saturday

Restaurants breakfast 8–11am, lunch 11:30am–2:30pm Monday to Friday, dinner 5–9:30pm daily; some open for brunch 8am to 1pm Saturday and Sunday

Bars 5pm–2am daily

Clubs 9pm–2am Wednesday to Saturday

Shops 10am–6pm Monday to Saturday, noon–5pm Sunday; some open to 8pm or 9pm Thursday and/or Friday

Supermarkets 9am–8pm; some open 24 hours

PUBLIC HOLIDAYS

Canada observes 10 national public holidays and more at the provincial level. Banks, schools and government offices close on these days.

SAFE TRAVEL

Canada is one of the safest countries in the world. Pickpocketing and muggings are rare, especially if you take commonsense precautions. Panhandling is common, but usually not dangerous or aggressive.

➡ Stay in your car at all times when photographing wildlife.

➡ Drink spiking is rare but solo travelers should be cautious.

➡ With the exception of cannabis, recreational drug use in Canada is illegal, including magic mushrooms, and police can stop you any time you're behind the wheel.

➡ Forest fires, though rare, are a possible threat and should be treated seriously.

TELEPHONE

Canada's phone system is extensive and landlines reach most places; however, cell service can be spotty. Truly remote areas may not have any phone service at all.

Cell Phones

➡ You should be able to buy a SIM card from local providers such as **Telus** (www.telus.com), **Rogers** (www.rogers.com) or **Bell** (www.bell.ca). Bell has the best data coverage.

➡ US residents can often upgrade their domestic cell phone plan to extend to Canada. **Verizon** (www.verizonwireless.com) provides good results.

➡ Reception is poor and often nonexistent in rural areas no matter who your service provider is. Some companies' plans do not reach all parts of Canada, so check coverage maps.

➡ SIM cards that work for a set period, such seven, 14, 20 or 30 days, can be purchased online, often with United States and Canada voice, SMS and data bundled together.

Domestic & International Dialing

➡ Canadian phone numbers consist of a three-digit area code followed by a seven-digit local number. In many parts of Canada, you must dial all 10 digits preceded by 1, even if you're calling across the street. In other parts of the country, when you're calling within the same area code, you can dial the seven-digit number only, but this is slowly changing.

➡ For international calls, dial ☎011 + country code + area code + local phone number. The country code for Canada is 1 (the same as for the USA, although international rates still apply for all calls made between the two countries).

➡ Toll-free numbers begin with ☎800, 877, 866, 855, 844 or 833 and must be preceded by 1. Some of these numbers are good throughout Canada and the USA, others only work within Canada, and some work in just one province.

TOURIST INFORMATION

➡ The **Canadian Tourism Commission** (www.canada.travel) is loaded with general information, packages and links.

➡ All provincial tourist offices maintain comprehensive websites packed with information helpful in planning your trip. Staff also field telephone inquiries and, on request, will mail out free maps and directories about accommodations, attractions and events.

VISAS

Currently, visas are not required for citizens of 46 countries – including most EU members, Australia and New Zealand – for visits of up to six months.

To find out if you need an eTA or are required to apply for a formal visa, go to www.cic.gc.ca/english/visit/visas.asp.

Visitor visas – aka Temporary Resident Visas (TRVs) – can now be applied for online at www.cic.gc.ca/english/information/applications/visa.asp. Single-entry TRVs ($100) are usually valid for a maximum stay of six months from the date of your arrival in Canada. In most cases your biometric data (such as fingerprints) will be taken. Note that you don't need a Canadian multiple-entry TRV for repeated entries into Canada from the USA, unless you have visited a third country.

A separate visa is required for all nationalities if you plan to study or work in Canada.

Visa extensions ($100) need to be filed at least one month before your current visa expires (www.canada.ca/en/immigration-refugees-citizenship/services/visit-canada/extend-stay.html).

BEHIND THE SCENES

SEND US YOUR FEEDBACK

We love to hear from travelers – your comments help make our books better. We read every word, and we guarantee that your feedback goes straight to the authors. Visit **lonelyplanet.com/contact** to submit your updates and suggestions.

Note: We may edit, reproduce and incorporate your comments in Lonely Planet products such as guidebooks, websites and digital products, so let us know if you are happy to have your name acknowledged. For a copy of our privacy policy visit **lonelyplanet.com/legal**.

WRITER THANKS

RAY BARTLETT

Thanks first and foremost, to Buck, for the chance to work on this, and to each of the editors who will peek at it afterwards, and to the great team of co-authors. Thanks as well to my family, friends, and to the incredible collage of folks I met along the way: Kristina, Vera, Rubí, Miro, Allan & Dan, Cat and Greg, Louise and Melva, Alice H, Molly and Spencer (congrats!), Morgan, William Flenders, Josh W, Char, the 'Lindsays', Riya, and many more.

OLIVER BERRY

Big thanks to Ben Buckner for the chance to return to write about Canada, to the LP editors for whipping my work into shape, and to my fellow writers for making this book what it is. Heartfelt thanks to Rosie Hillier for putting up with my wanderlust, and to Susie Berry for long-distance correspondence. Thanks also to Sam White, Justin Foulkes, Deborah Gill, Anna Louis and many others for useful Canadian tips and much-needed hospitality.

GREGOR CLARK

Heartfelt thanks to all of the kind Albertans and fellow travelers who shared their love and knowledge of Banff and Jasper – especially Karina Birch, Kate Williams, Ken Wood, Paul Krywicki, Erin Wilkinson, Ed and Vanessa, Shauna and Lindsay. Thanks also to the family and friends who helped me explore Banff and Jasper's trails: Chloe, Sophie, Wes and Ted, that means you! Couldn't have asked for a more delightful research crew.

SHAWN DUTHIE

It was great to re-connect with my home province and my deepest thanks to Vivek, Danny and Stefan for allowing me to sleep on your couch, driving too many kilometres to count and just making the research even more fun than usual. Of course, my biggest thank you is to my wife and son who put up with all my traveling!

STEVE FALLON

Un très grand merci to the folk who offered assistance, ideas

THIS BOOK

This 2nd edition of Lonely Planet's *Canada's Best Road Trips* guidebook was curated by Regis St Louis. It was researched and written by Ray Bartlett, Oliver Berry, Gregor Clark, Shawn Duthie, Steve Fallon, Carolyn Heller, Anna Kaminski, Adam Karlin, John Lee, Craig McLachlan, Liza Prado, Brendan Sainsbury and Phillip Tang. This guidebook was produced by the following:

Destination Editor Ben Buckner

Senior Product Editors Grace Dobell, Martine Power, Angela Tinson, Saralinda Turner

Product Editors Hannah Cartmel, Jenna Myers

Regional Senior Cartographer Corey Hutchison

Cartographer Julie Sheridan

Book Designers Gwen Cotter, Aomi Ito

Assisting Editors Sarah Bailey, James Bainbridge, Judith Bamber, Michelle Bennett, Joel Cotterell, Lucy Cowie, Melanie Dankel, Carly Hall, Victoria Harrison, Jennifer Hattam, Gabrielle Innes, Kellie Langdon, Jodie Martire, Lou McGregor, Christopher Pitts, Sarah Reid, Tamara Sheward, Simon Williamson

Cover Researcher Fergal Condon

Thanks to Sonia Kapoor, Alison Killilea, Catherine Naghten

and/or hospitality along the way, including Gabriel d'Anjou Drouin and Maxime Aubin in Québec City; Vicky Drolet in Malbaie; Sylvie Senécal & Pierre Lachance in Ville de Mont-Tremblant; and Carolyne Cyr and Pierre-André Guichoud in Ste-Adèle. *Et à mon cher 'pays d'hiver' qui a combattu le bon combat et gagné!* (And to my beloved 'land of winter' that fought the good fight and won!) As always, my share is dedicated to my now spouse and almost Quebecer, Michael Rothschild.

CAROLYN HELLER

Many thanks to all the friends and colleagues who shared their Québec tips, especially Kim Huard-Carette and Emily Dunn. Special thanks to Ben Buckner for signing me onto the Canada team, to Suzie Loiselle and Étienne Fiola for all the advice and the crêpes, and to Michaela Albert, ace travel buddy, snow hiker, and champion lobster eater.

ANNA KAMINSKI

Huge thanks to Ben for entrusting me with Nunavut, NWT and Manitoba, and to everyone who's helped me along the way. In particular: Theresa and the merry crew of medics, plus Stephen, Alan and Brian in Iqaluit, Markus in Pangnirtung, Joamie, Pootoogook and Silaqqi in Cape Dorset, Don and Christine in Fort Smith, Sherry in Valleyview, Jacob and Herb in Yellowknife, John and Gina in Fort Providence, Lois in Fort Simpson, Wayne at Checkpoint, and Minerva in Inuvik.

ADAM KARLIN

Big thanks: Ben Buckner, for getting me on this project, Anna Kaminski, my commiserator in chief, my fellow co-authors, Carolyn and Adam in St John's, Gordon in Bonavista, the construction crews of the New Wes Valley, Mom and Dad, my wild little Isaac, and my favorite traveling companions: Rachel, who can layer for anything, and Sanda, who endures the road better than her daddy.

JOHN LEE

Heartfelt thanks to Maggie for joining me at all those restaurants and for keeping me calm during the brain-throbbing final write-up phase of this project. Thanks also to Max, our crazy-whiskered ginger cat, for sticking by my desk and also reminding me to chase him around the house every once in a while. Cheers also to my brother Michael for visiting from England and checking out some local breweries with me: you really know how to go the extra mile.

CRAIG MCLACHLAN

A hearty thanks to all those who helped out on the road, but most of all, to my exceptionally beautiful wife, Yuriko, who maintained semi-control of my craft-beer intake.

LIZA PRADO

A shout out to the extraordinary LP team: Ben Buckner, the production crew, my co-authors – I'm so proud to be able to work with you. *Mil gracias* to Mom and Dad for your boundless support, love, and curiosity about places so close to home. Big thanks to Eva and Leo for waiting so patiently for 'Fun...With Mom.' And Gary, my love, there is absolutely no way I could do my job without you. Your support, your understanding, your cheerleading. Thank you, always.

BRENDAN SAINSBURY

Many thanks to all the skilled bus drivers, helpful tourist information staff, generous hotel owners, expert burger flippers, unobtrusive bears and numerous passers-by who helped me, unwittingly or otherwise, during my research trip. Special thanks to my wife Liz, my son Kieran and my mother-in-law Ammy for their company (and patience) on the road.

PHILLIP TANG

Thank you to Ben Buckner and the DEs for your expertise and legacy. *Muchas gracias a Lalo* (José Eduardo García Sánchez) *por tu apoyo y consejo sobre estilo y mucho más desde lejos.* Thank you to Felix, Nick Zhang and all the other Montréalers who offered guidance; and to Manuelle González Goretti for advice on the Eastern Townships and adventures in the Village.

ACKNOWLEDGE-MENTS

Climate map data adapted from Peel MC, Finlayson BL & McMahon TA (2007) 'Updated World Map of the Köppen-Geiger Climate Classification', *Hydrology and Earth System Sciences*, 11, 1633–44.

Front cover photograph: Icefields Parkway, Alberta, Stas Moroz/Shutterstock ©

INDEX

D

E

F

G

H

I

J

K

L

M

N

O

P

Q

R

S

T

U

V

W

Z

ADAM KARLIN

Adam has contributed to dozens of Lonely Planet guidebooks, covering an alphabetical spread that ranges from the Andaman Islands to the Zimbabwe Border. As a journalist, he has written on travel, crime, politics, archeology and the Sri Lankan Civil War, among other topics. He has sent dispatches from every continent barring Antarctica (one day!) and his essays and articles have featured in the BBC, NPR, and multiple non-fiction anthologies. Adam is based out of New Orleans, which helps explain his love of wetlands, food and good music.

JOHN LEE

Born and raised in the historic UK city of St Albans, John slowly succumbed to the lure of overseas exotica, and arrived on Canada's West Coast in 1993 to begin an MA in Political Science at the University of Victoria. Regular trips home to Britain ensued, along with stints living in Tokyo and Montréal, before he returned to British Columbia to become a full-time freelance writer in 1999. Now living in Vancouver, John specializes in travel writing and has contributed to more than 150 different publications around the world.

CRAIG MCLACHLAN

Craig has covered destinations all over the globe for Lonely Planet for two decades. Based in Queenstown, New Zealand, for half the year, he runs an outdoor activities company and a sake brewery, then moonlights overseas for the other half, leading tours and writing for Lonely Planet. Craig has completed a number of adventures in Japan and his books are available on Amazon. Check out www.craigmclachlan.com

LIZA PRADO

Liza has been a travel writer since 2003, when she made a move from corporate lawyering to travel writing (and never looked back). She's written dozens of guidebooks and articles as well as apps and blogs to destinations throughout the Americas. She takes decent photos too. Liza is a graduate of Brown University and Stanford Law School. She lives very happily in Denver, Colorado, with her husband and fellow LP writer, Gary Chandler, and their two kids.

BRENDAN SAINSBURY

Born and raised in the UK in a town that never merits a mention in any guidebook (Andover, Hampshire), Brendan spent the holidays of his youth caravanning in the English Lake District and didn't leave Blighty until he was 19. Making up for lost time, he's since squeezed 70 countries into a sometimes precarious existence as a writer and professional vagabond. In the last 11 years, he has written over 40 books for Lonely Planet from Castro's Cuba to the canyons of Peru.

PHILLIP TANG

Phillip grew up on a typically Australian diet of pho and fish'n'chips before moving to Mexico City. A degree in Chinese- and Latin-American cultures launched him into travel and then writing about it for Lonely Planet's *Canada*, *China*, *Japan*, *Korea*, *Mexico*, *Peru* and *Vietnam* guides. Writing at hellophillip.com, photos @mrtangtangtang, and tweets @philliptang.

OLIVER BERRY

Oliver Berry is a writer and photographer from Cornwall. He has worked for Lonely Planet for more than a decade, covering destinations from Cornwall to the Cook Islands, and has worked on more than 30 guidebooks. He is also a regular contributor to many newspapers and magazines. His writing has won several awards, including The Guardian Young Travel Writer of the Year and the TNT Magazine People's Choice Award. His latest work is published at www.oliverberry.com.

GREGOR CLARK

Gregor Clark is a US-based writer whose love of foreign languages and curiosity about what's around the next bend have taken him to dozens of countries on five continents. Chronic wanderlust has also led him to visit all 50 states and most Canadian provinces on countless road trips through his native North America. Since 2000, Gregor has regularly contributed to Lonely Planet guides, with a focus on Europe and the Americas.

SHAWN DUTHIE

Originally from Canada, Shawn has been traveling, studying and working around the world for the past 13 years. A love of travel merged with an interest in international politics, which led to several years of lecturing at the University of Cape Town and, now, as a freelance political risk consultant specialising in African countries. Shawn lives in South Africa and takes any excuse to travel around this amazing continent.

STEVE FALLON

A native of Boston, Massachusetts, Steve graduated from Georgetown University with a Bachelor of Science in modern languages. After working for several years for an American daily newspaper and earning a Master's degree in journalism, his fascination with the 'new' Asia and led him to Hong Kong, where he lived for over a dozen years, working for a variety of media and running his own travel bookshop. He has written or contributed to more than 100 Lonely Planet titles.

CAROLYN HELLER

Carolyn has been a full-time travel, food, and feature writer since 1996, writing for publications including LonelyPlanet.com, *Forbes Travel Guide*, *Boston Globe*, *Los Angeles Times* and *Viator Travel.* The author of several guidebooks, she's also contributed to 50+ travel and restaurant guides for Lonely Planet and other publishers. She's eaten her way across more than 40 countries on six continents.

ANNA KAMINSKI

Originally from the Soviet Union, Anna grew up in Cambridge, UK. She graduated from the University of Warwick with a degree in Comparative American Studies, a background in the history, culture and literature of the Americas and the Caribbean, and an enduring love of Latin America. Anna has contributed to almost 30 Lonely Planet titles. When not on the road, Anna calls London home.

OUR WRITERS

OUR STORY

A beat-up old car, a few dollars in the pocket and a sense of adventure. In 1972 that's all Tony and Maureen Wheeler needed for the trip of a lifetime – across Europe and Asia overland to Australia. It took several months, and at the end – broke but inspired – they sat at their kitchen table writing and stapling together their first travel guide, *Across Asia on the Cheap*. Within a week they'd sold 1500 copies. Lonely Planet was born.

Today, Lonely Planet has offices in the US, Ireland and China, with a network of more than 2000 contributors in every corner of the globe. We share Tony's belief that 'a great guidebook should do three things: inform, educate and amuse'.

REGIS ST LOUIS

Regis grew up in a small town in the American Midwest – the kind of place that fuels big dreams of travel – and he developed an early fascination with foreign dialects and world cultures. He spent his formative years learning Russian and a handful of Romance languages, which served him well on journeys across much of the globe. Regis has contributed to more than 50 Lonely Planet titles, covering destinations across six continents. His travels have taken him from the mountains of Kamchatka to remote island villages in Melanesia, and to many grand urban landscapes. When not on the road, he lives in New Orleans.

RAY BARTLETT

Ray has been travel writing for nearly two decades, bringing Japan, Korea, Mexico, Tanzania, Guatemala, Indonesia, and many parts of the United States to life in rich detail for top-industry publishers, newspapers, and magazines. His acclaimed debut novel, *Sunsets of Tulum*, set in Yucatán, was a Midwest Book Review 2016 Fiction pick. Among other pursuits, he surfs regularly and is an accomplished Argentine tango dancer. He currently divides his time between homes in the USA, Japan, and Mexico.

MORE WRITERS

Published by Lonely Planet Global Limited
CRN 554153
2nd edition – Oct 2022
ISBN 978 1 78868 351 7

10 9 8 7 6 5 4 3 2 1
Printed in China